The Ruffin Series No. 4
A Publication of the Society for Business Ethics

BUSINESS, SCIENCE, AND ETHICS

R. Edward Freeman and Patricia H. Werhane, Editors

The Society for Business Ethics

The Society for Business Ethics is a non-affiliated international Association whose objectives are:

- to promote the study of business ethics;
- to provide a forum in which moral, legal, empirical, and philosophical issues of business ethics may be openly discussed and analyzed;
- to provide a means by which those interested and concerned with business ethics may exchange ideas;
- to promote research and scholarship through the regular publication of a professional journal, *Business Ethics Quarterly*;
- to promote the improvement of the teaching of business ethics in universities and in organizations;
- to foster a better understanding between college and university administrators and those engaged in teaching and research in the field of business ethics;
- to help develop ethical business organizations; and
- to maintain a friendly and cooperative relationship among teachers, scholars, and practitioners in the field of business and organizational ethics.

The Society is pleased to acknowledge the financial support of Loyola University Chicago in the publication of *Business Ethics Quarterly*. Additional support is provided by the Olsson Center for Applied Ethics, University of Virginia, and by the Ruffin Foundation.

Ruffin Series No. 4: Business, Science, and Ethics

This special issue marks the fourth in a series from the Ruffin Lectures at the Darden Graduate School of Business Administration at the University of Virginia sponsored by the Ruffin Foundation and the Olsson Center for Applied Ethics at Darden. The Series is under the general editorship of R. Edward Freeman, Olsson Professor of Business Administration at the University of Virginia. Neither the Ruffin Lectures nor this volume would be possible without the continued dedication and hard work of the Olsson Center staff. Karen Musselman and Jenny Mead have gone far beyond the call of duty to make this possible. George Leaman, Greg Swope, and the staff of the Philosophy Documentation Center have made the editorial tasks much easier and more pleasant. Dean Bob Harris and Associate Deans James Freeland and Mark Reisler have given their unwavering support to the Ruffin Lectures and we are grateful to them. Finally, these lectures are published with the help and support of the Darden School Foundation and its two research centers: The Olsson Center for Applied Ethics and The Batten Institute. We thank our many contributors and sponsors for making this volume possible. This particular volume is the result of the vision and hard work of Bill Frederick, who has given tirelessly to make the conference and the volume a worthwhile endeavor.

Some time ago the Ruffin Foundation endowed a permanent lecture series in business ethics at the Darden School at the University of Virginia. The purpose of the endowment was to conduct a series of lectures every second or third year that would bring in experts on a particular topic in business ethics. The Series, edited by R. Edward Freeman, was originally published by Oxford University Press.

However, many of the contributors to the Series in the past have suggested that a journal publication of their contributions might speed up publication, make the papers more accessible to interested academics and practitioners, and provide a journal citation for young faculty who contribute to the Series collection. As a result, *Business Ethics Quarterly* agreed to take on the publication of this series, and *BEQ* was responsible for the first issue in the Ruffin Series. Beginning with the second volume, the Series has been published as a monograph of the Society for Business Ethics. However, as is the case for *Business Ethics Quarterly*, each essay in this collection has been blind-reviewed by peers in the field. We shall publish future Ruffin lectures in this same format and under the same stringent reviewing conditions. The Society for Business Ethics is pleased to be able to carry out this mission.

R. Edward Freeman
Patricia H. Werhane

INTRODUCTION

R. Edward Freeman and Patricia H. Werhane

This volume of the Ruffin Series in Business Ethics brings together the ideas of those in business ethics with some scientists working in biology, evolution, and evolutionary psychology. This volume represents the vision of William Frederick, who has argued for some time that business ethicists should learn more about the sciences and their implications for value creation and trade. The lectures address the question of what business ethicists can learn by paying attention to the sciences. Jessica C. Flack and Frans B. M. de Waal suggest that the origins of morality can be found in our evolutionary cousins: non-human primates. Paul Lawrence suggests that the human sense of morality is innate, or at least has evolved over a long period of time, to fulfill our need to bond with and care for others. Leda Cosmides and John Tooby argue that the evolutionary psychology framework can be useful for understanding business ethics in its account of "cheater detection," participation in collective action, and how our minds socially construct groups. William Frederick suggests that we come to see firms as natural phenomena. Edwin Hartman argues that we should take an Aristotelian approach to understanding nature and evolution. In addition there are papers by Joshua Margolis, Robert Solomon, Timothy Fort, David Messick, Saras Sarasvathy, Mollie Painter-Morland, Sandra Waddock, Joseph DesJardins, Ronald Mitchell, and Tara Radin.

Flack and De Waal's paper opens up new vistas for scholars in business ethics. While there has been much normative work on animal rights, almost no ethicists have suggested that we can look to the animal world for insight into our deepest moral intuitions. However, when one takes a pragmatist or Deweyan or fully Darwinian approach that the human and animal worlds are defined by differences of degree not kind, it is "natural" to ask how morality might have evolved, and what evidence is there in the world of our closest evolutionary cousins. Flack and de Waal suggest that we find instances of reciprocity and food sharing, reconciliation, consolation, and conflict management, all of which are used to create and enforce social cohesion. Furthermore they suggest that we find strategies based on sympathy, empathy and concern for the social.

While Flack and de Waal's paper is primarily concerned with setting forth the scientific findings, Robert Solomon and Joshua Margolis aptly show some of the implications for business ethics. Solomon puts the claim for the sentiments of sympathy and empathy in a philosophical context, and suggests that Flack and de Waal be read as claiming that human motivation is complicated, neither purely competitive nor altruistic, and that we need a finer grained understanding of the virtues and reason and emotion. Margolis suggests that the important point of this work is that it shows our capacity for moral action, even in the face of opposing forces and pressures. But, Margolis argues that how we are socialized may well dictate the kind of response in certain situations. For instance, if we are socialized to believe that business requires selfish and unethical behavior, our capacity for moral behavior may well go unused. Margolis concludes:

> The quest to understand human nature so as to develop institutions consistent with it is unavoidable accompanied by the ever-present danger of seeking in the evolutionary record of human nature incontrovertible confirmation of our preferred economic arrangements. It is worth risking this danger for the potential insight to be gained. Risking much for the sake of enlightenment also seems to be part of human nature, and the human tendency to cooperate will enable us to help one another remain open and honest.

Much in line with the spirit of Flack and de Waal, Professor Paul Lawrence's paper goes further and argues that based on work like that of Flack and de Waal, we can conclude a "unified explanation of human morality as an innate feature of human minds," and that "morality is an innate skill." Lawrence bases these conclusions on the work of evolutionary theorists, brain scientists, and the meta-theories of Antonio Damasio. Lawrence suggests that we need to understand four basic drives: (1) the drive to acquire; (2) the drive to bond; (3) the drive to learn; and, (4) the drive to defend one's self, possessions, loved ones and beliefs. Undoubtedly this theory is controversial. Certainly "innate" and "human nature" are inflammatory words these days, but the alternative of not understanding the implications of these scientific theories is not acceptable.

In his response to Lawrence, Tim Fort cautions that there is a cultural context to understanding and using these findings. He suggests that there are multiple ways to balance the four drives, and that there are interactions that need to be carefully delineated. Combining these ideas, he argues that the framework of "social contract" may serve well as a mechanism for integrating this scientific knowledge with our moral theory.

Professors Leda Cosmides and John Tooby present a number of important ideas from their work on cognitive programs in evolutionary psychology. They present three examples that have implications for business ethics: (1) a program for cheater detection that will have implications for how trade emerges and becomes stable or not; (2) a program based on the use of moral sentiments, which can be relevant to organizational behavior; and, (3) a program based on how our "minds socially construct groups, and how these can be harnessed to reduce racism and foster true diversity in the workplace." They take roughly the same approach as Flack and de Waal and Lawrence arguing that evolutionary psychology has much to teach ethicists about the way that human behavior has evolved. In addition their paper is an excellent starting point for those ethicists who want to explore these ideas in more depth, as they give a wonderful introduction to "what is evolutionary psychology."

David Messick responds that we need to add to these cognitive programs the fact that human beings are evaluative machines, making judgments about good and bad constantly. He suggests that we have an "innate tendency to differentiate good from bad, soothing from disturbing, positive from negative, approachable from aversive." Saras Sarasvathy is more critical of the whole approach. She suggests that her critique "has to do with the semantic bankruptcy of second-hand syntax borrowed from the physical and biological sciences and with the fact that such a debt seduces us to completely ignore history." She then focuses on the "ethics as adaptation" example of the cheater, and suggests that while it makes a good story, it does not generalize well. Sarasvathy also suggests that when quantities are difficult to measure and verify, then cheating will increase, since it will be hard to spot them. In short her critique calls for a finer grained analysis, embracing economics as an historical science, while leaving room for a social sphere where we are able to create more interesting and more useful selves and communities.

William Frederick continues the line of reasoning that he opened up in *Values, Nature and Culture in the American Corporation*. He suggests that we see the firm as an "evolutionary firm" capable of responding to environmental stimuli and changing. He suggests that there are five principal functions but emphasizes the Motivator/Driver and Moralizer/Valuator functions in this paper. Frederick believes that if one looks at work being done in neurosciences, thermodynamics, and complexity theory one finds evidence for extending these ideas to the firm. His central thesis is this:

> The moral traits, features, habits—and ultimately the moral problems, puzzles, and dilemmas—of the Evolutionary Firm are a product of contradictions embedded in diverse neural algorithms that motivate and activate the behavior of the firm's coalition members and thence, through them, the firm's aggregate operations. . . . The firm is reflexively immoral for reasons beyond the control of its participants while simultaneously preserving and promoting what is arguably the central moral principle—economizing—on which all life depends.

Frederick's paper is both comprehensive and integrative, giving us a full-fledged theory of the firm in evolutionary and scientific terms. He suggests that while moral analysis has an important role to play, it must begin with "what nature has bequeathed to business and humanity." In response, Mollie Painter-Morland suggests that all naturalistic theories such as Frederick's potentially run afoul of relativism and determinism. She then goes on to defend Frederick from these charges and argues that if we do ethics in the way the Frederick has suggested we have the potential to make ethics "become more than just

abstract ideals or pleasing principles." Sandra Waddock also provides an optimistic reinterpretation of Frederick's view adding a systemic orientation and a
developmental perspective. The first perspective visualizes "ecologizing" as
well as economizing, and the second recognizes that evolution is an ongoing
process, that is influenceable.

Edwin Hartman's paper offers a context for the reading of the other Ruffin
Lectures papers. He suggests an Aristotelian approach to the reading of these
papers, understanding that Aristotle believes that we are both rational and
communal creatures. He outlines Aristotle's view of eudemonia as an alternative to the now stale commentaries of humans as self-interested or altruistic.
Hartman argues:

> The Aristotelian response is this: "You are asking the wrong ques-
> tion. The right question is this: 'Why should I be the sort of person
> who takes pleasure in helping those who are in need?' And the an-
> swer to that is that in so doing you will fulfill your nature and achieve
> well-being, and contribute to a community in which others will co-
> operate with you in achieving well-being." And how do we know
> that? "Just look at human nature," Aristotle replies. "We are social
> creatures whose need and pleasure is to live in a community and
> exercise our rationality. Morality is in our best interests when we
> get our best interests right."

In response to Hartman, Lisa Newton suggests that naturalist society, at
least in the Aristotelian version, simply can't be achieved without external control, which contradicts the view that order must be freely chosen. She argues
that the overemphasis on reason, and the products of reason as reasonable is
dangerous, given the "disastrous proclivities of human nature." Robert Phillips
suggests that perhaps the entire program of naturalism, even the relatively benign Aristotelian version, rests on a distinction between "nature" and "culture"
that no self-respecting pragmatist (of which he counts Hartman as one) wants
to countenance. He then extends this critique to other Ruffin Lectures papers
and concludes that "the 'nature/culture' distinction is irrelevant to ethics."

A number of scholars chose to emphasize certain themes that were present
in some of the Ruffin Lectures. Joseph DesJardins examines the set of distinctions around "fact" and "value" and the attempt to draw normative conclusions
from empirical science. He suggests that the distinction between "explanation"
and "justification" can be useful, and that for the purposes of influencing human behavior we would better spend our time with the people we want to
influence, rather than the latest scientific discoveries. Ronald Mitchell applies
the ideas of evolutionary biology to entrepreneurship. He argues that the security seeking behavior which he believes underlies entrepreneurial behavior can
only be founded on the evolutionary morality in notions such as reciprocity,
consonance with basic drives, discouragement of free riding and good citizenship. Tara Radin argues that a naturalistic approach like the ones taken in the

papers in this volume can be used to build a foundation for stakeholder theory. She explores several apparent paradoxes and concludes that "the naturalistic approach to business is not the only approach; it is, however, one rich with potential and one difficult to ignore."

As we assemble the papers in this volume, we are reminded of an earlier Ruffin Lecture on business ethics and feminist theory.[1] While there was much controversy, the arguments and ideas that were presented had been absent in the conversation of business ethics, and such a state of affairs was unacceptable. Similarly, the ideas of biologists, evolutionary thinkers, complexity theorists, and others who find it useful to talk in scientific metaphors and languages have been absent from the conversation of business ethicists. These papers stand as a testament to the usefulness of engaging these ideas and in using them to describe and redescribe our business institutions and ourselves.

Note

1. Published as Andrea Larson and R. Edward Freeman, *Women's Studies and Business Ethics*, New York: Oxford University Press, 1997.

MONKEY BUSINESS AND BUSINESS ETHICS: EVOLUTIONARY ORIGINS OF HUMAN MORALITY

Jessica C. Flack and Frans B. M. de Waal

Abstract: To what degree has biology influenced and shaped the development of moral systems? One way to determine the extent to which
human moral systems might be the product of natural selection is to
explore behaviour in other species that is analogous and perhaps
homologous to our own. Many non-human primates, for example, have
similar methods to humans for resolving, managing, and preventing
conflicts of interests within their groups. Such methods, which include
reciprocity and food sharing, reconciliation, consolation, conflict intervention, and mediation, are the very building blocks of moral
systems in that they are based on and facilitate cohesion among individuals and reflect a concerted effort by community members to find
shared solutions to social conflict. Furthermore, these methods of resource distribution and conflict resolution often require or make use
of capacities for empathy, sympathy, and sometimes even community
concern. Non-human primates in societies in which such mechanisms
are present may not be exactly moral beings, but they do show signs
of a sense of social regularity that—just like the norms and rules underlying human moral conduct—promotes a mutually satisfactory
modus vivendi.

Introduction

Any animal whatever, endowed with well-marked social instincts, the
parental and filial affections being here included, would inevitably
acquire a moral sense or conscience, as soon as its intellectual powers
had become as well developed, or nearly as well developed, as in
man.—Charles Darwin, *The Descent of Man* (1982 [1871], pp. 71–2)

Thomas Huxley, in his famous lecture, *Evolution and Ethics* (Huxley, 1894),
advanced a view of human nature that has since dominated debate about
the origins of morality. Huxley believed that human nature is essentially evil—
a product of a nasty and unsympathetic natural world. Morality, he argued, is a
human invention explicitly devised to control and combat selfish and competitive tendencies generated by the evolutionary process. By depicting morality in

Previously published as: "'Any Animal Whatever': Darwinian Building Blocks of Morality
in Monkeys and Apes," by Jessica C. Flack and Frans B. M. de Waal. *Journal of Consciousness Studies* 7(1–2) (2000), pp. 1–29. Copyright © 2000 Imprint Academic, Exeter, UK.
© 2004 *Society for Business Ethics and the Darden School Foundation*   pp. 7–41

this way, Huxley was advocating that the search for morality's origins be decoupled from evolution and conducted outside of biology.

Proponents of Huxley's dualistic view of nature and morality abound today. Among them is the evolutionary biologist Richard Dawkins, who, in 1976, (p. 3) wrote

> Be warned that if you wish, as I do, to build a society in which individuals cooperate generously and unselfishly towards a common good, you can expect little help from biological nature. Let us try to teach generosity and altruism, because we are born selfish.

Another well-known evolutionary biologist, George C. Williams (1988, p. 438), also reaffirmed, with minor variation, Huxley's position when he stated, 'I account for morality as an accidental capability produced, in its boundless stupidity, by a biological process that is normally opposed to the expression of such a capability'. And recently, the philosopher Daniel Dennett (1995, p. 481), although admitting that it is conceivable that perhaps the great apes, whales, and dolphins possess some of the requisite social cognition on which morality depends, wrote

> My pessimistic hunch is that the main reason we have not ruled out dolphins and whales as moralists of the deep is that they are so hard to study in the wild. Most of the evidence about chimpanzees—some of it self-censored by researchers for years—is that they are true denizens of Hobbes' state of nature, much more nasty and brutish than any would like to believe.

But if, as Dawkins suggests, the origins of morality—of the human sense of right and wrong used by society to promote pro-social behaviour—are not biological, then what is the source of strength that enabled humanity to escape from its own nature and implement moral systems? And from where did the desire to do so come? If, as Williams suggests, morality is an accidental product of natural selection, then why has such a 'costly' mistake not been corrected or eliminated by the very process that inadvertently created it? Our inability to answer these questions about the origins and consequences of moral systems is an indication that perhaps we need to broaden the scope of our search. After all, the degree to which the tendency to develop and enforce moral systems is universal across cultures (Midgley, 1991; Silberbauer, 1991), suggests that moral systems, contrary to Huxley's beliefs, do have biological origins and are an integral part of human nature.

Morality indeed may be an invention of sorts, but one that in all likelihood arose during the course of evolution and was only refined in its expression and content by various cultures. If, as we believe, morality arose from biological origins, then we should expect at a minimum that elements of it are present in other social species. And indeed, the evidence we will present in this paper suggests that chimpanzees and other social animals are not the 'true denizens of Hobbes' state of nature' they are surmised to be by Dennett. It may well be that chimpanzees are not moral creatures, but this does not mean that they do not have elements of moral systems in their societies. If we are to understand how our moral systems evolved, we must be open to the idea that the sets of rules that govern how non-human animals behave in their social groups provide clues to how morality arose during the course of evolution. These simple rules, which emerge out of these animals' social interactions, create an element of order that makes living together a possibility, and in a liberal sense, reflect elements of rudimentary moral systems. The order that these sets of rules create is vital to maintaining the stability of social systems and probably is the reason why human morality (whether or not an evolutionary accident) has not been eliminated by natural selection (Kummer, 1979). Garret Hardin (1983, p. 412) captured the essence of this argument in a statement about the importance of justice—'The first goal of justice is to create a *modus vivendi* so that life can go on, not only in the next few minutes, but also indefinitely into the future.'

Had Huxley acknowledged that the origins of morality lay in biology but argued against searching within biology for the *specifics* of our moral systems, his case might have been more persuasive today. Such an argument would have at least fit the contemporary framework for addressing questions about why we are the way we are, which in the case of morality has been explored intensely (Nitecki and Nitecki, 1993, and contributions therein). Indeed, the only pertinent question seems to us: *To what degree* has biology influenced and shaped the development of moral systems? One way to determine the extent to which human morality might be the product of natural selection is to explore behaviour in other species that is analogous (similar traits that arose by convergent evolution due to the presence of similar selection pressures or evolutionary conditions), and perhaps homologous (traits that evolved in a common ancestor and that remain present in related species due to common phylogenetic descent) to our own.

Many non-human primates, for example, seem to have similar methods to humans for resolving, managing, and preventing conflicts of interests within their groups. Such methods, which include reciprocity and food sharing, reconciliation, consolation, conflict intervention, and mediation, are the very building blocks of moral systems in that their existence indicates, as Mary Midgley (1991, p. 12) wrote, 'a willingness and a capacity to look for shared solutions' to conflicts (see also Boehm, 2000). Furthermore, unlike strict dominance hierarchies, which may be an alternative to moral systems for organizing society, advanced methods of resource distribution and conflict resolution seem to require or make use of traits such as the capacity for empathy, sympathy, and sometimes even community concern. Conflict resolution that reflects concern for and possibly understanding of a predicament in which a fellow group member finds himself or herself provides for society the raw material out of which moral systems can be constructed.

Non-human primates in such societies may not be exactly moral beings, but they do show indications of a sense of social regularity that parallels the rules and regulations of human moral conduct (de Waal, 1996a; 1996b, chapter 3). In addition to conflict resolution, other key components or 'prerequisites' of morality recognizable in social animals are reciprocity, empathy, sympathy, and community concern. These components, which also include a sense of justice, and perhaps even the internalization of social norms, are fundamental to moral systems because they help generate connections among individuals within human and animal societies despite the conflicts of interests that inevitably arise. By generating or reinforcing connections among individuals, these mechanisms facilitate co-operative social interaction because they require individuals to make 'commitments' to behave in ways that later may prove contrary to independent individual interests (used throughout this paper in reference to those interests that are truly independent as well as in reference to those interests for which pursuit requires engaging in competition) that when pursued can jeopardize collective or shared interests (Frank, 1988; 1992).

Although many philosophers and biologists are sceptical that evolution can produce components of moral systems such as the capacity for sympathy and empathy or even the capacity for non-kin based co-operation that require the suspension of short term, independent interests, there also exists a tradition going back to Petr Kropotkin (1902) and, more recently, Robert Trivers (1971), in which the view has been that animals assist each other precisely because by doing so they achieve long term, collective benefits of greater value than the short term benefits derived from straightforward competition. Kropotkin specifically adhered to a view in which organisms struggle not necessarily against each other, but collectively against their environments. He strongly objected to Huxley's (1888) depiction of life as a 'continuous free fight'. Although some of Kropotkin's rationale was seriously flawed, the basic tenet of his ideas was on the mark. Almost seventy years later, in an article entitled 'The Evolution of Reciprocal Altruism,' Trivers refined the concepts Kropotkin advanced and explained how co-operation and, more importantly, a system of reciprocity (called 'reciprocal altruism' by Trivers) could have evolved. Unlike simultaneous co-operation or mutualism, reciprocal altruism involves exchanged acts that, while beneficial to the recipient, are costly to the performer. This cost, which is generated because there is a time lag between giving and receiving, is eliminated as soon as a favour of equal value is returned to the performer (see Axelrod and Hamilton, 1981; Rothstein and Pierotti, 1988; Taylor and McGuire, 1988).

According to Richard Alexander (1987), reciprocity is essential to the development of moral systems. Systems of indirect reciprocity—a type of reciprocity that is dependent on status and reputation because performers of beneficent acts receive compensation for those acts from third parties rather than necessarily from the original receiver—require memory, consistency across time, and most importantly, a sense of social regularity or consensual sense of right and wrong (Alexander, 1987, p. 95). It is not yet clear whether systems of indirect reciprocity exist in non-human primate social groups, but certainly there is evidence from studies on food-sharing, grooming, and conflict intervention that suggest the existence of reciprocal systems and, at least among chimpanzees, a sense of social regularity (e.g., Cheney and Seyfarth, 1986; de Waal, 1991; 1996a; 1996b, chapter 3; 1997a; 1997b; Silk, 1992).

Food Sharing, Reciprocal Exchange, and Behavioural Expectations in Primates

Food sharing is known in chimpanzees (Nissen and Crawford, 1932; Kortlandt, 1962; Goodall, 1963; Nishida, 1970; Teleki, 1973; Boesch and Boesch, 1989; de Waal, 1989b; 1997a; Kuroda *et al.*, 1996), bonobos (Kano, 1980; Kuroda, 1984; Hohmann and Fruth, 1993; de Waal, 1992b), siamangs (Fox, 1984), orangutans (Edwards and Snowdon, 1980), and capuchin monkeys (Perry and Rose, 1994; Fragaszy, Feuerstein, and Mitra, 1997; de Waal, 1997b; Rose 1997). It is an alternative method to social dominance and direct competition by which adult members of a social group distribute resources among themselves. Most food sharing requires fine-tuned communication about intentions and desires in order to facilitate inter-individual food transfers. The food transfers typically observed are passive, involving selective relinquishment of plant and animal matter more frequently than active giving (de Waal, 1989b). Three non-exclusive hypotheses have been forwarded to explain the proximate reasons why one individual would voluntarily allow another to take food.

Richard Wrangham (1975) suggested that food possessors share with other group members in order to deter harassment and reduce the possibility that, as possessors, they will become the recipients of aggression. This idea, known as the 'sharing-under-pressure' hypothesis, resembles Nicholas Blurton-Jones' (1987) 'tolerated-theft' model, according to which it is more common for possessors to let food be taken from them than for them to actually give it away. Blurton-Jones reasoned that possessors tolerate theft in order to avoid potentially risky fights.

The 'sharing-to-enhance-status hypothesis' has been used by Adriaan Kortlandt (1972) and James Moore (1984) to explain male chimpanzee food sharing and the displays that frequently accompany the treatment of objects in the environment such as captured prey. Both the act of sharing and the displays—for example, branch shaking—draw attention to the food possessor in a way that may raise his or her status in the group. Illustrative examples of this strategy can be found in Toshisada Nishida *et al.*'s (1992) description of a chimpanzee alpha male in the wild who kept his position through 'bribery' (i.e., selective food distribution to potential allies), and in de Waal's (1982) account of a male contender for the alpha position in a zoo colony, who appeared to gain in popularity by acquiring and distributing food to the group to which the apes normally had no access.

A similar hypothesis was developed for human food distribution by Kristen Hawkes (1990), an anthropologist, who suggested that men who provide food to many individuals are 'showing off'. Showing off in this manner, according to Hawkes, signals hunting prowess and generosity, two characteristics that may be attractive to potential mates or potential political allies.

A third hypothesis—the reciprocity hypothesis—proposes that food sharing is part of a system of mutual obligations that can involve material exchange, the exchange of social favours such as grooming and agonistic support, or some combination of the two. For example, de Waal (1982) found that subordinate adult male chimpanzees groom dominant males in return for an undisturbed mating session. Suehisa Kuroda (1984) and de Waal (1987) found indications that adult male bonobos exchange food with adolescent females in return for sex. The reciprocity hypothesis thus differs significantly from the sharing-under-pressure hypothesis because it addresses possessors and 'beggars' as potential long-term co-operators rather than merely as present competitors who use sharing to appease one another. It differs from the 'sharing-to-enhance-status' hypothesis because it emphasizes the co-operative nature of the relationship between possessors and beggars and, consequently, emphasizes how sharing benefits both the possessor and the beggar rather than just the possessor. One advantage of the 'sharing-to-enhance-status' hypothesis is, however, that it provides a testable proximate account of what social factors might motivate possessors to initially share with beggars, in that it suggests that possessors share because by doing so they increase their social status in the group. In fact, the 'sharing-to—enhance-status' hypothesis, although a partial explanation of sharing, is useful if considered in conjunction with the reciprocity hypothesis because it provides a proximate motivational explanation for why possessors allow some of their food to be taken by others. Consequently, this hypothesis is not necessarily in conflict with the reciprocity hypothesis, and may be an extension of it. Furthermore, the 'sharing-to—enhance-status' hypothesis, like the reciprocity hypothesis, involves the exchange of favours between individuals using apparently equivalent, although unequal, currencies: For example, a form of reciprocal exchange may emerge if A shares food with B, which makes A more popular with B resulting—as suggested by Hawkes—in agonistic support or matings.

De Waal (1989b; 1997a; 1997b) examined whether food itself is exchanged reciprocally over time or is shared in return for some social favour by investigating the food sharing tendencies of brown capuchin monkeys and chimpanzees. Results of the capuchin study indicated that female brown capuchins share food reciprocally. The methodology used in this study differed substantially from the chimpanzee study described next. The primary difference was that the capuchin's food sharing tendencies were examined in a dyadic context rather than in the presence of the entire group as in the chimpanzee study. As shown in Figure 1, adult capuchins were separated into pairs and placed into a test chamber divided into two sections by a mesh partition. One capuchin was allowed continuous access to a bucket of attractive food. The individual with access to the food was free to monopolize all of it or could move close to the mesh and share actively or passively by allowing his counterpart access to pieces he had dropped. The situation was then reversed so that the second individual had access to the attractive food (which was of a new type) and the first did not. The rate of transfer between pairs of adult female capuchins was found to be reciprocal while the rate of transfer between pairs of adult males was not. Males, however, were less discriminating than females in terms of with whom they shared, and more generous in the amount of food they shared. Although this study examined food-sharing in capuchins in an artificial environment created by the experimenters, the results were not anomalous—food sharing among unrelated adults has been observed both among capuchins in a colony at the Yerkes Regional Primate Centre as well as among wild capuchins (Perry and Rose, 1994; Rose, 1997).

In order to study how chimpanzees share food in a social context, a situation was created in which a monopolizable food source was available to individuals in the social group. To accomplish this, a captive group of chimpanzees at the Field Station of the Yerkes Regional Primate Research Centre was provided with branches and leaves that were tightly bundled together so that the possibility existed for some group members to keep all of the food for themselves. Based on an analysis of nearly 7,000 recorded interactions over food, de Waal found that food exchanges between nine adult group members were quite balanced per dyad so that, on average, individuals A and B shared the same amount with each other. If individual A, however, shared a particular day with individual B, this did not necessarily result in B being more likely to share with A the following day. Grooming, on the other hand, did affect the likelihood to share when sharing and grooming occurred on the same day. For example, A was less likely to share with B if A had also groomed B the same day, but A was

Mesh partition   →   Food bowl →

Figure 1
Schematic drawing of the pair-test setup. One subject at a time receives food from a bowl attached to the outside of the chamber. A mesh partition divides the test chamber, preventing direct access to the food by the other subject. In a rare instance of active sharing, a male (right) hands a piece of food to a female who reaches through the mesh to accept it. Both subjects visually monitor the transfer. This drawing (by the second author) was made from an actual video still. From de Waal (1997b).

more likely to share with B if it had been B who had groomed A earlier that day. Other data indicating that food possessors actively resisted approaches by individuals who had not previously groomed them bolstered this result. Lastly, individuals who were reluctant to share their food had a greater chance of encountering aggression when they themselves approached a food possessor.

Although the chimpanzee food-sharing study confirmed one part of the prediction of Wrangham's and Blurton-Jones' hypotheses that there should be a negative correlation between rate of food distribution and frequency of received aggression, de Waal (1989b; 1996b, pp. 152–3) considers his results inconsistent with the tolerated theft model. He found that most aggression is directed not against the possessors of food, as the tolerated theft model predicts, but against beggars for food. In fact, even the lowest-ranking adult possessors are able to hold on to food unchallenged due to the 'respect of possession' first noted, with astonishment, by Goodall (1971, chapter 16), who wondered why the alpha male of her community failed to claim food possessed by others, and actually had to beg for it (Goodall, however, noted that the apparent respect for possession she observed among chimpanzees only applied to animal matter and not to bananas or other kinds of vegetable matter. This led her to suggest another somewhat different, although not mutually exclusive, explanation that focused more on the motivational state of the possessor and the corresponding response to this by the beggars). Respect of possession exists also in other primates, and was experimentally investigated by Sigg and Falett (1985), Kummer and Cords (1991), and discussed by Kummer (1991).

In fact, in de Waal's (1989) study the observed negative correlation between an individual's food distribution rate and the probability of aggression received concerned this individual as an *approacher* rather than as food possessor. This suggests either that food distributors respond to stingy individuals by sharing less with them than with others *or* that individuals, who for whatever reason, are more likely to be aggressively rebuffed when approaching food possessors, in turn become more reluctant themselves when they possess food to share with others.

Thus, the food sharing data are most in line with the reciprocity hypothesis. It is conceivable, though, that receipt of a favour (whether it be a service such as grooming or an object, such as food) positively influences an individual's social attitude so that this individual is willing to share indiscriminately with everyone else in its group (Hemelrijk, 1994). This so-called 'good mood' hypothesis, however, is not supported by the data (de Waal, 1997a), which show that if A receives grooming from B, A is only more likely to share with B but not with others in the group. The exchange between grooming and food is, therefore, partner-specific.

These studies on capuchins and chimpanzees address whether reciprocity is calculated or a by-product of frequent association and symmetrical relationships (de Waal and Luttrell, 1988; de Waal, 1997a). Calculated reciprocity is based on the capacity to keep mental note of favours given and received. It is a more sophisticated and cognitively complex (and consequently less easily accepted) form of reciprocity than symmetry-based reciprocity, which occurs when individuals preferentially direct favours to close associates. Since association is a symmetrical relationship characteristic (if A associates often with B, B does so often with A), the distribution of favours automatically becomes reciprocal (for a more in-depth discussion of what constitutes symmetry-based reciprocity, see de Waal, 1996b, p. 157). Although important, such symmetry-based reciprocity is not as cognitively demanding as calculated reciprocity, which was shown above to occur in chimpanzees and possibly female capuchins.

Calculated reciprocity—unlike symmetry-based reciprocity—raises interesting questions about the nature of expectations. The possibility that chimpanzees withhold favours from ungenerous individuals during future interactions, and are less resistant to the approaches of individuals who previously groomed them (de Waal, 1997a) suggests they have expectations about how they themselves and others should behave in certain contexts.

Other evidence to suggest that some primates have expectations about how others should behave comes from studies of patterns of conflict intervention. Chimpanzees and some species of macaques exhibit what appears to be calculated reciprocity in beneficial interventions, or the interference by a third party in an ongoing conflict in support of one of the two conflict opponents (de Waal and Luttrell, 1988; Silk, 1992). Thus, if A intervenes in favour of B, B is more likely to intervene in favour of A. In de Waal's and Luttrell's study, chimpanzees, but not macaques, also exhibited reciprocity in harmful interventions, suggesting the existence of a so-called 'revenge system'. In other words, in the chimpanzee group under study there existed a significant correlation between interventions given and received so that if A intervened against B, B was more likely to intervene against A in the future. This retaliatory pattern was not found in stumptail and rhesus macaque groups. Silk (1992), however, found evidence for a revenge system among males in bonnet macaque society in that the males in her study group appeared to monitor both the amount of aggression that they received from and directed at other males. Although Silk's data and numerous anecdotes suggest that macaques do have the capacity to engage in revenge, it is likely that revenge of this sort is not commonplace due to the greater risks in a macaque society (compared to a chimpanzee society) associated with directing aggression at dominants.

Revenge of another sort—indirect revenge—does, on the other hand, appear to be relatively common in at least one macaque species. Indirect revenge occurs when recipients of aggression redirect their aggression at the uninvolved juvenile or younger kin of their opponents. In this way, these often low ranking macaques are still able to 'punish' their attackers but are able to do so without much cost to themselves (Aureli, Cozzolino, Cordischi and Scucchi, 1992). For example, Aureli and colleagues found that Japanese macaque recipients of aggression were significantly more likely to attack the kin of their former opponents within one hour after the original conflict had occurred than if no conflict had occurred at all. One could argue, as the authors pointed out, that it is possible that this increase in aggression towards an opponent's kin after a conflict may be due to a general rather than selective aggressive tendency that is triggered by fighting and thus does not reflect a revenge system. Additional analyses revealed, however, that this hypothesis is not supported by the data—the relative probability that the original recipient of aggression would attack, following the conflict, the kin of a former opponent was significantly higher than the probability that the original recipient of aggression would attack following the conflict any group member subordinate to it. The existence of this form of revenge in macaque society suggests that a macaque's capacity to be vindictive is constrained by its rank in society rather than by its cognitive abilities.

These examples of retributive behaviour indicate that some form of calculated reciprocity is present in primate social systems. This kind of reciprocity and the kinds of responses seen by chimpanzees in the food-sharing study exemplify how and why prescriptive rules, rules that are generated when members of a group learn to recognize the contingencies between their own behaviour and the behaviour of others, are formed. The existence of such rules and, more significantly, of a set of expectations, essentially reflects a sense of social regularity, and may be a precursor to the human sense of justice (de Waal, 1991; Gruter, 1992; see also Hall, 1964; Nishida, 1994).

Trivers (1971) daringly labelled negative reactions to perceived violations of the social code, *moralistic aggression*. He emphasized that individuals who respond aggressively to perceived violations of the social code help reinforce systems of reciprocity by increasing the cost of not co-operating and, even more importantly, by increasing the cost of cheating, or failing to return a favour. When one individual cheats another, that individual exploits a relationship that is based on the benefits the partners previously obtained by co-operating. By doing so, the cheater benefits himself or herself at the partner's expense and destabilizes the system of reciprocity. Moralistic aggression, which often manifests itself as protest by subordinate individuals or punishment by dominant individuals, helps deter cheating. Consequently, it contributes to the creation of order, an element essential to the maintenance of the stability or integrity of social systems (de Waal, 1996a; Hardin, 1983). If unchecked, however, moralistic aggression can also lead to a spiral of spiteful retaliation that confers advantage on neither the original defector nor the moralistic aggressor, as is the case when those seeking retributive justice exacerbate conflicts to such a degree that feuds develop (Boehm, 1986; de Waal, 1996b, chapter 4).

Conclusion: Monkeys and apes appear capable of holding received services in mind, selectively repaying those individuals who performed the favours. They seem to hold negative acts in mind as well, leading to retribution and revenge. To what degree these reciprocity mechanisms are cognitively mediated is currently under investigation, but at least for chimpanzees there is evidence for a role of memory and expectation.

Conflict Resolution

Conflicts are inevitable in social groups. They may be generated by disagreement over social expectations or simply by competition over access to resources. Regardless of what triggers conflicts, group-living individuals need mechanisms for negotiating resolutions to them and for repairing the damage to their relationships that results once conflicts of interests have escalated to the point of aggression. One of the simplest ways that conflicts are regulated and resolved is through the establishment of clear-cut dominance relations (see Carpenter, 1942; Mendoza and Barchas, 1983; Bernstein, 1981; Bernstein and Ehardt, 1985; de Waal, 1996b; for a review, see Preuschoft and van Schaik, in press).

Primates in hierarchical social systems typically have many methods by which they communicate who is dominant and who is subordinate. Subordinate rhesus macaques, for example, bare their teeth in a ritualized expression and often present their hindquarters to an approaching dominant group member. Such displays signal to the dominant individual that the subordinate recognizes the type of relationship they share, which consequently eliminates any question of ambiguity or need for aggression and promotes harmony and stability at the group level (de Waal, 1986). Interestingly, it appears that the bared-teeth expression is a *formal* dominance signal in despotic species, such as the rhesus macaque, in that it is almost exclusively displayed by subordinate individuals (de Waal and Luttrell, 1985; Preuschoft, 1999). In more egalitarian and tolerant macaque species, such as Tonkean macaques, power asymmetries between individuals are less evident than in despotic species, like rhesus macaques. Coinciding with this difference in power is a difference in use of the bared-teeth expression, which in Tonkean macaques is neither ritualized nor formal but common to both subordinate and dominant individuals (Thierry, Demaria, Preuschoft and Desportes, 1989).

Strict dominance relationships are often an effective means by which conflicts can be negotiated. When conflicts persist despite dominance relationships, or in primate species where dominance relations are relaxed or almost absent, there must be alternative ways to work out problems and repair relationships (this does not, however, imply that the development of egalitarian social systems led to the development of conflict management devices or vice versa, only that generally the two go together). One of the most important of these post-conflict behaviours is *reconciliation*. Reconciliation, which is defined as a friendly reunion between former opponents not long after a confrontation, is illustrated in the following description of an agonistic interaction between two chimpanzees and the post-conflict behaviour that followed (de Waal, 1989c, p. 41):

> . . . Nikkie, the leader of the group, has slapped Hennie during a passing charge. Hennie, a young adult female of nine years, sits apart for a while feeling with her hand the spot on the back of the neck where Nikkie hit her. Then she seems to forget about the incident; she lies down in the grass, staring into the distance. More than fifteen minutes

later, Hennie slowly gets up and walks straight to a group that includes Nikkie and the oldest female, Mama. Hennie approaches Nikkie with a series of soft pant grunts. Then she stretches out her arm to offer Nikkie the back of her hand for a kiss. Nikkie's hand-kiss consists of taking Hennie's whole hand rather unceremoniously into his mouth. This contact is followed by a mouth-to-mouth kiss.

Reconciliation enables the immediate, negative consequences of aggression to be counteracted and reduces the tension-related behaviour of recipients of aggression (de Waal and van Roosmalen, 1979; Aureli and van Schaik, 1991; de Waal and Aureli, 1996; Aureli, 1997). Perhaps more importantly, though, reconciliation enables former opponents to restore their relationship (Kappeler and van Schaik, 1992) and indeed one can increase the rate of reconciliation by experimentally enhancing the value of the relationship, e.g., by making the food-intake of two individuals dependent on their co-operation (Cords and Thurnheer, 1993). This form of post-conflict behaviour has been demonstrated in many primate species, each of which has its own typical 'peacemaking' gestures, calls, facial expressions and rituals, including, for example, kissing and embracing (see de Waal and Yoshihara, 1983; Cords, 1988; de Waal and Ren, 1988; York and Rowell, 1988; Aureli, van Schaik and van Hooff, 1989; Judge, 1991; Ren *et al.*, 1991; Kappeler, 1993). We label friendly post-conflict behaviour 'reconciliation' if we can demonstrate empirically that the former opponents are selectively attracted so that they tend to come together in this manner more than usual and more with each other than with individuals who had nothing to do with the fight. In order to determine the percentage of conflicts followed by reconciliation for individuals of a particular species, we compare the post-conflict period (PC) to a matched-control period (MC). We use the matched-control period because it enables us to determine whether the affiliation that takes place during the post-conflict period is triggered by the conflict, or if it is simply due to chance (for a detailed discussion of the PC/MC method, see Veenema, Das and Aureli, 1994). As seen in Figure 2, former stumptail macaque opponents affiliate considerably more in post-conflict periods than they do in the matched-control periods.

Although reconciliation has been observed in most primate species and appears to be a universal method of repairing disturbed relationships, the degree to which it is used differs across primate species in a pattern that may reflect the level of integration and cohesion in a primate society. For example, analysis of post-conflict/matched-control (PC/MC) data from 670 pairs of former stumptail macaque opponents with PC/MC data from 573 pairs of former rhesus macaque opponents, revealed that stumptail monkeys reconciled on average significantly more often (i.e., 51.6 per cent) than rhesus monkeys (i.e., 21.1 per cent) (de Waal and Ren, 1988). In general, individuals in despotic species reconcile less frequently after conflicts than individuals in more tolerant and egalitarian species, most likely because the strict dominance hierarchies that are present in despotic species constrain the development of strong symmetrical relationships among group members (de Waal, 1989a).

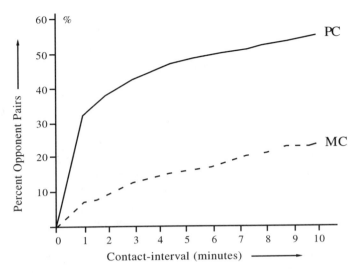

Figure 2
Cumulative percentage of pairs of opponents making their first nonagonistic body contact within a certain time interval. PC = post conflict observation, MC = matched control observation, N = number of pairs. From de Waal and Ren (1988).

Another way primates regulate and resolve conflicts of interests between group members is through conflict intervention. Although many studies have shown that interventions are related to coalition building and alliance formation, some interventions may have other functions as well (e.g., Reinhardt, Dodsworth and Scanlan, 1986; Bernstein and Ehardt, 1986; Boehm, 1994; Petit and Thierry, 1994; for reviews see Harcourt and de Waal, 1992). In some species, interventions by the highest ranking members of the social group end fights or at least reduce the severity of aggression that occurs during fights. The alpha male chimpanzee often plays such a role in fights involving females and/or juveniles in his group (de Waal, 1982). For example, if two juveniles are playing and a fight erupts, the alpha male just has to approach the area of the conflict to stop the fight. By doing so, he directly reduces the levels of aggression within the group, and also prevents the fight from escalating further by ending it before the juveniles' mothers intervene and possibly begin fighting themselves. Another example of this type of intervention in chimpanzees is given by the following excerpt from *Chimpanzee Politics* (1982, p. 124):

> On one occasion, a quarrel between Mama and Spin got out of hand and ended in biting and fighting. Numerous apes rushed up to the two warring females and joined in the fray. A huge knot of fighting, screaming apes rolled around in the sand, until Luit leapt in and literally beat them apart. He did not choose sides in the conflict, like the others; instead anyone who continued to fight received a blow from him.

This pattern of behaviour, often referred to as the 'control role' has been described in other species of primates as well, (e.g., Bernstein, 1964; Tokuda and Jensen, 1969; Reinhardt *et al.*, 1986), and is a type of arbitration. The most interesting types of interventions that fall under the control role heading are those that are impartial. Individuals who intervene without choosing sides seem to do so in order to restore peace rather than simply aid friends or family (de Waal and van Hooff, 1981; de Waal, 1982; Goodall, 1986). The ability to put one's own preferences aside in this manner is another indication that a rudimentary form of justice may exist in the social systems of non-human primates (Boehm, 1992; de Waal, 1996a; 1996b). On the other hand, one might argue that although such interventions ultimately may have the effect of restoring the peace and reducing overall levels of aggression in the group, it is possible that the intervener's intentions were simpler, and that he or she was motivated only by the desire to terminate an aversive stimulus—the noisy conflict—and not by any group-oriented motivation. Evidence from chimpanzees and macaques suggests, however, that this explanation for impartial interventions may be inadequate. Such interventions may indeed be motivated in part by a desire to terminate an aversive stimulus but, if that were the only motivation, we might expect the interventions to be severe and partial, and in favour of the individual with whom the intervener shares the best relationship. Furthermore, agonistic interventions, in particular, can trigger agonistic and nonagonistic involvement by other individuals and intense screaming by the target or targets of the intervention (Gouzoules, Gouzoules and Marler, 1984). Thus, interventions often temporarily exacerbate the aversive stimuli that supposedly the intervener sought to suppress.

Another type of intervention that falls under the control role is the protective intervention. Interventions in this group include those that occur on behalf of recipients of aggression. When expressed in this form, the control role can be viewed as a way that lower ranking or weaker (either physically *or* socially) individuals are protected from higher ranking, stronger (either physically *or* socially) group members.

A particularly salient example of the power of control animals to protect recipients of aggression in some primate societies that demonstrates not only the degree to which a control animal can influence the outcome of a conflict, but also that other individuals in the group recognize this capacity in certain individuals, comes from an experiment in which the composition of a pigtail macaque group was manipulated (Flack and de Waal, unpublished data). During this experiment, the three highest-ranking male pigtail macaques were removed for the day once per week and confined to their indoor housing. We studied the patterns of conflict intervention and aggression that occurred in the group when the males were present and when the males were absent. During removal periods, although confined to their indoor housing, the males had vocal and very restricted visual access to the group in that they were separated from the group by only a two foot long tunnel (to the indoor housing), divided in the middle by a metal door that did not completely seal off the indoor area from the outdoor area.

Three very low-ranking females typically received moderate levels of aggression from other group members when the males were present, but the males often intervened in these conflicts and, when this occurred, the aggression that had been directed at the females usually subsided. During the period when the males were removed, the intensity and frequency of aggression directed at these low ranking females increased substantially, and severe biting (biting for more than five seconds in duration), in particular, was more common. Several times, the aggression directed at these females became so severe that the investigator was forced to intervene.

Over the course of the study period, however, the females discovered a way to deal with the increase in severe aggression that they received when the high-ranking males were absent. This began when one female started running into the tunnel that separated the indoor housing from the outdoor housing. Once in the tunnel, the female solicited support from the males locked inside. The males, who could hear the conflict, were always waiting at the door. The female being attacked would scream, bare her teeth, and stick her arm though a small space in the door as her attackers were rushing forward. Each time this occurred, one of the males confined to the indoor housing would emit a threat bark, and the female would scream, clearly distressed by both her attackers and the threat, but not move from her position. Her attackers, however, would jump back and cease their abusive behaviour. The female would then lie prone in the tunnel for the next fifteen minutes or so, and each time her attackers attempted to bite her, a male inside would emit a threat bark and the attack would cease. The other two females, too, learned that when they were severely attacked they could appeal to the confined high-ranking males in this way, and as the study period progressed, this behaviour increased in frequency. Notably, no individuals ever escaped from aggression by running into the tunnel when the males were present in the group, presumably because doing so prohibited escape and thus was very dangerous.

Interestingly, among chimpanzees, the individual who plays this control role need not be the alpha male of the group. The control animal may be any group member who the community permits—in the sense that none of the individuals in the social group protests the control animal's involvement in the conflict nor prohibits the particular control animal from 'playing' his or her role (de Waal, 1996b, chapter 3). Pascale Sicotte (1995) described a similar mechanism for resolving conflicts in bi-male groups of mountain gorillas in which females and infants sometimes interposed themselves between two fighting silverbacks. These interpositions, which occurred in 10–25 per cent of conflicts between silverbacks, involved more than just passive or chance interference in the agonistic dyad by a third party. Sicotte only included as interpositions those third party interventions in which a previously uninvolved individual interacted nonagonistically with at least one of the two males engaged in conflict, and in which the course of the initial agonistic interaction between the males was modified because one of the opponents directed its attention towards the third party. Notably, in one of the two groups Sicotte studied, he found that interpositions significantly increased the time between the end of the fight in which it occurred, and the start of the next fight.

One other important method of conflict resolution that has been identified in primate groups is mediation. Mediation occurs when a third party to a conflict becomes the bridge between two former opponents who cannot seem to bring themselves to reconcile without external help. It is characterized in the following example (de Waal and van Roosmalen, 1979, p. 62).

> Especially after serious conflicts between two adult males, the two opponents sometimes were brought together by an adult female. The female approached one of the males, kissed or touched him or presented towards him and then slowly walked towards the other male. If the male followed, he did so very close behind her (often inspecting her genitals) and without looking at the other male. On a few occasions the female looked behind at her follower, and sometimes returned to a male that stayed behind to pull at his arm to make him follow. When the female sat down close to the other male, both males started to groom her and they simply continued when she went off.

In the above example of mediation, a female, who apparently is trying to reunite two former opponents in her social group, seems to show community concern in that she apparently cares about resolving a conflict in which she had no part and, more importantly, about restoring a disturbed relationship that is not her own. Although such examples are rare in primates, and perhaps unlikely in any but apes, a very similar pattern of behaviour to that illustrated by the example above was observed in stump-tail macaques (Flack, personal observation), suggesting that individuals in several species may have a sense of community concern that comes from having a stake in the quality of life within the group as a whole.

De Waal (1996b, p. 31) explained the evolution of community concern as follows:

> Inasmuch as every member benefits from a unified, cooperative group, one expects them to care about the society they live in, and to make an effort to improve and strengthen it similar to the way the spider repairs her web, and the beaver maintains the integrity of his dam. Continued infighting, particularly at the top of the hierarchy, may damage everyone's interests, hence the settlement of conflict is not just a matter of the parties involved, it concerns the community as a whole. This is not to say that animals make sacrifices for their community, but rather that each and every individual has a stake in the quality of the social environment on which its survival depends. In trying to improve this quality for their own purposes, they help many of their group mates at the same time. A good example is arbitration and mediation in disputes; standard practice in human

society—courts of law serve this function—but recognizable in other primates as well.

Two other patterns of behaviour in monkeys and apes illustrative of community concern are triadic reconciliation—the involvement of third parties in the reconciliation process—and the group-wide celebration that often follows the reconciliation of dramatic conflicts of chimpanzees (de Waal, 1992b; 1996b, chapter 4). These patterns of behaviour suggest that monkeys and apes devote time and energy to making sure their social group remains peaceful, perhaps because group members recognize the value that a harmonious coexistence can have to achieving shared interests. In this sense, community concern can be extremely beneficial to individuals within social groups—even if it requires subordinating independent interests (non-shared), at least on occasion, to community interests—so long as many common goals are shared among group members. This kind of community concern, however, does not require that monkeys and apes worry about how the community, as an abstract entity, is doing. It only requires that the individual works toward creating a community atmosphere that reflects his or her own best interests. Consequently, the evolution of community concern in individuals may not necessarily require group selection. Its evolution can most likely be explained using selection at the level of the individual (although it is possible that individual selection may perhaps provide only a partial explanation for the evolution of such behaviours—for more discussion of this matter, see Wilson and Sober, 1994, and this issue), particularly if we consider the other behaviours that probably co-evolved with community concern in order to mitigate the risks and reduce the short-term costs to individuals generated by investing in the community.

Punishment, for example, or the imposition of a cost or penalty by one individual (usually who has some authority or power over the other individual) on another for its behaviour (Bean, 1981), and perhaps indirect reciprocity and social norms, help offset the cost of placing community (shared) interests above individual (independent) interests. Punishment and indirect reciprocity facilitate the evolution of investment in community interests because they help deter cheating (as discussed earlier) and reinforce community-oriented behaviours by making it possible for reciprocity to become generalized—so that if one individual performs a favour for another, that favour may be returned by a third party (for discussion of punishment, see Boyd and Richerson, 1992; Clutton-Brock and Parker, 1995; for discussion of indirect reciprocity, see Alexander, 1987; Boyd and Richerson, 1989). As Axelrod (1986) discussed, an especially powerful mechanism by which cheating can be deterred emerges when punishment against defectors becomes linked with negative indirect reciprocity, or punishment of nonpunishers. This *metanorm*, as Axelrod calls it, makes the 'norm' against defection self-policing. Whether this occurs in non-human primates, however, remains to be empirically demonstrated.

There is, however, evidence from a recent study of play signalling patterns in juvenile chimpanzees that suggests primates may modify their behaviour in anticipation of punishment (Jeannotte, 1996). Lisa Jeannotte found that older play partners were significantly more likely to emit play signals, such as 'play face,' during play bouts that occurred in proximity to adults, particularly those adults who were mothers of younger play partners and who were themselves young, than was the case when these adults were absent. These results suggest that an older juvenile play partner may increase its play signalling in the presence of a young mother to make clear that its interaction with the younger play partner is benign and does not warrant intervention or punishment.

Another mechanism that might enable the evolution of community concern is docility, or the receptivity to social influence that is common to social primates and that is useful for acquiring valuable information without the need for direct experience or evaluation (Simon, 1990). Thus, if certain values, like community concern, are fostered in a particular social environment, then an individual, simply due to its docile disposition, may adopt and become committed to those values even though at times those values or sentiments may encourage a course of action that is counter to an individual's independent (non-shared) interests. In this way, community concern evolves as a by-product of selection for docility (for a related argument about a similar mechanism, the 'conformist transmission,' by which community concern might evolve, see Boyd and Richerson, 1985; 1992; Henrich and Boyd, 1998; see also Cronk, 1994 for a Marxian argument about how docility may actually make it possible in some moral systems for certain individuals to justify and perpetuate inequalities of power and access to resources).

Although at present, direct evidence for punishment, docility, and especially indirect reciprocity is scant or fragmented in the primate literature, such behavioural mechanisms by which collective action is facilitated do probably exist to varying degrees. The existence of these mechanisms, which are likely complementary rather than alternative methods that act in concert to produce stability in social systems (Henrich and Boyd, 1998), is indirectly supported by the presence of learned adjustment, succourant behaviour, empathy, and sympathy in non-human primates.

Conclusion: Despite inevitable conflicts of interests, a certain degree of stability must be maintained in primate societies so that individuals can realize their collective interests and make worthwhile their investments in sociality. Dominance relationships provide one simple way to regulate and order societies. Social systems with more level dominance relationships require additional mechanisms, however, such as reconciliation; consolation; impartial, protective, and pacifying interventions; and perhaps community concern. All of these mechanisms are present to varying degrees in monkeys and apes.

Empathy, Sympathy and Consolation

Although food-sharing, social reciprocity in general, and the different forms of conflict resolution seen in primates need not require a capacity for sympathy and empathy, it is likely that both are involved to some degree in all of these behaviours, and to a high degree in at least the more sophisticated forms of conflict intervention such as mediation. In order to help others, as the female in the mediation example was doing, individuals need to be concerned about and be able to understand others' needs and emotions.

Learned adjustment, which is common in primates, is a precursor to such behaviour in that it demonstrates the ability of monkeys and apes to change their behaviour as they become familiar with the limitations of those with whom they interact without requiring that these individuals understand why they should adjust their behaviour. Juvenile chimpanzees, for example, commonly restrict the degree of force they use in wrestling matches while playing with younger juveniles and infants (Hayaki, 1985). Monkeys and apes also adjust their behaviour in the presence of disabled group members (e.g., Fedigan and Fedigan, 1977; de Waal, 1996b, chapter 2; de Waal, Uno, Luttrell, Meisner and Jeannotte, 1996c). The adjustment may include increased social tolerance towards individuals who behave abnormally or intervention on behalf of disabled individuals who seem unaware of when they are involved in a dangerous predicament. Although the examples discussed above are most parsimoniously explained using learned adjustment, the possibility that cognitive empathy—the ability to comprehend the needs and emotions of other individuals—may provide a more accurate explanation for some of these behaviours needs to be explored in future studies.

An especially important area that needs investigation is how learned adjustment and cognitive empathy relate to the internalization of social norms. One study that begins to address this question is Jeannotte's previously mentioned study (1996) of play-signalling in juvenile chimpanzees in relation to social context and environment. Results of this study indicate that an older juvenile is not significantly more likely to play roughly when the age difference between it and its partner is small as opposed to large. Although this result seems to contradict findings from previous research that suggested that juvenile chimpanzees restrict the intensity of play when interacting with younger play partners, it does not necessarily do so. Jeannotte found that there was a strong correlation between the play intensity of one partner with that of the other. One likely explanation for this 'matching' is that it may be a consequence of restraint on the part of the older partner and escalation on the part of the younger partner (Hayaki, 1985).

Succourant behaviour, which includes care-giving and providing relief to distressed individuals who are not kin, is also an example of a category of behaviours that seem to require attachment to and concern for others and, in some cases, an understanding of other's needs and emotions (Scott, 1971).

Succourant tendencies develop in primates early in life; even infants respond to tension generated by aggression by mounting one another or by mounting kin or even the individuals involved in the agonism. Although these infants probably are not helping to reduce tensions between the individuals involved in the agonism by responding in this way, they may be comforting themselves. This simple need to comfort oneself after or during a fight in which the infant itself was not involved suggests that the infant perceives distress in others and reacts vicariously to it by becoming distressed itself. This 'emotional contagion' (Hatfield, Cacioppo and Rapson, 1993) may be the mechanism underlying the development of succourance and suggests that primates do have the ability to empathize.

Non-human primates may be able to empathize with one another in that other group member's feelings and actions emotionally affect them, but are non-human primates also concerned about individuals who appear distressed? In other words, do they sympathize with or just react to individuals in their group who are distressed? There is evidence suggesting that some primates do have concern for fellow group members; it comes from studies of consolation, or the appeasement of distressed individuals through affiliative gestures such as grooming and embracing by third parties following a fight (de Waal and van Roosmalen, 1979). The predominant and immediate effect of consolation—the alleviation of distress (de Waal and Aureli, 1996), is illustrated by the following example observed by Jane Goodall (1986, p. 361):

> An adult male challenged by another male often runs screaming to a third and establishes contact with him. Often both will then scream, embrace, mount or groom each other while looking toward the original aggressor. This . . . is how a victim tries to enlist the help of an ally. There are occasions, however, when it seems that the primary goal is to establish reassurance contact—as when fourteen-year-old Figan, after being attacked by a rival, went to hold hands with his mother.

In the above example, however, the recipient of aggression is *seeking* consolation. This type of consolation occurs in several primate species but may not require that the third party sympathizes with the recipient who approaches for reassurance (for other examples see Lindburg, 1973; de Waal and Yoshihara, 1983; Verbeek and de Waal, 1997). *Active* consolation, on the other hand, occurs when a third party approaches and affiliates with a recipient of aggression following a fight. Such action may require that the third party not only recognize the distress of the recipient of aggression but also be concerned enough about that individual to approach and appease it. Sometimes, for example, a juvenile chimpanzee will approach and embrace an adult male who has just lost a confrontation with his rival (de Waal, 1982).

There exist systematic data to support the conclusion that chimpanzees have the capacity to engage in active consolation (de Waal and Aureli, 1996). An analysis of 1,321 agonistic incidents among a captive group of seventeen chimpanzees housed in a large compound at the Field Station of the Yerkes Regional Primate Research Center revealed that significantly more affiliative contacts initiated by bystanders occurred immediately (within several minutes) after a conflict than after longer time intervals or in control periods not preceded by conflict. Furthermore, significantly more affiliative contacts initiated by bystanders occurred following serious incidents than mild incidents (this is particularly important because, if consolation occurs to alleviate distress, and if an individual's level of distress is proportional to the aggression intensity of the conflict in which it participated, then consolation should occur more frequently following serious aggressive incidents). And finally, bystanders initiated significantly more affiliative contact with the recipients of aggression than with the aggressors themselves.

In contrast to these findings for chimpanzees, researchers have been unable to quantitatively demonstrate active consolation in four macaque species (Aureli, 1992; Aureli and van Schaik, 1991; Judge, 1991; Aureli, Veenema, van Panthaleon van Eck and van Hoof, 1993; Aureli, Das, Verleur and van Hooff, 1994; Castles and Whiten, 1998; for a review, see de Waal and Aureli, 1996). This suggests that consolation may be limited to the great apes, possibly because it requires more sophisticated cognition than present in monkeys. Alternatively, it may be limited to apes because within their social systems, such behaviour is more advantageous and perhaps less costly than in monkey social systems in which approaching recipients of aggression, and areas of conflicts generally, can be dangerous due to the frequency with which aggression is redirected to bystanders in many monkey societies (de Waal and Aureli, 1996).

Conclusion: Moral sentiments such as sympathy, empathy, and community concern, engender a bond between individuals, the formation of which facilitates and is facilitated by co-operation. This bond is enabled by an individual's capacity to be sensitive to the emotions of others. Monkeys and apes are capable of learned adjustment, and have succourant tendencies, in that they comfort and console one another when distressed. But are they capable of genuine concern for others based on perspective-taking? There is some evidence to suggest that apes, like humans, are capable of cognitive empathy but its existence in monkeys remains questionable.

Implications of Primate Research for Understanding Human Morality

In the opening pages of *A Theory of Justice* (1971, p. 4), John Rawls elegantly states the central problem that plagues those human (and animal) societies in which implicit or explicit rules of conduct exist to make co-operation possible:

> . . . although a society is a co-operative venture for mutual advantage, it is typically marked by a conflict as well as by an identity of interests. There is an identity of interests since social cooperation

makes possible a better life for all than any would have if each were to live solely by his own efforts. There is a conflict of interests since persons are not indifferent as to how the greater benefits of their collaboration are distributed, for in order to pursue their ends they each prefer a larger to a lesser share.

This problem, as identified above by Rawls, has in practice no true solutions. Furthermore, the research on the natural history and social behaviour of our non-human primate relatives illustrates how both our capacity and tendency to pursue our independent interests and our capacity and tendency to pursue shared interests are natural and important, at least from a biological point of view (see de Waal, 1992a). This suggests that morality was not *devised* to subjugate the independent interests of individuals. Rather, a moral system *emerged* out of the interaction of the two sets of interests, thus providing a way to express both. This conclusion should not be mistaken as justification for using natural selection as a model for what we ought to do or *not* do. What we ought to do and how we decide this is a separate question from why and how moral systems arose.

It is particularly important that in our pursuit of the origins and purpose of moral systems we resist the temptation to let our moral views frame, and thus obscure, how in the end we describe and explain the moral standards embodied in implicit social contracts. Even more importantly, we need to be careful not to hold up as moral systems only those that in our view wholly subjugate the independent interests of individuals in favour of those interests that are shared, simply because we value that these systems suppress conflict and deliver consensus. Doing so precludes from consideration those systems that from an operational standpoint are moral systems, but that may not fit perfectly our moral views of what is right, of worth, or of value.

Humans, nonetheless, may be the only truly moral creatures. Although one could argue that several elements of human morality are present in non-human primates—particularly in apes—there is no evidence at this time to suggest that non-human primates have moral systems that mirror the complexity of our own. In some species, individuals, by interacting every day, may create a kind of social contract that governs which types of behaviour are acceptable and tolerable and which are punishable—yet these individuals have no way to conceptualize such decisions or abstract them from their context, let alone debate them amongst themselves. Consensus is only obvious in the absence of protest and prohibition.

Consensus achieved in this tacit manner, however, is not uncommon in our own species. This observation, in conjunction with the above research that suggests that an actual social contract of sorts arises out of interactions between group members in primate societies, makes plausible the idea that human morality is best understood as having arisen out of an implicit agreement among group members that enabled individuals to profit from the benefits of co-operative sociality.

Acknowledging that morality may have a social function and stressing that it may have emerged from such a social contract does not require that we accept this kind of 'actual' social contract as the medium through which we decide what is moral. Nor does it suggest that we revert to some form of Social Darwinism, an approach to deciding what we ought to do that was based not only on a misconceived, red-in-tooth-and-claw representation of natural selection, but worse, also on the idea that this interpretation of 'nature's way' should be used to guide (and justify) our own behaviour. Although we need to recognize that the social contract does in fact often represent the process by which we come to agree (as a group) what is acceptable, we also need to recognize that this is probably the case because the social contract is useful from an evolutionary perspective because it enables individuals in groups to reach consensus with minimal, if any, need for explicit co-ordination. Certainly, from a social perspective, one of the major limitations of any actual social contract is that such contracts do not necessarily produce the most 'moral' solutions to problems. The outcome such contracts produce is no more than a reflection of compromise, and of the behaviour that as a group we practice.

Another important observation about human behaviour made by David Hume (1739), Adam Smith (1759), and Edward Westermarck (1912) is that human morality is powerfully influenced by emotional responses and is not always governed by the abstract, intellectual rules upon which we have supposedly agreed. The primate research implicitly suggests that this emphasis on the role of emotions is both insightful and accurate—in primate groups individuals are motivated to respond to others based on the emotional reactions they have to one another's behaviour. That sympathy, based on empathy, seems to direct the emotional responses of some primates to others may reflect their ability to differentiate between self and other and, more significantly, to care for one another. Yet, the idea that emotion may be fundamental to morality contradicts what many philosophers—most significantly Immanuel Kant (1785)—have argued: That the human sense of right and wrong is more a consequence of rational processes than of emotional reactions. It would be quite erroneous, however, to equate moral emotions with a lack of rationality and judgement. The emotions discussed by Hume, Smith and Westermarck are actually very complex, involving retribution, reciprocity and perspective taking. The latter, as is now increasingly apparent from research into so-called Theory-of-Mind, involves complex mental abilities (for a review of Theory-of-Mind in non-human primates, see Heyes and Commentaries, 1998).

Darwin (1871; 1872), who was familiar with the thinking of Hume and Smith, advocated a perspective on human morality in line with these ideas in that he saw human nature as neither good nor bad but neutral. He recognized that moral systems enable individuals to reconcile what Hume saw as two sides to human nature—the dark, competitive side, which is dominated by greed and competition, and the 'sentimental,' co-operative side, which is marked by social instincts and compassion. To Darwin, this dualism in human nature arose from the evolution of two strategies (the individual and social) that together provided a method by which individuals can obtain limited resources. Thus, Darwin recognized that moral systems not only govern the expression and use of these strategies but also reflect their interaction.

Opposition to this more integrated view by some contemporary evolutionary biologists, such as Richard Dawkins and George Williams (see Introduction), leads us to propose that their views on morality be classified not as Darwinian but Huxleyan. For example, Dawkins recently reconciled human moral ideals with his interpretation of evolution by saying that we are entitled to throw out Darwinism ('in our political and social life we are entitled to throw out Darwinism, to say we don't want to live in a Darwinian world,' *Human Ethology Bulletin,* March 1997). Because Darwin himself perceived absolutely no contradiction or dualism between the evolutionary process and human moral tendencies (e.g., de Waal, 1996b; Uchii, 1996), such views represent a considerable narrowing of what Darwin deemed possible.

The Kantian view of morality as an invention of reason supplemented with a sense of duty remained pervasive despite Darwin's insights. Perhaps primate research that suggests that morality is a consequence of our emotional needs and responses as well as of our ability to rationally evaluate alternatives is strong enough to warrant making room for a more integrated perspective of morality that acknowledges its biological basis and emotional component as well as the role of cognition. Perhaps Hume and Kant were both correct.

The foundations of morality may be built on our emotional reactions to one another but morality itself is no doubt also tempered and sometimes modified by two additional factors. First, morality may be modified by our ability to evaluate the situation generating these emotional reactions. Second, it may be tempered by our understanding of the consequences that our responses to the behaviour that elicited the emotional reaction have for ourselves and others. A problem, however, remains even after we acknowledge that what generates in each of us an understanding of what is good or virtuous is a combination of two factors: 1) the emotional reaction and intuition of each individual that jumpstart the moral process, with 2) the cognitive-rational evaluations that enable the individual to determine what is right. The problem that remains despite this integration is how to translate the resultant conception in the individual of what is good to action at the community level. In human societies, as in animal societies, this is often achieved by some manifestation of the social contract. But as mentioned earlier, 'actual' social contracts, as rough compromises between competing agents, often with unequal powers and needs, may be unsatisfactory from a normative standpoint because they do not fully respect worth, value or rights.

Conclusion

Sympathy-related traits such as attachment, succourance, emotional contagion and learned adjustment in combination with a system of reciprocity and punishment, the ability to internalize social rules and the capacity to work out conflicts and repair relationships damaged by aggression, are found to some degree in many primate species, and are fundamental to the development of moral systems (Table 1).

Table 1

It is hard to imagine human morality without the following tendencies and capacities also found in other species. These tendencies deserve to be called the four ingredients of morality:

Sympathy Related
Attachment, succourance, and emotional contagion.
Learned adjustment to and special treatment of the disabled and injured.
Ability to trade places mentally with others: cognitive empathy.*

Norm Related
Prescriptive social rules.
Internalization of rules and anticipation of punishment.*
A sense of social regularity and expectation about how one ought to be treated.*

Reciprocity
A concept of giving, trading, and revenge.
Moralistic aggression against violators of reciprocity rules.

Getting Along
Peacemaking and avoidance of conflict.
Community concern and maintenance of good relationships.*
Accommodation of conflicting interests through negotiation.

*It is particularly in these areas—empathy, internalization of rules, sense of justice, and community concern—that humans seem to have gone considerably further than most other animals.

All of these elements of moral systems are tools social animals—including humans—use to make living together a possibility. These capacities help keep in check the inevitable competition among group members due to conflicting interests. More importantly, however, sympathy-related traits and the capacity to work out conflicts and repair relationships help promote cohesion, co-operation and social bonding, characteristics of a social group that may, from an evolutionary perspective, make group living a functionally effective strategy and, therefore, an attractive strategy in which individuals should invest resources. As the anthropologist Ruth Benedict wrote in 1934 (p. 251):

One of the most misleading misconceptions due to this nineteenth-century dualism was the idea that what was subtracted from society was added to the individual and what was subtracted from the individual was added to society. . . . In reality, society and the individual are not antagonists. His culture provides the raw material of which the individual makes his life. If it is meagre, the individual suffers; if it is rich, the individual has the chance to rise to his opportunity.

At the end of this paper, in which we have discussed the possible evolutionary building blocks of human moral systems, it is essential to also point out the limitations of biological approaches to human morality. After all, we have in the past seen attempts to derive moral rules directly from nature, resulting in a dubious genre of literature going back to Ernest Seton's (1907) *The Natural History of the Ten Commandments*. Other biblical titles have followed, principally in the German language, spelling out how moral principles contribute to survival (e.g., Wickler, 1971). Much of this literature assumed that the world was waiting for biologists to point out what is Normal and Natural, hence worth being adopted as ideal. Attempts to derive ethical norms from nature, however, are highly questionable.

Our position is quite different. While human morality does need to take human nature into account by either fortifying certain natural tendencies—such as sympathy, reciprocity, loyalty to the group and family, and so on—or by countering other tendencies—such as within-group violence and cheating—it is in the end the society that decides, over a period of many generations, on the contents of its moral system. There is a parallel here with language ability: The capacity to develop and learn a very complex communication system such as language is naturally present in humans, but it is filled in by the environment resulting in numerous different languages. In the same way, we are born with a moral capacity, and a strong tendency to absorb the moral values of our social environment, but we are not born with a moral code in place. The filling in is done by the social environment often dictated by the demands of the physical environment (de Waal, 1996b).

Interestingly, moral development in human children hints at the same emphasis on conflict resolution and reciprocity (principles of 'fairness') as emphasized above for non-human primates. Instead of the traditional, Piagetian view of morality imposed upon the child by the all-knowing adults, increasingly it is thought that children develop moral rules in social interaction with each other, particularly during the resolution of conflict (e.g., Killen and Nucci, 1995; Killen and de Waal, in press).

At the same time that our moral systems rely on basic mental capacities and social tendencies that we share with other co-operative primates, such as chimpanzees, we also bring unique features to the table, such as a greater degree of rule internalization, a greater ability to adopt the perspective of others, and of course the unique capacity to debate issues amongst ourselves, and transmit them verbally, including their rationale. To communicate intentions and feelings is one thing, to clarify what is good, and why, and what is bad, and why, quite something else. Animals are no moral philosophers.

But, while there is no denying that we are creatures of intellect, it is also clear that we are born with powerful inclinations and emotions that bias our thinking and behaviour. It is in this area that many of the continuities with other animals lie. A chimpanzee stroking and patting a victim of attack or sharing her food with a hungry companion shows attitudes that are hard to distinguish from those of a person taking a crying child in the arms, or doing volunteer work in a soup kitchen. To dismiss such evidence as a product of subjective interpretation by 'romantically inspired naturalists' (e.g.: Williams, 1989, p.190) or to classify all animal behaviour as based on instinct and human behaviour as proof of moral decency is misleading (see Kummer, 1979). First of all, it is uneconomic in that it assumes different processes for similar behaviour in closely related species. Second, it ignores the growing body of evidence for mental complexity in the chimpanzee, including the possibility of empathy.

One wonders if, on the basis of external behaviour alone, an extraterrestrial observer charged with finding the only moral animal on earth would automatically end up pointing at *Homo sapiens.* We think it unlikely that human behaviour in all its variety, including the occasional horror, will necessarily strike the observer as the most moral. This raises of course the question how and whether morality sets us apart from the rest of the animal kingdom. The continuities are, in fact, quite striking, and need to weigh heavily in any debate about the evolution of morality. We do hesitate to call the members of any species other than our own 'moral beings,' but we also believe that many of the tendencies and cognitive abilities underlying human morality antedate our species' appearance on this planet.

Acknowledgements

The authors thank Rudolf Makkreel and, especially, Leonard Katz for very helpful comments and suggestions. The first author thanks Meredith Small, Adam Arcadie, and Richard Baer, Jr. for patient and stimulating discussion about the evolution of morality.

Bibliography

Alexander, R. D. 1987. *The Biology of Moral Systems* (New York: Aldine de Gruyter).

Aureli, F. 1992. 'Post-conflict behaviour among wild long-tailed macaques (*Macaca-fascicu-laris*).' *Behavioural Ecology and Sociobiology* 31, pp. 329–37.

_____. 1997. 'Post-conflict anxiety in non-human primates: The mediating role of emotion in conflict resolution.' *Aggressive behaviour* 23, pp. 315–28.

Aureli, F., R. Cozzolino, C. Cordischi, and S. Scucchi. 1992. 'Kin-oriented redirection among Japanese macaques—an expression of a revenge system?' *Animal Behaviour* 44, pp. 283–291.

Aureli, F., M. Das, D. Verleur, and J. van Hooff. 1994. 'Postconflict social interactions among Barbary macaques *(Macaca sylvanus)*.' *International Journal of Primatology* 15, pp. 471–85.

Aureli, F., and J. van Hooff. 1993. 'Functional-aspects of redirected aggression in macaques.' *Aggressive behaviour* 19, pp. 50–1.

Aureli, F., C. J. van Panthaleon van Eck, and H. C. Veenema. 1995. 'Long-tailed macaques avoid conflicts during short-term crowding.' *Aggressive behaviour* 21, pp. 113–22.

Aureli, F., and C. P. van Schaik. 1991. 'Post-conflict behaviour in long-tailed macaques *(Macaca fascicularis)*. 2. Coping with the uncertainty.' *Ethology* 89, pp. 101–14.

Aureli, F., C. P. van Schaik, J. and van Hooff. 1989. 'Functional-aspects of reconciliation among captive long-tailed macaques *(Macaca fascicularis)*.' *American Journal of Primatology* 19, pp. 39–51.

Aureli, F., H. C. Veenema, C. J. van Panthaleon van Eck, J. and van Hooff. 1993. 'Reconciliation, consolation, and redirection in Japanese macaques *(Macaca fuscata)*.' *Behaviour* 124, pp. 1–21.

Axelrod, R. 1986. 'An evolutionary approach to norms.' *American Political Science Review* 80, pp. 1095–111.

Axelrod, R., and W. D. Hamilton. 1981. 'The evolution of co-operation.' *Science* 211, pp. 1390–96.

Bean, P. 1981. *Punishment: A Philosophical and Criminological Inquiry* (Oxford: Rutherford).

Benedict, R. 1989 (1934). *Patterns of Culture* (Boston: Houghton Mifflin Company).

Bernstein, I. S. 1964. 'Group social patterns as influenced by the removal and later reintroduction of the dominant male rhesus.' *Psychological Reports* 14, pp. 3–10.

_____. 1981. 'Dominance: The baby and the bathwater.' *Behavioural and Brain Sciences* 4, pp. 419–58.

Bernstein, I. S., and C. Ehardt. 1986. 'The influence of kinship and socialization on aggressive behaviour in rhesus monkeys *(Macaca fascicularis)*.' *Animal Behaviour* 34, pp. 739–47.

Bernstein, I. S., and C. L. Ehardt. 1985. 'Intragroup agonistic behaviour in rhesus monkeys.' *International Journal of Primatology* 6, pp. 209–26.

Blurton-Jones, N. G. 1987., 'Tolerated theft, suggestions about the ecology and evolution of sharing, hoarding, and scrounging.' *Social Science Information* 26, pp. 31–54.

Boehm, C. 1986. 'Capital punishment in tribal Montenegro: Implications for law, biology, and Theory of Social Control.' *Ethology and Sociobiology* 7, pp. 305–20.

_____. 1992. 'Segmentary warfare and the management of conflict: Comparison of east African chimpanzees and patrilineal-patrilocal humans.' In *Coalitions and Alliances in Humans and Other Animals,* ed. A. H. Harcourt and F. B. M. de Waal (Oxford: Oxford University Press), pp. 137–73.

_____. 1994. 'Pacifying interventions at Arnhem zoo and Gombe.' In *Chimpanzee Cultures*, ed. R. W. Wrangham, W. C. McGrew, F. B. M. de Waal, and P. G. Heltne (Cambridge, Mass.: Harvard University Press), pp. 211–26.

_____. 2000. 'Conflict and the evolution of social control.' *Journal of Consciousness Studies* 7 (1–2), pp. 79–101.

Boesch, C., and H. Boesch. 1989. 'Hunting behaviour in wild chimpanzees in the Tai National Park.' *American Journal of Physical Anthropology* 78, pp. 547–73.

Boyd, R., and P. J. Richerson. 1985. *Culture and the Evolutionary Process* (Chicago: University of Chicago).

_____. 1989. 'The evolution of indirect reciprocity.' *Social Networks* 11, pp. 213–36.

_____. 1992. 'Punishment allows the evolution of cooperation (or anything else) in sizable groups.' *Ethology and Sociobiology* 13, pp. 171–95.

Carpenter, C. R. 1942. 'Sexual behaviour of free-ranging rhesus monkeys, *Macaca mulatta*, 1: Specimens, procedures, and behavioural characteristics of oestrus.' *Journal of Comparative Psychology* 33, pp. 113–42.

Castles, D. L., and A. Whiten. 1998. 'Post-conflict behaviour of wild olive baboons. I. Reconciliation, redirection and consolation.' *Ethology* 104, pp. 126–47.

Cheney, D., R. Seyfarth. 1986. 'The Recognition of social alliances in vervet monkeys.' *Animal Behaviour* 34, pp. 350–70.

Clutton-Brock, T. H., and. G. A. Parker. 1995. 'Punishment in animal societies.' *Nature* 373, pp. 209–15.

Cords, M. 1988. 'Reconciliation of aggressive conflicts by immature long-tailed macaques.' *Animal Behaviour* 36, pp. 1124–35.

Cords, M., and S. Thurnheer. 1993. 'Reconciling with valuable partners by long-tailed macaques.' *Ethology* 93, pp. 315–25.

Cronk, L. 1994. 'Evolutionary theories of morality and the manipulative use of signals.' *Zygon* 29, pp. 81–101.

Darwin, C. 1965 (1872). *The Expression of Emotion in Man and Animals* (Chicago: University of Chicago Press).

_____. 1982 (1871). *The Descent of Man, and Selection in Relation to Sex* (Princeton, N.J.: Princeton University Press).

Dawkins, R. 1976. *The Selfish Gene* (Oxford: Oxford University Press).

_____. 1997. 'Interview.' *Human Ethology Bulletin* 12(1).

Dennett, D. C. 1995. *Darwin's Dangerous Idea: Evolution and the Meaning of Life* (New York: Simon and Schuster).

Edwards, S., and C. Snowdon. 1980. 'Social behaviour of captive, group-living orang-utans.' *International Journal of Primatology* 1, pp. 39–62.

Fedigan, L. M., and L. Fedigan. 1977. 'The social development of a handicapped infant in a free-living troop of Japanese monkeys.' In *Primate Bio-social Development: Biological, Social and Ecological Determinants*, ed. S. Chevalier-Skolnikoff and R. E. Poirier (New York: Garland), pp. 205–22.

Fox, G. 1984. 'Food transfer in gibbons.' In *The Lesser Apes*, ed. H. Preuschoft, D. J. Chivers, W. Y. Brockelman, and N. Creel (Edinburgh: Edinburgh University Press), pp. 32–32.

Fragaszy, D. M., J. M. Feuerstein, and D. Mitra. 1997a. 'Transfers of food from adult infants in tuffed capuchins (*Cebus apella*). *Journal of Comparative Psychology* 111, pp. 194–200.

Frank, R. 1992. 'Emotion and the costs of altruism.' In *The Sense of Justice: Biological Foundations of Law*, ed. R. D. Masters and M. Gruter (Newbury, Calif.: Sage Publications), pp. 46–67.

Frank, R. H. 1988. *Passions Within Reason: The Strategic Role of the Emotions* (New York: Norton).

Goodall, J. 1963. 'My Life Among Wild Chimpanzees,' *National Geographic*, 124, pp. 272–308.

———. 1971. *In the Shadow of Man* (Boston: Houghton Mifflin).

———. 1986. *The Chimpanzees of Gombe: Patterns of Behaviour* (Cambridge, Mass.: Belknap Press, Harvard University Press).

Gouzoules, S., H. Gouzoules, and P. Marler. 1984. 'Rhesus monkey (*Macaca mulatta*) screams: representational signaling in the recruitment of agonistic aid?' *Animal Behaviour* 32, pp. 182–93.

Gruter, M. 1992. 'An ethological perspective on law and biology.' In *The Sense of Justice: Biological Foundations of Law*, ed. R. D. Masters and. M. Gruter (Newbury Park, Calif.: Sage Publications), pp. 95–105.

Hall, K. R. L. 1964. 'Aggression in monkey and ape societies.' In *The Natural History of Aggression*, ed. J. Carthy and F. Ebling (London: Academic Press), pp. 51–64.

Harcourt, A. H., and F. B. M. de Waal, eds. 1992. *Coalitions and Alliances in Humans and Other Animals* (Oxford: Oxford University Press).

Hardin, G. 1983. 'Is violence natural?' *Zygon* 18, pp. 405–13.

Hatfield, E., J. T. Cacioppo, and R. L. Rapson. 1993. 'Emotional contagion.' *Current Directions in Psychological Science* 2, pp. 96–9.

Hawkes, K. 1990. 'Showing off: Tests of an hypothesis about men's foraging goals.' *Ethology and Sociobiology*. 12, pp. 29–54.

Hayaki, H. 1985. 'Social play of juvenile and adolescent chimps in the Mahale Mountains National Park, Tanzania.' *Primates* 26, pp. 343–60.

Hemelrijk, C. K. 1994. 'Support for being groomed in longtailed macaques, *Macaca fasicularis*.' *Animal Behaviour* 48, pp. 479–81.

Henrich, J., and R. Boyd. 1998. 'The evolution of conformist transmission and the emergence of between-group differences.' *Evolution and Human Behaviour* 19(4), pp. 215–41.

Heyes, C. M., and Commentators. 1998. 'Theory of mind in non-human primates.' *Behavioural and Brain Sciences* 21, pp. 101–48.

Hobbes, T. 1991 (1651). *Leviathan* (Cambridge: Cambridge University Press).

Hohmann, G., and B. Fruth. 1993. 'Field observations on meat sharing among bonobos (*Pan paniscus*).' *Folia Primatologica* 60, pp. 225–9.

Hume, D. 1978 (1739). *A Treatise of Human Nature* (Oxford: Oxford University Press).

Huxley, T. H. 1888. 'Struggle for existence and its bearing upon man.' *Nineteenth Century*, Feb., 1888.

_____. 1989 (1894). *Evolution and Ethics* (Princeton, N.J.: Princeton University Press).

Jeannotte, L. A. 1996. *Play-signaling in juvenile chimpanzees in relationship to play intensity and social environment.* Unpublished Master's Thesis (Atlanta, Ga: Emory University).

Judge, P. G. 1991. 'Dyadic and triadic reconciliation in pigtail macaques (*Macaca nemestrina*).' *American Journal of Primatology* 23, pp. 225–37.

Kano, T. 1980. 'Social behaviour of wild pygmy chimpanzees (*Pan paniscus*) of Wamba: A preliminary report.' *Journal of Human Evolution* 9, pp. 243–60.

Kant, I. 1947 (1785). 'Groundwork for the metaphysics of morals,' *The Moral Law* (London: Hutchinson).

Kappeler, P. M. 1993. 'Reconciliation and post-conflict behaviour in ringtailed lemurs, *Lemur catta*, and redfronted lemurs, *Eulemur fulvus rufus*.' *Animal Behaviour* 45, pp. 901–15.

Kappeler, P. M., and C. P. van Schaik. 1992. 'Methodological and evolutionary aspects of reconciliation among primates.' *Ethology* 92, pp. 51–69.

Killen, M., and L. P. Nucci. 1995. 'Morality, autonomy and social conflict.' in *Morality in Everyday Life: Developmental Perspectives*, ed. M. Killen and D. Hart (Cambridge: Cambridge University Press), pp. 52–86.

Killen, M., and F. B. M. de Waal. In press. 'The evolution and development of morality.' In *Natural Conflict Resolution*, ed. F. Aureli and F. B. M. de Waal (Berkeley: University of California Press).

Kortlandt, J. 1962. 'Chimpanzees in the wild.' *Scientific American* 206, pp. 128–39.

_____. 1972. *New Perspectives on Ape and Human Evolution* (Amsterdam: Stichting voor Psychobiologie). Kropotkin, P. 1972 (1902). *Mutual Aid: A Factor of Evolution* (New York: New York University Press).

Kummer, H. 1980. 'Analogs of morality among non-human primates.' In *Morality as a Biological Phenomenon*, ed. G. S. Stent (Berkeley and Los Angeles: University of California Press), pp. 31–49.

_____. 1991. 'Evolutionary transformations of possessive behaviour.' *Journal of Social Behaviour and Personality* 6, pp. 75–83.

Kummer, H., and M. Cords. 1991. 'Cues of ownership in long-tailed macaques, *Macaca fascicularis*.' *Animal Behaviour* 42, pp. 529–49.

Kuroda, S. 1984. 'Interaction over food among pygmy chimpanzees.' In The *Pygmy Chimpanzee*, ed. R. Susman (New York: Plenum), pp. 301–24.

Kuroda, S., S. Suzuki, and T. Nishihara. 1996. 'Preliminary report on predatory behaviour and meat sharing in tschego chimpanzees (*Pan troglodytes troglodytes*) in the Ndoki Forest, northern Congo.' *Primates* 37, pp. 253–59.

Lindburg, D. G. 1973. 'Grooming as a social regulator of social interactions in rhesus monkeys.' In *Behavioural Regulators of Behaviour in Primates*, ed. C. Carpenter (Lewisburg: Bucknell University Press), pp. 85–105.

Mendoza, S. P., and P. R. Barchas. 1983. 'Behavioural processes leading to linear hierarchies following group formation in rhesus monkeys.' *Journal of Human Evolution* 12, pp. 185–92.

Midgley, M. 1991. 'The origin of ethics.' In *A Companion Guide to Ethics*, ed. P. Singer (Oxford: Blackwell Reference), pp. 1–13.

Moore, J. 1984. 'The evolution of reciprocal sharing.' *Ethology and Sociobiology* 5, pp. 5–14.

Nishida, T. 1970. 'Social behavior and relationship among chimpanzees of the Mahale Mountains.' *Primates* 11, pp. 47–87.

————. 1994. 'Review of recent findings on Mahale chimpanzees.' In *Chimpanzee Cultures*, ed. R. Wrangham, W. C. McGrew, F. B. M. de Waal, and P. G. Heltne (Cambridge, Mass.: Harvard University Press).

Nishida, T., T. Hasegawa, H. Hayaki, Y. Takahata, S. Uehara. 1992. 'Meat-sharing as a coalition strategy by an alpha male chimpanzee?' In *Topics in Primatology, Vol. 1, Human Origins*, ed. T. Nishida, W. C. McGrew, P. Maler, and F. B. M. de Waal (Tokyo: University of Tokyo Press), pp. 159–74.

Nishida, T., and L. A. Turner. 1996. 'Food transfer between mother and infant chimpanzees of the Mahale Mountains National Park, Tanzania.' *International Journal of Primatology* 17, pp. 947–68.

Nissen, H. W., and M. P. Crawford. 1932. 'A preliminary study of food sharing behaviour in young chimpanzees.' *Journal of Comparative Psychology* 22, pp. 383–419.

Nitecki, M. H., D. V. Nitecki. 1993. *Evolutionary Ethics* (Albany, N.Y.: State University of New York Press).

Perry, S. 1997. 'Male-female social relationships in wild white-faced capuchins (*Cebus capucinus*).' *Behaviour* 134, pp. 477–510.

Perry, S., and L. Rose. 1994. 'Begging and food transfer of coati meat by white-faced capuchin monkeys *Cebus capucinus*.' *Primates* 35, pp. 409–15.

Petit, O., and B. Thierry. 1994. 'Aggressive and peaceful interventions in conflicts in Tonkean macaques.' *Animal Behaviour* 48, pp. 1427–36.

Preuschoft, S. 1999. 'Are primates behaviourists? Formal dominance, cognition, and free-floating rationales.' *Journal of Comparative Psychology* 113, pp. 91–5.

Preuschoft, S., and C, P. van Schaik. In press. 'Dominance and communication: Conflict management in various social settings.' In *Natural Conflict Resolution*, ed. F. Aureli and F. B. M. de Waal (Berkley, Calif.: University of California Press).

Rawls, J. 1971. *A Theory of Justice* (Oxford: Oxford University Press).

Reinhardt, V., R. Dodsworth, and J. Scanlan. 1986. 'Altruistic interference shown by the alpha female of a captive group of rhesus monkeys.' *Folia primatologica* 46, pp. 44–50.

Ren, R., K. Yan, Y. Su, H. Gi, B. Liang, W. Bao, and F. B. M. de Waal. 1991. 'The reconciliation behavior of golden monkeys (*Rhinopithecus roxellanae*) in small groups.' *Primates* 32, pp. 321–7.

Rose, L. M. 1997. 'Vertebrate predation and food-sharing in Cebus and Pan.' *International Journal of Primatology* 18, pp. 727–65.

Rothstein, S. I., and R. Pierotti. 1988. 'Distinctions among reciprocal altruism, kin selection, and cooperation and a model for the initial evolution of beneficent behavior.' *Ethology and Sociobiology* 9, pp. 189–209.

Scott, J.P. 1971. *Internalization of Social Norms: A Sociological Theory of Moral Commitment* (Englewood Cliffs, N.J.: Prentice-Hall).

Seton, E. T. 1907. *The Natural History of the Ten Commandments* (New York: Scribners).

Sicotte, P. 1995. 'Interpositions in conflicts between males in bimale groups of mountain gorillas.' *Folia primatologica*, 65, pp. 14–24.

Sigg, H., and J. Falett 1985. 'Experiments on respect of possession and property in hamadryas baboons *(Papio hamadryas)*.' *Animal Behaviour* 33, pp. 978–84.

Silberbauer, G. 1991. 'Ethics in small scale societies.' In *A Companion Guide to Ethics*, ed. P. Singer (Oxford: Blackwell Reference), pp. 14–29.

Silk, J. B. 1992. 'The patterning of intervention among male bonnet macaques: Reciprocity, revenge and loyalty.' *Current Anthropology* 31, pp. 318–24.

Simon, H. A. 1990. 'A mechanism for social selection and successful altruism.' *Science* 250, pp. 1665–8.

Smith, A. 1937 (1759). *A Theory of Moral Sentiments* (New York: Modern Library).

Taylor, C. E., and M. T. McGuire. 1988. 'Reciprocal altruism: Fifteen years later.' *Ethology and Sociobiology* 9, pp. 67–72.

Teleki, G. 1973. 'Group response to the accidental death of a chimpanzee in Gombe National Park, Tanzania.' *Folia primatologica* 20, pp. 81–94.

Thierry, B., C. Demaria, S. Preuschoft, and C. Desportes. 1989. 'Structural convergence between the silent bared-teeth display and the relaxed open-mouth display in the Tonkean macaque *(Macaca tonkeana)*.' *Folia primatologica* 52, pp. 178–84.

Tokuda, K., and G. Jensen. 1969. 'The leader's role in controlling aggressive behaviour in a monkey group.' *Primates* 9, pp. 319–22.

Trivers, R. 1971. 'The evolution of reciprocal altruism.' *Quarterly Review of Biology* 46, pp. 35–57.

Uchii, S. 1996. 'Darwin and the evolution of morality.' Paper presented at the Nineteenth-Century Biology International Fellows Conference, Centre for Philosophy of Science, University of Pittsburg. Published on Internet: www.bun.kyoto-u.ac.jp/~suchii/D.onM.html.

Veenema, H. C., M. Das, and F. Aureli. 1994. 'Methodological improvements for the study of reconciliation.' *Behavioural Processes* 31, pp. 29–37.

Verbeek, P., and F. B. M. de Waal. 1997. 'Postconflict behaviour of captive capuchins in the presence and absence of attractive food.' *International Journal of Primatology* 18, pp. 703–25.

de Waal, F. B. M. 1982. *Chimpanzee Politics: Power and Sex Among Apes* (London: Jonathon Cape).

———. 1986. 'Integration of dominance and social bonding in primates.' *Quarterly Review of Biology* 61, pp. 459–79.

———. 1987. 'Tension regulation and nonreproductive functions of sex among captive bonobos *(Pan paniscus)*.' *National Geographic Research* 3, pp. 318–35.

———. 1989a. 'Dominance "style" and primate social organization.' In *Comparative Socioecology: The Behavioural Ecology of Humans and Other Mammals*, ed. V. Standen and R. A. Foley (Oxford: Blackwell), pp. 243–64.

_____. 1989b. 'Food sharing and reciprocal obligations among chimpanzees.' *Journal of Human Evolution* 18, pp. 433–59.

_____. 1989c. *Peacemaking Among the Primates* (Cambridge, Mass.: Harvard University Press).

_____. 1991. 'The chimpanzee's sense of social regularity and its relation to the human sense of justice.' *American Behavioural Scientist* 34, pp. 335–49.

_____. 1992a. 'Aggression as a well-integrated part of primate social relationships: Critical comments on the Seville Statement on Violence.' In *Aggression and Peacefulness in Humans and Other Primates*, ed. J. Silverberg and J. P. Gray (New York: Oxford University Press), pp. 37–56.

_____. 1992b. 'Appeasement, celebration, and food sharing in the two *Pan* species.' In *Topics in Primatology, Vol. 1 Human Origins*, ed. T. Nishida, W. C. McGrew, P. Marler, and F. B. M. de Waal (Tokyo: University of Tokyo Press), pp. 37–50.

_____. 1993. 'Reconciliation among the primates: A review of empirical evidence and unresolved issues.' In *Primate Social Conflict*, ed. W. A. Mason and S. P. Mendoza (Albany: State University Press), pp. 111–44.

_____. 1996a. 'Conflict as Negotiation.' In *Great Ape Societies*, ed. W. C. McGrew, L. F. Marchant, and T. Nishid (Cambridge: Cambridge University Press), pp. 159–72.

_____. 1996b. *Good Natured: The Origins of Right and Wrong in Primates and Other Animals* (Cambridge, Mass.: Harvard University Press).

_____. 1997a. 'The chimpanzee's service economy: Food for grooming.' *Evolution and Human Behaviour* 18, pp. 375–86.

_____. 1997b. 'Food transfers through mesh in brown capuchins.' *Journal of Comparative Psychology* 111, pp. 370–78.

de Waal, F. B. M., and F. Aureli. 1996. 'Reconciliation, consolation, and a possible cognitive difference between macaques and chimpanzees.' In *Reaching into Thought: The Minds of the Great Apes*, ed. A. E. Russon, K. A. Bard, and S. T. Parker (Cambridge: Cambridge University Press), pp. 80–110.

de Waal, F. B. M., and D. L. Johanowicz. 1993. 'Modification of reconciliation behaviour through social experience: An experiment with two macaque species.' *Child Development* 64, pp. 897–908.

de Waal, F. B. M., and L. M. Luttrell. 1985. 'The formal hierarchy of rhesus monkeys: An investigation of the bared-teeth display.' *American Journal of Primatology* 9, pp. 73–85.

_____. 1988. 'Mechanisms of social reciprocity in three primate species: Symmetrical relationship characteristics or cognition.' *Ethology and Sociobiology* 9, pp. 101–18.

_____. 1989. 'Toward a comparative socioecology of the genus *Macaca*: Intergroup comparisons of rhesus and stumptail monkeys.' *American Journal of Primatology* 10, pp. 83–109.

de Waal, F. B. M., and M. R. Ren. 1988. 'Comparison of the reconciliation behaviour of stumptail and rhesus macaques.' *Ethology* 78, pp. 129–42.

de Waal, F. B. M, H. Uno, L. M. Luttrell, L. F. Meisner, and L. A. Jeannotte. 1996. 'Behavioural retardation in a macaque with autosomal trisomy and aging mother.' *American Journal on Mental Retardation* 100, pp. 378–90.

de Waal, F. B. M., and J. A. R. A. M. van Hooff. 1981. "Side-directed communication and agonistic interactions in chimpanzees." *Behaviour* 77, pp. 164–98.

de Waal, F. B. M., and A. van Roosmalen. 1979. 'Reconciliation and consolation among chimpanzees.' *Behavioural Ecology and Sociobiology* 5, pp. 55–66.

de Waal, F. B. M., and D. Yoshihara. 1983. 'Reconciliation and re-directed affection in rhesus monkeys.' *Behaviour* 85, pp. 224–41.

Westermarck, E. 1912. *The Origin and Development of the Moral Ideas* (London: Macmillan).

Wickler, W. 1981 (1971). *Die Biologie der Zehn Gebote: Warum die Natur für uns Kein Vorbid ist* (Munich: Piper).

Williams, G. C. 1988. 'Reply to comments on "Huxley's evolution and ethics in a sociobiological perspective."' *Zygon* 23, pp. 383–407.

Williams, G. C. 1989. 'A sociobiological expansion of "Evolution and Ethics."' *Evolution and Ethics* (Princeton, N.J.: Princeton University Press), pp. 179–214.

Wilson, D. S., and E. Sober. 1994. 'Reintroducing group selection to the human behavioural sciences.' *Behaviour and Brain Sciences* 17, pp. 585–654.

Wrangham, R. 1975. *The Behavioural Ecology of Chimpanzees in Gombe National Park, Tanzania.* Unpublished doctoral dissertation (Cambridge: Cambridge University).

Wrangham, R. W. 1979. 'On the evolution of ape social systems.' *Social Science Information* 18, pp. 335–68.

York, A. D., and T. E. Rowell. 1988. 'Reconciliation following aggression in patas monkeys (*Erythrocebus patas*).' *Animal Behaviour* 36, pp. 502–9.

RESPONSIBILITY, INCONSISTENCY, AND THE PARADOXES OF MORALITY IN HUMAN NATURE: DE WAAL'S WINDOW INTO BUSINESS ETHICS

Joshua D. Margolis

Abstract: Efforts to trace the evolutionary antecedents of human morality introduce challenges and opportunities for business ethics. The biological precedents of responsibility suggest that human tendencies to respond morally are deeply rooted. This does not mean, however, that those tendencies are always consistent with ends human beings seek to pursue. This paper investigates the conflicts that may arise between human beings' moral predispositions and the purposes human beings pursue.

Frans de Waal's path-breaking work (de Waal, 1996; Flack and de Waal, 2000) can prompt numerous debates, discussions, and lines of inquiry within the quarters of business ethics. In this article, I would like to draw on de Waal's research and his insights into human morality in three ways. First, I will use Enron and the attacks of September 11, 2001, to bring into sharp relief what I take to be essential points from de Waal's work, essential points that serve in particular as a foundation for the scholarly agenda in business ethics. Second, I will introduce a fundamental problem of ethical theory that follows from de Waal's work. This is the problem created by inconsistency between our naturally rooted moral sentiments and our reasoned, principled pursuit of the good. I will briefly describe three faces of this problem and the particular relevance of each face to business ethics. Third, I will outline some of the challenges to be tackled as we take up a tremendous intellectual opportunity de Waal has set before us: the opportunity to investigate and develop practices that fortify our natural moral predispositions and counter our natural immoral predispositions.

Human Responsibility

If we look at the two events that have captivated attention in the business world and beyond recently—the terrorist attacks of September 11, 2001, and the spectacular collapse of Enron, WorldCom, and other major corporations—we can find evidence for the many sides of human nature. I want to be quite careful not to equate the two events, or even to compare the level of the moral vice perpetrated by the terrorists and corporate executives.

However, the two events share a few features in common. We see, for example, just how calculating and ingenious human beings can be in advancing their own cause at the expense of others. In both cases, human beings have shown themselves especially ingenious in constructing organizational forms, and reinforcing norms, that facilitate wrongdoing. Human beings have also shown themselves to be remarkably resourceful in justifying a range of misdeeds.

But both episodes also have shown us just how deeply woven into our nature the moral inclinations that de Waal illuminates are. Even in the face of social pressure, hierarchical organization, monetary incentives, and personal ostracism, Sherron Watkins and Vince Kaminski (Emshwiller, 2002) spoke truth to power: that is, despite severe pressure at Enron, there were nonetheless individuals who felt deeply that something was wrong and needed to be stopped, and who objected. Such a response was even more pronounced at WorldCom, where three managers within the internal audit department disregarded pressures and personal costs to unearth the extent of accounting impropriety (Pulliam and Solomon, 2002).

With the attacks of September 11, there were of course rescue workers' acts of altruistic heroism, but even in the cutthroat world of Wall Street, there was evidence of indomitable human morality. Following the World Trade Center attack, the investment firm Sandler O'Neill found its competitors helping it get business, adding it to syndicated deals, lending personnel and space (Brooker, 2002)—all in an industry typically known for its unforgiving competition.

What I want to point out here is not the specific responses in each case to the adverse environment. Rather, I want to underscore the *fact* of human response. Even where personal costs of acting were great, and the benefits of retreat, ignorance, or abstention were great, human beings responded to moral pulls and tugs.

De Waal's work traces the origins of what we see in human responses to the attacks of September 11 and the corporate scandals: he traces the origins of our *capacity* for moral action. The power of de Waal's work lies, in part, in how he substantiates the fundamental responsibility of human beings—responsibility literally understood: how we as human beings are equipped with the ability to respond. Thanks to our biological inheritance, de Waal shows, human beings are poised to respond morally to others and to challenges posed by the environment. The specific shape our responses take depends upon the specific content of the moral code with which we are imprinted. The content of human beings' response—how we respond and why we respond in the way we do—depends upon the specific conception of right and wrong, good and bad, into which we have been socialized. But respond we do, and that capacity, de Waal shows, is part of our evolutionary heritage.

De Waal is quite cautious to note that unearthing natural predispositions differs from formulating justifiable normative guidelines. He takes care to state that one cannot derive ethical norms from natural predispositions, but neither can one deny those natural predispositions. Herein lies the implication for a scholarly agenda in business ethics. What needs constructing is a conception of what is right and good: a justifiable, captivating, and viable conception that nourishes and guides human beings' moral predispositions. It is not enough to say, "do what comes naturally," or "do what is natural to human beings." What is natural is that we seek to do what is right and good, all the while battling other natural tendencies that may take us in an opposite direction.

Business school graduates are clearly being imprinted with one set of ideas about what is right and good for those who occupy their roles. The Aspen Institute Initiative for Social Innovation through Business (Aspen Institute, 2001) published results of a survey that asked MBA graduates from the class of 2001 what a company's top priorities should be. While seventy-five percent responded "maximizing value for shareholders," seventy-one percent said "satisfying customers," thirty-three percent said "producing high quality goods and services," twenty-five percent said "creating value for their local communities," and five percent said "improving the environment." This indicates an impoverished conception of right and wrong, good and bad.

Business ethics can set out to supply coherent conceptions of what is right and good, conceptions that can appeal to the natural human thirst for substantive moral direction. The emphasis here is on plural conceptions, and it is on serious scholarly consideration of what managers' priorities ought to be. To be clear, the project is not to dictate the one right way, or to dismantle a concern with wealth creation. The project is to undertake serious and significant construction of, and debate about, what a company's priorities should be under varying conditions and how contests among vying objectives ought to be managed. Maximizing shareholder value is one worthy objective, and perhaps the preeminent objective, but to treat it—or any other objective—as self-evidently or presumptively preeminent is counterproductive. It chokes the necessary inquiry and vibrant discussion that can nourish the moral intuitions of managers.

As attempts are made to develop conceptions of the good for business and enrich individuals' sense of purpose, a significant challenge illuminated by de Waal's work is likely to arise. This is the problem of inconsistency.

The Problem of Inconsistency

There are three faces to the problem of inconsistency. As Frans de Waal's research suggests, human beings have certain moral predispositions—sympathy, cooperation, conflict resolution, and mutual aid, for example. As shorthand, I will refer to these as our moral sentiments. These moral sentiments give rise to the first face of the problem of inconsistency. Our moral sentiments may lead us, at times, to make decisions or engage in conduct that can find no justification in principle.

For example, philosophers (Blackburn, 2001; Herman, 2002; Murphy, 2000; Unger, 1996) have had difficulty constructing a principle to justify the distinction we seem to make intuitively in our sense of duty to rescue. We experience that sense when the person is in close proximity to us (a drowning child, for example) but do not experience that sense of duty when the person is not that close (such as a starving child in Bangladesh). It is still unclear whether such a distinction can be justified on principled grounds, though philosophers have tried and found candidate principles wanting.

So too with the classic trolley problem. Consider the widely publicized study conducted by a team of cognitive scientists, social psychologists, and philosophers at Princeton University, who examined the brain activity of individuals responding to moral dilemmas (Greene et al., 2001). They found that dilemmas with a personal component activated greater emotional processing than did dilemmas that were impersonal. There may be no principled difference between, in one case, re-routing a trolley through a flip of a switch, thus killing one person on the new track and, in the other case, pushing someone onto the tracks to halt the trolley. In both cases killing one person averts the death of five people. But the psychological experience surrounding these two dilemmas, and presumably surrounding the action itself, is quite different. The researchers found that dilemmas involving direct personal interaction activated those areas of the brain associated with emotion. Hence, the personal dilemmas elicited longer response times and even different responses—saving one life at the cost of five, for example—than did dilemmas that posed the same tradeoff in an impersonal way. Perhaps this is the next piece of evidence in tracing the biological roots of moral sentiments in human beings. Whether that is so or not, it does suggest that inconsistency may be a fact of our moral lives.

We have similar cases in business ethics. When United Nations Secretary General Kofi Annan calls for corporations to respond to the global AIDS crisis, especially the looming crisis in Africa, there is a sense that corporations ought to do something. There seems to be a duty of beneficence. So too with any number of social initiatives, from education to poverty amelioration. There is an intuitive sense that managers ought to marshal firm resources to respond in some way, at least to misery in their backyard, and managers who refuse, or owners who discipline managers who *do* respond beneficently, are often considered callous or lacking humanity. Nonetheless, it is difficult to find the principles to justify corporate responses, and in fact, the dominant principles militate against responding.

Finding the principled grounds for explaining stakeholder obligations (beyond instrumental reasons) seems to be this sort of problem as well. There is an intuitive sense that we have duties to certain stakeholders, and to certain stakeholders rather than others, but it has proven somewhat difficult to fully ground the normative justification of these duties and the difference in their priority (Phillips, 1997). Perhaps we need to become accustomed to the (unsettling) inconsistency between intuition, grounded in moral sentiment, and principle, grounded in rational theorizing (Haidt, 2001).

The second face of the problem of inconsistency arises when our moral sentiments collide with the purposes we pursue, purposes generated from a systematic and principled account of what constitutes the good and how we ought to live (Haidt, 2001: 819). Here it is helpful to use the distinction Ronald Dworkin (2000) draws between morality and ethics. Morality has to do with how we ought to treat other human beings, and ethics has to do with how we ought to live our lives and what purposes are worth pursuing. Using Dworkin's labels for convenience, morality corresponds in a rough way to the moral predispositions de Waal traces. Ethics refers to another aspect essential to human nature, it would seem: our capacity to deliberate and, in de Waal's words, "to clarify what is good, and why" (Flack and de Waal, 2000: 23).

Morality and ethics may collide. The worthy purposes we pursue and the means developed to pursue those purposes may sometimes collide with our natural predispositions toward sympathy, mutual aid, and fairness. The purposes deemed good may suffer, at times, if we adhere to the instinctive call of morality. So too, how we feel we ought to treat others may get trampled in the pursuit of valued purposes. To put it in the inimitable words of Jake Burton Carpenter, founder and CEO of Burton Snowboards, who announced in April 2002 the company's first-ever layoff in 25 years: "The people side of these moves suck, but if the market is telling us this is what it takes to continue to develop the best and most innovative product out there, we have to sacrifice and streamline so we don't compromise those objectives" (Ski Press Media, 2002).

These inevitable conflicts between our moral predispositions and the purposes that give life meaning and value deepen the work to be done in business ethics. Methods must be constructed for adjudicating creatively among these conflicts, where, for example, the economic institutions of capitalism, designed as they are to advance the purpose of social welfare through a system of maximizing wealth, albeit imperfect in many ways, may call for harm to be done to any number of individuals who must be let go from their jobs. Conceptual boundaries might also be developed to demarcate and prevent excesses: to limit the grave harm that can be done in the name of transcendent purposes, and to avoid the self-defeating paralysis that can come from heeding the moral sense too fastidiously. The aim should be to preserve both morality and ethics, to use Dworkin's categories, even if one of them must yield in a particular circumstance.

This introduces the third face of the inconsistency problem. How is judgment best nurtured in individuals who manage purposive entities, such as corporations, so they know when to override their moral sentiments and avoid paralysis, and when to honor those intuitions even at the expense of worthy purposes (Williams, 1983)?

For the business leaders trained in business schools, how is their human tendency toward sympathy, cooperation, and mutual aid best sustained alongside their commitment to steward a firm's resources and advance its purpose? How is judgment to be developed among those who will find themselves in wrenching situations, judgment refined enough so that they avoid excessive swings to one side or the other? And so they avoid becoming desensitized to their sense of right and wrong, good and bad, all in the name of a higher purpose? If one risk lies in managers' readiness to subjugate their moral sense to their role responsibility, or to their narrow self-interest, or to temptations of their position, then one starting point might be to take up a scholarly opportunity de Waal sets out.

Fortifying and Countering Human Tendencies

The opportunity and challenge for business ethics, in research and prescriptive work, is to identify ways, to use Flack and de Waal's words, to fortify the other-oriented, natural tendencies of human beings—our tendencies toward sympathy, reciprocity, and loyalty—and to counter our destructive tendencies, such as within-group violence and cheating (Flack and de Waal, 2000: 23). Much of business ethics indeed focuses on this line of inquiry, what Immanuel Kant referred to as moral anthropology (Kant, 1991: 44–45): searching for what in fact contributes to pro-social conduct and what elicits misconduct, and theoretically constructing possible institutional arrangements that elicit human beings' constructive qualities and inhibit our destructive qualities. However, this is a complicated endeavor. This call to fortify and counter presents several vexing challenges, which must be taken up in their own right.

Paradoxical Effects of Fortification

The very mechanisms introduced to fortify salubrious conduct and counter deleterious conduct may have paradoxical effects. Research done by Tenbrunsel and Messick (1999), for example, suggests that sanctioning systems designed to curtail competition and encourage cooperation may in fact elicit non-cooperative behavior. The mere presence of penalties may signal to individuals that they are engaged in one type of a situation—an economic contest, for example—rather than another—such as a cooperative endeavor. Human behavior then corresponds not to the content of the penalty but to our sense of what is appropriate in a situation marked by such a penalty (March, 1994). Mechanisms designed to deter targeted conduct may instead elicit behavior designed to circumvent those mechanisms.

Consequences of Purposive Institutions

Organizations that advance worthy purposes may frustrate, rather than fortify, pro-social tendencies; they may make destructive conduct more likely, rather than less. Fort (2001) has drawn on anthropology and ethology, for example, to suggest that 150 people is the maximum advisable size for human groups. Some corporations, such as W. L. Gore, operate with this limitation in mind. Research by Darley (1996) on the B. F. Goodrich brake fraud of the early 1970s, by Vaughan (1995) on the Challenger disaster, and by Jackall (1988) on corporate management indicate the cost of complex organization, not only to ethical principles, but to meaningful work and, potentially, even to human life. But complex organization also facilitates accomplishments otherwise beyond the reach of human endeavor.

Institutional arrangements that make large-scale projects possible and that make the realization of valued purposes possible may disrupt human beings' capacity to relate to others in a manner that advances our pro-social moral tendencies (Heimer, 1992). The reverse is also possible. Our moral predispositions may well get in the way of valued purposes that are equally sustaining of human life. The tendency to weigh the personal more heavily, as manifested in the study by Greene and colleagues (2001) mentioned above or in the effort expended on identifiable victims (Jenni and Loewenstein, 1997), may get in the way of advancing some moral purposes or the interests of depersonalized others. For example, Sull (1999) found that executives in the tire industry were much slower to close plants where they had worked, despite crushing overcapacity and sound economic rationale for closing the plants. In-group favoritism can be the source of discrimination (Brewer, 1996; Messick, 1998), and recent research by Bazerman, Loewenstein, and Moore (2002) indicates that a mere whiff of relationship is enough to bias accountants' judgments. Our capacity to aid those to whom we feel connected may well be the root of human moral sentiments, but it can be a counterproductive force as well.

This is not to deny the tremendous cost to those who suffer, from layoffs for example, or to grant a presumptive license to all acts conducted in the name of economic efficiency or material well-being. The problem with assuming economic efficiency to be the self-evident or pre-eminent objective is not that economic efficiency is somehow bad. Its importance ought not be belittled. The problem, in contrast, lies in the temptation to oversimplify or elide fundamental practical dilemmas, rather than acknowledge them and wrestle with them. Much careful work remains to be done to determine how morally conducive tendencies might be fortified and sustained. To draw on de Waal's terms (Flack and de Waal, 2000), what happens when our sympathetic tendencies conflict with our moral code, or with the reasoned judgment that emerges, perhaps tragically, from weighing the moral code against our sympathy and empathy?

Failure

Third of the vexing challenges is a question: what about when fortifying and countering fails? De Waal has marshaled significant evidence of the many ways in which animals repair disturbed relationships (Flack and de Waal, 2000: 11).

These practices of repair seem especially important in human affairs, particularly in business. While a fair amount of research and theory has been devoted to conflict resolution and intervention, less attention has been devoted to repairing disturbed relationships.

Because human beings are not solely benevolent; because we will inevitably violate our natural predispositions to cooperate, aid, and sympathize, sometimes for good reason, and sometimes not; because, quite simply, human beings are imperfect, we need a better understanding of how individuals and organizations do, can, and should repair disrupted relationships. When earnings projections are missed, thereby disappointing and even hurting shareholders, or employees are systematically exposed to an undisclosed hazard, or customers suffer harmful consequences from products, what is to be done?

Reconciliation, so common in primate society (Flack and de Waal, 2000: 10–12), seems far less common in the world of commerce, where proxy fights, shareholder suits, and product liability litigation seem the common response to past wrongs. These may well be the only available forms of viable recourse, and perhaps they represent human forms of reconciliation. If so, that is eerie and disappointing. After all, the origins of business, whether in barter, trade, or the joint stock company, reside in efforts to cooperate for mutual gain, even to bridge between different cultures. Investigating how injured parties and tattered relationships can and should be restored, especially when the ends of business cannot avoid all of these effects, seems like an essential area of inquiry. Fortifying human moral tendencies entails acknowledging our imperfections. Rather than simply justifying those imperfections or ignoring them (Darley, 1992: 216), we might learn from those imperfections and strengthen social bonds.

Conclusion

The work of Frans de Waal and other ethologists and biologists, so enlightening in its own right, leaves us with many possible paths of inquiry in business ethics. One of those paths is self-reflective, raising an anthropological question, in fact, about human behavior, specifically the behavior we engage in when importing Frans de Waal's work into business scholarship. What do we make of the recurring efforts to pin down human nature—especially in the quarters of business scholarship? What is the source of my—of our—interest in the possibility and content of human nature? What does the quest to discern human nature and its origins tell us about our nature as human beings? When we invoke the research of Frans de Waal, are we seeking confirmation for our chosen view of the world and confirmation of the economic institutions we prefer? Are we seeking reassurance that what we have is a world that is optimal in some sense? Or am I—are we—on a quest of inquiry and enlightenment, an open-ended journey, seeking guidance for developing economic institutions consistent with human nature? This search for human nature reflects our aspirations, and Frans de Waal's, but it inevitably inhabits one side of a double-edged sword, which we must live with if we are to draw on ethology and the biological sciences. The quest to understand human nature so as to develop institutions consistent with it is unavoidably accompanied by the ever-present danger of seeking in the evolutionary record of human nature incontrovertible confirmation of our preferred economic arrangements. It is worth risking this danger for the potential insight to be gained. Risking much for the sake of enlightenment also seems to be part of human nature, and the human tendency to cooperate will enable us to help one another remain open and honest.

Bibliography

Aspen Institute for Social Innovation through Business. 2001. *Where Will They Lead? MBA Student Attitudes about Business and Society.* New York: Aspen ISIB.

Bazerman, M. H., G. Loewenstein, and D. A. Moore. 2002. Why good accountants do bad audits. *Harvard Business Review* 80(11): 97–102.

Blackburn, S. 2001. *Being good: An Introduction to Ethics.* New York: Oxford University Press.

Brewer, M. 1996. In-group favoritism: The subtle side of intergroup discrimination. In *Codes of Conduct: Behavioral Research into Business Ethics*, ed. D. M. Messick and A. E. Tenbrunsel. New York: Russell Sage Foundation: 160–170.

Brooker, K. 2002. Starting over. *Fortune* 145(2): 50–65.

Darley, J. 1992. Social organization for the production of evil. *Psychological Inquiry* 3: 199–218.

———. 1996. How organizations socialize individuals into evil-doing. In *Codes of Conduct: Behavioral Research Into Business Ethics*, ed. D. M. Messick and A. E. Tenbrunsel. New York: Russell Sage Foundation: 13–43.

Dworkin, R. 2000. *Sovereign Virtue: The Theory and Practice of Equality.* Cambridge, Mass.: Harvard University Press.

Emshwiller, J. R. 2002. Enron official gave early warnings as early as '99. *Wall Street Journal* (March 18): A3.

Flack, J. C., and F. de Waal. 2000. "Any animal whatever": Darwinian building blocks of morality in monkeys and apes. *Journal of Consciousness Studies* 7(1–2): 1–29. See pages 7–41 in this volume.

Fort, T. 2001. *Ethics and Governance: Business as Mediating Institution.* New York: Oxford University Press.

Greene, J. D., R. B. Sommerville, L. E. Nystrom, J. M. Darley, and J. D. Cohen. 2001. An fMRI investigation of emotional engagement in moral judgment. *Science* 293 (September 14): 2105–2108.

Haidt, J. 2001. The emotional dog and its rational tail: A social intuitionist approach to moral judgment. *Psychological Review* 108: 814–834.

Heimer, C. 1992. Doing your job and helping your friends: Universalistic norms about obligations to particular others in networks. In *Networks and Organizations: Structure, Form, and Action*, ed. N. Nohria and R. G. Eccles. Boston, Mass.: Harvard Business School Press: 143–164.

Herman, B. 2002. The scope of moral requirement. *Philosophy and Public Affairs* 30 (3): 227–256.

Jackall, R. 1988. *Moral Mazes: The World of Corporate Managers*. New York: Oxford University Press.

Jenni, K. E., and G. Loewenstein. 1997. Explaining the "identifiable victim effect." *Journal of Risk and Uncertainty* 14: 235–257.

Kant, I. 1797/1991. *The Metaphysics of Morals*, trans. M. Gregor. New York: Cambridge University Press.

March, J. G. 1994. *A Primer on Decision Making: How Decisions Happen*. New York: The Free Press.

Messick, D. M. 1998. Social categories and business ethics. *Business Ethics Quarterly* Ruffin Series: Special Issue 1: 149–172.

Murphy, L. B. 2000. *Moral Demands in Nonideal Theory*. New York: Oxford University Press.

Phillips, R. A. 1997. Stakeholder theory and a principle of fairness. *Business Ethics Quarterly* 7(1): 51–66.

Pulliam, S., and D. Solomon. 2002. Uncooking the books: How three unlikely sleuths discovered fraud at WorldCom. *Wall Street Journal* (October 30): A1.

Ski Press Media. 2002. Snowboard shocker! Burton announces big layoffs (April 12).

Sull, D. 1999. The dynamics of standing still: Firestone Tire & Rubber and the radial revolution. *Business History Review* 73(3): 430–464.

Tenbrunsel, A. E., and D. M. Messick. 1999. Sanctioning systems, decision frames, and cooperation. *Administrative Science Quarterly* 44: 684–707.

Unger, P. K. 1996. *Living High and Letting Die: Our Illusion of Innocence*. New York: Oxford University Press.

Vaughan, D. 1995. *The Challenger Launch Decision*. Chicago: University of Chicago Press.

de Waal, F. 1996. *Good Natured: The Origins of Right and Wrong in Humans and Other Animals*. Cambridge, Mass.: Harvard University Press.

Williams, B. 1983. Professional morality and its dispositions. In *The Good Lawyer: Lawyers' Roles and Lawyers' Ethics*, ed. D. Luban. Totowa, N.J.: Rowman & Allanheld: 259–269.

SYMPATHY AS A "NATURAL" SENTIMENT

Robert C. Solomon

Abstract: In this essay, I want to reconsider sympathy as a "natural" emotion or sentiment. Adam Smith famously defended it as such (as did his friend David Hume) but both used the term ambiguously and in a different sense than we use it today. Nevertheless, it seems to me that Smith got it quite right, that the basis of morality and justice is to be found in the realm of affect rather than in theory and principles alone, and that sympathy is a "natural" or should we say a "basic" emotion. But that means that morality may not be an exclusively human characteristic, as many philosophers (including Smith and Hume) have assumed. But some contemporary thinking in psychology and philosophy makes that extension plausible.

Adam Smith, despite his reputation among businessmen as the father of the compassionless free market, might better be seen as the Philosopher of Compassion, or he would say, "sympathy." The "moral sentiment theorists" David Hume and Adam Smith in Scotland defended the centrality of the "natural" sentiment of *sympathy* in morals, distinguishing between sympathy and justice (which Hume declared not to be "natural" at all) but nevertheless arguing that the basis of morality and justice is to be found in our natural disposition to have certain other-directed emotions. This did not mean that morality is not, in part, a function of reason or, above all, a matter of "doing the right thing." Both Hume and Smith emerged as early champions of the importance of "utility." But it is clear that the right things don't usually get done for the wrong motives, and we don't usually think of ourselves or of others as just or moral if the right thing gets done for the wrong motives or if the wrong thing gets done for the right motives. But surely among the "right motives" are the sympathetic emotions. Contrary to at least one dominant strand of the Kantian tradition, to be moral and to be just does not mean that one must act *on principle*. A good motive for helping another person in need is "I feel sorry for him." A good motive for helping a friend is "because I care about her." But such motivation is clearly to be found, as Frans de Waal has so elegantly shown, in the lives of some social animals as well as in human society.[1]

The Nature of Sympathy: Adam Smith and David Hume

> How selfish soever man may be supposed, there are evidently some
> principles in his nature, which interest him in the fortune of others,
> and render their happiness necessary to him, though he derives noth-
> ing from it except the pleasure of seeing it. Of this kind is pity or
> compassion, the emotion which we feel for the misery of others. . . .
> The greatest ruffian, the most hardened violator of the laws of soci-
> ety, is not altogether without it.
> —Adam Smith (*Theory of the Moral Sentiments* (*TMS*) I, I, i)

Traditionally, moral sentiment theory was concerned with a family of "natural"
emotions, including benevolence, sympathy, compassion and pity. (Care and caring, instructively, were not part of the standard list.) These were often lumped
together and not infrequently treated as identical (for example, by Hume). In the
standard account of moral sentiment thinking, Francis Hutcheson's "moral sense"
theory is usually included as a moral sentiment theory, despite the fact that
Hutcheson explicitly denied any special moral role to the sentiments. Jean-Jacques
Rousseau is usually not included as a moral sentiment theorist, though he was
obviously one with them. With his Scottish colleagues he attacked the "selfishness" theories of Hobbes and Mandeville and argued for the naturalness of pity,
an emotion closely kindred to compassion in particular. But as developed by
Hume and Smith, in particular, the exemplary moral sentiment was *sympathy*.
This sentiment, I suggest, is an awkward amalgam of several emotional states
and dispositions, including compassion and what we have come to call "care."

In common parlance, sympathy means "feeling sorry for" someone, while
for many philosophers (notably Hume) it is conflated with benevolence. (Smith
tries to keep these distinct.) "Feeling sorry for" can be a sign of caring, but
surely a minimal one, as we can feel sorry for strangers and even our enemies.
Benevolence has much in common with the more activist concept of "caring
for," but benevolence has much greater scope than sympathy as such. We can
feel benevolence in the abstract (without any particular object) and benevolence for those whose feelings are utterly malicious or indifferent to us (e.g. in
being merciful to a condemned and still hateful wrong-doer, perhaps as an expression of our own largesse but out of benevolence nevertheless.) We often
use "sympathy" or the verb "sympathize" to register agreement or approval,
although none of these qualify as an adequate philosophical conception or a
correct dictionary definition of the term. Technically, sympathy (literally, "feeling with," like "com/passion") is the sharing of feeling, or, as a disposition, the
ability to share the feelings of others. Or, if one wants to insist that the emotions can be individuated only according to the persons who have them and
thus cannot be shared, one might say that sympathy is an "agreement of feelings" (Random House Dictionary), in the sense of "having the same [type of]
emotion." One need not "agree with" in the sense of "approve of" the feeling in
question, of course, any more than must always enjoy, like or approve of one's

own emotions. The feelings may agree but we need not; sharing a feeling is one thing but accepting or approving of the feeling something quite different. (In grade B movies, we might well share the offended hero's rather fascist sense of revenge, as we might share the envy of someone who has been similarly deprived while berating ourselves for just that feeling.) Presumably even intelligent animals lack this "second order" consciousness of self-approval and disapproval, but, nevertheless, they are demonstrably prone to the sharing of feelings, both joyous and otherwise.

Adam Smith uses the term in this technical way, as "agreement of emotion," but he does not thereby imply the agreement of any particular emotion or kind of emotion. Thus there is a serious ambiguity between sympathy as a specific sentiment and sympathy—or what we now call *empathy*— as a disposition to share sentiments (*whatever* sentiments) with others. Sympathy so conceived is thus not actually a sentiment at all but rather a *vehicle* for understanding other people's sentiments, "a fellow-feeling with any passion whatever" (*TMS* I.i.5.) Thus one can sympathize not only with the kindly and social moral sentiments but with such antisocial sentiments as envy and hatred as well. But sympathy for Smith is not an actual sharing of sentiments (in the sense of "having the same feeling") but rather an act of imagination by which one can appreciate the feelings of another person by "putting oneself in his place." "a principle which interests him in the fortunes of others" (*TMS* I.i.I.2) This, presumably, is also lacking in animals, for whom the idea of "imagination" is a bit of a stretch. Nevertheless, if Smith thus accounts for how it is that people are not essentially selfish or self-interested but are essentially social creatures who can act on behalf of others whose feelings they do not (and logically cannot) actually share, so, too, would this account apply to animals.

But can sympathy then be a motivating factor (in opposition to the equally natural and often more powerful sentiment of self-interest)? Smith's sympathy, according to his definition as "fellow-feeling," seems to be more concerned with comprehension than feeling as such, and comprehension is too close to the "comparison of ideas" to provide the "sentiments of pleasure and disgust" that play the role that sympathy is called to play in morals.[2] ("The approbation of moral qualities most certainly is not deriv'd from reason, or any comparison of ideas; but proceeds entirely from a moral taste, and from certain sentiments of pleasure and disgust, which arise upon the contemplation and view of particular qualities or characters" and "As we have no immediate experience of what other men feel, we can for no idea of the manner in which they are affected, but by conceiving what we ourselves should feel in the like situation." *TMS* I. i. I 2.) Sympathy cannot mean merely "comprehension" but, on the other hand, sympathy as shared feeling seems too strong for the role.[3] Smith is inconsistent. On the one hand, he wants a mechanism for "fellow-feeling," on the other, a motive for morals. It is not at all clear that he can have both, and it is arguable that neither provides an adequate analysis of sympathy as he discusses it.

Both Hume and Smith are dead-set against the Hobbesian view that people are motivated only by their own selfish interests and advocate the importance of distinctive, natural "social passions." Indeed, the core of their argument is, in Smith's terms, that "nature, when she formed man for society, endowed him with an original desire to please, and an original aversion to offend his brethren." (*TMS* III.2.6.) Moreover, "nature endowed him not only with a desire for being approved of, but with a desire of being what ought to be approved of, or of being what he himself approves of in other men." (*TMS* III.2.7.) It is not just sympathy but a whole complex of mutually perceiving and reciprocal passions that tie us together. Thus it does not take too much tinkering with Scottish moral sentiment theory to incorporate justice along with sympathy under its auspices and take the whole as a welcome alternative to both the "man is essentially selfish" thesis and the overly intellectual "justice is abstract rationality" view of most current justice theorists. This intermediary interpretation suggests that some sense of justice as well as sympathy is to be found in social animals as well as in human society. I have argued this at some length (regarding both wolves and chimpanzees) in my *A Passion for Justice*.[4]

Both Hume and Smith sometimes talk about sympathy as if it were no more than a generalized sense of altruism, a concern for others with no thought of benefit to oneself. But altruism like benevolence doesn't involve any sharing of feelings, as sympathy does, and Smith's phrase "fellow-feeling" too easily hides the distinction between "feeling for," "feeling with" and simple camaraderie, which is feeling oneself with but not necessarily feeling with the other. Altruism, on the other hand, might best be understood as the behavioral analog of benevolence, and sympathy is often used as a synonym for benevolence, a wishing well toward others, sympathy *for* others. This is the way that Hume often uses the term, and in the *Inquiry*, at least, he claims that this feeling "nature has made universal in the whole species."(*Inquiry* I) This is his way of denying the Hobbesian portrait of humanity as essentially selfish, and it is a mistake or at least unfair, I think, to attack Hume on the grounds that he is really an unreconstructed Hobbesian individualist who brings in "sympathy" only as a desperate measure to explain the non-coercive validity of morals.[5]

What both Hume and Smith are concerned to point out, against Hobbes, is that we genuinely and "naturally" do *care* about other people and we are capable of feeling *with* others as well as for ourselves. But it is obvious that animals, too, care about and care for others of their group, if not other members of their species.

Sympathy and Empathy Reconsidered

The word "empathy" is recent in origin, although there are antecedents (for instance, German *Verstehen*) that clearly anticipate some of its meaning. Empathy, in contemporary psychology, is defined as "an affective response that stems from the apprehension or comprehension of another's emotional state or condition, and that is identical of very similar to what the other person is feeling or would be expected to feel." (Nancy Eisenberg, in the authoritative *Handbook of Emotions*, second edition, "Empathy and Sympathy," pp. 677–691.) Eisenberg gives the example: "if a woman sees or hears about a person who is sad and feels sad in response she is experiencing empathy." (Handbook 677) But this is a response that can be readily viewed in social animals, and when Eisenberg notes that early use of the term was heavily cognitive and involved imaginatively "taking the role of the other," we can see how this meaning seriously limits the range of the emotion. Thus Eisenberg emphasizes the "affective" aspect of empathy and notes that it need not involve thinking at all. Nevertheless, it is important to distinguish empathy from just being upset or "personally distressed" and it minimally requires the "cognitive" separation of self and other. Infants, accordingly, cannot feel empathy although they can get very upset when their mothers are upset. Animals are an open question here. To what extent is their empathy with others a matter of what psychologists now (dubiously) call "emotional contagion" and to what extent does it involve some understanding of the other's situation? I should add that getting upset because someone else is upset need not be either sympathy or empathy. One's being upset may be wholly self-involved and even aversive (for instance, getting uncomfortable when someone regales you with his or her tale of woe and just makes you want to leave the room).

Sympathy, in contrast to empathy, is defined by Eisenberg as " an affective response that consists of feeling sorrow or concern for the distressed or needy other (rather than the same emotion as the other person)." By such a definition, it is clear that what Smith means by "sympathy" is empathy. Philosophically, sympathy is therefore a less interesting emotion than empathy. Indeed, it is empathy, not sympathy, that one might even question whether it is an emotion, rather than a capacity to have any number of emotions depending on the emotions of others. Sympathy is a straightforward emotion in the sense that it is a distinctive emotion, emotion dependent on the emotions of others, perhaps, but only a response to them, not in any sense an imitation or reproduction of them. Indeed, one might sympathize with another person and get his or her emotional situation completely wrong. Empathy, by contrast, seems to require that one does (in some sense) replicate the emotions of the other person.

Sympathy is an emotion, argues Peter Goldie, because it characteristically involves a distinctive emotional experience as well as characteristic emotional expression (though this can usually be read as such only in context) and it tends to motivate action (namely helping or at least nurturing behavior).[6] In the language of current emotion theory, the question is whether sympathy (compassion) counts as an "affect program," a scientifically respectable conception because it renders emotions almost wholly physiological. But Goldie's worry about facial expression is particularly significant because affect program theorists (Paul Ekman, Paul Griffiths) tend to eschew context. (Ekman's research consists largely of showing photographs of facial expressions, devoid of context or narrative.)

Expressions of sympathy would be unintelligible without context or narrative, indiscernible from mere sadness or distress. But in some animals as well as humans, we recognize (in appropriate contexts) the furrowed brow and worried eyes of sympathy. And in animals as well as in humans, sympathy motivates action, both directly and indirectly. Direct action tends to be something as simple and straightforward as reaching out in a calming or soothing gesture. Indirect action can be almost anything, depending on the context and the situation, so long as it is some sort of helping or sharing behavior and not merely self-interested or escapist (that is, avoiding the other rather than helping him).

Against some of the monstrous theories of human nature Smith and Hume confronted—Hobbes, Mandeville, etc.—they argued for a much more humane and admirable picture of human nature, one that greatly qualified and restricted the selfish aspects of humanity (for which Smith is mainly known, given a few famous comments in *Wealth of Nations*) and rendered human nature neither a "war of all against all" nor a buzzing beehive but a sympathetic community defined by fellow-feeling and an abhorrence of seeing one's fellow citizens in pain or suffering. What Professor de Waal has done is nothing less than extend similar arguments to at least some illustrious members of the animal kingdom other than humans. Animal life is not always "red in tooth and claw" and the process of evolution is not just about selfishness. Animal nature too is neither a "war of all against all" nor a mindless beehive but involves sympathetic communities characterized by fellow-feeling and abhorrence of seeing one's fellow creatures suffering.

Notes

1. Frans de Waal, *Chimpanzee Politics* (London: Cape, 1982) and *Good Natured* (Cambridge, Mass.: Harvard, 2002).

2. Patricia Werhane, *Adam Smith and His Legacy for Modern Capitalism* (New York: Oxford University Press, 1991).

3. Joseph Crospey, *Polity and Economy* (Westport Conn.: Greenwood Press, 1957), p. 12.

4. Robert C. Solomon, *A Passion for Justice* (Boston: Addison-Wesley, 1990). Reissued by Rowman and Littlefield (Lanham, Md.: 1995).

5. Alasdair MacIntyre, *After Virtue* (Notre Dame, Ind.: University of Notre Dame Press, 1981), pp. 214–215. Milton Friedman (characteristically): "Smith regarded sympathy as a human characteristic, but one that was itself rare and required to be economised." In "Adam Smith's Relevance for 1976," in *Selected Papers of the University of Chicago Graduate School of Business*, No. 50 (Chicago: University of Chicago Graduate School of Business, 1977), p. 16.

6. Peter Goldie, *Emotions* (Oxford: Oxford University Press, 1999), and in "Compassion: A Natural, Moral Emotion," in "Die Moralitaet der Gefuehle," special issue of *Deutsche Zeitschrift fur Philosophie* 4 (2002), ed. S. A. Doering and V. Mayer (Berlin: Akademie), pp. 199–211.

THE BIOLOGICAL BASE OF MORALITY?

Paul R. Lawrence

Abstract: The study of human morality has historically been carried out primarily by philosophers and theologians. Now this broad topic is also being studied systematically by evolutionary biologists and various behavioral and social sciences. Based upon a review of this work, this paper will propose a unified explanation of human morality as an innate feature of human minds. The theory argues that morality is an innate skill that developed as a means to fulfill the human drive to bond with others in mutual caring. This explanation has also been reported as part of a broader theory on the role of human nature in the shaping of human choices (*Driven*, Lawrence and Nohria).

Three major findings have emerged from recent study of the human brain. The first is the discovery of the locus and function of human drives. Neuroscientists have tentatively found that these unconscious drives are located in the limbic section of the brain, lying just below and behind the pre-frontal cortex to which the limbic modules are densely connected.[1] The second is the discovery of innate skill sets. Starting with the identification and study of a language skill set, more and more of these innate "starter-kits" for learning sophisticated skills are being found by evolutionary psychologists. Pinker has assembled probably the most complete list of these skill sets, some more speculative than others.[2] (See Exhibit 1, p. 77.) The third has been the development of meta-theories (drawing especially upon the work of Antonio Damasio) about how the various modules of the brain interact to produce high-level consciousness, choice and behavior.[3] All of these new findings have been made possible primarily by the use of the relatively new methodology of brain scanning and secondarily, the use of high-speed cameras to record the minute movements of the eyes of infants as they respond to various stimuli.[4] In addition the traditional experimental methods of psychologists have been reinvigorated by creatively designed experiments that bear directly on morality and fairness issues. This paper will bring this current knowledge about the brain to bear on the issue of human morality.

In pulling together these various strands of research, Lawrence and Nohria have essentially added the biological element to various pre-existing theories about human behavior that have been developed primarily by economists, psychologists and sociologists. The resulting *Four-Drive* theory draws its name from the four innate drives that we hypothesize are genetically pre-wired in the limbic area of the brain. We argue that these four drives operate independently of one another in the sense that fulfilling one does not fulfill the others. They all evolved by the well-known Darwinian mechanisms of natural selection and sex (mate) selection. All four drives, severally and jointly, serve the evolutionary challenge of gene survival and reproduction into the next generation.

Four-Drive Theory

We hypothesize that humans possess four drives. These are: the drive to *acquire* (D1) valued objects and pleasurable experiences; the drive to *bond* (D2) with individuals and with collectives in long-term, mutually caring relationships; the drive to *learn* (D3) and develop beliefs that make sense of the world; and finally, the drive to *defend* (D4) one's self, one's possessions, one's loved ones, and one's beliefs. The evidence we have found for the existence of these drives is presented in *Driven,* including an explanation of how and when the newer independent drives to bond and to learn evolved as the critical final step in distinguishing modern *Homo sapiens* from earlier archaic *Homo sapiens* and other primates. In addition we present evidence from neuroscience that the drive to defend is located in the amygdala module of the limbic area of the brain. Subsequent to the publication of *Driven*, we have also found tentative evidence from neuroscience that the drive to acquire is located in the nucleus accumbens and the drive to bond in parts of the hypothalamus.[5] All three of these modules are also found in the limbic area of the brain. The locus of the drive to learn has not yet been found but neuroscientists state that, "Part of the brain's internal environment is a ceaseless pressure to seek out new stimuli. This greed for information is one of the fundamental properties of the brain and it is reflected in our most basic reactions."[6]

We argue that these four drives are found in all humans with intact brains even though there may be variability in their strength. All of these drives are essentially insatiable, never out of action. Individuals judge how they are doing in fulfilling these drives in terms of their position relative to their reference groups. What the drives are pushing humans toward arrives on a one-at-a-time basis; that is, we achieve acquisitions, bonds, beliefs and defenses on a step-by-step basis throughout life. These drives provide the sense of purpose, meaning, and intentionality to all human behaviors.

We hypothesize that the various parts of the brain work together as follows: Neural signals from our sense organs are fed through the limbic modules and there pick up markers that code them as opportunities or threats to the fulfillment of these drives. These coded signals move on to the pre-frontal cortex, the seat of consciousness, where they are manifested as emotion-laden representations.[7] At this point the relevant skill sets and memories are activated and drawn into the working memory to aid in formulating a variety of action scenarios. These possible lines of response are weighted for their promise in fulfilling the drives (all four if possible) in the current situation. When the drives are in conflict, such as pushing for incompatible lines of action, more deliberation ensues in search of a more creatively integrated solution. In the end, a deliberate choice is made by an act of will that satisfices, not optimizes, in relation to the four drives. The chosen action plan is moved back through the limbic area to be energized and then sent to the motor centers for activation (see Exhibit 2, p. 78).

Morality as an Innate Skill

This simplified description of an extremely complex mental process lays the foundation for our central argument that morality has a biological basis. Morality, we believe, arises from the existence in humans of the drive to bond—in the strongest form of bonding found in any mammal. It is the emergence of this drive in humans that has led, in turn, to the evolution of a skill set for morality. As with the other drives, the drive to bond is the "end," the ultimate motive supplied by our biology, and the morality skill set is the "means" to this end, also supplied initially by our biology.

This exact formulation of morality was first articulated by Darwin himself. We will quote the relevant passages at some length since they have been neglected over the 125 years since they were written. Darwin wrote about the "social instincts" of humans. For instance Darwin wrote, "Every one will admit that man is a social being. We see this in his dislike of solitude, and in his wish for society beyond that of his own family. Solitary confinement is one of the severest punishments which can be inflicted."[8] Again, "The small strength and speed of man, his want of natural weapons, etc., are more than counterbalanced by his social qualities which lead him to give and receive aid from his fellow-men."[9] Darwin proceeds from such statements about the drive to bond directly to his explanation of the morality skill set in humans. "The following proposition seems to me in a high degree probable—namely, that any animal whatever, endowed with well-marked social instincts . . . would inevitably acquire a moral sense or conscience, as soon as its intellectual powers had become as well, or nearly as well developed, as in man. For, firstly, the social instincts lead an animal to take pleasure in the society of its fellows, to feel certain amount of sympathy with them, and to perform various services for them. . . . Secondly, as soon as the mental faculties had become highly developed, images of all past actions and motives would be incessantly passing through the brain of each individual; and that feeling of dissatisfaction, or even misery, which invariably result as often as it was perceived that the enduring and always present social instinct had yielded to some other instinct, at the time stronger, but [not] enduring in its nature."[10]

It is interesting that Darwin added a footnote to his thoughts about morals that takes strong exception to the position of John Stuart Mill, the dominant economist of the day and one of the founding fathers of modern economics. The footnote follows:

Mr. J. S. Mill speaks, in his celebrated work, "Utilitarianism" (1864, pp. 45, 46), of the social feelings as a "powerful natural sentiment." . . . He also remarks, "if, as in my own belief, the moral feelings are not innate, but acquired, they are not for that reason less natural." It is with hesitation that I venture to differ at all from so profound a thinker, but [since] it can hardly be disputed that the social feelings are instinctive or innate, [Mill's belief] that the moral sense is acquired by each individual during his lifetime is at least extremely improbable. The ignoring of all transmitted mental qualities will, as it seems to me, be hereafter judged as a most serious blemish in the works of Mr. Mill.

A number of contemporary scholars from different disciplines have repeated Darwin's point in multiple ways. James Q. Wilson, a political scientist, has expressed this idea in his book "The Moral Sense."[11] He writes, "We suggest that these [moral] principles have their source in the parent-child relationship, wherein a concern for fair shares, fair play, and fair judgments arises out of the desire to bond with others. All three principles are rational in a social and evolutionary sense, in that they are useful in minimizing conflict and enhancing cooperation. At some stage in the evolution of mankind— probably a quite early one—cooperative behavior became adaptive. Groups that could readily band together to forage, hunt, and defend against predators were more likely to survive than were solitary individuals."[12]

This explanation of morality is also offered by Frans deWaal. "This common benevolence nourishes and guides all human morality. Aid to others in need would never by internalized as a duty without the fellow-feeling that drives people to take an interest in one another. Moral sentiments came first; moral principles, second."[13]

E. O. Wilson also makes this point. He states, "Orthodox social theory holds that morality is largely a convention of obligation and duty constructed from mode and custom. The alternative view, favored by Westermarck in his writings on ethics, is that moral concepts are derived from innate emotions. . . . The evidence now leans strongly to Westermarck."[14]

This entire line of theorizing about morality has recently been pulled together in a comprehensive way by a psychologist, Jonathan Haidt. Haidt argues that human morals are based on intuition and emotions and are then subsequently elaborated and rationalized by reasoning. "The social intuitionist model . . . proposed that morality, like language, is a major evolutionary adaptation for an intensely social species, built into multiple regions of the brain and body, that is better described as emergent than as learned yet that requires input and shaping from a particular culture. Moral intuitions are therefore both innate and enculturated."[15]

The Rules of Innate Morality

So far we have discussed morals in a very general sense. Can progress be made by using deductive logic to reason carefully about the content, the specific moral rules that could have been established in human genetic memory? At this point a thought experiment, as philosophers would say, is relevant. If one strongly desires to establish a relationship of mutual caring with another, what kinds of behavior toward the other would help fulfill that desire? It is not a big step from the drive to bond to the practical rule that the key is to treat the other, most of the time, as oneself would desire to be treated in terms of the four innate drives. From this start we could deduce basic rules as follows:

In support of the other's drive to acquire
—help preserve, not steal or destroy, the other's property;
—facilitate, not frustrate, the other's pleasurable experiences.

In support of the other's drive to bond
—keep, not break, one's promises;
—seek fair, not cheating, exchanges,
—return a favor with a favor.

In support of the other's drive to learn
—tell truths, not lies;
—share, not withhold, useful information;
—respect, not ridicule, the other's beliefs, even in disagreement.

In support of the other's drive to defend
—help protect, not harm nor abandon, the other.

Based on this logic and on the existence of skill sets that support the other basic drives, we hypothesize that genetic rules such as these are built into the biology of all humans as an innate skill set that goes into action on all those occasions when bonding with another individual or a collective is a salient motive. These rules are, of course, not always followed since humans have other drives, such as the drive to acquire, that might lead humans to break the rules. But the true test of the hypothesis is not in the consistent observance of the rules, but rather whether humans experience a feeling of guilt, a "bad conscience," when they knowingly break the rules. While we have not found conclusive evidence of the existence of such particular innate moral rules in humans, the work of Haidt offers strong support.[16] With the use of the newer tools of neuroscience, more rigorous tests can be made. The basic moral ground rules taught by all the major religions seem similar and could be examined systematically as another test of the universality of these rules. We argue that the bonding drive and the associated moral skill set provide children with a significant head start toward learning the more elaborate and varied norms and values of the unique society into which they are born.

The most common punishment for violating social commitments is (as indicated by Darwin) social ostracism, the "silent treatment," and, at the extreme, solitary confinement, and even exile. Ostracism as a social norm enforcer is both powerful and low in cost. Infants almost instantly cry out in distress when their welcoming smile to an adult is responded to with a frozen stare. Another type of low-cost enforcer is derogatory words. Societies tend to save their most negative terms for social defectors. The words associated with violations of bonded relationships are cheater, liar, double-crosser, and, worst of all, traitor. The personal feelings associated with such accusations are intense shame and guilt. Our anticipation of these powerful negative feelings helps reinforce the bonding commitment. These basic moral senses appear in all children at such an early age that it seems they are, for all humans, an inbred skill set, akin to our language skill set. This skill set is our human conscience.

This way of thinking about morals moves beyond the conventional wisdom of the scientific community that science cannot or, at least, should not have anything to do with morals, ethics and values.[17] It clarifies that morals are such a central and pervasive aspect of human life that we badly need a scientific way of understanding them. Establishing that our morals have genetic roots can help us understand our past and give us more confidence in our future.

This description of human morals moves beyond the limited type of morals that have been observed in chimpanzees and some other mammals. In *The Moral Animal,* Robert Wright does an excellent job of pulling together and analyzing observations of this type.[18] With the important exception of the strong and lasting bond between mother and infant and the implicit morals of these relationships, chimpanzee alliances seem to be purely temporary expediencies. This is to be expected when relationships are based primarily on the narrow self-interest of the parties. These studies also reveal the prevalence of deception and trickery in the social relations of these primates. For example, chimps have been observed going to great trouble to appear to other chimps to hide food when they have actually already hidden the food in another place. Since humans have a drive to acquire as well as to bond, such opportunistic relationships obviously also occur among humans—but to a much lesser extent. Wright's analysis of chimpanzee morals clarifies that, if theirs is the only type of morality that our genetic heritage supports, then any substantial moral code among humans would have to be created almost exclusively by culture to override our genetic tendencies. The moral codes built upon human genes are more enduring and trustworthy.

Humans throughout history have created not only enduring alliances with other individuals starting with their kin but also enduring commitments to collectives. Humans are unique in conceptualizing, symbolizing and ritualizing their commitments to a large variety of collectives. The commitment to collectives appeared in hunter-gatherer societies as tribal loyalty. In modern times it appears most conspicuously as national patriotism. But well beyond these clear examples, humans make commitments to religious collectives, educational institutions, work organizations, local communities, and even many more mundane groups such as sports and social clubs. The combination of the drive to bond and related moral skills contributes in a decisive way to making humans unique.

One of the newest sources of evidence of the existence of a universal moral code in humans comes from the work of behavioral economists and anthropologists. A multi-cultural study of the idea of fairness has been conducted by this combination of scientists, largely sponsored by the National Science Foundation. These scholars have conducted careful experiments in fifteen small-scale non-industrial societies located in twelve countries around the globe.[19] These experiments set up an economic exchange between two strangers. The usual experiment is known as the "ultimatum game." The experimenters give a sizable amount of money, such as $50, to Player 1, known as the Proposer, who is instructed to offer some portion of the amount to Player 2, known as the Responder. The Responder is instructed to either accept the offer or refuse it. Refusal leads to the loss of the money to both players. If the offer is accepted both players get to keep their share. When this experiment is run with American undergraduates almost all Proposers offer between thirty and forty percent of the total and the Responders almost always reject anything below twenty percent. This type of response turned out to be typical in modern industrial societies that feature an abundance of market transactions.

When this experiment is run with a variety of different cultures, the cultural average of proposals runs from twenty percent to nearly fifty percent. No cultural group is reported to have offered a lower percentage, such as five percent, that neoclassical economics would predict to be offered, and, in turn, accepted. After all, reason the economists, a self-interested Responder would accept even a trivial offer since it is better than nothing, so no rational Proposer would offer anything more.

The variability between cultures seems to be related to the nature of the core technology that is the primary support of the people's livelihood and the principal cultural code governing any resulting exchanges. For example, the forest-dwelling families of the Machiguenga of Peru live in near-isolation, eking out a subsistence livelihood on a mix of slash-and-burn farming, hunting, foraging, and fishing. These people displayed more self-interest than college students did. They usually offered fifteen percent to twenty-five percent of the pot. Responders agreed to nearly all offers, including some below fifteen percent. This practice seems to be a response to their isolation and the lack of trading associated with their subsistence technology. In sharp contrast, the whale-hunting Lamalera of Indonesia made the most generous offers. A majority of Lamalera Proposers offered around half of their pot. Offers lower than fifty percent were frequently rejected. This seems to be consistent with the custom of these people to cut up any captured whale into portions for all the villagers with the successful hunters getting only a modestly larger portion of the whale. And the technical fact that these people have no way of refrigerating whale meat makes the custom very sensible.

The main point made by the principal researcher, Joseph Henrich of the Institute for Advance Study in Berlin, was captured by the *Science News* article's subtitle, "People everywhere put a social spin on economic exchanges." People everywhere seem to seek "fair" exchanges that make friends instead of enemies.

Forms of Human Sociality and Morality

Another line of cross-cultural research that throws light on the morality of exchanges has been done by Allan Fiske.[20] Fiske's work has focused on developing an overview of the skill sets that humans use to relate to one another, what he calls the basic, universal forms of sociality. He finds that all varieties of human relationships can be grouped into just four basic types with each type representing a social contract with its own moral ground rules.

To explain I will quote at some length from *Driven.*[21]

> Fiske made his initial observations on the four form of sociality while doing extensive fieldwork among the Moose people of Burkina Faso in West Africa, among the poorest people on earth. He has subsequently tested his findings not only in other African tribes but also in several advanced industrial countries. The four basic forms Fiske identified and named are; communal sharing (CS), authority ranking (AR), equality matching (EM), and market pricing (MP). Communal sharing (CS) is found universally in the primary family group. In this family group people largely follow the exchange rule, "From each according to their ability and to each according to their need." This social contract generally works fine in the nuclear family and is employed beyond the family only in an uneven way, sometimes to extended family. Communism was, in fact, an ill-fated experiment in trying to turn CS into an all-purpose ideology, far beyond the primary family group.
>
> Authority ranking (AR), by contrast, is a hierarchical relationship of inequality. In this mode humans negotiate, over time, a rank ordering among themselves as to who has more social importance, status or dominance over others. This is the "pecking order" that is so clearly evident in many animal species. Rank can be established in many ways—age, intelligence, brute strength, wealth, social skills and combinations of these attributes. Ranking relationships do involve a form of exchange between the parties even though it is unequal.
>
> Equality matching (EM), better known as long-term reciprocity, provides the ground rules that govern most peer relationships. This mode calls for an equality of exchange over an extended time period. You scratch my back, and then I have an obligation, sooner or later, to scratch yours. These are the ground rules for establishing lasting friendships. There is very strong evidence that all humans, in all cultures, use this form of sociality on a regular basis.

Finally, market pricing (MP) is exchange by bartering or by a ratio to some medium of exchange. This can be the price negotiation that occurs in a standard, one-time commercial transaction that is done, for example, with a used car salesman, a Middle East rug merchant or an African street merchant. This kind of bargaining involves bidding and counter bidding, often with bluffing and calling bluffs, while keeping one's rock-bottom or "reservation" price a secret. It lends itself to exchanges between strangers who do not expect to trade repeatedly. Fiske asserts that all humans seem to have a basic understanding of how to play this game.

Fiske presents evidence to support his hypothesis that these four modes are universal and innate among all humans. In addition, he presents limited anecdotal evidence that these four modes are manifested in maturing children, in the order they have been presented, in a spontaneous, uncoached manner starting roughly with three-year-olds for CS and proceeding to eight-year-olds for MP.

He develops the idea that each of these modes carries its own set of ground rules or moral codes that people expect to be observed or sanctions will follow. For example, fairness and equality of exchange over time are the key rules for the EM mode, while "buyer beware" during the negotiations but abide by the resulting agreement or contract are the key rules for MP. Communal Sharing invokes the rule of sharing generously with the others that are most closely bonded of one's kind, and placing the needs of the group on a par with personal needs. The morality of AR consists in an attitude of respect, deference, loyalty, and compliance by subordinates, complemented by the responsibility of the authority figure to provide protection for subordinates, a share of the resources available, and wise directive guidance.

In our terms, these four forms of social relations represent four skill sets or methods that people have innately available to them to develop and maintain bonded ties and simultaneously to exercise their drive to acquire. The rules that are the essence of each of the four modes define them as a particular kind of social contract. When people are acting in the MP or the AR modes, it is experienced as primarily a competitive relationship, oriented mostly to fulfilling the drive to acquire. When people are acting in EM or CS mode it is experienced primarily as a cooperative relationship, oriented mostly to fulfilling the drive to bond. Any given relationship between two people will always have some competitive elements and some cooperative elements. The weighting between the two aspects will depend on the history of the relationship and the immediate context of the current action.[22]

Brain-Scanning for Morality

Only recently has brain-scanning research begun to test for the presence of the drive to bond as an important element of the human brain. On July 18, 2002, the journal *Neuron* published the article, *A Neural Basis for Social Coopera-tion*.[23] The summary of the article stated, "Cooperation based on reciprocal altruism has evolved in only a small number of species, yet it constitutes the core behavioral principle of human social life. The iterated Prisoner's Dilemma Game has been used to model this form of cooperation. We used fMRI to scan thirty-six women as they played an iterated Prisoner's Dilemma Game with another woman to investigate the neurobiological basis of cooperative social behavior. Mutual cooperation was associated with consistent activation in brain areas that have been linked to reward processing. . . . We propose that activa-tion of this neural network positively reinforces reciprocal altruism, thereby motivating subjects to resist the temptation to selfishly accept but not recipro-cate favors."[24] And later, "Cooperative social interactions with nonkin are pervasive in all human societies and generally emerge from relationships based on reciprocal altruism. Such relationships arguable lay the foundation for the interdependence upon which societal division of labor is based. We have iden-tified a pattern of neural activation that may be involved in sustaining cooperative social relationships, perhaps by labeling cooperative social interactions as re-warding, and/or by inhibiting the selfish impulse to accept but not reciprocate an act of altruism."[25] There is reason to hope that this research is only the earli-est of a continuing use of brain scanning to help explain the nature of unconscious drives.

Immoral Behavior: The Enron Case

The discussion so far of the biological base of morality has failed to address one major issue—how to explain immoral behavior. If morality is an innate skill of humans, how can there be so many obvious instances of behavior that the world agrees are immoral? Since the theme of this Ruffin conference is *Business,* as well as *Science and Ethics,* it now seems appropriate to examine and attempt to explain, at least in a preliminary way, a conspicuous case of business immorality. We will focus on the business case that is currently in the spotlight, the Enron case. In this regard we will draw extensively, but not ex-clusively, from *The Collapse of Enron,* a case by Anne Lawrence[26]

The moral-rule breaking at Enron seems to have involved scores of top managers and to have spread to associated professional service and banking firms with Arthur Andersen being the most conspicuous. While the legality of the behavior of Enron executives remains to be decided in court, the verdict of the general public is already clear. In the court of public opinion the behavior of Enron executives is regarded as highly immoral whether or not it was legal. At the very least, the top management of Enron broke the bonds of trust with their employees, their stockholders and their customers. Can four drive theory with its related moral skill set help explain the Enron situation? It is clear that the senior managers at Enron broke the norms of responsible business behavior in an amazing number of ways. Evidence suggests that they hiked electricity prices through phony energy-futures transactions among their own subsidiaries, thereby defrauding energy customers including the state of California. They probably used inside information to time their sales of Enron stock and options while simultaneously advising employees to add Enron stock to their retirement accounts and also freezing sales from these accounts. They may have been using their leverage with investment banks to corrupt the professional judgment of stock analysts. They systematically used campaign contributions in an effort to corrupt government officials in all branchs of the federal government, especially the regulatory bodies from which they sought exemptions from regulation. They apparently seduced their Anderson accountants with large fees and generous perks to approve the moving of debt off the books, inflating revenues and other accounting abuses.

On March 3, 2003, the government released a 2000-page report by Neal Batson, an Atlanta lawyer who was appointed by the federal bankruptcy court in New York to investigate Enron's financial transactions. As reported in the Times,

> The Batson report reads like a pulp fiction novel for the financial world, replete with tales of manipulations, deceits and flat-out mistruths that resulted in one of the world's most powerful and respected companies misrepresenting its precarious—and ultimately fatal—position. . . . Batson also concludes in the report that the company relied on six complex accounting maneuvers to make its financial picture more attractive. Such techniques—including non-economic hedges, tax transactions and other devices—accounted for 96 percent of Enron's reported $979 million in net income for 2000. . . . They also allowed Enron to report debt of $10.2 billion instead of $22.1 billion.[27]

These actions, of course, grossly misrepresented their profitability and misled investors.

In terms of four-drive theory, the easy analysis would be that the senior people at Enron were expressing an excessive amount of the drive to acquire— that they were carried away with greed. This is undoubtedly true but it is by no means the whole story. Why did not their drive to bond with their own employees, their customers and their stockholders moderate their greed and activate their innate sense of moral behavior? Why did not the internal checks and balances, that we hypothesize were built into their minds, lead to a better balance between acquiring and bonding? How did the drives to learn and to defend play a part in their behavior? Can we state a credible hypothesis about what was going on in their minds that led to their actual behavior?

It is well known that the human mind is capable of generating a vast array of rationalizations for breaking moral rules. We can easily imagine some of the rationalizations that might have been employed by Enron executives to ease their consciences. "Everybody was doing it." "I didn't know I was getting involved until it was too late to get out." The list could go on. But these executives were sophisticated people. They must have realized that such reasons were only flimsy excuses that could hardly blot out their inner sense of guilt about the complex and extensive scam they were conducting. And we would repeat that the proper test for the existence of an innate moral sense is not whether moral rules are violated but whether the individual rule-breaker feels guilty. Again, can four drive theory be used to develop a more complete and robust explanation of the complex process by which Enron became the poster boy for corporate corruption?

We will start our analysis with what the record shows about the bonding process (D2) at Enron. Who were the important "others" with whom the top executives at Enron were psychologically bonded with mutual commitments to caring? We can get clues to this from the people they chose to recruit for senior manager positions. Enron focused its managerial hiring on the "best and brightest" among the MBAs from the top-rated business schools. They subjected all candidates to intensive reviews. "After an initial screening interview, candidates were brought to the Houston office for a 'Super Saturday,' during which they were individually interviewed for fifty minutes by eight interviewers, with only ten-minute breaks between interviews."[28] The interviewers were looking for those who were smartest, hardest working and most loyal to the top executives. The ones selected after this process must have been convinced that they were truly part of an elite group. If they came up with a creative new business plan that promised profits, they were with some regularity put in charge of a new division. Being part of this elite insider group meant that, by definition, all others were "outsiders." This set up a condition discussed in *Driven* that might have overridden the bonds that Enron executives might normally have felt with their ordinary stockholders, customers and lower-level employees. One of the simplest but most far-reaching skill sets that supports the human drive to bond is the ability to make a distinction between "us" and "them." In the technical language of biology, this skill is known as the *dyadic instinct*, the proneness to use two-part classifications in treating socially important arrays. To state the rule in its primal form there is an in-group to whom the social rules of moral behavior apply and an out-group to whom they do not apply because the "others" are thought of as something less than fully human. At the extreme this "us vs. them" distinction can even be used to rationalize genocide as well as slavery. In its mild form it can be used to exploit others who are "beyond the pale," "not our type," outside "our" social contract. It is the dyadic instinct that gives rise to such loyalty codes as, "We stick together to help and protect our close cronies against the outside world." It is a strictly limited application of the drive to bond, empathizing only with a narrowly defined group. At Enron it meant that many of the company's stakeholders were candidates for being treated as dumb suckers, eligible for fleecing and exploitation. After all, economic theory warns outsiders that "buyers should beware."

Tight executive bonding is closely related to the way the drive to learn (D3) was played out at Enron. Kenneth Lay, a founder and CEO, firmly believed in free markets and felt that the deregulation of the natural gas industry presented a great opportunity for the fledging company. He recruited Jeffrey Skilling from McKinsey to help him take advantage of this opportunity. Skilling brought with him an elaboration of Lay's belief in free markets that is known as neoclassical economics, or more popularly as laissez-faire capitalism. They both applied this theory to their business situation and undoubtedly indoctrinated other members of senior management. In its simple version it is the doctrine that totally unregulated markets provide the best means to a healthy, prosperous society. It argues that the general welfare is best served if each business firm exclusively pursues its own profits. It argues that *all* social relations are (or at least should be) governed by Fiske's market pricing (MP) form of sociality. For some it argues that corporate greed works out to be best for everyone. This statement would be closer to the truth if greed always took the form of people working harder and smarter to increase their production of useful goods and services and if profit always measured the difference between the value others placed on the extra production and its total cost. Unfortunately, situations like Enron, with its ninety-six percent phony profits, demonstrate that profit figures can grossly misrepresent the contribution they make to the general welfare.

It is highly dubious that this economic model in its pure form is, in fact, widely acted out in behavior. Most people sense that it can only predict some aspects of behavior. Amitai Etzioni and Robert Frank, among others, have documented the extensive predictive failures of the theory.[29] The "ultimatum game" line of research is but one example of work that indicates that, while the theory is certainly not entirely wrong, it is seriously incomplete. However, one ultimatum experiment that was run with college students came up with remarkably deviant results. In this particular experiment the Proposers made remarkably stingy offers and most of the Responders actually accepted them. On further inquiry it was learned that the subjects of the experiment were all taking a class in neoclassical economics. Their behavior was clearly an exception to the universal pattern reported above. Could the Enron executives have been a similar exception—a group of true believers in neoclassical economics as the sole theory for explaining all social relations? Was this the exclusive theory that their drive to learn had drawn them into? Is it possible that such a strong cultural belief could act as an intervening variable between moral rule breaking and a bad conscience?

In any event, Enron executives discovered that applying the free market doctrine to the natural gas industry was, in fact, very profitable for them. Their insider group of executives was becoming wealthy at a rapid pace. Their drive to acquire (D1) was being fulfilled. In *Driven* we offer the hypothesis that, when the drive to acquire is carried to the extreme of greed, it works in the same manner as the addictive process that has been studied to some extent by neuroscientists. It is known, for instance, that mind-altering drugs can activate neurotransmitters, such as serotonin, that generate feelings of happiness. There is also some limited evidence that events that provide humans with status or monetary rewards also stimulate the production of serotonin. Michael McGuire and his neuroscience collaborators at UCLA have found elevated serotonin levels in the leaders of college fraternities and athletic teams.[30] This suggests the possibility that the leaders of Enron had, step by step, become addicted to the "high" of making more and more money, of moving up the status ladder. We see abundant evidence that drug addicts will break the moral codes of society to get their "fix." Is it possible that the leaders of Enron were on a similar mental track? This hypothesis may or may not seen likely, but, in any event, it is probably testable. Serotonin levels can be measured.

But even the presence of a serotonin "high" can only explain how greed is reinforced, not whether a sense of guilt comes along with the serotonin. But one part of the four drive theory was certainly demonstrated by the Enron executives. The profits they made from the "gas bank" technique of selling long-term gas contracts to both gas producers and to gas users were not enough. Their drive to acquire was insatiable, and, perhaps reinforced by beliefs in totally free markets (D3) and their bonding only with the top team (D2), they went for more. They quickly began to apply the same technique to market after market: electricity, water, broadband, pulp and lumber, specialty chemicals, coal, aluminum, plastics and even emission credits. The only trouble was that these new markets did not have the same characteristics found in the natural gas market. For example, gas can be stored for later use and electricity cannot. Enron began to lose money in a big way. At this point, not too surprisingly, top management's drive to defend (D4) began to kick in.

The record shows that the response of the Enron executives to the accumulating losses was to cover them up. They went for flight rather than fight. Their methods were very complex and very clever, again revealing their opinion of their own brilliance. It was at this stage that they sought out the collusion of their auditors and bankers—by making them insiders to help hold up the stock price in the quest for more money. The accounting methods they employed have since been revealed: mark-for-market, a scheme for declaring profits in advance of realization; special purpose entities (SPEs) to move debt off the balance sheet; sham swaps to inflate revenue, etc. Finally, consider the guilt implicit in the behavior of Skilling in blocking any questions at meetings with analysts about the dubious Enron partnerships and the instances of brokers being abruptly fired by their employing banks when Enron complained that they were advising clients to sell their Enron stock. The longer term problem with all of these methods was obvious: one cover-up required additional cover-ups, one after the other, until the inevitable collapse.

So the question still remains, did the top Enron executives, who, it is estimated, sold $1.1 billion in Enron stock shortly before the implosion, feel guilty about their actions or not? We would argue that their sense of guilt was made obvious by the elaborate and extended effort they made to cover up their actions. And tragically, in the very process of cover-up they committed their more egregious immoral acts. The great magnitude of the rewards they received for cheating their various stakeholders would have only increased their feeling of guilt. The problems at Enron started with the formation of their elite insider group, moved on to the hubris of the insiders in their abilities and their fixation on a limited guiding theory. They were grossly over-confident. The limits of their theory were revealed when it was applied in the wrong business environment. Their response to the mounting losses was to try to run and hide. They lost their opportunity to face up to their losses, cut out the unprofitable lines of business and struggle to met their obligations. Only further research will more rigorously test these hypotheses derived from four drive theory and offer either confirming or non-confirming evidence from Enron and other cases.

The issue of corporate corruption is increasingly being recognized as central to establishing healthy economies around the world. The slowness of the economic reform process in Russia is widely attributed to corporate and state corruption. Russia is still rated as the last of the industrialized countries in this regard. Even the Russian Union of Industrialists and Entrepreneurs has appealed to the Putin government for more comprehensive, enforceable regulations to improve business conditions. The World Bank is now treating the issue of corruption as a major impediment to economic development in emerging economies. And, lest we ignore the issue in the United States, its latest rating as bribe-givers is only 5.5 on a ten-point scale, only in the mid-range of industrialized countries.

Psychopaths—People With No Conscience?

There is growing evidence that the only humans who consistently feel no conscience, no remorse from actions that are widely perceived as immoral, are psychopaths with a brain deficiency. The Boston papers recently carried the story of an extreme example of such psychopathic behavior. A man who worked as a medical technician was convicted of injecting HIV-positive blood into the arm of his twelve-year-old son, apparently as a way of avoiding child support payments. Knowledge about this type of exceptional human behavior is being gradually developed. The compilation of this evidence has been done most recently by Robert Hare in his aptly titled book, *Without Conscience*. He estimates that there are currently two million psychopaths in North America. "Their hallmark is a stunning lack of conscience; their game is self-gratification at the other person's expense."[31] He states, "A frightful and perplexing theme that runs through the case histories of all psychopaths [is] a deeply disturbing inability to care about the pain and suffering experienced by others—in short, a complete lack of empathy, the prerequisite for love. In a desperate attempt to explain this lack, we have turned first to family background, but there is little to help us there. It is true that the childhood of *some* psychopaths were characterized by material and emotional deprivation and physical abuse. But for every adult psychopath from a troubled background there is another whose family life apparently was warm and nurturing, and whose siblings are normal, conscientious people with the ability to care deeply for others. Furthermore, most people who had horrible childhoods do not become psychopaths."[32] The disturbing symptoms appear very early in the lives of psychopaths. More and more evidence of this kind supports the conclusion that such people have a genetic brain disorder. In four drive terms they are behaving like individuals without a drive to bond with others. Hare has developed a list of the symptoms of the psychopath as follows: Glib and superficial, egocentric and grandiose, lack of remorse or guilt, lack of empathy, deceitful and manipulative, shallow emotions, impulsive, poor behavior controls, need for excitement, lack of responsibility, early behavior problems, and adult antisocial behavior.[33] The use of this list probably offers the best guide to the diagnosis of psychopaths currently available. Unfortunately the list is subject to different interpretations and cannot claim to generate a firm and conclusive diagnosis. There is hope, however, that by the use of brain scanning methods such a definitive diagnosis can be achieved. How the world could best deal with identified psychopaths is not at all clear.

Conclusion

If our primary hypothesis about the innate nature of a moral sense in all humans is supported by additional research, it would throw significant light on the broader topic of social control and moral behavior in many contexts. It would help our understanding of how the issues of morality are played out at every level from the individual, to the small group, to the firm, to the nation state, and even to the international arena. We would argue that the four drives provide at the individual level an internal pressure to find action plans in every situation that serve all four drives simultaneously in contrast to the pursuit of one or two drives at the expense of the others. This means that the outcome is not determined by our innate drives—choice for the individual is still real. It is obvious that these internal checks and balances are not foolproof in producing civil, pro-social actions. Humans are free to make immoral decisions. People can be swept into excesses in regard to each of the four drives. People have known throughout history that our internal sense of right and wrong, while providing the foundation for human moral behavior, needs to be reinforced by rules at all social levels to constrain serious deviance. All face-to-face human groups develop norms of behavior, a form of social contract that acts to constrain choices of individual members. Withholding social interaction and social approval is used to enforce these codes. At the level of the organization, formal rules are enacted as constraints that constitute a social contract specifying the terms of membership and employment. At the level of the state, humans have evolved a complex set of laws as well as informal codes of conduct that specify the rules that are enforced by public opinion, and by the police and the courts. This includes rules to constrain the behavior of business institutions. Even at the international level, humans are now creating laws that are only beginning to be enforced by UN policing and international courts. The continuing record of violent warfare between nations makes abundantly clear the urgent need for strengthening these international institutions.

Perhaps the word "rogue" can be applied to deviant moral behavior at all these levels from the rogue individual (such as the HIV blood injector cited above), to the rogue group (such as the group of top managers at Enron) to the rogue organization (such as the Mafia), to the rogue state (history as well as current events supply a number of candidates). Clearly social control of rogue behavior is a complex matter that occupies a great deal of human attention. Regulation is needed at each collective level because of the limitations of our inbred moral compass. However, it is all too easy to legislate an excessive amount of control that robs people of their sense of freedom of choice. The key must be to construct the minimum kind of constraints at each level of society to avoid the exploitation and abuse of others, without overly constraining the freedom of individuals and institutions. There will always be tension over where to draw this line in specific situations. The Enron example, however, provides evidence that the current regulations concerning business fraud are inadequate. The Batson study cited above reports that, in spite of the magnitude of misstated profits and the frequency of violations of accounting principles, as long as the auditors approved the figures, Enron and its leaders probably cannot be convicted of criminal fraud.

Humans, as individuals, are not designed to win, once and for all, the battle for pro-social, moral behavior. However, the human brain is designed in such a way that it forces us to choose right from wrong, or the greater good from the lesser, in our everyday activities. The more people are educated to the reality of these moral issues and are encouraged, for their own long-term good as well as that of others, to seek the moral path, the fewer constraints will be needed at higher levels. As humans, we also are capable of designing institutions at multiple levels that wisely constrain, not too much or too little, those individuals that are inclined to deviate significantly from the moral path. As humans, we are capable of developing bonds of caring with all humans worldwide and we are gradually moving in that direction. We are capable of continually pushing forward our learning and understanding of ourselves and our world and avoiding the mental traps of false and limited belief systems. We are capable of creating business firms and other institutions that can multiply the creativity and productivity of their members so as to continually enlarge the fund of resources and services for human use. We are capable of finding conflict resolution methods that satisfy our drive to defend in non-violent ways.

Finally, we would note that the human choice process, built into our brains by the independence of the drives, introduces a permanent, irreducible element of uncertainty to the prediction of human behavior. As a result we can only predict general tendencies. This is inevitably frustrating to scientists that always are seeking predictability. As scientists, we need to accept the fact that, as with electrons, we can only predict human behavior in terms of probabilities. And as humans, we should be eternally grateful for the uncertainty created by the human bonding drive and moral skills. Without these innate elements in human brains, we would all be very predictable psychopaths.

Exhibit 1

Human Skill Sets Hypothesized by Stephen Pinker[34]

1. Intuitive mechanics: how objects can be manipulated.
2. Intuitive biology: how plants and animals work.
3. Numbers.
4. Mental maps for large territories.
5. Habitat selections.
6. Danger: understanding major hazards; snakes, heights, etc..
7. Food: what is good to eat.
8. Contamination: intuitions about contagion and disease.
9. Monitoring of current bodily well being.
10. Intuitive psychology: predicting other people's behavior
11. A mental Rolodex: a data base on important individuals.
12. Self-concept.
13. Justice: sense of rights, obligations, etc..
14. Kinship.
15. Mating.

Exhibit 2

A Schematic Representation of How the Mind Works

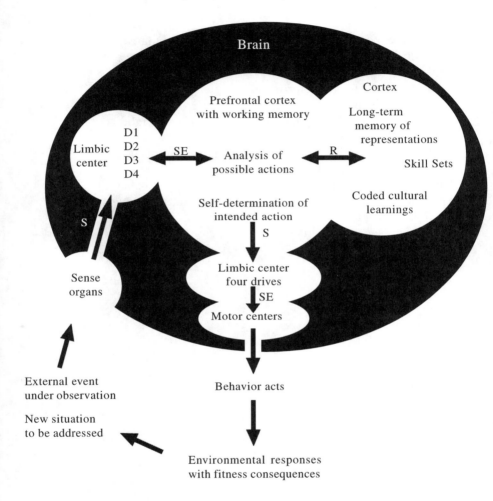

S = Signals
D = Drives
SE = Signals with emotional markers
R = Representations

Notes

1. Carter, R. 1998. *Mapping the Mind.* Berkeley: University of California Press.
2. Pinker, S. 1994. *How the Mind Works.* New York: Norton.
3. Damasio, A. 1994. *Descartes' Error: Emotion, Reason, and the Human Brain.* New York: Putnam.
4. Gropnick, A., A. Meltzoff, P. Kuhl. *The Scientist in the Crib.* New York: Harper Collins, 1999.
5. Ratey, J. J. 2001. *A User's Guide to the Brain.* New York: Vintage, pp. 117 and 315.
6. Carter, *Mapping the Mind*, p. 20.
7. Damasio, *Descartes' Error.*
8. Darwin, C. 1998 (1874). *The Descent of Man.* Amherst, N.Y.: Prometheus Books, p. 111.
9. Ibid., p. 65
10. Ibid., p. 101.
11. Wilson, J. Q. 1993. *The Moral Sense.* New York: Free Press.
12. Ibid., p. 70.
13. de Waal, F. 1996. *Good Natured: The Origin of Right and Wrong in Humans and Other Animals.* Cambridge, Mass.: Harvard University Press. p. 87.
14. Wilson, E. O. 1998. *Consilience: The Unity of Knowledge.* New York: Knopf, p. 179.
15. Haidt, J. 2001. "The Emotional Dog and Its Rational Tail: A Social Intuitionist Approach to Moral Judgement." *Psychological Review* 108(4): 814–834.
16. Ibid.
17. Gould, S. J. 1999. *Rocks of* Ages. New York: Ballantine.
18. Wright, R. 1994. *The Moral Animal.* New York: Vintage Books, 1994.
19. Bower, B. 2002. "A Fair Share of the Pie." *Science News* 161(7) (Feb. 16).
20. Fiske, A. P. 1991. *Structures of Social Life: The Four Elementary Forms of Human Relations.* New York: The Free Press.
21. Lawrence, P., and N. Nohria. 2002. *Driven: How Human Nature Shapes Our Choices.* San Francisco: Jossey-Bass, pp. 161–164.
22. Fiske, *Structures of Social Life*, p. 408.
23. Rilling, J. K., D. Gutman, T. Zeh, G. Pagnonik, G. Berns, and C. Kilts. 2002. "A Neural Basis for Social Cooperation." *Neuron* 35 (July 18): 395–405.
24. Ibid., p. 395.
25. Ibid., p. 403.
26. Lawrence, A. 2003. *The Collapse of Enron, A Case.* New York: McGraw-Hill/Irwin.
27. International Herald Tribune. 2003. "Enron's Accounting Binge Chronicled." Kurt Eichenward, from the *New York Times* (March 7), p. 13.
28. Lawrence, A., *The Collapse of Enron*, p. 6.
29. Etzioni, A. 1988. *The Moral Dimension: Toward a New Economics.* New York: Free Press.
30. McGuire, M., M. Raleigh, and G. Brammer. 1982. "Sociopharmacology." *Annual Review of Pharmacological Toxicology* 22: 643–661.
31. Hare, R. 1993. *Without Conscience.* New York: Guilford Press.
32. Ibid., p. 6.
33. Ibid., p. 34.
34. Pinker, *How the Mind Works*, p. 420.

A DEAL, A DOLPHIN, AND A ROCK: BIOLOGICAL CONTRIBUTIONS TO BUSINESS ETHICS

Timothy L. Fort

Abstract: In this response to Paul Lawrence's Ruffin Lecture, I assess the benefits of integrating biology into business ethics including the way in which biology counteracts conventional economic descriptions of human nature. Section II looks at the dangers of the project and offers the notion of Multilevel Selection Theory as a way to address the notion of how one balances various biological drives. Section III concludes by suggesting that in order to optimally integrate biology, one should attend to contractual notions (the deal) as well as a Sisyphean quest to engage in the task of integration. In doing so, we should also remember to draw upon the dolphin in each of us, that part that takes pleasure in doing moral acts.

In this response, I do not wish to challenge Professor Paul Lawrence's interpretation of the biological findings that lead him to characterize human behavior as the product of four insatiable drives of Acquisition, Bonding, Learning, and Defending.[1] I do wish to reinforce the reasons for welcoming these kinds of scientific findings to the field of business ethics. I also want to attempt to do something that must inevitably occur if a scientific field is to be integrated with a normative field such as business ethics. That is, biology provides us with a much better ability to comprehend how to understand ethical (or unethical) business behavior, but its use depends upon an understanding of the possible comparisons one makes between biology and organizational theory. Those comparisons can be assisted, I believe, by Multilevel Selection theory.

I. The Benefits of Finding a Biological Base of Morality

There are two main benefits for linking human behavior to a hard science such as biology. The first relates to its usefulness as an antidote to the perception of human nature as being irreducibly that of a ruthless, self-interested acquisition of material goods. The second relates to the heft biology brings to attempts to convince doubters of the inescapable reality of ethics in human life.

Economists are often more willing to consider human nature than for social scientists philosophies and it is a view befitting Dostoyevsky in its darkness.[2]

Perhaps the most famous articulation of it comes from the influential institutional economist, Oliver Williamson, who defines opportunism as "self-interest seeking with guile" and assumes that trait to be a ubiquitous feature of human nature.[3] The neoclassical understanding of human nature is that it is beholden to self-interest and that it can be accounted for in some type of financial metric.

Professor Lawrence's theory poses large problems for this approach. Professor Lawrence messes things up when he talks about innate drives of, yes, acquiring material and sensory goods (who would doubt that this drive does exist) but also drives of bonding, defending, and learning. Professor Lawrence's theory is Dostoyevkian too, but not in the dark sense I have linked to the economists, but instead in terms of the complexity of life.[4] If there are multiple drives, then there are multiple things to take account of. Particularly given identifiable drives of bonding and learning, human nature is imbued with a predisposition toward compassion and empathy as well as cognitive advancement through education. This contribution by itself is worth welcoming to the field of business ethics.

The second benefit the science Professor Lawrence brings to the debate is "hardness." Even to a receptive audience, ethics talk can be viewed as being "soft" and for this reason, to the extent the life sciences can demonstrate the rootedness of a moral or social sense, the harder it is to dismiss. For example, recently, I attended a lecture by a prominent organizational theorist who discussed the importance of compassion in business organizations. The basic point of the lecture was that human beings do, in fact, respond to pain in very real ways. One of the first questions, however, was whether this compassionate sense should be encouraged by management because, in a Darwinian sense, it may not prove to be competitive. Professor Lawrence's theory, I think, helps to anchor such theories of compassion in something that can't be brushed aside. Indeed, such biological evidence provides a platform on which we ethicists can stand to demonstrate that considerations of ethical principles are part of our human identity and need to be taken account of.

Although I have tried to understand a good deal of the biological contributions to ethical theory, I do not believe that I am in a position to evaluate the adequacy of Professor Lawrence's argument about whether there are four as opposed to three or six drives. However, I would like to note that this theory appears highly compatible with that of the business ethics thinker who has done more work than anyone in trying to link the sciences with ethics: William Frederick.

Frederick also proposes a theory of four "value clusters" that are embedded in all life.[5] Frederick's economizing cluster, whereby individuals or organizations (human or nonhuman) convert raw materials into useful energy seems akin to Lawrence's drive for acquisition of material goods and sensory experiences. Frederick's notion of power-aggrandizing, in which individuals and organizations carve out areas, territorial and otherwise, of status and power is akin to Lawrence's drive of defending one's self and one's possessions.

Frederick's notion of ecologizing value clusters in the sense of the deep interlinkages that support life in a long, evolutionary horizon is a broad notion of the drive to bond. Finally, Frederick's notion of techno-symbolic values, which are the essence of human cognitive ability to invent, philosophize, and develop culture is akin to Lawrence's drive of learning.

This is not to conflate the work of these two scholars. Frederick works on a larger time horizon and incorporates thermodynamic physics. Lawrence is tightly focused on human behavior within organizations. These perspectives make it impossible to line them up too closely. For instance, Lawrence's notion that the drive to defend includes concern for one's loved ones might more easily fit in an ecologizing rather than power-aggrandizing value cluster for Frederick. I do not make the comparison in order to argue that these approaches are the same, but to note that there is a consilience to dividing the world, and human nature, into these kinds of categories that seems to hang together.

II. The Dangers of Biologicizing Human Nature

Having pointed out some of the benefits of bringing biology into the business ethics game, it is equally important to point out some dangers. The first has to do with the accuracy with which science or any other field can describe the way the world works and what that means for normative thought. The second has to do with the extent to which human beings are able to consciously balance the four drives and, in particular, the appropriate level for comparing evolutionary notions to organizational theory.

Can Biology Accurately Describe the World?

The first concern is whether science can accurately describe the way the world is. Professor Lawrence notes the confidence with which scientists believe that they have discovered unconscious drives in the "limbic section of the brain, lying just below and behind the pre-frontal cortex."[6] The concern is that a few centuries ago, Descartes, working with the best science of the time, believed that he had located the soul in the pineal gland.[7] To avoid misunderstanding, I have no doubt that the scientific methods of the twenty-first century are light years ahead of that of those who thought the soul was in the pineal gland. But, I have my doubts as to whether further scientific advances fifty years from now won't disrupt today's findings.

In a sense, this is not a big deal. For purposes of determining whether or not Enron executives violated duties to their employees and shareholders, I don't think the precise location of these drives is significant. In another sense, however, it is a big deal. Biology's leverage to contribute to the field of ethics is largely dependent upon its prowess in depicting accurately the way the world works. Utilizing this kind of leverage is not new in normative thought. For millennia, cosmology has described, in different ways, the way in which the world works whether that be in a fall from a perfect creation or whether be in balancing a yin-yang duality of existence. Yet ontological conceptions change and there needs to be a sense of contingency associated with any confidence in determining how the world works.

B. Multilevel Selection Theory and Appropriate Balancing of Drives

The second concern regards the extent which human beings can consciously balance these four drives. Professor Lawrence poses the question of what rules we might follow, with respect to the four drives, if we desire a relationship of mutual caring with another person. His response, reciprocity-derived formulations of each drive with a test of one has a guilty conscience if they break one of those rules, seems reasonable and even compelling if research can confirm an innate sense of conscience. He proposes that balancing these four drives is something that can be done on an individual, organizational, national, or even global level.[8] How does one do that? Are the lessons of balancing individual manifestations of four-drive theory the same as they are for a nation-state? Obviously, this is a question that requires treatment well beyond that of a brief response paper, but I would like to suggest some things to consider.

Recognizing that there could be a differing way to apply the balancing of these four biological drives is important and is, moreover, consistent with a notion known as Multilevel Selection Theory. Multilevel Selection Theory can be described as recognizing that evolutionary competition and adaptation exist on a variety of levels, including perhaps, the socioeconomic level.[9] Darwin recognized this possibility.[10] Thus there may well be evolutionary kinds of competition between social systems as well as between genes. One could, then, compare the way genes evolve to the way social systems evolve and make assessments as to the likelihood of the potential fitness of the subject to be analyzed on the basis of comparison with other kinds of evolution. Of course, this what the Social Darwinists, such as Hubert Spencer, did in a way that so troubles ethicists as to make any use of biology deeply suspicious.[11] Multilevel Selection Theory, however, is more subtle that the approach of Social Darwinism. It stands for the idea that it is possible to study the adaptive behavior of various kinds of groups just as one might study the adaptive behavior of individuals, but without making groups and individuals into the same thing.[12] Evolutionary principles can be applied, but it is important to know what is being compared.

Alasdair MacIntyre implicitly uses a form of Multilevel Selection Theory in his somewhat surprising turn to biology as a resource for virtue ethics. MacIntyre is able to avoid the problems of the specific locus of various human drives while preserving the contribution such findings can make to ethical thinking by arguing that it is important to make appropriate kinds of comparisons. In critiquing Heidegger's grouping of humans on the one hand and all non-humans on the other, MacIntyre argues that such an approach fails to distinguish the crucial differences among various kinds of animals.[13] Earthworms and crabs, on the one hand, and dolphins, apes and dogs, on the other do not differ insignificantly. Dolphins, apes, and dogs differ from other animals and are more similar to human beings because, as MacIntyre argues, they have greater neocortex development in terms of the ratio of neocortex size to body bass. As a result, these animals have at least prelinguistic capacities.[14]

MacIntyre grasps the critical point that it is important to seek meaningful comparisons. He also engages in a level of comparison that emphasizes the socialness of humanity as being hardwired while preserving the cultural reality that other characteristics are malleable according to the community in which one learns, or fails to learn, virtues. These kinds of multilevel distinctions prevent an uncritical acceptance of hardwired behavior. Human socialization is not simply biology but culture as well.[15]

Culture shapes individual fitness as well as the group's collective fitness. Culture is also the product, in significant part, of individual choices. Thus, it is a mistake to think that human societies, whether clans, nation-states, or corporations, operate according to deterministic, naturalistic, evolutionary processes identical to that of cells and genes. But the importance of a group's fitness to an individual's own fitness is apparent in both cases. Individual relationships with the community can be identified, but their particular manifestations differ at differing levels of adaptation.

1. Possible Ways to Balance the Four Drives

With this in mind, there are at least three things that have to be considered if this balancing is to occur. First, there is a question as to whether human beings can, in fact, balance these things or whether evolution, genes, and history (or perhaps God) do the balancing. Two very different scholars who utilize evolutionary principles to bolster their moral prescriptions, F. A. Hayek, and William Frederick, are very dubious about the possibility of conscious balancing. Hayek refers to it as a "fatal conceit" to think that human beings can devise some kind of overarching social contract that will achieve social justice.[16] Frederick explicitly eschews the notion of balancing arguing that nature is not "in balance" but that various value clusters are always in contention.[17] Thus, the first concern is whether a social contract comprehending all of these biological drives is possible or whether this balancing occurs on a level beyond that of human consciousness.

Second, if it is possible to construct such a social contract, what form might it take? The notion of checks and balances is a constant, in some form, throughout human history; indeed, it might be described as a hardwired feature of human organization restraining individuals and small group. Even in highly autocratic pre-Western societies, such as Hawaii, where it was death to a commoner to have the shadow of the *Moi'i* (the king) fall upon him, commoners had rights believed to be exercised through nature and its bounty by the gods.[18] There was a social contract, but it was one rooted in a cultural evolution that connected human moral failings to cycles of nature. The "contract" arguably "worked" for the centuries in which Hawaii had its own form of "splendid isolation"[19] until western contract transformed moral principles such as *kapu* into nothing more than positivist restrictions created by the elite to exploit the poor.[20] The balance of the contractual system of checks and balances was thrown out of whack by the removal of the understanding of natural judgment on the actions of the ruler and, in doing so, significant suffering resulted.[21]

The form the balancing takes and the rules and principles applicable to a cultural setting thus seem to have everything to do with culture as opposed to biology, but the principle of some system of checks and balances may be inherent in cultural organization. If so, then there is a question as to the relative contribution biology can make to the terms of a just social contract as opposed to traditional legal and philosophical experience. This is not to dispute the possibility that contracting may be a hardwired feature of human nature as Leda Cosmides proposes.[22] Biological hardwiring may specify the kinds of things that philosophers and theologians should take account of as opposed to other things that are not so "real." If this is the case, then biology and traditional normative thought can work hand in hand. They can do so by turning to contracting philosophies and strategies in the confidence that, in doing so, we are playing on an aspect of human nature deeply rooted in our evolutionary capacity to survive that has proven the test of time. Moreover, by using Multilevel Selection Theory as a constraint to sift through various contracting possibilities so that the right kinds of contracts are applied to the appropriate level of human organization, one can integrate our social and emotional proclivities through what I have called "banded contracts" – contracts among the members of the band[23] and link the lessons learned from those banded contracts to global contracts to them our tendency to declare war on other tribes. Put in more traditional business ethics terms, it could well be that theories focusing on sentiments maybe more appropriate in dealing with interpersonal issues whereas notions of social contracts have more weight in conceiving of duties among strangers or institutions.

The simple points, however, are (1) that social contract thinking depends on an ontological understanding of the way in which the world works and (2) adjusting a social contract to reflect the changing understanding of the way the world works requires an ability to understand that biology may describe a certain level of human interaction, but leave open a great deal of political, moral, economic, and ethical specification through the judgments we exercise as to the appropriate kinds of contracts relevant to particular situations.

Third, in Professor Lawrence's paper and even more explicitly in his book, there is a temptation to view larger governmental units as evidence of this contract that can transcend the limitations of the narrowness and often the narrow-mindedness of people in smaller groups. In other words, a larger social contract embodying the common principle and ethical rules beneficial to all of humanity has significant benefits to humanity and is worth attempting to construct. I want to suggest, however, that allegiance to larger governmental units may not be all that beneficial.

2. Why Large Groups Might Not Be Beneficial

One reason they might not be beneficial is, in fact, for biological reasons. As I have argued at some length, there is both a strand of natural law as well as biological support for the notion that human beings learn their moral values in relatively small groups.[24] Borrowing from the traditions of Catholic Social Thinking and its interpretation of natural law, I have argued that in mediating institutions, where there is face-to-face interaction with others and where one is able to comprehend the consequences of one's actions, morality is formed.

Studies on the development of language capability by Robin Dunbar tend to support this notion.[25] Dunbar's studies show that the neocortex of primates correlates with the size of the primate grouping; once a group reaches a certain size, the group splits.[26] Extrapolating from existing evidence, Dunbar argues that the maximum number of human beings with whom a person can have some degree of personal relationship is only about 150.[27] Dunbar's finding is further substantiated by anthropological studies that show when group sizes increase beyond certain threshold levels, the number of disputes in those groups increase not arithmetically for every new person added, but exponentially.[28] Indeed, returning to natural law, the argument of Catholic Social Thought is that in such large groupings, one loses a sense of moral efficacy and transfers one's engagement with moral duties to a far-away bureaucracy.[29]

A second reason to be concerned about allegiance to large groups is that large groups may even encourage the kinds of violence we wish to avoid. This is not to romanticize hunter-gatherers as peaceful nomads. The work of Lawrence Keeley demonstrates that there was a great deal of violence in pre-history.[30] At the same time, there have been anthropological studies of peaceful societies done by David Fabbro, who summarizes them as having, among others, these characteristics: being relatively small, with little hierarchy, face-to-face interaction, non-violent values, gender equity, participation in decision-making, and relatively remote.[31] Moreover, even Keeley who argues for large, transcending kinds of organizations to limit tribal fights, not that even when adjusting for population changes, the so-called civilized twentieth century killed twenty times more people in warfare than in our tribal past.[32]

It seems that a critical contribution that subjects such as biological anthropology, evolutionary psychology, biology itself, and perhaps other sciences is to make us aware that we must exercise great care in constructing the right kinds of checks and balances in the right time and place. In other words—to use the insights of Multilevel Selection Theory—the kind of contracts must link to the appropriate level of communal analysis To repeat, it may well be that we need relatively small groups to develop notions of empathy and caring so that we internalize virtuous rules but that in order to prevent tribal warfares we need construction of other kinds of organizations that are attentive to the dangers of human nature but which also leave room for empathy-sustaining mediating institutions.

III. A Deal, A Dolphin, and a Rock

Professor Lawrence's paper leaves us with the possibility of three ways in which we may be able to consider the contributions biology may make to normative thinking and how those contributions helps to solve intractable problems of immoral behavior. The first way is the topic of the previous few pages: is there a contractual way of balancing, individually, organizationally, socially, and globally the four drives inherent in our nature? This is the "deal" approach. Is there a social contract that could be agreed upon, leaving aside philosophical arguments as to what an agreed-upon social contract is? Despite the concerns I have raised about this approach in the previous pages, it is hard to think that it could not be our moral responsibility to engage in such contractual creation of a world in which certain duties are agreed to for the welfare of all humanity and to limit the kinds of violence and terrorism that plagues us.

The second way is that of Sisyphus. Professor Lawrence ends with a Camus-like comment when he states that "[h]umans, as individuals, are not designed to win, once and for all, the battle for pro-social, moral behavior. However, the human brain is designed in such a way that it forces us to choose right from wrong, or the greater good from the lesser, in our everyday activities."[33] This seems akin to Camus's interpretation of the Myth of Sisyphus in which Camus argues that rather than being punished for never getting the rock to the top of the mountain, Sisyphus should be content (or perhaps resigned to his plight) because he knows what it is he should do: push the rock.[34] Similarly, it seems that the plight of those interested in promoting behavior that sustains "pro-social" behavior is to content ourselves with the scientifically substantiated ability to engage in that quest and to take courage from our innate capacities to undertake this challenge. This is not insignificant and we ethicists should be grateful to Professor Lawrence and others who translate difficult scientific concepts that can be applied in our field.

The third way is one that is not touched on, but which seems most appropriate for the subject. My first reaction in seeing questions about whether biology should have something to say about ethics is to exclaim "what's the big deal: what about Aristotle?" Indeed, Aristotle was a biologist as well as an ethicist and there has been a good deal of constructive engagement between contemporary Aristotelians and evolutionary biologists. Larry Arnhart's book, *Darwinian Natural Right: The Biological Ethics of Human Nature*[35] explicitly connects Aristotle and Darwin in a highly provocative way. MacIntyre, as already mentioned, has also connected biology with his reconceptualization of virtue theory.

MacIntyre roots his theory in the realization that, as animals, we have a dependent nature. Not only in our infancy, but at other times of life, we rely on the benefices of others. While there may be a human social instinct, we need communities and cultures to teach us virtues so that we can see the value of supporting those who are vulnerable even when we cannot see the reciprocal benefits for us. This is a capacity to want to achieve goods beyond material gain. We thus see each of us as disabled and therefore dependent on others and it is a local community—a mediating institution, to use my term—where we learn to see this and are inspired to build up on this natural proclivity.

We may not always be able to understand the purpose of the virtue of helping those who are vulnerable, but the purpose of a community is to teach the good of that virtue. Dolphins, for instance, are also highly intelligent creatures with a sophisticated means of communication. Like the brain mass to body mass ratio that was so important to the Dunbar studies, dolphins too have a large brain mass ratio. They use this brain power to hunt fish in a series of strategies, to communicate about their successes and to propose course alterations of course. MacIntyre then correlates this behavior with that of human beings in writing that "like human beings, dolphins take pleasure in those activities which are the exercise of their powers and skills. When Aristotle says that there is pleasure in all perceptual activity and that the pleasure supervenes upon the completed activity, what he asserts seems to be as true of dolphins as of human beings."[36]

MacIntyre goes on to argue that dolphins' ability to take such pleasure and pride in a prelinguistic fashion may not make them able to provide reasons for what they do, but the realization that they do take pleasure and pride in such activities blurs the sharp line that might be thought to exist separating human behavior from nonhuman behavior.[37] The dolphin, in some way, emotionally connects with the rule of behavior beneficial to the dolphin and its school. The sentiment is reinforced by a "feedback" mechanism of food itself. What is important, it seems, is that prelinguistic communication of information and of feelings of emotion are present in highly intelligent animals. This strikes me as similar to the moral sentiments relied upon by Professor Lawrence and which have been developed with considerable depth by Frans de Waal with respect to bonobos.[38]

Perhaps our biological nature is attuned to certain sentiments that human brain wattage is able to translate into notions of duty and obligation. It is certainly the case that human beings do, in fact, construct large organizations and there is reason to believe that doing so provides people with the ability to accomplish things that they might not otherwise do and to connect people, such as through allegiance to a nation or an ideal such as freedom, that they might not otherwise be able to do. But it is also important to recognize the need for layers of identification. Without the allegiance to family, how does a person understand what duty to the world means? Without allegiance to a neighborhood and the obligation to help those who need help in the neighborhood, how does an executive really understand her obligations to employees? In short, while social contractual construction of a system of checks and balances has a great deal of merit to it there is also a need to attend to the dolphin in us and to nourish communities that provide the flesh and blood experience that refines sentiments into virtues.

Conclusion

Biologists and traditional ethicists will have disagreements just as Kantians will disagree with Aristotelians. For too long, however, the study of human nature has been put to the side as being too difficult to achieve a consensus. Perhaps biological groundings will help that study and perhaps we will all advance because of it. It is my hope that there will be more discussions like this and more contributors like Paul Lawrence.

Notes

1. Paul Lawrence, *The Biological Base of Morality?* in BUSINESS, SCIENCE, AND ETHICS 59–79 (2004), at 60.

2. *See* Timothy L. Fort, *The Brothers Karamazov: Responsibility and Business Ethics* in THE MORAL IMAGINATION: HOW LITERATURE AND FILM CAN STIMULATE ETHICAL REFLECTION IN THE BUSINESS WORLD (Oliver Williams, ed. 1998) (describing the brooding darkness in Dostoyevsky).

3. OLIVER WILLIAMSON, MARKETS & HIERARCHIES: ANALYSIS AND ANTITRUST IMPLICATIONS 7, 9 (1975).

4. Fort, *supra* note 2 (describing Dostoyevsky's painting of life in its complexities).

5. *See generally*, WILLIAM C. FREDERICK, VALUES, NATURE, AND CULTURE IN THE AMERICAN CORPORATION (1995).

6. Lawrence, *supra* note 1, at 59.

7. EDWARD O. WILSON, CONSILIENCE: THE UNITY OF KNOWLEDGE 98–99 (1998).

8. Lawrence, *supra* note 1, at 74.

9. GEOFFREY M. HODGSON, ECONOMICS & EVOLUTION: BRINGING LIFE BACK INTO ECONOMICS 175–76 (1996).

10. David Sloan Wilson, *Altruism and Organism: Disentangling the Themes of Multilevel Selection Theory*, 150 NATURALIST S122 (Supp. 1997).

11. WILSON, *supra* note 7 at 184 (responding to attempts of scientists to disassociate themselves from Social Darwins).

12. Timothy L. Fort & James J. Noone, *Banded Contrast, Mediating Institutions, and Corporate Governance: A Naturalist Analysis of Contractual Theories of the Firm*, 62 LAW & CONTEMP. PROBS. 163, 176 (1999).

13. *See generally*, ALASDAIR MACINTYRE, DEPENDENT RATIONAL ANIMALS (1999).

14. *Id.* at 24–28.

15. *Id.* at 1–4; 63–86.

16. *See generally*, F. A. HAYEK, THE FATAL CONCEIT (1988).

17. FREDERICK, *supra* note 5, at 149.

18. VALERIO VALERI, KINGSHIP & SACRIFICE: RITUAL IN ANCIENT HAWAII 91 (Paula Wissing, trans. 1985).

19. LILIKALA KAME'EIHIWA, NATIVE LAND AND FOREIGN DESIRES: PEHEA LA E PONO AI? 48 (1992) (satirizing the "splendid isolation" frequently applied to England, which "discovered" Hawaii).

20. ALASDAIR MACINTYRE, AFTER VIRTUE: A STUDY IN MORAL THEORY 107 (1981).

21. MARSHALL SAHLINS, ISLANDS OF HISTORY 142–43 (1985).

22. Leda Cosmides & John Tooby, *Evolutionary Psychology and the Emotions* in THE HANDBOOK OF EMOTIONS 2nd. (M. Lewis & J. Haviland, eds. 2000).

23. Fort & Noone, *supra* note 12.

24. TIMOTHY L. FORT, ETHICS AND GOVERNANCE: BUSINESS AS MEDIATING INSTITUTION 39–86 (2001).

25. *See generally,* ROBIN DUNBAR, GROOMING, GOSSIP, AND THE EVOLUTION OF LANGUAGE (1996).

26. *Id.* at 57–63.

27. *Id.* at 69–79.

28. Gregory A. Johnson, *Organization Structure and Scalar Stress* in THEORY AND EXPLANATION IN ARCHEOLOGY 389, 389–42 (Colin Renfew et al., eds. 1982).

29. JAMES T. BURTCHAELL, C.S.C., PHILEMON'S PROBLEM: THE DAILY DILEMMA OF THE CHRISTIAN (1973).

30. LAWRENCE KEELEY, WAR BEFORE CIVILIZATION 117–22 (1996).

31. David Fabbro, *Peaceful Societies: an Introduction* 15 J. PEACE RES. 67 (1978).

32. KEELEY, *supra* note 30, at 181.

33. Lawrence, *supra* note 1, at 75.

34. Albert Camus, *The Myth of Sisyphus* in ALBERT CAMUS, THE MYTH OF SISYPHUS & OTHER ESSAYS 91 (Justin O'Brien, trans. 1955). My thanks to Bob Soloman for encouraging a less sanguine interpretation of Camus than I originally offered.

35. (1998.)

36. MACINTYRE, *supra* note 13, at 26.

37. *Id.* at 51.

38. FRANS DE WAAL, CHIMPANZEE POLITICS: POWER AND SEX AMONG APES (1982); FRANS DE WAAL, GOOD NATURED: THE ORIGIN OF RIGHT AND WRONG IN HUMANS AND OTHER ANIMALS (1996).

KNOWING THYSELF: THE EVOLUTIONARY PSYCHOLOGY OF MORAL REASONING AND MORAL SENTIMENTS

Leda Cosmides and John Tooby

Abstract: "Ought" cannot be derived from "is," so why should facts about human nature be of interest to business ethicists? In this article, we discuss why the nature of human nature is relevant to anyone wishing to create a more just and humane workplace and society. We begin by presenting evolutionary psychology as a research framework, and then present three examples of research that illuminate various evolved cognitive programs. The first involves the cognitive foundations of trade, including a neurocognitive mechanism specialized for a form of moral reasoning: cheater detection. The second involves the moral sentiments triggered by participating in collective actions, which are relevant to organizational behavior. The third involves the evolved programs whereby our minds socially construct groups, and how these can be harnessed to reduce racism and foster true diversity in the workplace. In each case, we discuss how what has been learned about these evolved programs might inform the study and practice of business ethics.

Introduction: Human Nature and Ethics

Human beings have moral intuitions. Assume, for a moment, that some of these reflect the operation of reliably developing neural circuits, which implement programs that are species-typical and therefore cross-culturally universal. That is, assume that some forms of moral reasoning and moral sentiment are produced by elements of a universal human nature. Does this justify them ethically?

Of course not. Natural selection favors designs on the basis of how well they promote their own reproduction, not on how well they promote ethical behavior. If this is not obvious, consider the fate of a mutation that alters the development of a neural circuit, changing its design away from the species standard. This new circuit design implements a decision rule that produces a radically different ethical choice in a particular type of situation: help rather than hurt, cooperate rather than free ride. Will this new decision rule, initially present in one or a few individuals, be eliminated from the population? Or will it be retained, increasing in frequency over the generations until it replaces the old design, eventually becoming the new species standard?

The fate of the mutant decision rule will be jointly determined by two ethically blind processes: chance and natural selection. Chance is blind not only to ethics, but to design: it cannot retain or eliminate circuit designs based on their consequences. Natural selection, however, is not blind to design. The mutant design and the standard design produce different ethical choices; these choices produce different consequences for the choosers, which can enhance or reduce the average rate at which they produce offspring (who carry the same design). If the mutant decision rule better promotes its own reproduction (through promoting the reproduction of its bearers), it will be favored by selection. Eventually, over the generations, it will become the new species-standard. The decisions it produces—ethical or otherwise—will become the "common sense" of that species.

This is the process that, over eons, constructed our human nature. As a result, human nature is comprised of programs that were selected for merely because they outreproduced alternative programs in the past. There is nothing in this process to ensure the production of decision rules or moral sentiments that track the desiderata of an ethically justifiable moral system. So why should ethicists care about human nature?

Human nature matters for three reasons. First, outcomes matter. Many ethicists are concerned with how to create a more just and humane society, starting in the workplace. But what policies are capable of achieving this? Whereas some moral philosophers argue that an outcome is ethical if the procedure that produced it was ethical (e.g., Nozick, 1975), others argue that certain outcomes are ethically better than others and that policies and rules of interaction should be chosen—at least in part—according to how well they achieve ethical outcomes (e.g., Bentham, 1789; Rawls, 1971; Sen, 1999). When outcomes matter, policy choices need to be made in light of human nature. What incentives encourage people to contribute to a public good, such as clean air? If people are starving and need to be fed, will collective incentive systems succeed in feeding them? If racial equality in the workplace is the goal, will this be best achieved by seminars designed to ferret out negative stereotypes in the attitudes of participants? Or will this increase hostility, making matters worse?

The nature of human nature matters for a second reason: It may place constraints on what can be considered a moral imperative. An action cannot be morally required unless it is possible to perform. But when it comes to human behavior, the meaning of *possible* is complicated (see Conclusions). Consider the following example. Corporations have many internal rules regulating procedures, a (large) subset of which are not safety rules. Yet violations of these rules can produce cascades of consequences that end up being ethically catastrophic (think Homer Simpson at the nuclear plant). Perhaps people should be alert to such violations; perhaps this should be a moral imperative, in the same way that monitoring the safety of one's child is. The mind is designed to monitor for breaches of safety rules (Fiddick, Cosmides, and Tooby, 2000; Stone et al., 2002), and certain conditions, such as impending parenthood, seem to hyperactivate this system (Leckman and Mayes, 1998, 1999). But what if the human mind lacks cognitive mechanisms that spontaneously monitor for violations of procedural rules when these are not, in any obvious way, about safety? If this were true, could a person be held ethically responsible for not noticing such a breach? As we will see, this example is not as science-fictional as it may seem.

There is yet a third reason that ethicists should care about human nature: Ethicists are human beings. If the human cognitive architecture contains programs that generate moral intuitions in humans, then it generates moral intuitions in humans who are ethicists. These evolved programs cause certain moral intuitions to be triggered by particular situations. Yet this in no way justifies those moral intuitions—see above. Indeed, on reflection, some of these moral intuitions may be found wanting (yes, the ability to reflect is also made possible by evolved programs; see Leslie, 1987; Frith, 1992; Baron-Cohen, 1995; Cosmides and Tooby, 2000a). If outcomes matter to ethical judgments, then ethicists need to focus on the real world consequences of alternative policies, and not have their judgment unduly affected by moral sentiments that are nothing more than read-outs of evolved programs that were generated by an amoral process.

Justified or not, people's moral sentiments are a fact of life that anyone in business will need to accommodate. Far more needs to be known about the evolutionary psychology of moral reasoning and moral sentiments, but a start has been made. Below we present a brief overview of where evolutionary psychology fits in the intellectual landscape. Then we present empirical findings from evolutionary psychology relevant to three different topics: social exchange, collective action, and the social construction of groups. Some findings, like the results about social exchange, rest on a large evidentiary base that also includes cross-cultural tests. Others are newer, and more tentative. We offer these findings not as the last word on each topic, but as food for thought. For each topic, we briefly discuss possible implications for business ethics. Our intention is not to present well-worked out ethical theories in these sections. Instead, they are offered in the spirit of brain storming, as an exercise in how research in evolutionary psychology might eventually inform ethical theory and practice.

What is Evolutionary Psychology?

In the final pages of the *Origin of Species*, after Darwin had presented the theory of evolution by natural selection, he made a bold prediction: "In the distant future I see open fields for far more important researches. Psychology will be based on a new foundation, that of the necessary acquirement of each mental power and capacity by gradation." More than a century later, a group of scientists—Martin Daly, Margo Wilson, Don Symons, John Tooby, Leda Cosmides, David Buss, Steve Pinker, Gerd Gigerenzer—began to work out exactly how Darwin's fundamental insights could be used as a foundation on which to build a more systematic approach to psychology (for review, see Tooby and Cosmides, 1992; see also Symons, 1979; Cosmides and Tooby, 1987; Daly and Wilson, 1988; Buss, 1989; Pinker, 1997; Gigerenzer, 2000). We were motivated by new developments from a series of different fields:

Advance #1. The cognitive revolution was providing, for the first time in human history, a precise language for describing mental mechanisms, as programs that process information.

Advance #2. Advances in paleoanthropology, hunter-gatherer studies and primatology were providing data about the adaptive problems our ancestors had to solve to survive and reproduce and the environments in which they did so.

Advance #3. Research in animal behavior, linguistics, and neuropsychology was showing that the mind is not a blank slate, passively recording the world. Organisms come factory-equipped with knowledge about the world, which allows them to learn some relationships easily, and others only with great effort, if at all. Skinner's hypothesis—that learning is a simple process governed by reward and punishment—was simply wrong.

Advance #4. Evolutionary game theory was revolutionizing evolutionary biology, placing it on a more rigorous, formal foundation of replicator dynamics. This clarified how natural selection works, what counts as an *adaptive* function, and what the criteria are for calling a trait an *adaptation*.

We thought that, if one were careful about the causal connections between these disciplines, these new developments could be pieced together into a single integrated research framework, in a way that had not been exploited before because the connections ran between fields rather than cleanly within them. We called this framework *evolutionary psychology*.[1] The goal of research in evolutionary psychology is to discover, understand, and map in detail the design of the human mind, as well as to explore the implications of these new discoveries for other fields. The eventual aim is to map *human nature*—that is, the species-typical information-processing architecture of the human brain.

Like all cognitive scientists, when evolutionary psychologists refer to "the mind," they mean the set of information-processing devices, embodied in neural tissue, that are responsible for all conscious and nonconscious mental activity, and that generate all behavior. And like other psychologists, evolutionary psychologists test hypotheses about the design of these information-processing devices—these programs—using laboratory methods from experimental cognitive and social psychology, as well as methods drawn from experimental economics, neuropsychology, and cross-cultural field work.

What allows evolutionary psychologists to go beyond traditional approaches in studying the mind is that they make active use in their research of an often overlooked fact: That the programs comprising the human mind were designed by natural selection to solve the adaptive problems faced by our hunter-gatherer ancestors—problems like finding a mate, cooperating with others, hunting, gathering, protecting children, avoiding predators, and so on. Natural selection tends to produce programs that solve problems like these reliably, quickly, and efficiently. Knowing this allows one to approach the study of the mind like an engineer. You start with a good specification of an adaptive information-processing problem, then you do a task analysis of that problem. This allows you to see what properties a program would have to have in order to solve that problem well. This approach allows you to generate testable hypotheses about the structure of the programs that comprise the mind.

From this point of view, there are precise causal connections that link the four developments above into a coherent framework for thinking about human nature and human society (Tooby and Cosmides, 1992). These connections (C-1 through C-6) are as follows:

C-1. Each organ in the body evolved to serve a function: the intestines digest, the heart pumps blood, the liver detoxifies poisons. The brain is also an organ, and its evolved function is to extract information from the environment and use that information to generate behavior and regulate physiology. From this perspective, the brain is a computer, that is, a physical system that was designed to process information (*Advance #1*). Its programs were designed not by an engineer, but by natural selection, a causal process that retains and discards design features on the basis of how well they solved problems that affect reproduction (*Advance #4*).

The fact that the brain processes information is not an accidental side-effect of some metabolic process: The brain was designed by natural selection *to be* a computer. Therefore, if you want to describe its operation in a way that captures its evolved function, you need to think of it as composed of programs that process information. The question then becomes, what programs are to be found in the human brain? What are the reliably developing, species-typical programs that, taken together, comprise the human mind?

C-2. Individual behavior is generated by this evolved computer, in response to information that it extracts from the internal and external environment (including the social environment) (*Advance #1*). To understand an individual's behavior, therefore, you need to know both the information that the person registered *and* the structure of the programs that generated his or her behavior.

C-3. The programs that comprise the human brain were sculpted over evolutionary time by the ancestral environments and selection pressures experienced by the hunter-gatherers from whom we are descended (*Advances #2 and #4*). Each evolved program exists because it produced behavior that promoted the survival and reproduction of our ancestors better than alternative programs that arose during human evolutionary history. Evolutionary psychologists emphasize hunter-gatherer life because the evolutionary process is slow—it takes tens of thousands of years to build a program of any complexity. The industrial revolution—even the agricultural revolution—are mere eyeblinks in evolutionary time, too short to have selected for new cognitive programs.

C-4. Although the behavior our evolved programs generate would, on average, have been adaptive (reproduction-promoting) in ancestral environments, there is no guarantee that it will be so now. Modern environments differ importantly from ancestral ones—particularly when it comes to social behavior. We no longer live in small, face-to-face societies, in semi-nomadic bands of 50-100 people, many of whom were close relatives. Yet our cognitive programs were designed for that social world.

C-5. Perhaps most importantly, the brain must be comprised of many different programs, each specialized for solving a different adaptive problem our ancestors faced—i.e., the mind cannot be a blank slate (*Advance #3*).

In fact, the same is true of any computationally powerful, multi-tasking computer. Consider the computer in your office. So many people analyze data and write prose that most computers come factory-equipped with a spreadsheet and a text-editor. These are two separate programs, each with different computational properties. This is because number-crunching and writing prose are very different problems: the design features that make a program good at data analysis are not well-suited to writing and editing articles, and vice versa. To accomplish both tasks well, the computer has two programs, each well-designed for a specific task. The more functionally specialized programs it has, the more intelligent your computer is: the more things it can do. The same is true for people.

Our hunter-gatherer ancestors were, in effect, on a camping trip that lasted a lifetime, and they had to solve many different kinds of problems well to survive and reproduce under those conditions. Design features that make a program good at choosing nutritious foods, for example, will be ill-suited for finding a fertile mate. Different problems require different evolved solutions.

This can be most clearly seen by using results from evolutionary game theory (*Advance #4*) and data about ancestral environments (*Advance #2*) to define adaptive problems, and then carefully dissecting the computational requirements of any program capable of solving those problems. So, for example, programs designed for logical reasoning would be poorly-designed for detecting cheaters in social exchange, and vice versa; as we will show, it appears that we have programs that are functionally specialized for reasoning about reciprocity and exchange.

C-6. Lastly, if you want to understand human culture and society, you need to understand these domain-specific programs. The mind is not like a video camera, passively recording the world but imparting no content of its own. Domain-specific programs organize our experiences, create our inferences, inject certain recurrent concepts and motivations into our mental life, give us our passions, and provide cross-culturally universal frames of meaning that allow us to understand the actions and intentions of others. They cause us to think certain very specific thoughts; they make certain ideas, feelings, and reactions seem reasonable, interesting, and memorable. Consequently, they play a key role in determining which ideas and customs will easily spread from mind to mind, and which will not. That is, they play a crucial role in shaping human culture.

Instincts are often thought of as the diametric opposite of reasoning. But the reasoning programs that evolutionary psychologists have been discovering (i) are complexly specialized for solving an adaptive problem; (ii) they reliably develop in all normal human beings; (iii) they develop without any conscious effort and in the absence of formal instruction; (iv) they are applied without any awareness of their underlying logic, and (v) they are distinct from more general abilities to process information or behave intelligently. In other words, they have all the hallmarks of what we usually think of as an instinct (Pinker, 1994). In fact, one can think of these specialized circuits as *reasoning instincts*. They make certain kinds of inferences just as easy, effortless and "natural" to us as humans, as spinning a web is to a spider or building a dam is to a beaver.

Consider this example from the work of Simon Baron-Cohen (1995), using the Charlie task. A child is shown a schematic face ("Charlie") surrounded by four different kinds of candy. Charlie's eyes are pointed toward the Milky Way bar (for example). The child is then asked, "Which candy does Charlie want?" Like you and I, a normal 4 year old will say that Charlie wants the Milky Way—the candy Charlie is looking at. In contrast, children with autism fail the Charlie task, producing random responses. However—and this is important—when asked which candy Charlie is looking at, children with autism answer correctly. That is, children with this developmental disorder can compute eye direction correctly, *but they cannot use that information to infer what someone wants.*

We know, spontaneously and with no mental effort, that Charlie *wants* the candy he is *looking at*. This is so obvious to us that it hardly seems to require an inference at all. It is just common sense. But "common sense" is caused: it is produced by cognitive mechanisms. To infer a mental state (*wanting*) from information about eye direction requires a computation. There is a little inference circuit—a reasoning instinct—that produces this inference. When the circuit that does this computation is broken or fails to develop, the inference cannot be made. Those with autism fail the Charlie task because they lack this reasoning instinct.

As a species, we have been blind to the existence of these instincts—not because we lack them, but precisely because they work so well. Because they process information so effortlessly and automatically, their operation disappears unnoticed into the background. These instincts structure our thought so powerfully that it can be difficult to imagine how things could be otherwise. As a result, we take normal behavior for granted: We do not realize that normal behavior needs to be explained at all.

For example, at a business school, all aspects of trade are studied. Business school scholars and students take for granted the fact that, by exchanging goods and services, people can make each other better off. But this kind of cooperation for mutual benefit—known in evolutionary biology as reciprocity, reciprocal altruism, or social exchange—is not common in the animal kingdom. Some species—humans, vampire bats, chimpanzees, baboons—engage in this very useful form of mutual help, whereas others do not (Cashdan, 1989; Isaac, 1978; Packer, 1977; de Waal, 1989; Wilkinson, 1988).

This rarity is itself telling: It means that social exchange is not generated by a simple general learning mechanism, such as classical or operant conditioning. All organisms can be classically and operantly conditioned, yet few engage in exchange. This strongly suggests that engaging in social exchange requires specific cognitive machinery, which some species have and others lack. That is, there are good reasons to think we humans have cognitive machinery that is functionally specialized for reasoning about social exchange—reasoning instincts that make thinking about and engaging in social exchange as easy and automatic for humans as stalking prey is for a lion or building a nest is for a bird.

But what, exactly, are these programs like? The research we have been conducting with our colleagues on the cognitive foundations of social exchange—of trade—suggests that the programs that allow social exchange to proceed in humans are specialized for that function, and include a subroutine that one can think of as an instinct that causes a certain kind of moral reasoning: the detection of cheaters.

The Cognitive Foundations of Trade

Selection pressures favoring social exchange exist whenever one organism (the provisioner) can change the behavior of a target organism to the provisioner's advantage by making the target's receipt of a provisioned benefit *conditional* on the target acting in a required manner. This mutual provisioning of benefits, each conditional on the others' compliance, is what is meant by social exchange or reciprocation (Cosmides, 1985; Cosmides and Tooby, 1989; Tooby and Cosmides, 1996). Social exchange is an "I'll scratch your back if you scratch mine" principle: X provides a benefit to Y conditional on Y doing something that X wants.

Robert Trivers, W. D. Hamilton, Robert Axelrod, and other evolutionary researchers used game theory to understand the conditions under which social exchange can and cannot evolve (Trivers, 1971; Axelrod and Hamilton, 1981; Boyd, 1988). For adaptations causing this form of cooperation to evolve and persist—that is, for reciprocation to be an evolutionarily stable strategy (ESS)—the behavior of cooperators must be generated by programs that perform certain specific tasks well. For example these programs would need design features that would (i) allow cooperators to detect cheaters (i.e., those who do not comply or reciprocate), and (ii) cause cooperators to channel future benefits to reciprocators, not cheaters (Trivers, 1971; Axelrod and Hamilton, 1981; Axelrod, 1984).

In other words, reciprocation cannot evolve if the organism lacks reasoning procedures that can effectively detect cheaters (i.e., those who take conditionally offered benefits without providing the promised return). Such individuals would be open to exploitation, and hence selected out. Based on such analyses, Cosmides and Tooby hypothesized that the human neurocognitive architecture includes *social contract algorithms*: a set of programs that were specialized by natural selection for solving the intricate computational problems inherent in adaptively engaging in social exchange behavior, including a subroutine for cheater detection.

Conditional Reasoning

Reciprocation is, by definition, social behavior that is conditional: you agree to deliver a benefit *conditionally* (conditional on the other person doing what you required in return). Understanding it therefore requires conditional reasoning.

Indeed, an agreement to exchange—a social contract—can be expressed as a conditional rule: *If A provides a requested benefit to or meets the require-ment of B, **then** B will provide a rationed benefit to A.* A cheater is someone who illicitly takes the benefit specified in the social contract; that is, someone who violates the social contract by taking the benefit without meeting the provisioner's requirement.

Because engaging in social exchange requires conditional reasoning, in-vestigations of conditional reasoning can be used to test for the presence of social contract algorithms. The hypothesis that the brain contains social con-tract algorithms predicts a sharply enhanced ability to reason adaptively about conditional rules when those rules specify a social exchange. The null hypoth-esis is that there is nothing specialized in the brain for social exchange: This predicts no enhanced conditional reasoning performance specifically triggered by social exchanges as compared to other contents.

A standard tool for investigating conditional reasoning is Wason's 4-Card Selection Task (Wason, 1966, 1983; Wason and Johnson-Laird, 1972). Using this task, Cosmides, Tooby, and their colleagues conducted an extensive series of experiments to address the following questions:

1. Do our minds include cognitive machinery that is *specialized* for reason-ing about social exchange? (alongside some other domain-specific mechanisms, each specialized for reasoning about a different adaptive domain involving conditional behavior?) Or,
2. Is the cognitive machinery that causes good conditional reasoning gen-eral—does it operate well regardless of content? (a blank slate-type theory; Pinker, 2002).

This second, blank-slate view was in trouble before we even started our investigations. If the human brain had cognitive machinery that causes good conditional reasoning regardless of content, then people should be good at tasks requiring conditional reasoning. For example, they should be good at detecting violations of conditional rules. Yet studies with the Wason selection task had already shown that they are not. The Wason task asks you to look for potential violations of a conditional rule (*If P then Q*), such as "If a person has Ebbing-haus disease, then that person is forgetful" (see Figure 1 [p. 100], panel a). The rule is accompanied by pictures of four cards, each representing one person—a patient in this case. For each card, one side tells whether the patient in question has Ebbinghaus disease, and the other side tells whether that patient is forget-ful. However, you can see only one side of each card, so your information about each patient is incomplete. The question: Which card(s) would you need to turn over to find out if there are patients whose situation violates the rule?

Figure 1

a. General Structure of a Descriptive Problem

Consider the following rule: If P then Q.
The cards below have information about four situations. Each card represents one situation. One side of a card tells whether *P* happened, and the other side of the card tells whether *Q* happened. Indicate only those card(s) you definitely need to turn over to see if any of these situations violate the rule.

b. General Structure of a Social Contract Problem

Consider the following rule:

standard form:
If you take the *benefit*, then you satisfy the *requirement*.

switched form:
If you satisfy the *requirement*, then you take the *benefit*.

If   P   then   Q

The cards below have information about four people. Each card represents one person. One side of a card tells whether a person accepted the benefit, and the other side of the card tells whether that person satisfied the requirement. Indicate only those card(s) you definitely need to turn over to see if any of these people are violating the rule.

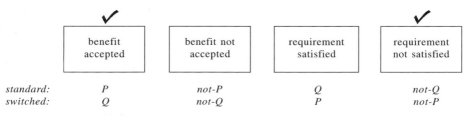

	benefit accepted	benefit not accepted	requirement satisfied	requirement not satisfied
standard:	P	not-P	Q	not-Q
switched:	Q	not-Q	P	not-P

Legend for Figure 1. The Wason selection task. The conditional rule (If *P* then *Q*) always has specific content. *Panel A*. The general structure of the task in logical terms. Check marks indicate the logically correct card choices. *Panel B*. The general structure of the task when the content of the conditional rule expresses a social contract. It can be translated into either logical terms (*P*s and *Q*s) or social contract terms (benefits and requirements). Here, check marks indicate the correct card choices if one is looking for cheaters: the *benefit accepted* card and the *requirement not satisfied* card (regardless of the logical category to which these correspond). For example, (i) "If you give me your watch, I'll give you $100" and (ii) "If I give you $100, then you give me your watch" express the same offer to exchange—the same social contract. Standard form is where the benefit to the potential cheater appears in the antecedent clause (*P*); switched is where the benefit appears in the consequent clause (*Q*). Thus, if I were the potential cheater, then (i) is standard form [because the benefit to me (getting your watch) appears in the antecedent clause, *P*)] and (ii) is switched form. In either case, my taking your watch without giving you the promised payment would count as cheating. Whereas these cards fall into the logical categories *P* & *not-Q* for a rule expressed in standard form, they fall into the logical categories *Q and not-P* for a rule expressed in switched form. *Q* & *not-P* is not a logically correct response. It is, however, the adaptively correct, cheater detection response when the benefit is in the consequent clause.

One card says "has Ebbinghaus disease" (i.e., *P*), one says "does not have Ebbinghaus disease" (*not-P*), one says "is forgetful" (Q), and one says "is not forgetful" (*not-Q*). A conditional rule like this is violated whenever *P* happens but *Q* does not happen (in this case, whenever someone has Ebbinghaus disease but is not forgetful). To respond correctly, you would need to check the patient who has Ebbinghaus disease and the patient who is not forgetful (i.e., *P* & *not-Q*). Yet studies in many nations have shown that reasoning performance on descriptive rules like this is low: only five to thirty percent of people give the logically correct answer, even when the rule involves familiar terms drawn from everyday life[2] (Cosmides, 1989; Wason, 1966, 1983; Wason and Johnson-Laird, 1972).

Are people also poor at detecting cheaters? To show that people who do not spontaneously look for violations of conditional rules can do so easily when the conditional rule expresses a social contract and a violation represents cheating would be (initial) evidence that the mind has reasoning procedures specialized for detecting cheaters.

That is precisely the pattern found. People who ordinarily cannot detect violations of if-then rules can do so easily and accurately when that violation represents cheating in a situation of social exchange. Given a conditional rule of the general form, "If you take benefit B, then you must satisfy requirement R" (e.g., "If you borrow my car, then fill up the tank with gas"), people will check the person who accepted the benefit (borrowed the car; *P*) and the person who did not satisfy the requirement (did not fill the tank; *not-Q*)—the individuals that represent potential cheaters (see Figure 1, panel b, standard form). The adaptively correct answer is immediately obvious to almost all subjects, who commonly experience a pop-out effect. No formal training is needed. Whenever the content of a problem asks one to look for cheaters in a social exchange, subjects experience the problem as simple to solve, and their performance jumps dramatically. In general, sixty-five to eighty percent of subjects get it right, the highest performance found for a task of this kind (for reviews, see Cosmides and Tooby, 1992, 1997, 2000b; Fiddick, Cosmides, and Tooby, 2000; Gigerenzer, 1992; Platt and Griggs, 1993).

It is not familiarity. This good performance has nothing to do with the familiarity of the rule tested. First, familiarity does not enhance performance for descriptive rules. Second (and most surprising), people are just as good at detecting cheaters on culturally unfamiliar or imaginary social contracts as they are for ones that are completely familiar, providing a challenge for any counterhypothesis resting on a general-learning skill acquisition account. An unfamiliar, culturally alien rule—e.g., "If a man eats cassava root, then he must have a tattoo on his face"—can elicit excellent cheater detection. All one needs to do is embed it in a scenario that says that the people involved consider eating cassava root to be a benefit; the rule then implies that having a tattoo is the requirement one must satisfy to be eligible for that benefit (Cosmides, 1985, 1989; Gigerenzer and Hug, 1992; Platt and Griggs, 1993).

It is not logic. Further experiments showed that subjects do not choose *P* & *not-Q* on social contract problems because these problems activate *logical* reasoning. Instead, they activate a differently patterned, specialized, logic of social exchange (Cosmides and Tooby, 1989).

Formal logic (i.e., the propositional calculus) is content-independent: a logical violation has occurred whenever *P* happens and *Q* does not happen. In contrast, cheater detection requires the search for illicitly taken *benefits*. It does not matter whether this benefit is in the antecedent clause *(P)* or the consequent clause *(Q)*: regardless of logical category, one must check the person who accepted the benefit and the person who did not meet the requirement. It is possible to construct a social exchange problem for which formal logic and social exchange logic predict different answers. When this is done, subjects overwhelmingly follow the evolved logic of social exchange. They investigate anyone who has taken the benefit and anyone who has not satisfied the requirement that it was contingent upon, even if this results in a logically incorrect answer, such as *Q and not-P*. (See Figure 1, panel b, on switched social contracts; Cosmides, 1985, 1989; Gigerenzer and Hug, 1992).

It is not a general ability to reason about permission rules (not a deontic logic). Detecting cheaters on social contracts was an important adaptive problem for our ancestors; so was detecting when people are in danger because they have failed to take appropriate precautions (Fiddick, Cosmides, and Tooby, 2000). Experimental results show that people are good at detecting violations of these two classes of conditional rules (precautions have the general form, *"If one is to engage in hazardous activity H, then one must take precaution R"*; Fiddick, Cosmides, and Tooby, 2000; Stone et al., 2002). Note, however, that social contracts and precautionary rules are instances of a more general class, *permission rules*. A permission rule is a conditional rule specifying the conditions under which one is permitted to take an action. They have the form "If action A is to be taken, then precondition C must be met" (Cheng and Holyoak, 1985). There are, however, permission rules that are neither social contracts nor precautionary rules. Indeed, we encounter many rules like this in everyday life—bureaucratic or corporate rules often state a procedure that is to be followed without specifying a benefit (or a danger). Despite their ubiquity in modern life, people are not good at detecting violations of permission rules when these are neither social contracts nor precautionary rules (Cosmides and Tooby, 1992; Manktelow and Over, 1991; Barrett, 1999; see below).

The Design of Social Exchange Mechanisms

Many cognitive scientists have now investigated social contract reasoning, and many of the predicted design features have been tested for and found. For example:

1. One needs to understand each new opportunity to exchange as it arises, so social exchange reasoning should operate even for unfamiliar social

contract rules. That is the case: Cheater detection occurs even when the social contract is wildly unfamiliar (see above).

2. The mind's automatically deployed definition of cheating is tied to the perspective one is taking (Gigerenzer and Hug, 1992). Given the rule "If an employee is to get a pension, then that employee must have worked for the firm for over 10 years," different answers are given depending on whether subjects are cued into the role of employer or employee. The former look for cheating by employees, investigating cases of P and not-Q (employees with pensions; employees who have worked for fewer than 10 years); the latter look for cheating by employers, investigating cases of not-P and Q (employees with no pension; employees who have worked more than 10 years).

3. To elicit cheater detection, the rule must specify a benefit: if there is no benefit, then it is not a social contract. Consider, for example, the following two rules granting conditional permission: (i) "If you are to go out at night, then you must tie a small rock to your ankle" versus (ii) "If you are to take out the garbage at night, then you must tie a small rock to your ankle." For our subject population, going out at night is seen as a benefit, but taking out the garbage is not. People succeed at (i) but not at (ii), even though both are rules granting conditional permission (of the form, "If you are to take *action A*, then you must satisfy *requirement R*). When *action A* of a permission rule is difficult to interpret as a conditional benefit (as in ii),[3] people have trouble detecting violations (Cosmides and Tooby, 1992; Manktelow and Over, 1991; Barrett, 1999).

4. For the reasoning enhancement to occur, the violations must potentially reveal cheaters: individuals who violate the rule *intentionally*. When detecting violations of social contracts would reveal only innocent mistakes, enhancement does not occur (Barrett, 1999; Cosmides and Tooby, 2000b; Fiddick, 1998, in press).

5. Excellence at cheater detection is not a skill elicited by extensive participation in an advanced market economy. Consistent with its being a species-typical ability, social contract reasoning effects are found across cultures, from industrial democracies to hunter-horticulturalist groups in the Ecuadorian Amazon (Sugiyama, Tooby, and Cosmides, 2002).

Perhaps the strongest evidence that there is a neural specialization designed for cheater detection is the discovery that cheater detection can be selectively impaired by brain damage, without impairing other reasoning abilities. R.M., a patient with extensive brain damage, was given a large battery of Wason tasks that were formally identical and matched for difficulty. His ability to detect violations of precautionary rules was very good, but his ability to detect cheaters on social contracts was very impaired (Stone et al., 2002). If performance on social contract and precautionary rules were a byproduct of some more general ability to reason, then damage to that more general mechanism would impair reasoning on both types of problem—not just on social contract problems.

These findings are all direct predictions of the hypothesis that there are neurocognitive mechanisms specialized for reasoning about social exchange. They are not predicted by other views. Alternative hypotheses to explain reasoning on the Wason selection task have been proposed (e.g., Cheng and Holyoak, 1985; Manktelow and Over, 1991; Sperber, Cara, and Girotto, 1995), but none so far can account for this array of results (for reviews, see Cosmides and Tooby, 1992, 1997, 2000b; Fiddick, Cosmides, and Tooby, 2000).

Cognition, institutions, and culture. An advanced market economy would be impossible for a species lacking social contract algorithms. Although necessary, possession of these cognitive programs is not a sufficient condition for the emergence of a market economy. Other institutions (i.e., "rules of the game"; North, 1990) and sociocultural conditions need to be co-present. Examples include a wide, consensually shared numerical counting system, a culturally accepted medium of exchange (which reduces transaction costs compared to barter), a division of labor making exchange more profitable, wide-broadcast information systems that signal scarcity of resources (e.g., prices), and institutions that enforce contracts and punish cheaters (e.g., rule of law). When these modern cultural institutions are combined with social contract algorithms designed for an ancestral world, what should we expect?

Implications for Understanding Business and Business Ethics

Cheating on an agreement to trade is obviously an ethical violation. The research discussed above suggests that our minds are well-designed for detecting this form of ethical violation. However, the cognitive machinery that does this was designed for small-scale, face-to-face societies: hunter-gatherer bands in which you lived in close contact with the same group of individuals day in and day out, and where it was relatively easy to see whether the conditions of a social contract had been met. Detecting cheaters in a large market economy may be far more difficult.

Too many people for the mind to process. Modern corporations employ hundreds or thousands of people, most of whom are strangers to one another. The working interactions of these individuals is governed by implicit and explicit agreements to provide services to one another, to the corporation, to suppliers, clients, and customers. But the more people are involved, the more difficult detecting cheaters should be. There are two reasons for this.

The first is cognitive load. More interactants and interactions means more opportunities to cheat, each of which needs to be monitored. Data from modern hunter-gatherers and hunter-horticulturalists show that individuals usually limit themselves to a rather small number of regular exchange partners within their larger group (Gurven, 2002; Gurven et al., 2000; modern hunter-gatherer bands average 50 people, including children (Lee and DeVore, 1968). A memory system designed for this level of interaction would need separate slots for each interactant, each slot able to store a certain amount of data about one's history of interaction with that person (Cosmides and Tooby, 1989). But how many person-slots is the memory system equipped with, and how much information can each hold (and for how long)? No one knows the answer to these questions yet. But monitoring the large number of persons and interactions in a modern corporation might overload the system, especially if these person-slots turn out to be limited in their number and capacity to hold information.

The second difficulty arises from lack of transparency. Hunter-gatherers have little privacy: if the neighbor my family has been helping comes back from a hunt with lots of meat, this will be seen and everyone will know, making nonreciprocation socially difficult for him. But when many people are interacting in complex ways, it can be difficult to tell when someone is failing to fully satisfy the responsibilities for which they are paid a salary. Has an employee generated enough ideas for ad campaigns or succeeded at improving public relations? Some tasks require the production of abstract goods that are difficult to quantify. Are profits really that high and debt that low? Complex numerical accounting systems are necessary in a market economy, but hardly transparent.

These problems can be mitigated by creating small internal working groups (on a more hunter-gathererish scale), and by creating more transparent and public systems for keeping track of who has done what for whom. Both are obvious solutions that many companies have converged on.

No design for detecting procedural violations. Cheater detection is most strongly activated when two conditions are jointly met: (i) the rule specifies a contingent *benefit* that a potential violator could illicitly obtain, and (ii) one suspects the rule will be violated *intentionally*. There is, of course, a connection between these two: the prospect of gaining a benefit at no cost provides an incentive to cheat that may tempt one to intentionally violate a social contract.

In this light, consider these ordinary procedural rules that one might encounter in a business:

(i) "If the invoice is from the appliances department, then route it through accounting division B."

(ii) "If you are going to contact a disgruntled client, first notify the manager."

Both rules are deontic (i.e., rules prescribing the conditions under which one is entitled or obligated to do something). But neither is a social contract because neither specifies a *benefit* that one is entitled to only if a requirement has been met (the pleasures of routing appliance invoices are difficult to fathom, and most people dread speaking to disgruntled clients). Moreover, such rules are more likely to be broken through inattention or negligence, rather than on purpose (what is there to gain?). When rules do not regulate access to benefits and violations are likely to be mistakes, cheater detection is barely activated; under these circumstances, fewer than thirty percent of people detect violations (Barrett, 1999; Cosmides and Tooby, 2000b).

Yet, depending on the downstream consequences, failure to comply with rules like these may ultimately waste resources or even endanger consumers. In many cases, the public—and the business itself—would be better served if such violations were detected. This is more likely to happen when people's attention is spontaneously drawn to situations that might involve violations, and the research discussed above shows that this is more likely to happen when rules are restated or reframed as social contracts (or else as precautionary rules, see above). For example, rule (i) could be prefaced with the explanation that the ovens, stoves and dishwashers in the appliance department are very expensive, high profit items, and division B specializes in making sure consumers make payments on these items on time. This background enables one to reframe the rule as, "If the consumer is to buy an expensive item from us, then they must pay for it in a timely manner"—a classic social contract. Rule (ii) could be prefaced with an explanation that dealing with disgruntled customers can be difficult or, if they are litigious, hazardous to the company, and notifying the manager is a precautionary measure taken because the manager may have some timely advice to give. This background reframes the rule as a classic precautionary rule, one of the other domains for which our minds are designed to detect violations.

The agency problem can bedevil attempts to reframe. A benefit to the company is not necessarily a benefit to one of the company's agents; agents who do not see the company's costs and benefits as such are unlikely to spontaneously attend to potential cases of cheating by employees or clients. In some cases, reframing the action specified in the rule as a benefit or hazard may be difficult, for example, when the rationale for the rule is too obscure or when the benefits to be gained are too many steps removed from the action that the rule permits or obliges.

It is important that people be alert to the possibility of rule violations when these might have negative ethical consequences. The best way to do this is for companies to work with human nature, rather than against it. The more procedural rules can be reframed as social contracts or precautions, the more one will engage employees' spontaneous attention to potential rule violations. To the extent such reframings are possible, ethicists advising businesses might want to suggest them.

Moral Sentiments: The Desire to Punish Free Riders on Collective Actions

Dyadic cooperation is sometimes seen in the animal kingdom. Far rarer are collective actions: cooperation between three or more individuals to achieve a common goal. Yet this form of multi-individual cooperation is common in our own species. It occurs not only in modern circumstances, but in hunter-gatherer and hunter-horticulturalist societies as well. Common examples include intergroup conflict—band-level warfare—cooperative hunting, and certain community-wide projects, such as shelter-building.

In these circumstances, sets of individuals cooperate to achieve a common goal, and they do so even when that goal is a public good—that is, even when the rewards to individuals are not intrinsically linked to individual effort. This has been, and continues to be, a puzzle to both economists and evolutionary biologists. When faced with the decision to participate in a collective action, there are two choices: free ride or participate. Ever since Mancur Olson's trenchant analysis, rational choice theorists have understood that free riding generates a higher payoff than cooperation: Participants and free riders get the same benefit—a successful outcome—but free riders do not incur the cost of participation (Olson, 1965). This incentive to free ride results in a paradoxical outcome: Participation unravels and the project fails, even though each individual would have been better off if the project's goal had been successfully achieved.

Evolutionary biologists find cooperation in collective actions puzzling for a different, but related, reason. In evolutionary biology, the different payoffs to alternative choices are relevant only if they cause differential reproduction of alternative designs (alternative programs) that cause those choices. The fact that collective action is rare in the animal kingdom means that most organisms *lack* programs that cause participation: free riding, therefore, is the default choice. If payoffs to collective action translate into reproductive advantages, then how could designs causing participation have gained a toe-hold in a universe dominated by non-participants? Those who participated in a successful collective action would have experienced an increase in their fitness, but free riders would have benefited even more (by getting the benefits of the achieved goal without suffering the costs of participation). The currency is differential reproduction of participant- versus free-riding designs; this means that individuals equipped with programs that caused free-riding would have out-reproduced those equipped with programs that caused participation. Consequently, free-rider designs would have been selected for, and any participation-designs that arose in a population would have been selected out. If so, then why do we see individual human beings routinely and willingly participating in collective actions? Is this a byproduct of adaptations that evolved for some other purpose, or did evolution produce mechanisms designed to cause this form of cooperation?

There may not be adaptations designed for regulating participation in collective actions. But if there are, programs that cause participation would need to be equipped with strategies that eliminated the fitness advantage of free riders. Without such features, designs causing participation could not be evolutionarily stable strategies (Maynard Smith, 1982). Price, Cosmides, and Tooby (2002) have proposed that punitive sentiments toward free riders are generated by an adaptation in participant designs whose function is to eliminate the fitness advantage free rider designs would otherwise enjoy. They tested this hypothesis against a labor recruitment theory and rational choice theory.

Alternative Theories of Adaptive Function of a Moral Sentiment

All functional theories, evolutionary or economic, propose that one's willingness to participate in a collective action will be a function of how much one expects to individually benefit from its success. But theories diverge in their predictions about the conditions that should trigger punitive sentiments toward free riders (as well as the conditions that should trigger pro-reward sentiments toward participants).

The adaptive function of a program is the reason it evolved: the selective advantage that, over evolutionary history, caused the program in question to be favored over alternative ones. If *eliminating free rider fitness advantages* were the adaptive function of punitive sentiments toward free riders, then several predictions (E-1 through E-6) follow about the design of the motivational system that triggers them:

E-1. An individual's own participation should be the specific factor that triggers punitive sentiments toward free riders. This is because (ancestrally) *only those individuals who contributed were at risk* of incurring lower fitness relative to free riders.

E-2. The more an individual contributes, the greater the adverse fitness differential s/he potentially suffers relative to free riders. Hence a sentiment designed to prevent outcompetition by free riders should key the *degree* of punitive sentiment toward free riders to the individual's own willingness to participate: The more one participates, the more punitive one should feel toward free riders.

E-3. Those who have an interest in the goal being achieved should be more willing to participate. However, punitive sentiment should track willingness to participate, even after controlling for self-interest in the group goal.

Indeed, if eliminating the free rider's fitness advantage were the adaptation's only function, then:

E-4. After controlling for willingness to participate, any relationship between perceived benefit and punitive sentiment should disappear.

E-5. Willingness to participate should predict punishment, but not sentiments in favor of rewarding participants. (When reward induces a free riding underproducer to join a collective action, this preserves the underproducer's relative fitness advantage compared to the producer design that is doing the rewarding).

E-6. Consequently, pro-reward sentiments should not track punitive sentiments, especially among those most willing to participate.

The *labor recruitment theory* is an alternative hypothesis about the adaptive function of punitive sentiments toward free riders on collective actions. According to this hypothesis, punitive sentiments were designed by evolution to encourage more participation in a collective action, in an effort to increase the probability that the common goal is successfully achieved. This hypothesis leads to many of the same predictions as rational choice theory, to wit:

L-1. Those most likely to benefit from achievement of a group goal should differentially act to induce others to participate. Self-interest in the group goal should trigger punitive sentiments, and the greater one's self-interest in that goal, the more punitive one should feel toward free riders.

L-2. Self-interest should independently predict punitive sentiment (even after controlling for willingness to participate). Encouraging self-sacrifice by others provides the largest net benefit—even for a free rider.

If encouraging participation by others were the adaptation's only function, then:

L-3. After controlling for self-interest, there should be no relationship between willingness to participate and punitive sentiment.

L-4. Pro-reward sentiment should track punitive sentiment. (Nothing in the problem of labor recruitment privileges the carrot over the stick as a means of inducing participation.)

L-5. Punitive sentiment should be sensitive only to labor needs, not to free riders per se. Once manpower needs are met, the system should be indifferent to the prospering of free riders.

L-6. The system should be indifferent to whether a non-participant is a free rider or not. Self-interest in the group goal should trigger punitive sentiment toward *any* non-participant who could help achieve the goal by participating, including people who do not benefit from the collective action and people who are considered exempt (e.g., women in warfare).

L-7. Those who contribute anything less than the optimal amount should be targets of punishment (even if they are contributing at the same level as everyone else).

Price et al. (2002) compared these predictions to results from experimental economics games (e.g., Fehr and Gächter, 2000a,b; Yamagishi, 1986), and to results of a survey they conducted assessing attitudes toward participation in a collective action. This survey (which was conducted prior to September 11, 2001) asked subjects to imagine that the United States was mobilizing for war, and to indicate how strongly they agreed or disagreed with a number of statements. In addition to other variables, subjects were asked how willing they would be to participate ("If I got drafted for this war, I would probably agree to serve"), how much they felt they would benefit from the group goal being achieved ("If the USA won this war, it would be very good for me as an individual"), how punitive they would feel toward nonparticipants ("If a U.S. citizen resisted this draft, I'd think they should be punished"), and how much they felt participants should be rewarded ("If a drafted U.S. citizen agreed to serve in this war, I'd think they should be rewarded").

The Adaptive Function of Punitive Sentiments: What Do the Results Say?

The survey results were surprisingly clear cut. They supported all the predictions that follow from the hypothesis that punitive sentiments evolved to eliminate the fitness advantage that would accrue to a free-rider design (E-1 through E-6). Moreover, the results contradicted all the predictions of the labor recruitment hypothesis that they could address (L-1 through L-4). The other predictions, L-5 through L-7, were contradicted by results from public goods games in experimental economics (Fehr and Gächter, 2000a,b; see Price et al for discussion).

In short, willingness to participate was the specific trigger for punitive sentiments toward free riders: the more willing one was to participate, the more punitive one felt toward free riders. Willingness to participate independently predicted punitive sentiment, even after controlling for self-interest in the group goal (partial $r = .55, .62$, for two different scenarios). In contrast, self-interest in the group goal did not independently predict punitive sentiment, once the effects of willingness to participate were statistically removed.

Engineering criteria are used to recognize adaptations and deduce their functions. To discover the function of a system, one looks for evidence of special design—a design that achieves an adaptive function precisely, reliably, and economically. The motivational system that generates punitive sentiments toward free riders showed evidence of special design for eliminating the fitness advantages of free riders. For example:

1. The participation-punishment link was *selective*. Willingness to participate predicted punitive sentiment, not pro-reward sentiment.
2. The trigger for the punitive response was *precise*: Willingness to participate was the only variable to independently predict punitive sentiment. Punitiveness was not independently predicted by self-interest in the group goal or by various demographic variables.
3. The punitive response was *specific*: Willingness to participate predicted punitive sentiment toward *free riders*; once this effect was controlled for, it did not predict punitiveness more generally (toward criminals, for example).
4. The punitive response was *uniform*: The participation-punishment link was just as strong in women as in men, despite the fact that women are considered exempt from the military draft.

The empirical data from this and the public goods games contradict the predictions of rational choice theory (see Table 1). Recently, Price replicated the selectivity, precision, and specificity of the participation-punishment link using behavioral data in a totally different circumstance: an economic collective action. The subjects were Shuar hunter-horticulturalists in the Ecuadorian Amazon, a group of men participating in a collective action to cultivate and sell a sugar cane crop (Price, Barrett, and Hagen, under review). This study produced the same results as the American survey. E-1 through E-6 were supported with about the same effect sizes, providing further evidence that the motivational system that generates punitive sentiments toward free riders on collective

Table 1. Rational Choice Theory (RCT) and Moral Sentiments Toward Free Riders: Predictions versus Results

1. **RCT:** People should not punish when costs of doing so cannot be recouped. **But they do.** (e.g., Fehr and Gächter, 2000a,b)

2. **RCT:** Targets should be people who could increase their own level of cooperation to the benefit of the rational agent. So punish anyone who contributes *less than the optimum* (even if they contributed at the group average). **Yet such people are *not* punished.** (Fehr and Gächter, 2000a,b)

3. **RCT:** Self-interest in group goal *should* predict punitive sentiment. **But it does not.** (Price, Cosmides, and Tooby, 2002)

4. **RCT:** Willingness to participate should not trigger punitive sentiment *independent* of expected gain (sunk cost fallacy). **But it does.** (Price et al., 2002)

5. **RCT:** Reward should track punitive sentiment. **But it does not.** (Price et al., 2002)

Perhaps rational choice leads you to support group norms that are in your interest. But . . .

6. **RCT:** Self-interest in group goal plus willingness to participate should trigger punitive sentiment only when both are high (to avoid advocating your own punishment). **But this is not the case.** (Punitive sentiment is triggered by willingness to participate, regardless of self-interest; Price et al., 2002.)

7. **RCT:** Those who are exempt are free to punish, so there should be no willingness-punitive sentiment link in those who are exempt (e.g., women). **Yet there is.** (Price et al., 2002)

8. **RCT:** Those who are willing to participate should advocate rewarding participants (they would get the reward!). **But willingness does *not* predict pro-reward sentiment.** (Price et al., 2002)

actions was designed by natural selection to eliminate the fitness advantage that free riders would otherwise enjoy. Additionally, the Ecuadorian study, like the American one, produced evidence that directly contradicts the labor recruitment and rational choice theories.

Carrots and Sticks are Not Fungible

The claim that punitive sentiments did not evolve to solve labor recruitment problems does not imply that the human mind lacks *any* programs designed to address this problem. Indeed, Price's data suggested the presence of a motivational system designed to encourage participation: one that generates sentiments in favor of *rewarding* participants. Pro-reward sentiments were independently predicted by self-interest in the group goal. The trigger for reward sentiments was precise (only one variable, self-interest in achievement of the goal, independently predicted them) and the response triggered was specific (self-interest predicted only reward sentiments, not punitive ones).

Thus, in collective actions, the motivation to punish and the motivation to reward appear to be triggered by different variables and generated by two different systems. Most economic analyses treat reward and punishment as fungible, mere increases and decreases in utility. But this dissociation between punitive and pro-reward sentiments suggests that the carrot and the stick are not just two sides of the same coin. In a collective action, the desire to use the carrot is triggered by different circumstances than the desire to use the stick.

When Punishment is Not Possible

Ancestrally (as now), punishment is not always an option. When this is so, a participant design can avoid outcompetition by free riders if it is equipped with a feature that monitors for the presence of under-contributors and drops its own level of participation when they are present. Research on contributions to public goods in experimental economics shows that people continuously monitor the state of play, adjusting their behavior accordingly (Fehr and Gächter, 2000a,b; Kurzban, McCabe, et al., 2001). If they can, they inflict punishment on under-contributors right away (which has the secondary consequence of allowing levels of cooperation to spiral up toward the welfare-maximizing optimum of 100 percent contribution to the common pool; see Price et al., for analysis). When there is no opportunity to punish, they ratchet back their own contribution to something like the average level. As this monitoring and adjustment process iterates, contributions gradually diminish to rational choice theory expectations (Kurzban, McCabe, et al., 2001). But this iterative ratcheting back does not reflect the emergence, through learning, of rational choice: when a new collective action begins, the very same people start out contributing to the common pool at relatively high levels (about sixty percent of their endowment; rational choice theory predicts zero percent).

Implications for Business Ethics

The first thing to note is that, if the above results hold up, they indicate that punitive sentiments toward free riders in collective actions evolved for a function that, from an economic point of view, makes no sense: eliminating the fitness differential between participant-designs and free-rider designs in a distant, ancestral past. Prior to the evolution of cognitive adaptations favoring participation in collective action, no minds were designed for participation (by definition). Without adaptations promoting participation, non-participation would have been the default strategy: free riding would have been the state of nature.

But that was then, and this is now. If selection did favor adaptations for participating in collective actions, there are strong reasons to assume that, by now, these would be universal and species typical (Tooby and Cosmides, 1990). When free riding occurs now, it probably reflects a contingent choice strategy that everyone has, embedded within a set of programs that would make any of us participate in a collective action under circumstances that were more individually auspicious. Designs that cause nothing but free riding—the original selection pressure causing participants to evolve punitive sentiments toward free riders—may no longer exist in the human population.

Punishment of free riders may be "irrational" in the rational choice sense of "rational," especially in a modern world full of anonymous strangers. But that does not matter if your goal is to understand behavior. Our evolved psychology may have been designed for a vanished world, but it generates our behavior nonetheless. People remain more afraid of spiders and snakes—ancestral dangers—than of cars and electric outlets, even though the latter pose a greater threat in the modern world. Whether it is sensible now or not, our psychology is designed so that the more we contribute to a collective action, the more punitive we will feel toward those we perceive as free riders.

Adaptations for a small world. Adaptations for participating in collective actions evolved in the context of a small social world of perhaps 20–100 people, many of whom were relatives (natural selection easily allows the evolution of mechanisms for delivering benefits to relatives noncontingently; Hamilton, 1964). As Mancur Olson pointed out in the context of labor unions, voluntary collective actions are more likely to succeed when they involve small groups rather than large ones—not surprising to an evolutionary psychologist. This occurs, he argued, because there are many compensatory benefits for those who join such groups, not merely the benefit to be gained from achieving the collective goal. His descriptions of these activities are strongly reminiscent of the risk pooling and mutual aid one sees in hunter-gatherer bands of similar size.

Large consumer and environmental advocacy groups are engaged in collective action projects, the intent of which is to curb what are seen as ethical violations by business. But large collective actions, Olson pointed out, are more difficult to sustain without the use of coercive force. An evolved psychology as described by Price et al. has additional implications for large collective action groups like these, especially for the morale and political attitudes of volunteers.

Morale. Idealistic people eagerly anticipate working toward noble goals with public advocacy groups. Nevertheless, many volunteers (and even paid workers) are lost to "burn-out": a catastrophic drop in morale triggered by the perception that one is doing all the work while most people free ride (often accompanied by bitterness—punitive sentiment?—toward non-participants, who are disparaged as "apathetic" or worse). The very experience of working hard for a collective good should trigger negative sentiments toward those who are not "involved." The loss of interest in making further contributions is also expected: These are private groups that lack the ability to punish free riders, a circumstance that triggers the iterative ratcheting back strategy.

Political attitudes. Less obviously, the two motivational systems—punitive sentiments triggered by degree of participation versus pro-reward sentiments triggered by self-interest in the group goal—might color the political solutions favored by various groups. For example:

Producing cleaner air is a classic public good. In an effort to reduce air pollution, one could advocate a pro-reward policy (e.g., tax incentives for businesses that contribute to the goal by reducing their pollution) or a punitive policy (e.g., fines levied on businesses that do not reduce their pollution). Which is more effective is an empirical matter, and the goal of clean air is best served by choosing the most effective policy. (N.B.: the authors have no opinion about which is best). But the very act of participating in a collective action triggers punitive sentiments toward free riders (businesses that do not reduce their pollution), not pro-reward sentiments toward participants (businesses that do reduce their pollution). Indeed, the more energetically one works for an environmental advocacy group, the more punitive one should feel toward businesses who do not curtail their pollution and toward fellow citizens who do not contribute to the group's work. Once this moral sentiment is activated, policies that impose sanctions and laws that mandate contributions toward the goal (through taxes and state agencies) may seem more reasonable and just. Indeed, individuals who, before joining an environmental advocacy group, had favored pro-reward policies might have a change of heart after joining. Once they are actively participating, they can be expected to experience an ethical tug in the direction of punitive sanctions and enforced contributions, and away from policies that reward businesses for curtailing pollution.

Working with human nature. Are there ways of harnessing these moral sentiments in the service of reducing negative externalities such as pollution? Clean air is a public good, but the individuals charged with enforcing pollution standards are government bureaucrats at agencies like the EPA, who have nothing in particular to gain by enforcement—not even the pleasure of cleaner air, if they live far from the polluters (see agency problem, above). Imagine a slightly different system: "pollution courts," where companies that had contributed to the public good by demonstrably reducing their own pollution levels had standing to both present evidence of pollution by their free-riding competitors and request the imposition of fines. Might this give companies an incentive to (i) prove they deserve standing (by lowering their own pollution levels), and (ii) investigate cases of pollution, thereby reducing the EPA's burden? Could this system wipe out the profit advantage the free riding polluter has over companies that voluntarily curtail their pollution?

Ethics and the organization of production. Price (personal communication, 2003) reports that the Shuar collective action in sugar cane cultivation ultimately failed. Everyone who participated was guaranteed an equal share of the proceeds from selling the crop, and there were consensually agreed upon fines for not showing up to clear the fields. But the fines had no bite: instead of being levied after each work episode (each episode in which participation occurred and could be monitored), the fines were to be deducted from each individual's profit once the crop was harvested and sold. The iterative ratchet effect ensued. Over time, participation in the cultivation effort dwindled to the point where the project failed and there were no proceeds to share. It is worth noting that everyday life among the Shuar involves norms promoting generosity and sharing at levels rarely seen in the West.

Communitarian methods of organizing production have a strong ethical pull for many people, including moral philosophers. Equal division of profits can seem fair (under the assumption that everyone is contributing equally) or at least humane (under the assumption that everyone who is capable of contributing is doing so). The fairness of these compensation schemes is predicated on the assumption that no one free rides. Their efficacy is predicated on the assumption that if free riding does occur, contributors will continue to work at the same level—there will be no iterative ratchet effect. Are these reasonable assumptions? Ethicists need to consider whether certain methods of compensation invite free riding and dwindling participation, given the kind of minds we have.

Farms, factories, restaurants—all involve multi-individual cooperation and hence collective action. The question is, are these projects organized as public goods (everyone benefits equally, regardless of their level of participation)? Or are payoffs organized such that effort is rewarded and free riding is punished? In the former Soviet Union, three percent of the land on collective farms was held privately, so local farming families could grow food for their own consumption and privately sell any excess. Yet estimates at the time were that this three percent of land produced forty-five percent to seventy-five percent of all the vegetables, meat, milk, eggs, and potatoes consumed in the Soviet Union (Sakoff, 1962). The quality of land on the collectively-held plots was the same; their low productivity was due to the iterative ratchet effect. People shifted their efforts away from the collective to the private plots. Without these private plots, it is likely that the people of the Soviet Union would have starved. Would this outcome have been ethically acceptable? Is a compensation procedure humane if its predictable consequence is mass suffering?

Workplace Diversity: When (and Why) Do People Notice and Remember Race?

Any given individual is a member of many different social categories: Leslie might be a boss, an engineer, a woman, a wife, a mother, an African-American, a church-goer. But when you meet Leslie, what do you notice and remember about her? That is, which category memberships do you encode?

Social psychologists can tell, using a memory confusion protocol (Taylor, Fiske, Etcoff, and Ruderman, 1978). This method uses errors in recall to unobtrusively reveal whether subjects are categorizing target individuals into groups and, if so, what dimensions they are using to do so (see Figure 2, p. 116). This method has revealed that, when adults encounter a new individual, they encode that individual's race, sex, and age (Taylor et al., 1978; Hewstone, Hantzi, and Johnston, 1991; Stangor, Lynch, Duan, and Glass, 1992; for review and discussion, see Brewer, 1988; Fiske and Neuberg, 1990; Hamilton, Stroessner, and Driscoll, 1994; Messick and Mackie, 1989). These dimensions can be encoded

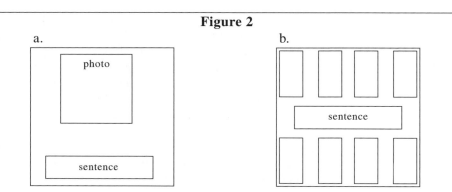

Figure 2

Legend for Figure 2. The memory confusion protocol uses errors in recall to unobtrusively reveal whether subjects are categorizing target individuals into groups and, if so, what dimensions they are using to do so. Subjects are asked to form impressions of individuals whom they will see engaged in a conversation. They then see a sequence of sentences, each of which is paired with a photo of the individual who said it (see panel a). Afterwards, there is a surprise recall task: the sentences appear in random order, and subjects must attribute each to the correct individual (see panel b). Misattributions reveal encoding: Subjects more readily confuse individuals whom they have encoded as members of the *same* category than those whom they have categorized as members of *different* categories. For example, a citizen of Verona who had encoded coalition membership would make more within-category errors—errors in which s/he confused, say, a Capulet with a Capulet (or a Montague with a Montague)—than between-category errors—ones in which s/he confused a Capulet with a Montague or vice versa (this relationship will hold for data that are corrected to equalize base rates).

without other individuating information; for example, one might recall that one's new client or colleague is a young, white woman, without remembering anything else about her—her name, her hair color, her hometown.

Until recently, it appeared that race—along with sex and age—was encoded in an automatic and mandatory fashion. The encoding of race was thought to be spontaneous and automatic because the pattern of recall errors that indicates race encoding occurred in the absence of instructions to attend to the race of targets, and across a wide variety of experimental situations. It was thought to be mandatory—encoded with equal strength across all situations—because every attempt to increase or decrease the extent to which subjects encode the race of targets had failed (Taylor et al., 1978; Hewstone et al., 1991; Stangor et al., 1992). Until recently, no context manipulation—whether social, instructional, or attentional—had been able to budge this race effect. Such results led some to propose that race (along with sex and age) is a "primary" or "primitive" dimension of person perception, built into our cognitive architecture (e.g., Messick and Mackie, 1989; Hamilton et al., 1994).

Automatic Race Encoding is a Puzzle

For millions of years, our ancestors inhabited a social world in which registering the sex and life-history stage of an individual would have enabled a large variety of useful probabilistic inferences about that individual (e.g., adolescent girl; toddler boy). So natural selection could have favored neurocomputational machinery that automatically encodes an individual's sex and age. But "race" is a different matter.

Ancestral hunter-gatherers traveled primarily by foot, making social contact geographically local (Kelly, 1995). Given the breeding structure inherent in such a world, the typical individual would almost never have encountered people drawn from populations genetically distant enough to qualify as belonging to a different "race" (even if one could make biological sense of the concept; geneticists have failed to discover objective patterns in the world that could easily explain the racial categories that seem so perceptually obvious to adults; for reviews, see Hirschfeld, 1996; Cosmides, Tooby, and Kurzban, 2003). If individuals typically would not have encountered individuals of other races, then there could have been no selection for cognitive adaptations designed to preferentially encode such a dimension, much less encode it in an automatic and mandatory fashion.

For this reason, "race" is a very implausible candidate for a conceptual primitive to have been built into our evolved cognitive machinery. Race encoding may be a robust and reliable phenomenon, but it cannot be caused by computational machinery that was designed by natural selection for that purpose. This means that race encoding must be a side-effect of machinery that was designed by selection for some alternative function. If that machinery and its function are known, one might be able to create social contexts that diminish or eliminate race encoding.

Encoding Coalitional Alliances

In our view, no part of the human cognitive architecture is designed specifically to encode race. With our colleague, Robert Kurzban, we hypothesized that encoding of race is a byproduct of adaptations that evolved for an alternative function that was a regular part of the lives of our foraging ancestors: detecting coalitions and alliances (Kurzban, Tooby, and Cosmides, 2001). Hunter-gatherers lived in bands, and neighboring bands frequently came into conflict with one another (Ember, 1978; Manson and Wrangham, 1991; Keeley, 1996). Similarly, there were coalitions and alliances within bands (Chagnon, 1992), a pattern found in related primate species and likely to be far more ancient than the hominid lineage itself (Smuts et al., 1987; Wrangham and Peterson, 1996). To negotiate their social world successfully, anticipating the likely social consequences of alternative courses of action, our ancestors would have benefited by being equipped with neurocognitive machinery that tracked these shifting alliances.

Tracking alliances. Consider a program designed to infer who is allied with whom under ancestral conditions. What clues might that program use to do this? What factors in the world should it encode?

Alliance tracking mechanisms should notice patterns of coordinated action, cooperation, and competition. This is the primary database from which alliances can be inferred. But acts of cooperation and competition—behaviors that reveal one's coalitional allegiances—do not occur all the time. Like all behaviors, they are transitory. Alliance tracking machinery could form a better map of the political landscape if it were designed to use these rare revelatory behaviors to isolate additional cues that are correlated with coalitional behavior, but are more continuously present and perceptually easier to assay. This cue-mapping would allow one to use the behavior of some people to predict what others are likely to do.

Cues come in many forms. Some are intentional markers of one's coalitional alliances: war paint, gang colors, political buttons, for example. Other cues are incidental markers. Ethnographically well-known examples include accent and dialect, manner, gait, customary dress, family resemblance, and ethnic badges. If alliance tracking programs detect correlations between allegiance and appearance, then stable dimensions of shared appearance—which may be otherwise meaningless—would emerge in the cognitive system as markers of social categories. Coalitional computation would increase their subsequent perceptual salience, and encode them at higher rates. Any readily observable feature—however arbitrary—should be able to acquire social significance and cognitive efficacy when it validly cues patterns of alliance.

Modern conditions. In societies that are not completely racially integrated, shared appearance—a highly visible and always present cue—can be correlated with patterns of association, cooperation, and competition (Sidanius and Pratto, 1999). Under these conditions, coalition detectors may perceive (or misperceive) race-based social alliances, and the mind will map "race" onto the cognitive variable *coalition*. According to this hypothesis, race encoding is not automatic and mandatory. It appeared that way only because the relevant research was conducted in certain social environments where the construct of "race" happened, for historical reasons (Hirschfeld, 1996), to be one valid probabilistic cue to a different underlying variable, one that the mind *was* designed to automatically seek out: coalitional affiliation (Kurzban, 2001; Kurzban, Tooby, and Cosmides, 2001; Sidanius and Pratto, 1999; Tooby and Cosmides, 1988).

Dynamic revision. Patterns of alliance often change when new issues arise whose possible resolutions differentially affect new subsets of the local social world. Consequently, coalitions shift over time, varying in composition, surface cues, duration and internal cohesion. To track these changes, cue validities would need to be computed and revised dynamically: No single coalitional cue (including cues to race) should be uniformly encoded across all contexts. Furthermore, arbitrary cues (such as skin color) should pick up—and lose—significance only insofar as they acquire predictive validity for coalitional membership.

There is a direct empirical implication of the hypothesis that race is encoded by alliance tracking machinery and that this machinery dynamically updates coalition cues to keep up with new situations. Consider a salient coalitional conflict in which race is *not* correlated with coalition membership. Two things should happen: (i) Arbitrary shared appearance cues that do predict coalition membership should be strongly encoded, and (ii) race encoding should decrease.

Is Coalition Encoded?

Using the memory confusion protocol, Kurzban, Tooby, and Cosmides (2001) confirmed both predictions. They first showed that people do automatically encode the coalitional alliances of targets. The targets were males, some black, some white; each made statements suggesting allegiance with one of two antagonistic coalitions. Crucially, race was not correlated with coalitional affiliation.

Subjects encoded coalitional alliance even in the absence of shared appearance cues—merely from patterns of agreement and disagreement. But when a shared appearance cue—jersey color—was added, coalition encoding was boosted dramatically, to levels higher than any found for race. (N.B. Jersey color is not encoded at all when it lacks social meaning [Stangor et al., 1992].)

Race as a Proxy for Coalition?

The results further showed that, as predicted, race encoding is not mandatory. When coalition encoding was boosted by a shared appearance cue, there was an accompanying decrease in race encoding, which was diminished in one experiment and eliminated in another. Other tests showed that the decrease in race encoding could not be attributed to domain-general constraints on attention.

Subjects had a lifetime's experience of race predicting patterns of cooperation and conflict. The decreases in these experiments occurred in response to only 4 minutes of exposure to an alternative world where race did not predict coalitional alliance. This is expected if (i) race is encoded (in real life) because it serves as a rough-and-ready coalition cue, and (ii) coalition cues are revised dynamically, to reflect newly emerging coalitions. There are many contexts that decrease racial *stereotyping* (inferences); creating alliances uncorrelated with race is the first social context found that decreases race *encoding*.

The results suggest that the tendency to notice and remember "race" is an easily reversible byproduct of programs that detect coalitional alliances. When the relevant coalitional conflict was uncorrelated with race, the tendency to notice and remember the race of the individuals involved diminished, and sometimes even disappeared. These results suggest that the social construct "race" is a byproduct of programs that evolved to look not for race *per se*, but for coalitional alliances. In a sense, the creation of multiracial coalitions "erased race" in the minds of our subjects.

Implications for Business Ethics: Harmony in the Workplace

There is no doubt that racial discrimination occurs; for an alarming and fascinating compendium of data on this point, we recommend *Social Dominance*, by Sidanius and Pratto (1999; their theoretical analysis is both interesting and relevant to business ethicists). The question is, how can the situation be improved?

It is often assumed that the way to promote harmonious cooperation in the workplace is to first eradicate racial stereotypes. Sensitivity training courses are created, the goal of which is to make people of one race aware of the negative inferences they make about people of another race, and to highlight the overt and subtle ways in which individuals of that race are discriminated against. Note, however, that this very process divides people into two different camps (e.g., "whites" and "blacks"), a process that social psychologists know promotes ingroup favoritism and outgroup derogation (Sherif et al., 1961; Tajfel et al., 1971; Brewer, 1979). It *reinforces* the social construction of racial groups as opposing coalitions. However well-intentioned sensitivity courses may be, if race is a proxy for coalition, they may turn out to exacerbate racial problems rather than mitigate them.

Kurzban, Tooby, and Cosmides' results suggest an intriguing alternative. Instead of trying to eradicate racism to get cooperation, companies might be able to use cooperation to eradicate racism. In making and marketing a product, companies create many small task-oriented teams: multi-individual cooperative coalitions. Creating teams where race does not predict team membership should decrease attention to race. At least that is what happened in the Kurzban experiments: when coalition membership could not be predicted by race, there was a decrease in people's attention to race.

We do not yet know the parameters and boundaries of Kurzban et al.'s "erasing race" effect. For example, do the coalitions have to be perceived as in conflict with one another, or does each merely have to be composed of individuals coordinating their behavior with one another in pursuit of a common goal? The creation of multiracial corporate teams could have the desired effect, however, even if it turns out that an element of conflict is necessary—that is, even if erasing race requires the construction of a (nonracial) *us* and *them*. After all, the fact that every company has competitors in the marketplace provides the raw material for thinking in terms of opposing "teams," as surely as the NFL does: Our marketing team versus theirs, our sales department versus theirs. The creation of groups where race does not predict alliances may be a way that companies can improve race relations and diversity, a method that works with human nature rather than against it.

Conclusions

What is ethically achievable depends on what is humanly possible. But what *is* humanly possible? When people think about limits to human action, external constraints come to mind: a stone too heavy to lift, a bullet too fast to dodge. But human action—behavior—is muscle movements, and muscle movement is caused by sophisticated cognitive programs. If this is unclear, consider that most movement disorders—paralysis, epileptic seizures, the tics and shouted epithets of Gilles de Tourette's syndrome, the shakes of Parkinson's disease— are caused by injury to or disorders of the cognitive programs that move muscles, not injury to the muscles themselves (Frith, 1992). In discussing what actions are humanly possible, we should start taking the cognitive programs that *cause* action into account.

Some of these are motivational programs, designed to start and stop our muscles in particular ways as a function of the situations we face. Standing still while watching a lion lunge toward one's throat may be impossible for a normal, brain intact human being. Our motivational systems were *designed* to mobilize evasive action in response to a lunging lion, and no sane ethical system would exhort a person to do otherwise.

Similarly, the human mind may have motivational systems that are *designed* to lower the amount of effort one expends on a collective action as a function of whether others are free riding. There may be no way to over-ride this gumption drain except by applying extreme coercive force—and thus engaging a different motivational system. Yet threatening someone's life is not an ethically neutral course of action. A better solution might be to avoid organizing the project as a public good in the first place.

The human mind may have a computational system that is *designed* to construct an *us* and a *them* under certain circumstances. Moral exhortation may not be enough to counteract the consequences of this social construction. Indeed, it may drive negative attitudes toward *them* underground, changing what people profess without changing their attitudes (Greenwald and Banaji, 1995). A better solution might be to create a new "us": a team comprised of Capulets *and* Montagus, of "blacks" *and* "whites." The experience of participating in such a coalition may diminish attention to the old divisions and reshape attitudes spontaneously, without moral exhortation.

The human mind may be attuned to detecting cheaters yet lack systems designed to seek out other kinds of ethical violations. Penalizing failures to notice such violations may be useless. A better solution might be to reframe ethical rules to take advantage of the human mind's natural abilities to detect cheaters and to attend to violations of precautionary rules.

Soft versus hard solutions. In their attempts to create a more just and ethical society, most people take the approach advocated by Katherine Hepburn's character, Rose Sayer, in *The African Queen*. When Charlie Allnut (Humphrey Bogart) tries to excuse some piece of bad behavior by saying "it's only human nature," Hepburn replies "Nature, Mr. Allnut, is what we are put in this world to rise above." Her words conjure the image of a Manichean struggle, in which "willpower" is deployed to counteract the low and degrading forces of our evolved human nature.

We think this is a losing strategy. Our minds are indeed equipped with over-ride programs—willpower, if you will (Baron-Cohen, Robertson, and Moriarty, 1994; Frith, 1992). But if override is necessary, the battle is already half lost. Far better are "soft" policies, solutions like the ones suggested above. These create situations that activate and deactivate the evolved programs that motivate ethical and unethical behavior.

Why call these solutions "soft"? Boxers are trained to meet the opponent's moves with countervailing force: a "hard," Hepburn approach. In soft martial arts, like aikido, one is trained to achieve goals by exploiting the moves that the opponent is already making. Equipped with an understanding of human nature, it may be possible to train people in ethical aikido: the art of designing policies that achieve ethical goals by taking advantage of the moves that our human nature is already prepared to make. But to do this, we must first know ourselves.

Notes

This paper was first delivered in April 2002 as a Ruffin Lecture on Business Ethics and Science, at the Olsson Center for Applied Ethics, Darden School of Business Administration, University of Virginia. We thank Bill Frederick, Ed Freeman, and the participants for many stimulating conversations. We also thank Douglass North and the Mercatus Center for inviting us to participate in their Social Change workshops; the ideas and excitement of those workshops informed many of our thoughts herein. We are especially grateful to Vernon Smith, who introduced us to the field of experimental economics and showed us its relevance to research in evolutionary psychology. We dedicate this paper to the late Robert Nozick, friend and mentor.

    1. Ethology integrated advances #2 and #3; sociobiology integrated 2-4; evolutionary psychology integrates 1-4 into the framework described in C-1 through C-6.

    2. Most choose either P alone, or P & Q. They are not reasoning correctly from a biconditional interpretation; if they were, they would choose all four cards (a rare response).

    3. And when the rule does not activate an alternative cognitive adaptation, as precautionary rules do; see Fiddick, 1998; Fiddick, Cosmides & Tooby, 2000).

Bibliography

Axelrod, R. 1984. *The evolution of cooperation.* New York: Basic Books.
Axelrod, R., and W. D. Hamilton. 1981. The evolution of cooperation. *Science* 211: 1390–1396.
Baron-Cohen, S. 1995. *Mindblindness: An essay on autism and theory of mind.* Cambridge, Mass.: MIT Press.
Baron-Cohen, S., M. Robertson, and J. Moriarty. 1994a. The development of the will: A neuropsychological analysis of Gilles de la Tourette's Syndrome. In *The self and its dysfunction: Proceedings of the 4th Rochester symposium*, ed. D. Cicchetti and S. Toth. Rochester, N.Y.: University of Rochester Press.
Barrett, H. C. 1999. Guilty minds: How perceived intent, incentive, and ability to cheat influence social contract reasoning. 11th Annual Meeting of the *Human Behavior and Evolution Society*, Salt Lake City, Utah.
Bentham, J. 1789. *An introduction to the principles of morals and legislation.* London: T. Payne.

Boyd, R. 1988. Is the repeated prisoners' dilemma a good model of reciprocal altruism? *Ethology and Sociobiology* 9: 211–222.

Brewer, M. 1979. Ingroup bias in the minimal intergroup situation: A cognitive motivational analysis. *Psychological Bulletin* 86: 307–324.

————. 1988. A dual process model of impression formation. In *Advances in Social Cognition* 1, ed. T. Srull and R. Wyer: 1–36.

Buss, D. M. 1989. Sex differences in human mate preferences: Evolutionary hypotheses tested in 37 cultures. *Behavioral and Brain Sciences* 12: 1–49.

Cashdan, E. 1989. Hunters and gatherers: Economic behavior in bands. In *Economic Anthropology*, ed. S. Plattner. Stanford, Calif.: Stanford University Press.

Chagnon, N. 1992. *Yanomamo (4ᵗʰ edition)*. Fort Worth, Tex.: Harcourt.

Cheng, P., and K. Holyoak. 1985. Pragmatic reasoning schemas. *Cognitive Psychology* 17: 391–416.

Cosmides, L. 1985. Deduction or Darwinian Algorithms? An explanation of the "elusive" content effect on the Wason selection task. Doctoral dissertation, Harvard University. *University Microfilms #86-02206*.

————. 1989. The logic of social exchange: Has natural selection shaped how humans reason? Studies with the Wason selection task. *Cognition* 31: 187–276.

Cosmides, L., and J. Tooby. 1989. Evolutionary psychology and the generation of culture, Part II. Case study: A computational theory of social exchange. *Ethology & Sociobiology* 10: 51–97.

————. 1992. Cognitive adaptations for social exchange. In *The adapted mind: Evolutionary psychology and the generation of culture*, ed. J. Barkow, L. Cosmides, and J. Tooby. New York: Oxford University Press.

————. 1997. Dissecting the computational architecture of social inference mechanisms. In *Characterizing human psychological adaptations* (Ciba Foundation Symposium #208). Chichester: Wiley: 132–156.

————. 2000a. Consider the source: The evolution of adaptations for decoupling and metarepresentation. In *Metarepresentations: A multidisciplinary perspective*, ed. D. Sperber. Vancouver Studies in Cognitive Science. New York: Oxford University Press: 53–115.

————. 2000b. The cognitive neuroscience of social reasoning. In *The New Cognitive Neurosciences, Second Edition* (chapter 87), ed. M. S. Gazzaniga. Cambridge, Mass.: MIT Press: 1259–1270.

Cosmides, L., J. Tooby, and R. Kurzban. In press, 2003. Perceptions of race. *Trends in Cognitive Sciences*.

Daly, M., and M. Wilson. 1988. *Homicide*. New York: Aldine.

Ember, C. R. 1978. Myths about hunter-gatherers. *Ethnology* 27: 239–448.

Fehr, E., and S. Gächter. 2000a. Cooperation and punishment in public goods experiments. *American Economic Review* 90: 980–994.

————. 2000b. Fairness and retaliation: The economics of reciprocity. *Journal of Economic Perspectives* 14: 159–181.

Fiddick, L. 1998. *The deal and the danger: An evolutionary analysis of deontic reasoning*. Doctoral dissertation, Department of Psychology, University of California, Santa Barbara.

Fiddick, L. 2004 (in press). Domains of deontic reasoning: Resolving the discrepancy between the cognitive and moral reasoning literatures. *The Quarterly Journal of Experimental Psychology*, 57A.

Fiddick, L., L. Cosmides, and J. Tooby. 2000. No interpretation without representation: The role of domain-specific representations and inferences in the Wason selection task. *Cognition* 77: 1–79.

Fiske, S., and S. Neuberg. 1990. A continuum of impression formation, from category-based to individuating processes: Influences of information and motivation on attention and interpretation. In *Advances in Experimental Social Psychology* 23, ed. M. Zanna (Academic Press): 1–74.

Frith, C. 1992. *The Cognitive Neuropsychology of Schizophrenia*. Hillsdale, N.J.: Erlbaum.

Gigerenzer, G. 2000. *Adaptive thinking: Rationality in the real world*. New York: Oxford.

Greenwald, A. G., and M. R. Banaji. 1995. Implicit social cognition: Attitudes, self-esteem, and stereotypes. *Psychological Review* 102: 4–27.

Gurven, M. In press. To give and to give not: The behavioral ecology of human food transfers. *Behavioral and Brain Sciences* (http://www.bbsonline.org/Preprints/Gurven-06282002/Gurven.pdf).

Gurven, M., K. Hill, H. Kaplan, A. Hurtado, and R. Lyles. 2000. Food transfers among Hiwi foragers of Venezuela: Tests of reciprocity. *Human Ecology* 28(2): 171–218.

Hamilton, D., S. Stroessner, and D. Driscoll. 1994. Social cognition and the study of stereotyping. In *Social cognition: Impact on social psychology*, ed. P. G. Devine, D. Hamilton, and T. Ostrom. San Diego: Academic Press: 291–321.

Hamilton, W. D. 1964. The genetical evolution of social behaviour. *Journal of Theoretical Biology* 7: 1–52.

Hewstone, M., A. Hantzi, and L. Johnston. 1991. Social categorization and person memory: The pervasiveness of race as an organizing principle. *European Journal of Social Psychology* 21: 517–528.

Hirschfeld, L. 1996. *Race in the Making*. Cambridge, Mass.: MIT Press.

Isaac, G. 1978. The food-sharing behavior of protohuman hominids. *Scientific American* 238: 90–108.

Keeley, L. 1996. *War before civilization: The myth of the peaceful savage*. Oxford: Oxford University Press.

Kelly, R. 1995. *The Foraging Spectrum*. Washington, D.C.: Smithsonian Institution Press.

Kurzban, R. 2001. The social psychophysics of cooperation: Nonverbal communication in a public goods game. *Journal of Nonverbal Behavior* 25: 241–259.

Kurzban, R., K. McCabe, V. Smith, and B. J. Wilson. 2001. Incremental commitment and reciprocity in a real time public goods game. *Personality and Social Psychology Bulletin* 27(12): 1662–1673.

Kurzban, R., J. Tooby, and L. Cosmides. 2001. Can race be erased?: Coalitional computation and social categorization. *Proceedings of the National Academy of Sciences* 98(26) (December 18, 2001): 15387–15392.

Leckman, J., and L. Mayes. 1998. Maladies of love—an evolutionary perspective on some forms of obsessive-compulsive disorder. In *Advancing research on developmental plasticity: Integrating the behavioral science and neuroscience of mental health,* ed. D. M. Hann, L. C. Huffman, I. I. Lederhendler, and D. Meinecke. Rockville, Md.: NIMH, US Dept. of Health and Human Services: 134–152.

————. 1999. Preoccupations and behaviors associated with romantic and parental love: Perspectives on the origin of obsessive-compulsive disorder. Obsessive-Compulsive Disorder 8(3): 635–665.

Lee, R., and I. DeVore, eds. 1968. *Man the Hunter.* Chicago: Aldine.

Leslie, A. 1987. Pretense and representation: The origins of "theory of mind." *Psychological Review* 94, 412–426.

Manktelow, K., and D. Over. 1991. Social roles and utilities in reasoning with deontic conditionals. *Cognition* 39: 85–105.

Manson, J., and R. Wrangham. 1991. Intergroup aggression in chimpanzees and humans. *Current Anthropology* 32(4): 369–390.

Maynard Smith, J. 1982. *Evolution and the theory of games.* Cambridge: Cambridge University Press.

Messick, D., and D. Mackie. 1989. Intergroup relations. *Annual Review of Psychology* 40: 45–81.

North, D. 1990. *Institutions, Institutional Change and Economic Performance.* New York: Cambridge University Press.

Nozick, R. 1975. *Anarchy, State, and Utopia.* Cambridge, Mass.: Harvard University Press.

Olson, M. 1965. *Logic of Collective Action: Public Goods and the Theory of Groups.* Cambridge, Mass.: Harvard University Press.

Packer, C. 1977. Reciprocal altruism in *Papio annubis. Nature* 265: 441–443.

Pinker, S. 1994. *The language instinct.* New York: HarperCollins.

————. 1997. *How the mind works.* New York: Norton.

————. 2002. *The Blank Slate.* New York: Norton.

Platt, R., and R. Griggs. 1993. Darwinian algorithms and the Wason selection task: A factorial analysis of social contract selection task problems. *Cognition* 48: 163–192.

Price, M., H. C. Barrett, and E. Hagen. Under review. Collective action and punishment in the Ecuadorian Amazon.

Price, M. E., L. Cosmides, and J. Tooby. 2002. Punitive sentiment as an anti-free rider psychological device. *Evolution and Human Behavior* 23: 203–231.

Rawls, J. 1971. *A theory of justice.* Cambridge, Mass.: Harvard University Press.

Sakoff, A. 1962. The private sector in Soviet agriculture. *Monthly Bulletin of Agricultural Economics* 11: 9.

Sen, A. 1999. *Development as freedom.* New York: Knopf.

Sherif, M., O. Harvey, B. White, W. Hood, and C. Sherif. 1961. *Intergroup conflict and cooperation: The robbers cave experiment.* Norman: University of Oklahoma Book Exchange.

Sidanius, J., and F. Pratto. 1999. *Social Dominance.* New York: Cambridge University Press.

Smuts, B., D. Cheney, R. Seyfarth, R. Wrangham, and T. Struhsaker. 1987. *Primate Societies*. Chicago: University of Chicago Press.

Sperber, D., F. Cara, and V. Girotto. 1995. Relevance theory explains the selection task. *Cognition* 57, 31–95.

Stangor, C., L. Lynch, C. Duan, and B. Glas. 1992. Categorization of individuals on the basis of multiple social features. *Journal of Personality & Social Psychology* 62: 207–218.

Stone, V., L. Cosmides, J. Tooby, N. Kroll, and R. Knight, R. (2002). Selective Impairment of Reasoning About Social Exchange in a Patient with Bilateral Limbic System Damage. *Proceedings of the National Academy of Sciences* (August, 2002).

Sugiyama, L., J. Tooby, and L. Cosmides. 2002. Cross-cultural evidence of cognitive adaptations for social exchange among the Shiwiar of Ecuadorian Amazonia. *Proceedings of the National Academy of Sciences* (August, 2002).

Tajfel, H., M. Billig, R. Bundy, and C. Flament. 1971. Social categorization and intergroup behavior. *European Journal of Social Psychology* 1: 149–178.

Taylor, S., S. Fiske, N. Etcoff, and A. Ruderman. 1978. Categorical bases of person memory and stereotyping. *Journal of Personality and Social Psychology*. 36: 778–793.

Tooby, J., and L. Cosmides. 1988. The evolution of war and its cognitive foundations. *Institute for Evolutionary Studies Technical Report* 88-1.

————. 1990. On the universality of human nature and the uniqueness of the individual: The role of genetics and adaptation. *Journal of Personality* 58: 17–67.

————. 1996. Friendship and the Banker's Paradox: Other pathways to the evolution of adaptations for altruism. In *Evolution of Social Behaviour Patterns in Primates and Man. Proceedings of the British Academy* 88, ed. W. G. Runciman, J. Maynard Smith, and R. I. M. Dunbar: 119–143.

Trivers, R. 1971. The evolution of reciprocal altruism. *Quarterly Review of Biology* 46: 35–57.

de Waal, F. 1989. Food sharing and reciprocal obligations among chimpanzees. *Journal of Human Evolution* 18: 433–459.

Wason, P. 1966. Reasoning. In *New Horizons in Psychology*, ed. B. Foss. Harmondsworth: Penguin.

————. 1983. Reasoning and Rationality in the selection task. In *Thinking and Reasoning: Psychological Approaches,* ed. J. S. B. T. Evans. London: Routledge & Kegan Paul.

Wason, P., and P. Johnson-Laird. 1972. *Psychology of Reasoning: Structure and Content*. Cambridge, Mass.: Harvard University Press.

Wilkinson, G. 1988. Reciprocal altruism in bats and other mammals. *Ethology and Sociobiology* 9: 85–100.

Wrangham, R., and D. Peterson. 1996. *Demonic males: Apes and the origins of human violence*. Boston: Houghton Mifflin.

Yamagishi, T. 1986. The provision of a sanctioning system as a public good. *Journal of Personality & Social Psychology* 51, 110–116.

HUMAN NATURE AND BUSINESS ETHICS

David M. Messick

Abstract: While there seems to be little controversy about whether there is a biological or evolutionary basis for human morality, in business and other endeavors, there is considerable controversy about the nature of this basis and the proper populations in which to study this foundation. Moreover, I suggest, the most fundamental element of this basis may be the tendency of humans and other species to experience the world in evaluative terms.

The part of the business school curriculum that is the most resistant to scientific developments is, in my opinion, the area of business ethics. Much of the business enterprise is concerned with finding economically useful applications of new scientific ideas, whether those ideas deal with biotechnology, chaos theory, or group decision making. The field of business ethics has been slow to incorporate new scientific ideas into its structure, claiming that normative theory is distinct from and independent of descriptive theory. So the papers in this conference come as a fresh breeze that bares the scent of change and of challenge. What is the relevance of natural science to business ethics? In particular, what is the relevance of the science of behavior, human and other primate behavior, for conceptions of ethics, in business and elsewhere? The papers in volume make a fine foray into this cluster of issues. The papers share a commitment to taking seriously behavioral and psychological research as well as the fact that we, as a species and as builders of organizations, evolve. This evolution is systematic and understandable.

Psychologists have understood the importance of evolution in shaping our social nature for many decades. Donald Campbell's 1975 presidential address to the American Psychological Association (Campbell, 1975) dealt specifically with this issue. It had the intriguing title, "On the conflicts between biological and social evolution and between psychology and moral tradition," a title that made clear his claim that social and biological evolution, both of which must be taken seriously, are often at odds, and that there was a tension between psychology and moral tradition (which Campbell links to biological and social evolution, respectively). The audacious question Campbell posed in this article was whether biological evolution was capable of selecting for the levels of self-denying social behaviors that are witnessed in sophisticated modern society (which has since come to be called "ultrasociality"). His answer was that natural selection at the individual level was incapable of producing such levels of sociality and that they must have been supported by social evolution, specifically the evolution of moral traditions.

For many reasons, Campbell's conclusions were controversial, but they awakened the field of psychology and behavioral science generally to the importance of understanding the origins of our social and moral natures and to the interplay between biological and social evolution as shaping processes (e.g., Wispe and Thompson, 1976; Boyd and Richerson, 1985).

I think it is fair to say that most psychologists accept that many forms of social behavior have a genetic or "hard-wired" foundation. Our ability to use language is a good example. Other examples include play, imprinting, and the distress of mutual gaze (of looking at the eyes of an organism that is looking at you). Of the latter, I recall that a colleague who kept a research colony of rhesus monkeys asked visitors not to stare at the monkeys when they visited the colony for fear that the monkeys would respond emotionally and possibly injure themselves. Reciprocity in various forms is surely built in, whether it is mutual grooming in cats or food sharing in vampire bats. The concept of reciprocal altruism as described by Trivers (1971) is more controversial and will be mentioned presently. There is good reason to think that empathy, vicarious emotionality, is hard-wired in some way, if for no other reason than the sensitivity of human babies to the sound of a baby crying. Flack and de Waal (this volume) also discuss evidence that other primates display empathetic capabilities. In 1998 I offered the hypothesis that the differentiation between "us" and "them," what social psychologists call inter-group discrimination, was basic (Messick, 1998). Like language, I suggested, the structure is basic, but the content varies from situation to situation. "We" could be men, Democrats, North Americans, psychologists, university professors, enophiles, or stamp collectors. "They" would be the complement. While the content of the "we" categories would be very different depending on whether one was thinking of men or stamp collectors, there would be some structural similarities. In-groups would be seen as more heterogeneous and out-groups as more homogeneous, for example. In-groups would be seen as more positive than out-groups. And so on.

Cosmides (this volume) suggests that evolution has provided humans with "programs" that help steer us through our social relationships and undergird some of our moral sentiments. She discusses three such programs: cheater detection in social exchange, punitive sentiments toward free riders in collective actions, and coalitional impulses. The latter of these programs is closely related to the inter-group schema I wrote about. While there is little doubt that the processes Cosmides refers to occur, there is great doubt that these are separate, independent processes, and that they have been sculpted by a process of natural selection. Furthermore, there appears to be at least one major piece of the behavioral foundation that is missing.

Research on the cheater detection concept has been innovative and persuasive that the social context of a simple reasoning task makes a huge difference in the accuracy of problem solvers (Cosmides, 1989). The data supporting the other two "programs" are far less compelling and are subject to alternative explanations. This is not the place for a detailed evaluation of the experimental evidence underlying the coalitional hypothesis and the punitive stance to free riders but it is relevant to note that these "mechanisms" may be less independent than supposed by Cosmides (this volume). What I mean is that a free rider may well be someone who is presumed to be a member of "us" about whom we maintain expectations of loyalty, participation, and positive regard. Collective action, in other words, may only be expected of "our" coalition. And when a "we" group forms, collective action may be one of the many consequences that are created by its formation. The literature on this important topic is massive. The recent compilation by Sedikides, Schopler, and Insko (1998) provides a useful introduction.

The element that I find missing in Cosmides' account of the cognitive scaffolding we have evolved is in her reliance on purely cognitive rather than emotive mechanisms. The computer analogy focuses us on the processing of information. We detect cheaters. We recognize free riders. We perceive fellow coalition members. I think there is a logic that may be implied but that is unstated or understated in this suggestions and that is that the reason these processes are important is because cheaters make us mad, and free riders (who may also be cheaters to an implicit deal) anger us, and we are on guard and vigilant with regard to "them" because they might be dangerous or harmful. In other words, what seems to be the driving force in the evolutionary "programs" that Cosmides describes is emotion, either anger or fear. And at the very most basic level, these emotions imply a more basic psychological process, namely one of evaluating things or making preferences.

It is arguably one of the most basic of human capacities to make judgments of good and bad. Furthermore, this capacity is the foundation of human morality, if we take morality to be any of a number of systems for making judgments about what is right or wrong. The basic capacity was documented decades ago in the pioneering research of Osgood, Suci, and Tannenbaum (1957). These authors developed a scale for measuring the "meanings" of concepts, a scale that they called the *semantic differential*. Concepts could be rated on a series of bipolar scales, like "strong-weak," "good-bad," "beautiful-ugly," and "active-passive." The ratings on a large series of such scales were then statistically analyzed to see which clusters of scales were intercorrelated in order to identify the underlying dimensions of judgment. The results of many studies conducted in all parts of the globe indicated that the most basic dimension was an evaluative dimension, a "good-bad" dimension of judgment. This fundamental fact has never, to my knowledge, been challenged.

Humans are not unique in seeing the world through an evaluative lens. The basic facts of instrumental conditioning include the specification of stimuli that are positive (good) or negative (bad) reinforcers. Basic approach or avoidance tendencies reflect a similar outlook on the world. We, and other mammals, do not just perceive the world in terms of its colors, smells, sounds, feels, and tastes, we also either like or dislike those sensations and perceptions. We move toward positive things and away from negative ones. We tend to repeat actions that produce positive outcomes and we tend not to repeat actions that produce negative consequences. So do rats and pigeons and apes.

It is surprising that many theorists who discuss the ways in which our psychology has been shaped by evolutionary processes either ignore or take for granted this fundamental tendency of evaluation. One treatment which does not do so is offered by Premack and Premack (2003). These researchers take an approach which differs from both Cosmides and from de Waal and his colleagues. Cosmides and her colleagues seek empirical support for their generalizations from research with human (near) adults—college students. De Waal and his colleagues focus mainly on non-human primates to make inferences about the basic ingredients for moral systems and judgments. Premack and Premack (2003) focus on human infants.

They propose that much of human cognitive architecture is composed of specific "modules" which guide learning about specific domains of experience. Modules are "innate devices that guide the infant's learning in all domains that are basic to human knowledge" (p. 18). There is a physical module that guides our learning about the physical world, a psychological module that guides our learning about the animate (intentional) world, and modules for space, language, music, and number. With regard to morality, they hypothesize that there is no module, but that the sense of morality is built from three dispositions that are basic. The first is empathy, the tendency to alleviate the distress of others. The second is a tendency for children to instruct each other, a disposition they refer to as pedagogy. And the third is assigning value, specifically assigning value to social interactions. Touching and caressing are positive, hitting and pushing are negative. These judgments can be witnessed in children as young as ten months old, according to the authors.

I agree completely with Cosmides (and de Waal) that we do not enter this world as empty moral vessels to be filled by our social environments. There is structure there that guides our interaction with this environment and that shapes and colors the growth of our beliefs and values. The precise description of this structure is a matter of controversy, but one element that I take as non-controversial is that one piece of it is the innate tendency to differentiate good from bad, soothing from disturbing, positive from negative, approachable from aversive. Sugar is sweet and skin punctures are painful. Other evaluative judgments may be only slightly less hard-wired.

Bibliography

Boyd, R., and P. J. Richerson. 1985. *Culture and the Evolutionary Process.* Chicago: University of Chicago Press.

Campbell, D. T. 1975. "On the Conflicts Between Biological and Social Evolution and Between Psychology and Moral Tradition. *American Psychologist* 30: 1103–1126.

Cosmides, L. 1989. The Logic of Social Exchange: Has Natural Selection Shaped How Humans Reason? Studies with the Wason Selection Task. *Cognition* 31: 187–276.

Cosmides, L., and J. Tooby. 2004. "Knowing Thyself: The Evolutionary Psychology of Moral Reasoning and Moral Sentiments," in *Business, Science, and Ethics*, ed. R. E. Freeman and Patricia H. Werhane (Charlottesville, Va.: Philosophy Documentation Center): 91–128.

Flack, J. C., and F. B. M. de Waal. 2004. "Monkey Business and Business Ethics: Evolutionary Origins of Human Morality," in *Business, Science, and Ethics*, ed. R. E. Freeman and Patricia H. Werhane (Charlottesville, Va.: Philosophy Documentation Center): 7–41.

Messick, D. M. 1998. "Social Categories and Business Ethics." *Business Ethics Quarterly*, The Ruffin Series, No. 1: 149–172.

Osgood, C. E., G. J. Suci, and P. H. Tannenbaum. 1957. *The Measurement of Meaning.* Urbana: University of Illinois Press.

Premack, D., and A. Premack. 2003. *Original Intelligence.* New York: McGraw-Hill.

Sedikides, C., J. Schopler, and C. A. Insko. 1998. *Intergroup Cognition and Intergroup Behavior.* Mahwah, N.J.: L. Erlbaum Associates.

Trivers, R. L. 1971. "The Evolution of Reciprocal Altruism." *Quarterly Review of Biology* 36: 35–57.

Wispe, L. G., and J. N. Thompson, Jr. 1976. The War Between the Words: Biological versus Social Evolution and Some Related Issues. *American Psychologist* 31: 341–384.

FOUNDING MORAL REASONING ON EVOLUTIONARY PSYCHOLOGY: A CRITIQUE AND AN ALTERNATIVE

Saras D. Sarasvathy

Abstract: In this paper I develop a critique of the strong adaptationist view inherent in the work of Leda Cosmides and John Tooby, as presented at the Ruffin Lectures series in 2002. My critique proceeds in two stages. In the first stage, I advance arguments as to why I find the particular adaptation story that the authors advance for their experimental results unpersuasive even when I fully accept the value of their experimental results. In the second stage, I grant them their adaptation story and critique the implications of such stories for business ethics and for future research. In sum, I argue against recasting key problems in the social sciences to fit the use of tools developed in the so-called "hard" sciences. Instead, I urge that we deal with these problems on their own terms, i.e. through their basis in and dependence on deliberate social action.

Cosmides and Tooby (2000) seek to clarify and illuminate our understanding of how we reason—particularly how we reason about social interaction laced with moral intonations. The method they have chosen involves connecting laboratory experiments with some evidence from the larger body of evolutionary theories including paleo-anthropology and behavioral ecology. My critique of their position has to do with the semantic bankruptcy of second-hand syntax borrowed from the physical and biological sciences and with the fact that such a debt seduces us to completely ignore history. Economics as social physics has for a long time done disservice both to society and physics, by disregarding the variety and reality of empirical evidence in the social sphere on the one hand, and on the other, by failing to acknowledge that physical concepts such as "entropy" "invariance" and "symmetry principles" lose their precision and become meaningless when carried over into what William James would call the "blooming buzzing confusion" of human affairs. Similarly the conceptualization of "Economics as evolutionary biology" or business ethics as consequences of evolutionary adaptation endangers our roots in historical reality while at the same time falling prey to an oversimplified, tautological and superficial understanding of evolutionary adaptation. Moreover, such oversimplification understates the pluralistic views of eminent evolution theorists, including those of Darwin himself, particularly with regard to the richness and variety of non-adaptive and non-selective explanations.

In the interest of limiting the scope of this article, I am going to undertake a critique of just one example of the "ethics as adaptation" story—i.e., the cheater detection mechanism (Cosmides and Tooby, 2000). But, with minor modifications, all my arguments can be applied to the other mechanisms and subroutines in the studies. I have organized my critique in two stages. In the first stage, I will advance arguments as to why I find the particular adaptation story that the authors advance for their experimental results unpersuasive even when I fully accept the value of their experimental results. In the second stage, I will grant them their adaptation story and critique the implications of such stories for business ethics and for future research.

I concur with, and congratulate the authors on their experimental results. While the Wason tests used in their experiments are novel and interesting, their results are entirely in line with earlier experimental work in cognition and decision making *without invoking an adaptation story*. Cognitive scientists and others have known since the fifties—if not earlier—that problem isomorphs or changes in the domain of logically similar problems do create differential outcomes. This can be seen even in toy problems such as the Tower of Hanoi and the fisherman problems. In other words, problem representations matter (Simon, 1975). Their results are also in line with those of Robin Dunbar who showed that we are better at dealing with social interaction than with scientific argumentation (1996).

To summarize the results of over forty years of related experimental work— we suck (if I may use the technical term!) at solving problems based on formal calculi such as the ones involving constrained optimization or propositional logic or any experientially meaningless problem representation. So what can we conclude from this in terms of the adaptationist story? To begin to answer that, let us examine closely just one of the numerous threads in the tangle of experiments over the last forty years. In the 60s and 70s Bar-Hillel (1980), Tversky and Kahnemann (1982), and others conclusively established the general incompetence of humans in solving statistical choice problems involving base rates. In short, when problems are cast in terms of choosing balls from bins, or deciding which doors to open and other stylized scenarios, human beings consistently ignored base rates. Yet as Gigerenzer, Hell, and Blank (1988) showed, when the same base-rate fallacy problem was cast as a football (soccer) wager, the proportion of people who do take into account base rates increased dramatically. The moral is not that we evolved to wager on football games. The sober lesson is that meaningful framing based on informative descriptions rooted in previous experiences does a lot more to help solve problems than precise axiomatics or stylistic representations of logical rigor. As Gigerenzer argues rather simply and elegantly, we are capable of "intuitive statistics" whether such an intuition "evolved" in the adaptationist sense or not. Arguments such as Gigerenzer's, so long as they rest on the *sufficiency* of evolutionary explanation, may be useful irrespective of the "truth" of their adaptationist claims. The complications of adaptive *necessity* however, whether embodied in a collection of subroutines or neural circuitry or genes or whatever else, are merely excess material, cluttering our explanations and getting in the way of our understanding.

So without further belaboring the point about our incompetence in using content-free formal logic to any desirable extent, let us examine a different aspect of the experimental results in this study. May be the key result here is not that we are bad at content-free logics, but that we are surprisingly good at "cheater detection"—which is after all the real issue at hand in this study. Let us for the moment accept the result—i.e. the existence of a particular "subroutine" in our brains. Does it follow that this mechanism—or more accurately, ability—adaptively evolved over thousands of millennia to solve particular social interaction problems such as the rather implausible ones used in the study?

I submit that the authors make a case for this through the following three points:

1. Throughout our evolutionary history, humans have had to solve similar social contract problems;
2. Cheaters can benefit by not keeping to their end of the bargains (get some thing for nothing); and,
3. People who can detect cheaters have an advantage over those who cannot.

Ergo, we, the survivors come equipped with a mechanism to detect cheaters. This may make for an adaptation *story*—and I will argue later that even the story is implausible at best. But it certainly does not make for a good adaptation *theory*. In the simplest case, as I understand it, a true adaptation theory (not story) begins with a heterogeneous population. The population may be grouped into two sets. At any point in time, we can associate an average numerical fitness with each set; the fitness is typically computed based on a set of common measurements (energy consumption, gestation period etc.). If one set has a higher fitness than the other, then other things being equal, it is possible to show that the members of that set may be expected to have greater reproductive success. If, for the time under consideration, we can explain the difference in proportions of the two sets as a result of the fitness values measured or estimated for that period, then we may say we have an adaptation theory. Furthermore, it is not enough for an adaptation theory to show something exists—it has to be able to trace its adaptive history as a changing distribution of the population over time.

Typically, the adaptive explanation is couched in terms of regression analysis (this can provide an explanation based on observables rather than on nebulous concepts like "fitness"), but there are weaker alternatives like game theoretic modeling, stochastic modeling, and/or computer simulations. In using these though, there are some important caveats: What is being explained cannot be used as an explanatory variable. Mere existence is not evidence of superior fitness. Superior fitness does not guarantee survival. Also, today's success may be someone's dinner tomorrow! In sum, evolution is about sufficient conditions for survival not necessary ones.

The adaptive explanation for the results of the study under consideration here does not meet the criteria for an adaptation theory. For example, I've seen no proof for the minimal requirement that the ability to solve Wason problems is inheritable. Or for the requirement that this ability leads to improved reproductive success. But perhaps I am unfairly pushing the argument beyond its scope. As the authors have explained elsewhere, inheritability is not an issue for their studies since they merely use the adaptationist explanation to generate hypotheses. If so, then what is the basis of their claim, "I will present experimental findings suggesting that our minds contain evolved mechanisms specialized for reasoning about problems"? Furthermore, using a theory to generate hypotheses that are not falsified in the results is the same as using the theory for explaining the results, especially since no alternative explanations based on history are even considered or explored. And even more importantly, no alternative hypotheses involving explicit *design* of social contracts to detect and punish cheaters based on collective historical experience were generated and eliminated. Hence I will now try and develop an alternate hypothesis based on history and social action rather than biology.

To do that, I will release the authors from the rigor required of an adaptation *theory* and examine their arguments as a *story* of adaptation instead. Here's how such a story might go: Imagine a group of pre-historic hominoids, some of whose brains are "programmed" with the cheater detection subroutine, or with punitive sentiments against non-participants, and others whose brains are not so "programmed." Then according to the adaptationist argument, the ones with the subroutine have an evolutionary advantage and over millennia increase in numbers in the population until the others who do not have the subroutine become virtually extinct. Fast forwarding through to the present, I am simply overwhelmed by the historical evidence that the exact opposite to the predicted outcome seems to have occurred. According to Thomas McCraw, (1997) as late as the eighteenth century, less than four percent of homo sapiens appear to have managed to convince the other ninety-six percent of us that we should hand over the products of our work and even the very essentials of our freedom to their will and disposition. The few cheaters in our midst appear to have successfully sold the majority of us a variety of bad goods and broken promises. Be it the divine rights of kings, the absolute rule of the husband in the household, well-deserved incarnations of the higher castes in India, or the sub-human status of African slaves in the New World, most of us have been unable to detect the "cheaters" in our midst. For practically all of recorded history, a few political charlatans in cahoots with a handful of religious leaders have sold us "requirements unfulfilled" and have paid for our lives and liberties with "benefits undelivered." It is not all that better today. Whether it is divorce rates or dot-com bubbles, we are still for the most part unable to detect "cheaters" in any non-trivial sense. So based on the historical evidence, I could argue that we do not have any evolved cheater detection mechanism at all and that is why we need to develop them through conscious action, such as collective bargaining, legislative initiatives, contractual due diligence and other explicit mechanisms of fair trade *designed* for defining and detecting cheaters, not evolved in any sense in our brains.

What about the counter-argument that the authors are not claiming that the presumed cheater detection mechanisms are omniscient, or capable of resolving complex social contract problems? But then, of what use is a cheater-detection mechanism that can solve toy Wason problems, but is incapable of detecting cheaters who, by spinning unverifiable social contracts, can obtain significant advantages including *reproductive* advantages for themselves (for example, a simple examination of caste rules in India shows very clearly how higher castes have claimed such advantages). All in all, the historical evidence is overwhelmingly against any adaptationist arguments to explain the laboratory results in this study.

But, of course, the results stand on their own and need explanation. What would an alternative explanation of the results be? Let us look at the particular experiment involving the transportation to Boston as opposed to the stolen watch. The reason I fail to detect the logical flaw while solving the transportation to Boston problem is that it is content-irrelevant and even meaningless in my own previous experience: it is reminiscent of calculus problems that urge you to solve problems involving cooling rates of cups of coffee, or sliding ladders or the crazy fly oscillating between trains heading for a collision! But when someone takes my watch and gyps me for the price, I can easily detect it because both my own previous experience and my memory of our collective experience in history points to this being a cheater problem. Since trade and contractual exchange constitute one of the oldest phenomenon in all cultures—even tribes at war with each other in ancient times would stop fighting at the end of each day so they could trade with each other!—trade matters to us. Taking the cab or train does not matter all that much—in fact when going to Boston all I care about is not having to drive.

And so most human beings would "get" any problem couched in simple terms of trade or contracts or promises to be fulfilled, with one major caveat. Fair trade assumes that value can be measured and clearly verified upon delivery. When the exact same problem of trade involves quantities such as martyrdom and loyalty and marital fidelity, we will find that the so-called cheater detection subroutine fails us miserably. This can easily be verified by conducting the same experiment as the current authors did except replacing the propositional calculus based descriptive rules with contracts involving non-measurable and unverifiable quantities and subsequently using measurable and verifiable quantities such as dollars. That is exactly the task of market transactions, to design mechanisms to make services rendered and benefits derived easier to measure and verify and trade in.

Therefore, the falsifiable alternative hypothesis I am putting forward here is: *When quantities to a contract are difficult to measure and verify, people will fail to spot cheaters; when the same quantities are made verifiable and measurable, they will quickly develop new cheater detection mechanisms—right there in the lab—in social time, not evolutionary time.* Furthermore, the more tightly tied the quantities and qualities to be measured are to our actual *lived* experience—i.e., our own past history and the collective cultural history we are raised in, the quicker we will develop cheater detection mechanisms. To give the most recent and raw of all such examples, if the young suicide bombers in the Middle East could somehow *verify* whether the fundamentalist cleric really delivers heaven and sixty-three virgins in exchange for their so-called martyrdom, we would find that they will very quickly develop a "cheater" subroutine that keeps them from making the trade in the first place. In sum, the development of this "mechanism" or ability need not be a consequence of millions of years of evolution, but a simple consequence of Lamarckian learning originating in our immersion in particular social groups.

Besides the inherent pitfalls of transferring arguments from biological adaptation and the massive historical evidence against it, there is another set of arguments why the adaptationist explanation for the results observed in the study is not very compelling. Recall the observation that Borges (1962) made in his essay "The fearful sphere of Pascal." He said: "It may be that universal history is the history of the intonations given a handful of metaphors." Ever since we have posited the existence of the brain, scholars have used metaphors to describe its workings and how it came to be. And with the supreme genius of the obvious, have (perhaps understandably) used the hottest and hippest of the tools of their time as their primary metaphors. The brain is a clock in the age of the clock; genes are messages and the brain the telegraph in the age of Darwin and Bell; and of course, the mind is but the hardware implementation of evolved subroutines in the age of the Turing machine and the double helix. In other words, it is one thing to consider an information processing system as a useful way to theorize about the mind; and quite another to posit actual subroutines that "explain" its functioning. To paraphrase the words of Herbert Simon, the author of the metaphor of mind as information processing system: "The mind is an ink blot. It is whatever you see in it."

Furthermore, even if any such subroutines do exist, it still does not follow (as I argued above) that they were evolved specifically to solve any particular problem. Also, even if they *did* evolve to solve particular problems, there may still be a variety of other alternatives that impact their existence and function. In the most rigorous of adaptation theories, proof for the existence of particular mechanisms or subroutines may at best illustrate their evolutionary sufficiency— proving evolutionary necessity is another matter altogether. In fact, better scholars than I, including eminent geneticists and evolutionary scientists such as Gould and Lewontin have powerfully argued against the Cosmides and Tooby (1994: 328) claim that "there is only one class of problems that evolution produces mechanisms for solving: *adaptive* problems." For example the mechanisms may be able to identify and solve new problems that had nothing to do with their evolution; or they may have no function whatsoever since the problem they evolved to solve is no longer relevant.

Evolutionary theorists (For example, Gould and Lewontin, 1979; Gould and Vrba, 1982) have identified several non-adaptive mechanisms including exaptations, serendipities, and redundancies. In the spirit of reasoning through metaphor, let us look at the history of technology as an analogue to the history of evolved "mechanisms" in the brain. The history of technological evolution too is filled with exaptations, serendipities, and redundancies. To give you just one example for each of these non-adaptive mechanisms: Viagra was developed while in search of anti-coagulants (exaptation); penicillin because someone neglected cleaning out a lab dish (serendipity); and the VCR embodies a collection of innumerable features that no one ever uses (redundancy). Similarly I could argue that any evolutionary history of neurological subroutines is also most likely strewn with exaptations, serendipities, and redundancies. So where is the compelling case to believe that the cheater detection mechanism or any other subroutine has adaptively evolved to solve any particular problem in our evolutionary history? All that the results tell us is that for reasons we can only speculate about, we are very good at solving social interaction problems as opposed to other logically equivalent problems that do not make sense in terms of our life experiences and that we do not in some way care about.

At this point, I would like to move to the second phase of my critique where I examine the consequences of *accepting* the adaptationist argument for business ethics and our future research. If we accept the idea that evidence for the existence of any particular "mechanism" or "subroutine" or a "grammar of social interchange" is also evidence for its adaptive usefulness in evolutionary selection, we fall into the implicit Panglossian ethic of the "just-so-story." Such an ethic, and I insist that it is indeed an ethic, goes as follows: *If something has adaptively evolved into existence, it deserves to exist—it has in some way "earned" its existence in an evolutionary sense. Otherwise, by default, it would not have come to be.* Translated into modern economics, this ethic would imply that since Enron has made it to the top ten of the Fortune 500 companies, it deserves to exist and may even be emulated, instead of being summarily eliminated.

While this might appear as an unfair flippancy on my part in interpreting the arguments in the paper in favor of an adaptationist explanation, I would urge that the implication I derive is not that far-fetched. If our rational powers or subroutines for reasoning about particular domains are inevitably and exclusively created through adaptive evolution, and not through learned historical experience and ongoing meaningful exchanges of ideas and goods, what would be the basis for our ethics in general and business ethics in particular?

In a powerful, but non-technical thesis titled "Biology as ideology" R. C. Lewontin (1991) argues my case far more eloquently and in greater detail. And the concluding paragraph of his thesis lays out for us the inescapability of social action as the primary basis for the creation both of our individual identities as well as the spatial and temporal contexts within which those identities get forged and become meaningful: *History far transcends any narrow limitations that are claimed for either the power of genes or the power of the environment to circumscribe us. Like the House of Lords that destroyed its own power to limit the political development of Britain in the successive Reform Acts to which it assented, so the genes, in making possible the development of human consciousness, have surrendered their power both to determine the individual and its environment. They have been replaced by an entirely new level of causation, that of social interaction with its own laws and its own nature that can be understood and explored only through that unique form of experience, social action.*

To look to biology or other so-called "hard" sciences to tell us what to do in the social sphere is (to paraphrase McCloskey, 2000) to busy ourselves with games in the sand-box while time runs out on the human condition. As ethicists and economists, we can only so long shirk the hard chores that need to be tackled in our own domain by distracting ourselves with the cool toys fashioned by other disciplines. The physicist's metaphors ask us to equilibrate between forces outside our control; the biologist's to adapt to an environment not of our making; and the theologian's to answer to a divinity we cannot question. I suggest it is time we took ownership of the problems in our disciplines and allowed the problems to drive our search for solutions instead of fabricating pseudo-problems that we can then pound into alignment with the tools others have developed for other purposes. I posit social action—organized through conversation, community, and commerce—as a powerful alternative tool to the physicist's equilibrium, the biologist's fitness, and the theologian's salvation for the conduct and future course of human affairs. And in the particular realm of business ethics, I hope we can embrace economics predominantly as a historical science that wields linguistic tools through which we can negotiate better societies into existence—both in the academy and the world outside it.

In the hope of such a possibility for the uses of our reason, whatever its origins may be, it might be worth re-reading the poets.

"Possibilities"
A week ago on longer clocks than ours
a supernova in Orion lit
the sky like a full moon. The dinosaurs
might have looked up and made a note of it
but didn't, and the next night it blinked out.
The next day from a metaphoric tree
my father's father's beetle brow and snout
poked through the leaves. Just yesterday at three
he spoke his first word. And an hour ago
invented God. And, in the last hour, Doubt.

I, because my only clock's too slow
for less than hope, hope he will not fall out
of time and space at least for one more week
of the long clock. Think, given time enough,
what language he might yet learn to speak
when the last hairs have withered from his scruff,
when his dark brows unknit and he looks out,
when the last ape has grunted from his throat.

—John Ciardi

Acknowledgment

I would like to thank Ed Freeman for giving me the opportunity to write this critique; Anil Menon for incisively reviewing several earlier drafts and being an invaluable comrade-in-arms; and, Ed Hartman for providing thought-provoking critical comments that have helped re-shape the final version in important ways.

Bibliography

Bar-Hillel, M. 1980. "The Base-Rate Fallacy in Probability Judgments." *Acta Psychologica* 44: 211–233.

Borges, Jorge Luis. 1962. *Labyrinths: Selected Stories & Other Writings*. New Directions.

Cosmides, Leda, and John Tooby. 1994. "Better than Rational: Evolutionary Psychology and the Invisible Hand." *The American Economic Review* 84(2) (May): 327–332.

_____. 2000. "The Cognitive Neuroscience of Social Reasoning." In *The New Cognitive Neurosciences*, ed. Michael S. Gazzaniga. MIT Press.

Dunbar, Robin. 1996. *Grooming, Gossip and the Evolution of Language*. Cambridge, Mass.: Harvard University Press.

Gigerenzer, Gerd, Wolfgang Hell, and Hartmut Blank. 1988. "Presentation and Content: The Use of Base Rates as a Continuous Variable." *Journal of Experimental Psychology: Human Perception and Performance* 14: 513–525.

Gould, Stephen J., and Richard C. Lewontin. 1979. "The Spandrels of San Marco and the Panglossian Paradigm: A Critique of the Adaptationist Programme." *Proceedings of the Royal Society of London* 205: 281–288.

Gould, Stephen J., and Elizabeth S. Vrba. 1982. "Exaptation: A Missing Term in the Science of Form." *Paleobiology* 8(1): 4–15.

Lewontin, Richard C. 1991. *Biology as Ideology: The Doctrine of DNA*. New York: Harper Collins.

McCloskey, Deirdre. 2000. *How to Be Human (Though an Economist)*. Ann Arbor: University of Michigan Press.

McCraw, Thomas K. 1997. *Creating Modern Capitalism*. Cambridge, Mass.: Harvard University Press.

Simon, Herbert A. 1975. "The Functional Equivalence of Problem Solving Skills." *Cognitive Psychology* 7: 268–272.

Tversky, Amos, and Daniel Kahneman. 1982. "Judgment and Uncertainty: Heuristics and Biases." In *Judgment and Uncertainty*, ed. D. Kahneman, P. Slovic, and A. Tversky. New York: Cambridge University Press: 3–20.

THE EVOLUTIONARY FIRM
AND ITS MORAL (DIS)CONTENTS

William C. Frederick

Abstract: The business firm, called here the Evolutionary Firm, is shown to be a phenomenon of nature. The firm's motives, organization, productivity, strategy, and moral significance are a direct outgrowth of natural evolution. Its managers, directors, and employees are natural agents enacting and responding to biological, physical, and ecological impulses inherited over evolutionary time from ancient human ancestors. The Evolutionary Firm's moral posture is a function of its economizing success, competitive drive, quest for market dominance, social contracting skills, and the neural algorithms found in the minds of its executives and directing managers. Behavioral, organizational, and societal contradictions arise from the normal expression of these nature-based executive impulses, so that the business corporation cannot simultaneously satisfy society's moral expectations and perform its nature-dictated economic functions.

Introduction and Overview

This paper outlines a concept of the Evolutionary Firm and its moral significance. The business firm, to be called the Evolutionary Firm (EF), is shown to be a phenomenon of nature. This is tantamount to saying that the business firm's motives, productivity, organization, strategy, markets, and its moral significance are a function of—a direct outgrowth of—evolutionary natural forces. The people who work within the Evolutionary Firm—owners, managers, employees—are themselves natural agents responding to a variety of biological, physical, and ecological impulses that were laid down in the genetic substrate, inherited from human ancestors over long periods of evolutionary time, elaborated through successive generations of the *Homo* genus, and channeled to various ends and purposes by human culture. Their decisions and policies are molded, sometimes haphazardly, other times effectively, by complex environmental natural forces over which they exert little or no direct rational control but which require highly attuned pragmatic skills. The normative significance of the EF—its moral deficits and credits—is understood only after peeling back the successive organizational and behavioral strata laid down through evolutionary time to reveal the values, ethics, and moral precepts left standing by natural selection.[1]

The Evolutionary Firm: An Overview

All business firms—large or small, domestically sheltered or globally exposed, giant corporation or neighborhood proprietor, prospector for minerals or producer of complex software, hawker of goods or service provider—are Evolutionary Firms. They are made so by responding to insistent, unyielding pressures of nature that impel them to be what they are and to do what they do. Natural selection has implanted motives deep within the firm's core structure, has given it the gift of creativity and productivity, has laid down organizational pathways, has enabled it to maneuver (though perilously) across competitive landscapes, and, *mirabile dictu*, has imbued it with a troubling, vexatious moral impulse.

Figure 1
THE EVOLUTIONARY FIRM'S FIVE CORE FUNCTIONS

MOTIVATOR/DRIVER The central motive of business operations
INNOVATOR/GENERATOR The source of innovation and productivity
ORGANIZER/COORDINATOR The firm's organizational systems
ENABLER/STRATEGIZER Strategic management to achieve business goals
MORALIZER/VALUATOR Moral impulses operative within the firm

The Evolutionary Firm therefore displays five principal operations and core functions (see Figure 1). The Motivator/Driver function and the Moralizer/Valuator function will be emphasized in this account, the former because it conditions all other activities and features of the EF, the latter because it expresses the EF's moral stature. The other three functions—Innovator-Generator, Organizer-Coordinator, and Enabler-Strategizer, especially their bearing upon the firm's moral status—are discussed briefly later in the paper.

Lying behind, supporting, and activating each of these five functions are distinctive, identifiable natural processes that enable the firm to operate as an entity and to carry out its distinctive role in human society (see Figure 2, p. 148):

Thermodynamics defines and sustains the principal business motive of economizing.
Symbolic cerebral codes and programs drive business productivity and innovation.

Two natural components—*symbolic language networks* and *coercive power systems*—make up the firm's organizational architecture.
Complex ecosystem dynamics dictate the firm's search for a sustainable strategy.
Embedded neural algorithms (the brain's "hard-wiring") activate conflicting moral impulses within the firm.

To anticipate much of what is to follow, the paper's central thesis can be put this way: *The confluence and contradictions among these underlying natural forces produce the distinctive, peculiar moral proclivities and ethical dilemmas of the Evolutionary Firm.*

Two Theoretical Puzzles

Before going on to describe how the Motivator-Driver shapes the actions and policies of the business firm, a precautionary note is in order. The concept of the Evolutionary Firm being proposed here rests on two very basic premises which must be proven or demonstrated if the concept is to be valid. Each can be put in the form of a question.

Is the Evolutionary Firm subject to natural selection? We know that *organisms* evolve through a combination of genetic transmission, genetic mixing, random mutations, and natural accidents and events, all occurring as the organism interacts with its environment. Those traits that promote an organism's reproduction and gene replication are selected for over evolutionary time. Can a similar kind of organic process exert influence on business firms, shaping their form and function? If so, what are the organic components on which natural selection works? Are they the people, i.e., the human organisms, who are identified with the firm? If they are in fact the firm's organic constituents, does natural selection operate on them as *individuals,* or as *a coalition* of organisms? This is a question that has long dogged Darwinian theorists: what unit of life does natural selection work on: Genes? Individuals? Groups? (Wright 1994: 186–188; Dennett 1995: 320–331; Ridley 1996: 175–188)

This puzzle is equivalent to asking whether the firm exists apart from the participants in it. Can "the firm," as opposed to the people in it, be seen, or heard, or touched? Does "it" move around, do things, interact with "its" environment? Is "it" born? Does "it" die? Is "it" alive in an organic sense? If it is none of these things, then how can it be said to be organic and thus subject to natural selection pressures? The firm's individual organic people display these traits, but can the same be said for the firm when it is considered as an entity *sui generis*? What is the evolutionary "it-ness" of a business firm? What is genetic or organic about the firm?

The position throughout the remainder of this paper is that the firm has organic (and nonorganic) parts but is not itself organic or genic. The firm's organic core is a coalition—an alliance, a collective, a team—of biological

Figure 2
THE EVOLUTIONARY FIRM'S NATURAL SUBSTRATE

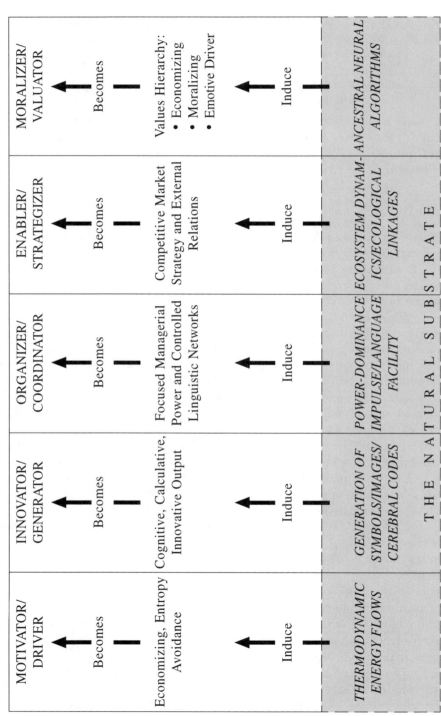

agents (i.e., people) who act collectively and symbolically as an adaptive unit, displaying a suite of organic behaviors and interacting with environment as do all organisms, and is thus subject to selection. The human members of the coalition include owners, directors, managers, employees, consultants, and others who enable the firm to do its work. In most firms, especially the larger ones, multiple coalitions exist, often with overlapping memberships; ideally, they cooperate in pursuing the firm's goals but frequently compete with each other. As biological agents acting in behalf of the firm, these human (organic) coalitions are subject to natural selection pressures. More will be said about the adaptive behavior of these coalitions later on.

The second major theoretical issue to be resolved concerns the moral traits of the Evolutionary Firm. *Can the values and moral principles operative in the Evolutionary Firm be a product of nature?* More generally, is morality, or a moral potential, implicit in nature and evolution? On what grounds can it be said that what humans now call "morality" is only another manifestation of evolutionary processes operating over long time spans?

It is well established that a wide range of biological organisms, including humans, engage in behaviors that display moral potential (Ridley 1996; Flack and de Waal 2000). Reciprocated altruistic acts, support of close kin, agreements among strangers to cooperate in social exchange, symbiotic linkages among cooperating organisms—all of these fall within the meaning given by humans to "moral" behavior. That the individual organic agents who populate the business firm are capable of engaging in such normatively tinged activities cannot be doubted. Can the same thing be said of the coalition of biological agents (owners, managers, employees, et al.) who inhabit the Evolutionary Firm? Are the moral-like effects generated between *individuals* also reproduced within the *coalitional* behavior of the biological agents who make up the firm? If so, is there an emergent quality of the firm's behavior that is simultaneously a function of natural processes and recognizable as morality?

If this were so, it would not be equivalent to saying that nature defines morality or that it is itself moral. Moral value (and its converse) is a human conceptual invention, an assigned quality, made possible by human judgment, which is itself a natural process. Morality is not *in* nature but emerges from judgments about natural processes that affect human welfare.[2] At the same time, the judgments that *are* morality are themselves a function of identifiable natural forces—in this case, the brain's cognitive and emotive capabilities—that make such judgments possible. Morality is in this sense a reflexive relationship between natural process and human judgment. This moral reflexivity recognizes no impenetrable boundary separating moral judgment from nature and is neither hampered nor restrained by such an imagined barrier. Human moral judgment, being a function of nature, is easily at home with its procreator.

The argument here will be that evolutionary change produces biologically adaptive (and maladaptive) behaviors whose consequences are judged by humans to be either moral or immoral. Beyond and in addition to these moral proclivities associated directly with organic adaptation are the many ethical themes generated by human experience as lived in highly diverse sociocultural settings. However, these cultural themes, too, are subject to a natural evolutionary calculus, to be briefly noted later on.

The Firm's Motivator/Driver Function

Outwitting Entropy through Economizing

The primary natural force responsible for business motives is found within the operation of thermodynamic laws. These physical processes set the basic conditions under which all living organisms exist and sustain themselves over time. Put as simply as possible, all life entities must acquire and process sufficient energy to begin life, build their basic cellular structure, and develop whatever growth potential is present in their genetic makeup. By capturing energy and incorporating it within themselves, living beings are responding to what physicists call the first and second laws of thermodynamics (Coveney and Highfield 1990; Goldstein and Goldstein 1993; Haynie 2001).

The first law says that the total amount of energy present in any closed system remains constant through time, thereby leaving it to the organism's skill and ability to capture enough energy for its purposes. The classic statement of thermodynamics laws, developed during the nineteenth century, posits a closed system containing a constant amount of energy. As will be subsequently explained and argued, this stricture is relaxed in the present account, inasmuch as few of the life units and their ecosystems to be discussed, including the business firm, are closed but are instead open to their respective environments. This openness becomes a key element in their survival, enabling them to import and export energy.

The second law says that the use of energy always converts it into some less useful form. The tendency of energy to be degraded until it is no longer available to do work is called *entropy*. All life entities, including the business firm, are driven to find and use energy.[3] In doing so, they produce entropy in the form of degraded energy, wastes, and pollution. Within the living space firms occupy, their constant need is to absorb energy, using it to build and maintain an organizational structure, and letting the energy drive the firm onward, striving to stay ahead of the entropy wave that they themselves are helping to create. Entropy constantly bears down upon all living entities. Evading or avoiding or postponing it is essential.[4]

The search for energy to exceed entropy and for organizational order to repel disorder and dissolution is ceaseless in the life of the Evolutionary Firm because entropy carries the danger of increasing faster than the firm can absorb energy to do its work. This means that a business firm can be overwhelmed by entropy—*unless it can export its entropy into the surrounding environment*. In that case, it can be someone else's problem. The greater the order created in the firm to promote its goals and deter internal entropy, the more disorder and entropy are created in the firm's environment: decimated rainforests, depleted soils, ripped up landscapes, clear-cut forests, degraded water sources, fouled air, "downsized" workers, junked obsolete technology, weakened indigenous industries, corrupted civil governments, etc.[5] The firm, in this sense, is at war with society. The only way a firm can sustain itself over time is to have a favorable energy-to-entropy ratio. *To achieve such a favorable ratio is the central driving force—the core motivator—of business activity.* Business's "bottom line" is set by thermodynamic nature, not by accountants, stockholders, or Wall Street's financial analysts, who act only as nature's calculators and numerators.

The formula then would be: Take advantage of the first law to acquire the needed energy. Then outwit the second law by increasing the firm's efficiency and dumping your degraded energy where you don't have to deal with it any more. By doing that, you can have your energy cake and eat it too. That is precisely what business firms do, or at least try to do, all the time. It's called *economizing*: an attempt to acquire enough energy (in the form of capital, technology, natural resources, people, information, skills) to produce something of marketable value (goods, services, information), using revenues and borrowed funds to build and maintain an organizational structure and expand the firm's operations, while minimizing costs.

Economizing is the core bedrock function of business firms everywhere. As a life entity—as a coalition of biological agents acting collectively—the firm must economize if it is to exist, function, and grow. In that respect, it mirrors the selfsame economizing activity that is found in every living organism. It draws energy in, uses it productively, and expels the entropic wastes outward into its environment. All organic life taken collectively does this repeatedly. Indeed, it is an imperative if there is to be life at all. Within the Evolutionary Firm itself, economizing is such a powerful, unyielding, natural imperative that it takes precedence over all other incentives and motives. Presenting a favorable "bottom line" is every manager's goal. Shareholders expect, Wall Street presses for, institutional holders demand, and directors yearn for positive economizing results.

The larger significance of business economizing, aside from its importance for each individual firm, is that the societies who host such firms depend upon this vital process if there is to be human collective life. In this regard, it is possible to say that the economizing business firm is one of nature's most brilliant, though flawed, inventions.

Thermodynamic Selection versus Natural Selection

From a thermodynamics point of view, a business firm is an aggregation of energy forms carrying out economizing functions. The energy may take several different forms. It can be the *organic energy*, mental and physical, of the people who work there. Or a firm's energy can reside partly in its *physical structures, buildings, and equipment. Process materials* such as electricity, water, air, geological derivatives, organic substances/derivatives make up another part of the energy inventory, for all of these make work possible. One active energy component is *technology*, both physical machinery and abstract symbolic, computerized processes. Add in *organizational structure/pathways/linkages*, and *information/ knowledge/data banks* through which the firm does its work. If the firm is to economize successfully, the costs of all of this incoming and aggregated energy— labor, materials, information, capital, technology—must be minimized, as must the costs of using the energy for production, organization, and distribution.

As noted earlier, the firm as a whole is not an organism, although it has organic parts. Unlike its organic constituents, the firm has no DNA, no immune system, no tissue repair, no central nervous system. Its organizational economizing is extra-cellular and extra-organismic in form and structure while still employing the various kinds of biophysical energy it acquires and controls. Firms lack the reproductive-replicative functions of cellular-organic entities, and in that sense the firm departs dramatically from the organic norm of generational genetic succession. Its goal is simpler and more stark: to push entropy away from itself, as far away and for as long as possible. The firm shares this goal with all living organic entities who could not themselves live to pass their genes on to future generations if they did not first meet the test posed by entropy.

The firm's active *organic* core is a coalitional undertaking, a group of interacting (and at times competing and quarrelsome) biological agents whose collective efforts seek economizing results. While acting in behalf of the firm, these interlinked biological agents and the activities they undertake are subject to selection pressures. They may succeed or fail, survive or perish, be selected for or selected against, face the same entropic degradation as any organic being that tries to economize.

The kind of selection that operates on the business firm as a whole is what I shall call *thermodynamic selection*, which occurs when the firm either successfully responds to entropic pressures by economizing, or fails to do so. In this sense, the entire firm—all of its functioning parts, its technology, its organizational systems, its resources, and not just its individual organic components—is being selected for or against. The same challenge confronts all organic entities, including the very first ones to have appeared on Earth: "[T]hese first beings would have metabolized and incorporated energy, nutrients, water, and salts into their developing selves . . . to postpone return to thermodynamic equilibrium" (Margulis and Sagan 1995: 62). Failure of the firm to economize leads to a loss of order (financial and organizational) and its subsequent demise, called "bankruptcy" in the business lexicon, or "thermodynamic equilibrium" in physics. When this occurs to *a living organism*, it is called *natural selection* and may be traceable to a genome lacking some important adaptive trait. *Thermodynamic selection*, on the other hand, affects *all organized entities* whether they are living or nonliving, while natural selection occurs only among biological organisms. Thermodynamic selection is the broader, overarching (and primordial) process, leaving natural selection to be seen as one variety in a larger system of evolutionary selection.[6]

The Growth Imperative

A thermodynamic specter haunts the lives of all who occupy places within and outside the Evolutionary Firm—its directors, managers, employees, stakeholders, and dependent communities. Because the EF, as a successful economizer, may generate entropy in proportions equaling or even exceeding the levels of incoming energy, information, and order, it feels the pressure of thermodynamic selection keenly. It risks having its pollutants outrun its production, its costs exceed its revenues. Howsoever efficient its use of energy, entropic wastes may pile up at an even faster pace. As technology and information (other forms of energy) seem to lift it out of the entropic slough, the firm's organizational systems may (and often do) impede the acceptance of the new technologies while information overload (e.g., torrents of e-mail messages) clogs communications and usage channels. Order and regularity may slide toward disorder and chaos. As economizing flags and entropy looms, excess personnel are let go ("downsized"), inefficient plants are closed or moved to low-cost nonunionized areas or Third World locales, services are outsourced, budgets are trimmed, managers are put on notice to reduce costs—or else.

Entropy is a voracious beast with an unlimited appetite. Feeding its maw is a case of hope struggling against fate. Vaguely but uneasily aware they are up against an implacable enemy, the EF's managers must search for ways to enhance productivity while reducing or foregoing costs. They turn first to expansive growth. Their laboratories and product development departments bring out new products; their marketing programs seek to undercut rivals by increasing the firm's market share; their global strategists explore and exploit ever-widening markets around the world; they flog their suppliers to reduce costs and speed deliveries ("just-in-time"); their shrewd financial analysts identify ways to diminish competitive pressures by merging with or acquiring competitors, or to expand through technology-sharing alliances, market-sharing joint ventures, let's-not-compete partnerships, or government bail-out deals. Presumably, though often dubiously, such expansive arrangements are claimed to enhance the firm's productivity, profits, and overall economizing. While the true verdict may be long in coming, the firm enjoys a peaceful and joyous interregnum when it is believed that the entropic monster has been sated, at least until its stomach is heard to rumble again. Expansive growth in this sense is an unavoidable extension of the EF's basic economizing impulse. Stasis risks decline and eventual dissolution.[7]

Growth of the EF can be greatly enhanced if ways can be found to discard its ever-increasing entropic load into the environment of the communities in which it operates. As its growth creates jobs and produces new products and services—thus improving the firm's and the community's economic stature— so too does the community become the EF's sink for degraded energy, setting up a two-way exchange between firm and ecosystem: energy in, energy and entropy out. The EF's borders, its outer boundaries, its membranous outlines are entirely porous and nonconfining, and in this sense the firm is an open system able both to engulf energy and belch out the unwanted degraded forms remaining after its economizing efforts that are welcomed by all. Business and society are thus locked in an inescapable embrace enjoyed by both in the short run (jobs and growth) but by neither in the longer run (when new technologies displace employees and disrupt communities, and the firm encounters the limits of entropic disposal). This flow, this firm-environment exchange literally keeps the firm viable while simultaneously showering its sphere of operations with both life-supporting jobs and new products, as well as life-diminishing entropic wastes.

Discipline and Renewal

Undergirding and reinforcing the centrality of economizing as the EF's Motivator/Driver is the training and disciplining of the business professionals who together make up the directing and controlling coalition. Corporate culture is honed, shaped, and cultivated in ways that drive home the necessity of possessing, displaying, and improving high levels of cost consciousness, a dedication to the firm's well-being even at cost to one's own self, displaying an enthusiasm for and a loyalty to the firm's policy goals and strategic moves, and on occasion concealing, distorting, and falsifying information otherwise detrimental to the firm's ongoing operations.

The list lengthens of companies successful in inculcating such values in coalition members: Enron's go-go culture was enthusiastically embraced by employees throughout the company (Banerjee 2002); Arthur Andersen's auditors were key players in preparing less-than-fully truthful financial reports for a number of firms and ordering the destruction of files sought by government investigators; Xerox, WorldCom, Dynegy, Global Crossing, Lucent Technologies, PNC Financial Services, Tyco, and between 150 and 200 other companies have "restated earnings" under pressure from regulatory officials, meaning they falsified earlier reports.

Such attitudes and values supportive of corporate culture are not infrequently found to be highly prized in management training schools of universities—a kind of MBA boot camp—where tomorrow's elite corporate soldiery ("a few good men") are sought by a company's "recruiters." Thus, fresh sources of energy flood into the lower levels of the EF, where they will be channeled to promote the company's central economizing purposes.[8]

The Firm's Moralizer/Valuator Function

The modern large-scale business corporation—the Evolutionary Firm—is imbued with behaviors and operations that acquire a moral tone as a consequence of their impact on human affairs. The firm gives moral effect to, *and* is a moral expression of, identifiable natural forces that embed a moralizing function deep within the firm's structure and being.

In thus showing a moral face, the EF draws on three distinct but overlapping kinds of innate brain-based neuronal circuitry. Evolutionary psychologists and cognitive neuroscientists often call these hard-wired circuits "algorithms," which are problem-solving or sense-making procedures. Sometimes, they are labeled "neural modules," which are groups of interacting neurons that are activated when certain distinct kinds of environmental situations arise. Those hard-wired modules most prominent in defining the firm's Moralizing/Valuator function are *economizing algorithms, symbiotic-moralizing algorithms,* and *emotive algorithms,* each to be described below. (A fourth set of algorithms expresses power-dominance predispositions, thus supporting a wide range of normatively questionable corporate actions, to be identified later on.)

A company's coalition members—its directors, managers, employees, et al.—draw upon a suite of these algorithmic possibilities, some impelling them towards economizing goals, others seeking cooperative-symbiotic actions, and still others evoking a range of strong emotions that condition, channel, and solidify decisions taken in behalf of the firm. From this melange of interacting, overlapping, algorithmically-driven behaviors emerges the moral substrate of the EF upon which it judges itself and is judged by others. Whether it will be considered to be acting in morally acceptable ways or, to the contrary, to be partially or grossly immoral, depends largely (but not entirely) on the particular ideological-sociocultural context from which such judgments are launched. More fundamentally, though, the basis on which the EF can be seen to display moral content is its effect on the survival, adaptation, and qualitative efflorescence of those people and communities who come within its orbit as a Darwinian survival machine struggling against the entropic tides of a thermodynamic universe.

The central thesis of the paper can now be stated: *The moral traits, features, habits—and ultimately the moral problems, puzzles, and dilemmas—of the Evolutionary Firm are a product of contradictions embedded in diverse neural algorithms that motivate and activate the behavior of the firm's coalition members and thence, through them, the firm's aggregate operations.* For these reasons, the EF is not only its own worst enemy but cannot avoid moral condemnation by others both inside and outside the firm. The firm is reflexively immoral for reasons beyond the control of its participants while simultaneously preserving and promoting what is arguably the central moral principle—economizing—on which all life depends. Nature has indeed played a cruel trick on humankind. Just how it was done takes us deeper into the business firm's Moralizer-Valuator function.

Evolutionary Algorithms

Leda Cosmides, frequently collaborating with John Tooby, has been the leading advocate of the view that modern human behavior owes much to our ancestral past, especially the experiences of hunter-gatherers who lived during the Pleistocene

(Ice Age) era from two million years ago to fifty thousand years ago (Cosmides and Tooby 1992). It was during this period that the modern human brain took shape and became the powerful computational tool we now possess. In confronting and resolving the many different kinds of survival and adaptational problems that arose, the hunter-gatherer brain became specialized, developing domain-specific neural algorithms that matched the challenges presented by the Pleistocene environment. Our modern brains bear the deep imprint of our ancient forebears. We are wired for Pleistocene times while living in the Age of the World Wide Web. The peculiar moral problems of the EF are one result.

The three major sets of neural algorithms inherited from ancestral times that activate the Moralizer-Valuator function in the modern business corporation are depicted in Figure 3.

Economizing Algorithms

Much of this story has already been told above. The energy capture required for adaptation, survival, and outwitting entropy in ancestral times took the form of hunting, gathering, and scavenging. Social systems in the form of family, clan, band, and tribe extended humans' economizing reach (Flannery 1995). Faced with real problems, risks, and dangers requiring judgment, skills, prediction, and cause-and-effect understanding, pragmatic reasoning schemas emerged as sense-making and problem-solving methods (Cheng and Holyoak 1985; Reader and Laland, forthcoming; Finlay et al. 2001). Each of these three economizing modes—energy capture, social system building, and pragmatic reasoning—was a response to one or more environmental challenges. Over long periods of evolutionary time, brains capable of confronting and resolving such challenges evolved. As Cosmides has argued, brain form follows function; so if the brain has a set of neural modules that enable it to economize, it is because such challenges were successfully met in the ancestral past. *It is that same brain that drives the economizing actions and motives of the coalition members of the modern business corporation.* As evolutionary biologist Ernst Mayr says, "the human brain seems not to have changed one single bit since the first appearance of *Homo sapiens*, some 150,000 years ago" (Mayr 2001: 252).

Symbiotic-Moralizing Algorithms

Behavior that draws people together in common cause through cooperation, mutual defense, nurturance, caring, and sympathetic bonding has long been typical of the human experience. Frans de Waal (1996; 2001) and other primatologists have effectively demonstrated similar behavior among chimpanzees, bonobos, and (to a lesser extent) gibbons and orangutans (Whiten and Boesch 2001), thus extending its origins far back in evolutionary time. One well known evolutionary biologist, Lynn Margulis (Margulis and Sagan, 1986; 1995), has argued that life itself, especially some of its earliest forms, emerged from a process of symbiogenesis when simple, primitive life-precursors were joined

Figure 3
ANCESTRAL ALGORITHMS OF THE BUSINESS MIND

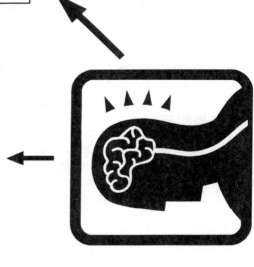

EMOTIVE Algorithms

* Cue/Orchestrate Responses to Environmental Stimuli
* Drive/Sustain Behavioral Responses
* Behavioral-Attitudinal Residues and Imprints

SYMBIOTIC-MORALIZING Algorithms

* Care-bonding
* Inclusive Fitness
* Reciprocal Altruism
* Social Exchange/Social Contracts

ECONOMIZING Algorithms

* Energy Intake
* Internal System Building
* Growth
* Entropy Avoidance
* Pragmatic Reasoning Schemas

together into viable units capable of metabolizing energy drawn from the environment. *Care-bonding* of parent and offspring, while not found among all living creatures, is presumed to have been selected for among many mammalian groups, thus leading to the formation of human family groupings (Wilson 1993), with chimpanzees again leading the way. Kinship bonds that produce an *inclusive fitness* for close kin are present among the social insects and other organisms, as well as humans (Ridley 1996). *Reciprocal altruism*—acting to promote the reproductive interest of others, even against one's own similar interests, and even for unrelated strangers—is another form of mutualistic behavior appearing in the ancestral record (Mayr 2001). So, too, is mutually advantageous *social exchange* an ancient practice among humans, leading to the emergence of *social contract algorithms* (Cosmides 1989; Cosmides and Tooby 1999; Frederick and Wasieleski 2002), primitive trade, early markets, and eventually modern market exchanges (Polanyi, Arensberg, and Pearson 1957; Bohannan and Dalton 1965; Dalton 1967; Braudel 1982). All of these symbiotic linkages find additional reinforcement in a whole host of other *ecological mutualisms*, many of them summarized in Frederick (1995, chap. 6).

Over long stretches of evolutionary time when ancient peoples repeatedly encountered environmental situations favorable to the activation of these symbiotic-moralizing impulses, and especially when they carried adaptive and reproductive advantage, brain circuitry to support such cooperative, symbiotic behaviors emerged to become a part of both Pleistocene and modern-day brains. Behavior that acknowledged the dependence of individuals on one another to promote their own and their collective interests thus entered the human realm very early. Only at a much later time did it acquire the label of "moral" behavior.[9] Today's Evolutionary Firm harbors traces of these ancient symbiotic-moralizing algorithms, even in the midst of furious, intense economizing that often overrides and ruptures their mutualistic tendencies. It is precisely at that algorithmic crossroads where one finds the most intractable moral dilemmas of today's Evolutionary Firm.

Emotive Algorithms

Neuroscientific study of the emotions remains at a very early, even primitive stage of scientific investigation, so there is considerable uncertainty about emotion's meaning, origin, function, and relationship to other parts of the algorithmic human brain. The twentieth century alone recorded more than 90 definitions of "emotion" (Plutchik 2001). Some cognitive neuroscientists (Panksepp 1998; Damasio 1994; 1999) begin with the brain's physical structure, attempting to identify the incredibly complex interactions that occur among the tangle of several billion neurons and thereby to pinpoint the precise locales where various emotional impulses seem to arise. Others, many of them psychologists (Ledoux 1991; Cosmides and Tooby 2000), propose functional theories about emotions that surge outward from the brain to spill over into human behavior. Both groups agree that emotions, however defined and wherever located, play a central, vital, even directive role in human behavior. If that is so, the implications for the behavior found in business firms are profound indeed.

The position here will be that the human brain houses a set of emotive algorithms formed during ancient times as our ancestors interacted with an environment filled with dangers, threats, unforeseen and unforeseeable risks, as well as opportunities and potential windfalls that could boost survival and reproductive chances. According to Jaak Panksepp (2000: 144), who has traced their likely locales in the brain, the predominant emotions that emerged over evolutionary time were "FEAR/anxiety, RAGE/anger, PANIC/separation, LUST/sexuality, CARE/nurturance, PLAY/joy, and SEEKING/exploration [i.e., curiosity]." His research reveals the presence in contemporary human brains of neural algorithms expressing each of these emotional states, with overlap among and between some of them. Robert Plutchik's (1994; 2001) list of "eight bipolar emotions" is closely similar: joy/sorrow, anger/fear, acceptance/disgust, surprise/expectancy, with many subtle combinations, permutations, and intensities being possible.

Their presence within the modern human brain would have to mean that such emotions are potentially capable of becoming—and are likely to be—a part of everyday life in the modern corporation, expressed primarily by members of the firm's human coalition as they interact with each other and as they come in contact with others outside the firm. But for what purposes and towards what ends are these evolutionarily embedded emotive algorithms expressed as they surface in day-to-day business operations? If they originally emerged and were selected for their functional usefulness as survival-and-reproductive capabilities in ancient times, do they continue to do so today, say, in the actions of corporate directors, managers, and employees?

Here, the views of Leda Cosmides are most useful. She hypothesizes that the brain's emotional programs orchestrate the responses an organism must make when confronted with environmental challenges if it is to survive, adapt, and reproduce.

> Emotion programs . . . have a front end that is designed to detect evolutionarily reliable cues that a situation exists (whether or not these cues reliably signal the presence of that situation in the modern world). When triggered, they entrain a specific set of subprograms: those that natural selection "chose" as most useful for solving the problems that situation posed in ancestral environments. . . . Far from being internal free agents, these programs have an unchanging structure regardless of the needs of the individual or her circumstances, because they were designed to create states that worked well in ancestral situations, regardless of their consequences in the present. (Cosmides and Tooby 2000: 93)

Jaak Panksepp concurs: "There appears to be a set of circuits situated in intermediate areas of the brain . . . that have been conceptualized as sensory-motor emotional command circuits. That is, they orchestrate coherent behavioral, physiological, cognitive, and affective consequences . . . . They are emotions like fear, anger, sadness, joy, affection and interest" (Panksepp 2000: 143). "Prior to the emergence of complex cognitive strategies, animals may have generated most of their behavior from . . . primitive emotional systems. . . . These simpleminded behavioral solutions were eventually superseded by more sophisticated cognitive approaches" (Panksepp 1998: 135).

Another cognitive psychologist goes further: "For important adaptive tasks, emotion can be more efficient than cognition. . . . Emotions, like motivations, are substantially domain-specific and are part of the heuristics in the [Darwinian] adaptive toolbox" (Gigerenzer 2001: 138).

Among the factors that can thus be directly influenced, shaped, and channeled by emotive algorithms are, quoting Cosmides, "perception; attention; inference; learning; memory; goal choice; motivational priorities; categorization and conceptual frameworks; . . . behavioral decision rules; communication processes; . . . affective coloration of events . . .; situation assessments, values, and . . . self-esteem . . . ." (Cosmides and Tooby 2000: 93). Translate each of these into the language and work of the business firm, and you have the equivalent of emotions cuing and conditioning almost every aspect of work life—from goals to motives to rules to values and to the many behavioral and attitudinal subtleties of what is now known as corporate culture. Likewise, Panksepp's rage, fear, lust, panic—as well as care, play, and exploratory curiosity-seeking—surge through the ranks of the corporate citizenry unceasingly, providing channels of expression and communication through which the firm's work is done.

The Evolutionary Firm's instrumental economizing and its moralizing impulses are thus orchestrated, even directed, by and through emotive algorithms of ancient lineage. For example, the pride and confidence stemming from *authoritative* knowledge-based skills and accomplishment can be matched (and often is offset or cancelled) by the exultant hubris generated by holding and wielding *authoritarian* dominance power. Or the joy and comfort found when cooperative team efforts pay off can quickly sour and turn into anger, frustration, disappointment, and cynicism when a power hierarchy's demands or a bureaucracy's smug sluggishness take precedence. One way to strip away the emotional ties that sometimes develop within corporations is to change official language. For example, Boeing Company at one time referred to employees as members of "a family" but then switched to calling them "team" members, causing one twelve-year veteran engineer to say, "You can lay off a team member, but to get rid of a family member is a little harder to do." Boeing subsequently found ways to shed thirty thousand "team members" (Goodin 2001: A-8).

Similarly, the pleasures of achieving goals, however well done, fade into bitterness and anxiety in face of layoffs and downsizing demanded by a faceless command structure seeking to preserve its power and domination through ever more effective economizing. Rage, anger, fear, panic, disgust, vengeance flicker through the corporate structure like small bolts of lightning, while executives find reasons and passions to justify decisions made in the name of economizing and power-holding. No better example exists than Enron. As Cosmides reminds us, a firm's biological agents are *"far from being internal free agents,"* driven as they are by "an unchanging [ancestral] structure *regardless of the needs of the individual . . . in the present"* (Cosmides and Tooby 2000: 93, emphasis added). Hence, evolution's legacy in the form of emotive algorithms takes its toll on the very people who carry them and whose behavior they cue and orchestrate.

On a more positive note, corporate managers have been urged to recognize and accept the emotional nature of employees when planning major organizational changes, recruiting rather than denying their feelings and emotional needs (Fox and Amichai-Hamburger 2001). Another study demonstrates that a deliberately induced policy of encouraging emotional interactions with customers creates positive attitudes about a company and hence pays large economizing dividends (Pugh 2001). What has been called "emotional intelligence" helps organizational members adapt to change, and an organization's "emotional capability" is one measure of its strategic success (Huy 1999). Reinforcing these findings is recent evidence from neuroscience that moral judgments are affected by the amount of emotional engagement people have when facing a given moral dilemma (Greene et al. 2001; Blakeslee 2001).

Algorithmic Moral Contradictions

In these several ways, both practitioners and students of the modern corporation confront the moral dilemmas, and the moral opportunities, posed by nature's ways: a veritable tangle of overlapping, inconsistent, and ultimately contradictory neural algorithms lying at the heart (and in the brain) of today's business practitioners.

> Contradiction No. 1: Economizing circuits drive the firm and its members to fend off life-threatening entropy, although these very actions generate an increasing wave of entropy and chaotic disorder that disrupts and sometimes tears asunder a community's symbiotic linkages. Thus, economizing algorithms contravene and contradict symbiotic-moralizing algorithms.

> Contradiction No. 2: Symbiotic-moralizing circuits impel coalition members towards cooperative, mutualistically supportive organizational behaviors that clash with and often lose out to the dominant economizing impulses, if they are not actually put in the service of the firm's economizing goals and its managers' self-aggrandizing behavior. Thus, symbiotic-moralizing algorithms vital to the organization's operations contravene and contradict both economizing and power-aggrandizing algorithms.

> Contradiction No. 3: Emotive circuits cue a range of adaptive reactions to the risks, dangers, and opportunities presented by a high-velocity competitive market environment, stirring up intense

emotional storms that can and do threaten both the achievement of economizing goals and the organizational acceptance of mutualistically advantageous symbiotic operations. Thus, emotive algorithms contravene and contradict both economizing and symbiotic-moralizing algorithms.

These nature-induced moral contradictions embody the EF's central ethical dilemma. Two million years of human evolution and genetic embedding have laid them at the corporation's doorstep and implanted them in the modern business mind. They must be recognized for what they are and for the behavioral constraints they bring to a search for ethical resolutions.

How the Evolutionary Firm Makes Choices

One may ask if there is a priority system that sorts out and regulates the inevitable tensions among the urges and impulses generated within the minds of business practitioners. The EF can be expected to have an array of algorithmic possibilities on which it can draw, all of which are accessed through the biological-agent members of the firm's dominant coalition. We also know that the coalition is normally constrained to act collectively in behalf of the firm's economizing goals. In doing so, the coalition's human members are subject to *natural* selection, which favors those traits and features that support the members' own reproduction and gene replication. But in the case of groups of organisms—here, the collective interests of the entire firm—*thermodynamic* selection favors behavioral practices that extend the economizing life of the firm in face of ever-threatening entropic decline. In short, if the firm is to survive, be self-sustaining, and grow to its full economizing potential, it *must* conform to what I shall call the Logic of Evolutionary Effect (LEE).

The Logic of Evolutionary Effect embraces both natural selection *and* thermodynamic selection. As noted earlier, thermodynamic selection pressures are necessarily the more comprehensive, more persistent, more compelling of the two kinds of selection because they select for the structural and functional features that permit life to begin and persist (Margulis and Sagan, 1986; 1995). Only when that metabolic state has been attained can natural selection that primes the reproductive and gene replicative processes go forward.

The Logic of Evolutionary Effect works its influence on *all* algorithms found within the human brain, including the three types discussed here: economizing, moralizing, emotive. Those with positive thermodynamic effect will be selected for, i.e., favored and sustained. *In the case of the Evolutionary Firm, economizing algorithms are consistently selected and favored by LEE*, and they thus have emerged as the dominant motivating force behind the firm's decisions, operations, strategies, and policies. Moralizing algorithms appear to be selected only when producing an economizing effect for the firm or when their entropic drag is slight. Emotive algorithms occupy a somewhat middle ground inasmuch as they may cue behaviors conducive to economizing outcomes, and thus be selected, or they may in some instances orchestrate actions that plunge the firm into passionate controversy, conflict, and possible dissolution.

The EF's consistent focus on economizing ("profits before people," "greed before good," "good ethics is good business"), along with the subordinate position it assigns to morality ("moral muteness," "codes of ethics"), plus strenuous efforts to abolish emotional expressions from the workplace ("love," "lust-sexuality," "displays of temper")—all are strong hints of an algorithmic priority system set by nature itself, and which constrains and moderates the choices made by business practitioners. Typically, these choices place the highest priority on economizing.

Those who despair of this state of affairs can take comfort from the variations that occur around the EF's priority norm of economizing. The Moralizer/Valuator function of any particular business firm varies with the diversity of its biological agents who, though not entirely free agents, are nevertheless inheritors of variable genetic traits and the predispositions they engender. The algorithms passed on through evolution represent statistical averages and probabilities generalized over many generations. They induce predispositions to behavior, not precise behavioral regimes. They outline possibilities, not certainties or rigid routines. For any given person, their operational effect is therefore unpredictable except in a very general sense. When multiplied by the numbers and types of people found within any given business firm at any given point of time, the lack of predictability of their moral state is magnified by several orders of magnitude.[10] The dominant inner core of the EF's human coalition—the directors, executives, and managers—may itself display a diversity of algorithmic inheritance that can cause the firm to lurch from one strategic (and moral) stance to another. Most employees are kept in line by training and disciplined supervision, but because they too are the inheritors of neural algorithms they can be a rich source of independence, creativity, moral imagination, resistance, and even rebellion, including an occasional whistle-blower. Primary stakeholders—suppliers, dealers, consultants—bring additional attitudes and inclinations that may fit uneasily and roughly (or well) into the economizing grooves gouged out by nature.

For all of these reasons—each one itself a product and expression of natural algorithmic impulses—the EF's strict economizing focus may be constrained and redirected by some varying combination of moralizing and emotive algorithmic forces. After all, Malden Mills CEO Aaron Feuerstein's humane decisions at a moment of financial crisis reflected a different proportion and mixture of economizing, moralizing, and emotion than those made by Enron CEOs Jeffrey Skilling and Kenneth Lay and CFO Andrew Fastow, whose self-aggrandizing decisions brought a powerful firm to the brink of financial disaster. Longtime students of corporate social responsibility recognize the difference between Johnson & Johnson's life-saving decisions during the Tylenol contamination crisis when consumer welfare was ranked higher than short-run profits, and the more recent defective-tire fiasco at Ford-Firestone where the economic and legal standing of both firms seemed to outweigh official concern and regret for the loss of human lives.

The lesson here is not that innate predispositions can be summarily denied or that human agents are completely free to pick and choose among the algorithms that nature has implanted in their genomes. The Logic of Evolutionary Effect has set a probabilistic pattern, created a framework, designed a system, and assigned priorities to the work of the Evolutionary Firm. Business practitioners are bound to act, make decisions, and set policies guided by these broad evolutionary guidelines, especially where (or because) economizing tends to dominate corporate operations. The diversity that is reflected in the varying algorithmic patterns of the firm's biological agentry is the source—a kind of escape valve—that registers whatever degree of decision-making latitude one finds among those who occupy key positions in the collective whole.

The Moral Force of the EF's Other Nature-Based Functions

As should already be evident from the above discussion, the centrality of economizing as the principal driving force of business creates a great wash of moral dilemmas for those both inside and outside the firm. These are the most wrenching, most intractable ethical problems posed by the Evolutionary Firm. However, the story does not end there, for the EF's other functions also carry moral weight, which can be briefly identified but not fully discussed here.

The Innovator/Generator function (as shown in Figure 2, above) is derived from an underlying natural process: the spontaneous generation of symbolic representations by the human central nervous system, particularly the neocortex that houses the brain's principal cognitive, calculative capability. From that neurological seat arise the tools, language, and behavioral guides that enable the firm to economize, innovate, and achieve a productive output. Here, too, resides the brain's "wild card," the source of new insights, the fount of creativity, the imaginative intelligence that generates new ways of seeing, thinking, and solving problems. These cerebral symbolic processes are the leading edge of human adaptation, the principal means we have of surviving and flourishing in an evolving world. As a human generative force housed within a corporate shell, this uniquely creative symbolic pulse gives the Evolutionary Firm its principal moral and social justification. Its never-ending innovations— from silicon chips to World Wide Web, from cell phones and DVD to pacemakers and computers-on-a-molecule—energize and vivify an essential economizing process, greatly amplifying the adaptive range of life options available to the human species. Turned outward towards the burgeoning needs of a global society, rather than being focused exclusively on the EF's own goals, this generative force holds great moral promise for a better human future. Take note, those who would redesign the Evolutionary Firm.

The EF's Organizer/Coordinator function is based upon two underlying natural features. One is a power-dominance natural impulse that is *emotively driven*; the other a system of linguistic linkages *cognitively driven*. Power-dominance organizes the firm as a vertical status hierarchy; language and data flows organize it technologically and horizontally. Both systems tie the firm's coalition members together and help coordinate their workplace activities. The resultant network focuses power, information, and decision making in a managerial elite that seeks to aggrandize its own interests and (where possible) those of the firm.

Some of the most intransigent moral dilemmas of the EF center on the use of dominance and power by a corporate elite that is often unmindful of the needs, interests, and welfare of others within and outside the corporation. Even a company's economizing goals are often made to yield to the self-aggrandizing urges and impulses of top-level executives, hence undermining the principal adaptive morality of the firm itself. Executive insiders of now-defunct Global Crossing cashed out $1.3 billion of their personal holdings in the company as it slid toward bankruptcy and ruin, even outdoing Enron's insiders who dumped about $1 billion worth of that company's stock under similar circumstances (Bryan-Low 2002). As his company was collapsing and its stock losing value, Enron's CEO sold $20 million of Enron stock *back to the company* while telling other investors and Enron employees that their own holdings would soon have "a significantly higher price" (Norris and Barboza 2002). In another case, Enron Broadband executives spent $2 billion setting up high-speed transmission cables across the U.S., but as one source later reported, "Enron Broadband was a colossal [financial] catastrophe." However, Broadband's CEO got $72 million by selling off his stock, and the firm's president took in $35 million the same way. Another Enron subsidiary lost $17 million in 2001's third quarter, then it was put up for sale at a $200 million loss, while its chairman walked away with $75 million from stock sales (Fields 2002).

In all likelihood, the radical conflicts of interest between executives and their firms reveal the active presence of a fourth kind of neural algorithm driving the business mind: a power-dominance circuitry that predisposes to the capture, retention, and magnification of power and influence, to be wielded first for personal gain and secondarily for the company's benefit. Evolutionary psychologist Denise Cummins (1998) traces this behavioral predisposition to ancestral times: "[S]pecial reasoning architecture evolved [among apes and humans] to handle problems that are repeatedly encountered by individuals living in dominance hierarchies, problems that directly impact survival rates and reproductive success" (Cummins 1998: 30). She points out that in a social world organized along dominance lines, the keys to success and survival came in two different forms: obliging others, and guile. Guile apparently won the day at Enron, WorldCom, et al.

An Enabler/Strategizer function reflects the complex, nonlinear ecosystem landscape on which the EF must maneuver if it is to survive, adapt, and expand its sphere of economizing influence. Mutualisms—life-supporting symbiotic linkages—abound within all ecosystems; indeed, they literally define what an ecosystem is at its core (Wilson 1992, chaps. 9 and 10). A firm's economizing success depends almost entirely on identifying, forming, and developing mutually beneficial ecological alliances with others, whether firms, governments, or institutional stakeholders of all varieties. Its economizing goals are achievable only through such ecologizing strategies. Finding, keeping, and expanding an economic niche calls for pushing back the chaotic disorder that is typical of such environments and for developing pragmatic intelligence to match the competitive challenges encountered. Complexity theory's "strange attractors" that orient the EF within an ever-shifting competitive marketplace are nothing more nor less than the firm's values and moral/immoral commitments, and these will determine whether the firm survives at the edge of chaos or plunges into uncontrolled chaotic-entropic disorder (Frederick 1998). This possibility alone should motivate an active search for values that sustain not just the EF but all others whose fate is tied to its fortunes.

In the end, it is worth remembering that the modern Evolutionary Firm remains one of nature's ongoing evolutionary experiments—a mere 200+ years in the making—with the long-run outcome not yet clear. The average life expectancy of a typical large-scale corporation today is forty to fifty years; only a handful have lived more than a century (de Gues 1997). Most smaller-scale firms last less than ten years: in the U.S. seventy to ninety percent of small firms fail in the first ten years, in the UK around seventy percent, and forty-eight to sixty-eight percent in Canada are gone before a decade is out (Stanworth et al. 1998; Monk 2000). Configured as it is, the Evolutionary Firm's long-run prospects do not seem too promising. It may not be important that the Evolutionary Firm as we know it today lives to see the end of the present century, but if it fades away nature will need to replace its several functions with equally vigorous ones housed in another organizational shell because in its present form the EF sustains huge swaths of humanity through its economizing vigor, even though it does so with sometime grievous moral consequences.

Whatever Happened to Culture?

In this account which has leaned so heavily on nature for an explanation of business behavior, it is reasonable for one to ask: But what about culture? Should we not heed the anthropologist who, for almost as long a time as Charles Darwin, has explained human behavior as a manifestation, not of biology or physics, but of culture? Has not the concept of corporate culture, now well into its third decade of use, proved to be a valuable way of tracking, understanding, and perhaps even improving business behavior? Must the natural sciences displace, or even *re*place, the social sciences in order to advance our understanding of the business firm?

To this challenge, there are two answers, neither of which can be adequately discussed on this occasion. A first observation is that the standard social science model that favors a *tabula rasa* concept of human learning, behavior, and development is being seriously eroded by the research of cognitive neuroscientists, evolutionary psychologists, geneticists, evolutionary biologists, primatologists, and paleontologists (Tooby and Cosmides 1992). Human behavior is now understood to be a function of natural systems—brains (Calvin 1998), genes (Dawkins 1989), climate (Calvin 1990; 2002), geography (Diamond 1998), ecology (Wilson 1992), anciently embedded ancestral impulses (Cosmides and Tooby 2000)—including even the basic grammars of language (Pinker 1994), the comprehension of music and artistic-aesthetic expressions (Jourdain 1997; Sloboda 1985; Barrow 1995), mathematical intelligence (Stewart 1995), and other traits once explained in purely cultural terms. The twentieth century saw the rise, domination, and decline of culture as an analytic tool (Degler 1991). The palette from which scholars now paint a human portrait is far richer in color, depth, and perspective than previously possible. The decline of culture and the rise of biology can be seen as an advance, as a filling out of the picture we seek to draw of the human—and business—experience.

The reason that makes it possible to celebrate rather than to regret today's greater reliance on the natural sciences—and this is the second answer to the basic question about culture's relevance—is the close, indeed, the inescapable kinship of nature and culture. Cognitive neuroscience now makes it possible to understand culture as an elaboration, an extension, a magnification, an amplification of cerebral symbol-making of almost unbounded human potential (Deacon 1997; Tattersall 2002). Culture in this view *is* nature. Not only can we now grasp Frans de Waal's (2001) point that our primate progenitor-cousins are capable of cultural behavior but we can in that way understand culture's debt to nature, as well as the lack of clear boundary between the two.

Corporate culture is truly a powerful analytic concept to both understand what goes on in business firms and to help managers do their daily work effectively. The EF's five nature-based functions undergird and make up the core of its corporate culture. Rather than a cloak that conceals nature's grip on the business mind, corporate culture illustrates the close bond between biological nature and symbolic culture.

Concluding Thoughts and Future Directions

Moral inquiry about business must begin with the Evolutionary Firm's Motivator-Driver function. Business firms are first and foremost economizing organizations, made that way by nature. All the wishful thinking in the world—even the most sophisticated philosophic speculations—will not make that feature go away. The firm's moral problems arise from contradictions rooted in behavioral impulses of the human psyche in interaction with an entropic universe.

Culture and reason can channel, moderate, and reconfigure—but cannot eliminate—these behavioral predispositions. Virtuous character can confront but not seriously deflect the natural course of embedded neural algorithms. Social contracts can design but cannot enforce or guarantee fair exchanges. Stakeholder claims on the corporation cannot exceed or violate the firm's entropic limits. Philosophic principles and ideals not consistent with the firm's natural architecture cannot be expected to prevail.

What then are the lessons for business ethicists to be found within the natural realm? Should one simply throw over the familiar ways of thinking, pre-Darwinian though they may be, that presently guide ethics inquiry? Does the naturalization of normative inquiry represent a revolution, perhaps even the emergence of a new Kuhnian paradigm? Those with long memories or great age may recall John Dewey's plea, issued in 1920, for a "reconstruction in philosophy" that would situate philosophers more securely within an activist, pragmatic, progressive, evolutionary realm of inquiry (Dewey 1920). Alas, his petition was both ignored and rejected, and the hoped-for "reconstruction" did not occur—that is, not within conventional philosophy circles. But the post-1920 world of affairs rolled over human societies everywhere, leaving philosophers and the general public adrift without secure normative guidance in times of inflation, depression, dictators, war, social upheaval, genocide, and the use of hideous military technology.

Is there here a possible parallel with today's business ethics inquiry? "Reconstructions" of the kind Dewey had in mind rarely occur in academia, as all would surely agree, nor is one of that magnitude imminent in business ethics. But a funny thing happened to the pre-1920 philosophers. While they weren't looking, the world around them changed. They continued, at least in their own minds, to be "right" but no one cared. Today, one wonders if that might be true of our own field of business ethics. One hears the favorite mantras chanted over and over—corporate social responsibility, Aristotelian virtues, Kantian rights, Rawlsian justice, duties to stakeholders, corporate citizenship, etc., *ad infinitum*. At the same time, one witnesses the actions of Enron, Global Crossing, WorldCom, Tyco, and many other less spectacular scandals, rip-offs, cheating, embezzling, misinformation, fraud, etc. It causes one to ask: Is anyone out there in the business world listening to business ethicists? Have they become today's pre-1920s philosophers: "Right," but no one cares?

Does this mean that one should give up on moral analysis of business? By no means. What it means is that we must *begin* with what nature has bequeathed to business and to humanity. Within that bequest, one finds a brain marvelously attuned to meeting environmental challenges and finding ways to adapt, survive, create, experiment, explore, imagine, and expand the quantity and quality of life. That brain has carried *Homo sapiens* to its present state in evolutionary time, far and well beyond our Pleistocene ancestral base. Its very flexibility, creativity, and emotionality hints—and haunts one's hopes and dreams—that it can point the way to a better moral life for the Evolutionary Firm and for human society.

Isn't it time we looked Nature in the eye? Without blinking?

Notes

1. An increasing number of authors draw on research from the natural sciences to explain business and economic behavior: Ken Baskin (1998) uses DNA as a metaphor of corporate decision making; Gareth Morgan (1997) says organizations behave like living organisms; Nigel Nicholson (1998) points out that much organizational behavior is modeled on biological impulses; Barbara Pierce and Roderick White (1999) find analogies between organization types in simian social groups and certain types of business organization; Thomas Petzinger, Jr. (1999) describes entrepreneurial firms as complex adaptive systems seeking niches on fitness landscapes; Paul Hawken, Amory B. Lovins, and L. Hunter Lovins (1999) say an environmentally sustainable corporate strategy can be achieved by basing production on processes found in nature; Timothy Fort (2001) uses research on the cortex-imposed size limitations of viable human groups to argue for scaled-down corporate governance systems more expressive of human morality; Andrew Henderson, Ithai Stern, and Jungzheng Ding (2001) say the survival and death of individual firms and products can be explained by natural selection; Sandra Waddock (2002) recognizes ecology as the biological basis of global corporate citizenship; Paul Lawrence and Nitin Nohria (2002) propose that four nature-based drives underlie most organizational and business behavior; Michael Rothschild (1990), Matthias Ruth (1993), and Jane Jacobs (2000) are but three among several economists who use natural forces to explain the operation of economic systems.

2. Such moral judgments are not limited to questions of human welfare alone, as evidenced by the longstanding affinity between humans and domesticated animals, the ancient religious practice of totemism, and the more recent interest in preserving the diversity of non-human organic species and protecting laboratory animals subject to scientific research. Zoos, commercial (tourist) aquaria, unintended netting of dolphins, slaughter of baby seals, various kinds of hunting traps and snares, and, of course, human carnivorous eating habits have all come in for their share of moral disapproval.

3. In common usage, "energy" tends to mean the heat and work produced by petroleum, coal, electric generation, gasoline stocks, natural gas, nuclear power, and power generated by wind, water, and sun, and they are indeed among our most important sources of energy. However, in thermodynamics theory, energy has a much broader meaning and takes many different forms. Essentially, *energy is defined as the ability to perform work*. For long periods, *human muscle power* was a prime source of energy used for human purposes, supplemented much later by the work of domesticated draft animals. The *mechanical power* made possible by tools made of stone, bone, and wood was subsequently elaborated and extended through the industrial period, putting ever greater amounts of work energy into human hands. Today, *computational power* supports and makes possible entirely new forms of work, greatly multiplying the total energy that can be put to human uses. *Information* itself is a form of energy, whether patented formulas, data banks, business strategy plans, marketing programs, or financial analyses—all can be used to get work done. Another form taken by energy is the amount of *order* present in a given system, such as the organizational order of a business firm. One measure of entropy is the amount of disorder or randomness present within a system, with maximum entropy leading to complete disorder, dispersal of energy, and total randomness of all elements that were formally organized or ordered into a system. A system that has reached maximum entropy is also known as being in a state of thermodynamic equilibrium, and it is to avoid this kind of equilibrium that business firms engage in economizing operations.

4. In more formal theoretical language, one researcher has described the operation of these natural laws this way: "All processes occurring in the ecosystem, physical, biological or economic, are constrained by the first and second law of thermodynamics. The first law states that mass and energy are conserved in an isolated system. According to the second law, however, transformation of energy is always inefficient in natural processes. *As a result, materials and energy use can never be 100% efficient and will always result in the generation of waste products.* The first and second law of thermodynamics constitute core concepts of thermodynamics that govern material and energy use in the economic system and its environment" (Ruth 1993: 204, emphasis added; cf. Schneider 1988).

5. These are some of the negative effects of "globalization," i.e., the rapid expansion and penetration of "foreign" ecosystems by the world's premier economizing corporations. As an invader species, these firms typically disrupt long-established, settled community routines and life-support arrangements in the host ecosystems. Whether the economizing benefits introduced by the invaders offset the host community's social and economic costs is a question of great complexity not easily decided, although there is no lack of very strong opinions voiced on either side. In any event, the phenomenon of new entrants into ecosystems is widespread in nature and has been for a very, very long time, so there is little of fundamental distinction to be found in the current "globalization" trend.

6. Thermodynamic selection (attaining either self-sustaining order or suffering chaotic disorder) also can and does occur among nonliving, nonorganic organized entities, such as certain chemical solutions, weather phenomena (e.g., a tornado or a hurricane), and the digitized agents in computer-simulated games or models. Speaking of archaic prebiotic chemical reactions during Earth's formative period, Lynn Margulis and Dorion Sagan say this: "Catalysts were important *before life* because they worked against randomness to produce order and pattern in chemical processes. . . . Some of these 'dead' autocatalytic reactions form patterns whose increasing complexity over time is reminiscent of life" (1986: 53, emphasis added). Thus, thermodynamic selection, affecting even nonliving chemical compounds, predates natural selection that, by definition, began only when living organisms appeared on Earth. Additionally, an even more ancient, primordial type of prebiotic evolution—in this case, the progressive emergence of the elementary particles, elements, chemicals, and minerals in the early universe—laid out the pathways and constraints along which biological evolution would subsequently flow (Lima-de-Feria 1995: 97–105). After all, the elements and molecular components that make up the universe had been evolving some ten to twelve billion years before the Earth was formed some five billion years ago, and another half-billion years then passed before the earliest life forms appeared on Earth. That's a very long evolutionary period when thermodynamic processes preceded the beginning of natural selection and, more importantly, continued thereafter and to the present day as a selection process.

This state of affairs that has produced two different concepts of selection—one thermodynamic, the other natural—is largely a product of the tendency of biologists to underemphasize, ignore, or even to shun physics. Their urgent focus on Darwinian theory, especially the genetics of neo-Darwinism, is understandable and has produced remarkable understanding of organic life, although their exclusive focus on the gene as the key unit of evolution has resulted in an overly narrow interpretation of the broader selection processes that produce change and order over evolutionary time.

7. Enron is not the only company that comes to mind. Media giant John Malone has been described in these words by *The Wall Street Journal*:

Mr. Malone spent 25 years building the biggest cable-TV operation in the U. S., becoming one of the most powerful and feared men in the entertainment industry before selling his Tele-Communications Inc. in 1999 for $46 billion to AT&T Corp. Now he is back, trying to do the same thing across the Atlantic. A series of deals already made or pending . . . [would make] him the biggest cable operator there. . . . Such a role in the U. S. helped earn him the sobriquet "Darth Vader" in some quarters. "These are not investments for wimps," Mr. Malone said in a recent interview. (Peers and Karnitschnig 2002)

8. No business school to my knowledge consciously teaches its students to be dishonest, although some school-approved marketing, accounting, and financial techniques lend themselves to dishonest use. Such pressures to bend the truth usually develop on the job as companies confront various competitive pressures or self-induced financial crises. Nevertheless, business schools that put almost exclusive emphasis on the tools of accounting, finance, marketing, economics, and quantitative analysis and who simultaneously either fail to teach business ethics or deemphasize its importance by making it an elective course produce graduates who are at a magnified risk of succumbing to on-the-job demands for unethical behavior. For a brief primer on the ethical pitfalls lurking in various accounting techniques, see a *Wall Street Journal* report on "creative accounting" by Ken Brown (2002), quoting an accounting professor who says, "That's what creative accounting is, it's trying to alter perceptions of business performance."

9. Hominoid primates, especially chimpanzees and bonobos, as well as a much wider range of other species, display behavior functionally similar to actions that humans define as moral or normative, and one leading primatologist (de Waal 1996) argues that these behaviors are an evolutionary parallel to human morality. In saying that morals and values are a humanly assigned quality, I accept de Waal's position while also maintaining that *Homo sapiens* and perhaps earlier hominid varieties have self consciously and deliberately assigned moral meanings to the behaviors that their primate predecessors were and are able to act out only by less-than-fully-deliberative means. More recently de Waal (2001) has extended his argument that chimpanzees and bonobos manifest the kind of imitative and learned behavior that constitutes culture, a view he shares with others (Wrangham et al. 1994; Whiten and Boesch 2001).

10. The many typical variations in the values held by the individual members of any given business firm were called "X-factor values" in *Values, Nature, and Culture in the American Corporation* (Frederick 1995), with the "X" denoting the uncertain and often unknowable numbers and types of values present within the whole. The workplace diversity is a function of race, gender, age, personality type, role taken at work, religion, natal locale, ethnic marker, intelligence, education, etc.

Bibliography

Banerjee, Neela. 2002. "At Enron, Lavish Excess Often Came Before Success." *New York Times*, February 26, 2002: C1.

Barrow, John D. 1995. *The Artful Universe*. Oxford: Oxford University Press.

Baskin, Ken. 1998. *Corporate DNA: Learning from Life*. Boston: Butterworth-Heinenman.

Blakeslee, Sandra. 2001. "Watching How the Brain Works as it Weighs a Moral Dilemma." *New York Times*, September 25, 2001: D3.

_____. 2002. "Scientists Find Retina Cells Responsible for Setting Biological Clock." *Pittsburgh Post-Gazette*, February 8: A-3. Reprinted from *New York Times*.

Bohannan, Paul, and George Dalton, eds. 1965. *Markets in Africa: Eight Subsistence Economies in Transition*. New York: Anchor Books, Doubleday.

Braudel, Fernand. 1982. *Civilization and Capitalism: 15th–18th Century, Volume II: The Wheels of Commerce*. New York: Harper & Row.G30

Brown, Ken. 2002. "Creative Accounting: How to Buff a Company." *Wall Street Journal*, February 21, C1, C18.

Bryan-Low, Cassell. 2002. "Insiders at Global Crossing Sold Shares Before Collapse." *Wall Street Journal*, February 6, C22.

Calvin, William H. 1990. *The Ascent of Mind: Ice Age Climates and the Evolution of Intelligence*. New York: Bantam Books.

_____. 1998. *The Cerebral Code: Thinking a Thought in the Mosaics of the Mind*. Cambridge, Mass.: MIT Press.

_____. 2002. *A Brain for All Seasons: Human Evolution and Abrupt Climate Change*. Chicago: University of Chicago Press.

Cheng, Patricia W., and Keith J. Holyoak. 1985. "Pragmatic Reasoning Schemas." *Cognition* 17: 391–416.

Cosmides, Leda. 1989. "The Logic of Social Exchange: Has Natural Selection Shaped How Humans Reason? Studies With the Wason Selection Task." *Cognition* 31: 187–276.

Cosmides, Leda, and John Tooby. 1992. "Cognitive Adaptations for Social Exchange." In *The Adapted Mind: Evolutionary Psychology and the Generation of Culture*, ed. Jerome H. Barkow, Leda Cosmides, and John Tooby. New York: Oxford University Press.

_____. 1999. "The Cognitive Neuroscience of Social Reasoning." In *The Cognitive Neurosciences*, ed. Michael S. Gazzaniga. Boston: MIT Press.: 1259–1270.

_____. 2000. "Evolutionary Psychology and the Emotions." In *Handbook of Emotions*, 2nd edition, edited by Michael Lewis and Jeannette M. Haviland-Jones. New York: Guilford Press, pp. 91–115.

Coveney, Peter, and Roger Highfield. 1990. *The Arrow of Time: A Voyage Through Science to Solve Time's Greatest Mystery*. London: W. H. Allen.

Cummins, Denise Dellarosa. 1998. "Social Norms and Other Minds: The Evolutionary Roots of Higher Cognition." In *The Evolution of Mind*, ed. Denise Dellarosa Cummins and Colin Allen. New York: Oxford University Press: 30–50.

Dalton, George, ed. 1967. *Tribal and Peasant Economies: Readings in Economic Anthropology*. Garden City, N.Y.: Natural History Press.

Damasio, Antonio. 1994. *Descartes's Error: Emotion, Reason, and the Human Brain*. New York: G. P. Putnam.

_____. 1999. *The Feeling of What Happens: Body and the Emotions in the Making of Consciousness*. New York: Harcourt, Brace.

Dawkins, Richard. 1989. *The Selfish Gene*. Oxford: Oxford University Press.

Deacon, Terrence W. 1997. *The Symbolic Species*. New York: W. W. Norton.

Degler, Carl. N. 1991. *In Search of Human Nature*. New York: Oxford University Press.

de Geus, Arie. 1997. *The Living Company*. Boston: Harvard Business School Press.

Dennett, Daniel C. 1995. *Darwin's Dangerous Idea: Evolution and the Meanings of Life*. New York: Simon & Schuster.

Dewey, John. 1950. *Reconstruction in Philosophy*. New York: New American Library. (Originally published in 1920 by Henry Holt.) See especially Dewey's new introduction written for the 1950 edition.

Diamond, Jared. 1998. *Guns, Germs, and Steel: The Fates of Human Societies*. New York: W. W. Norton.

Fields, Gregg. 2002. "Enron Execs Profited on Stock While Divisions Took a Bath." *Pittsburgh Post-Gazette*, February 12, A-8.

Finlay, Barbara L., Richard B. Darlington, and Nicholas Nicastro. 2001. *Behavioral and Brain Sciences*, April. As reported in *Science Times*, 161(11): 166, March 16, 2002. A study demonstrating that the so-called executive brain responsible for complex thinking evolved faster than other parts of the brain and was the major factor leading to larger human brains.

Flack, Jessica C., and Frans B. M. de Waal. 2000. "'Any Animal Whatever': Darwinian Building Blocks of Morality in Monkeys and Apes." *Journal of Consciousness Studies* 7(1–2): pp. 1–29. See also pp. 7–41 in this volume.

Flannery, Kent V. 1995. "Prehistoric Social Evolution." In *Research Frontiers in Anthropology*, ed. Carol R. Ember and Melvin Ember.

Fort, Timothy L. 2001. *Ethics and Governance: Business as Mediating Institution*. New York: Oxford University Press.

Fox, Shaul, and Yair Amichai-Hamburger. 2001. "The Power of Emotional Appeals in Promoting Organizational Change Programs." *Academy of Management Executive* 15(4): 84–94.

Frederick, William C. 1995. *Values, Nature, and Culture in the American Corporation*. New York: Oxford University Press.

———. 1998. "Creatures, Corporations, Communities, Chaos, Complexity." *Business & Society* 37(4): 358–389.

Frederick, William C., and David M. Wasieleski 2002. "Evolutionary Social Contracts." *Business and Society Review* 107(3).

Gigerenzer, Gerd. 2001. "The Adaptive Toolbox: Toward a Darwinian Rationality." In *Evolutionary Psychology and Motivation*, ed. Jeffrey A. French, Alan C. Kamil, and Daniel W. Leger. Nebraska Symposium on Motivation, vol. 47. Lincoln: University of Nebraska Press: 113–143.

Goldstein, Martin, and Inge Goldstein. 1993. *The Refrigerator and the Universe*. Cambridge, Mass.: Harvard University Press.

Goodin, Dan. 2001. "Christmas? Bah! Humbug!" *Pittsburgh Post-Gazette*. December 15: A-8.

Greene, Joshua D., R. Brian Sommerville, Leigh E. Nystrom, John M. Darley, and Jonathan D. Cohen. 2001. "An fMRI Investigation of Emotional Engagement in Moral Judgment." *Science* 293 (September): 2105–2108.

Hawken, Paul, Amory B. Lovins, and L. Hunter Lovins. 1999. *Natural Capitalism: Creating the Next Industrial Revolution*. Boston: Little, Brown.

Haynie, Donald T. 2001. *Biological Thermodynamics*. Cambridge: Cambridge University Press.

Henderson, Andrew D., Ithai Stern, and Jungzheng Ding. 2001. "An Evolutionary Perspective on Internal and External Selection." Academy of Management Conference, Washington, D.C.

Huy, Quy Nguyen. 1999. "Emotional Capability, Emotional Intelligence, and Radical Change." *Academy of Management Review* 24(2): 325–345.

Jacobs, Jane. 2000. *The Nature of Economies*. New York: Modern Library.

Jourdain, Robert. 1997. *Music, the Brain, and Ecstasy: How Music Captures Our Imagination*. New York: William Morrow.

Lawrence, Paul R., and Nitin Nohria. 2002. *Driven: How Human Nature Shapes Our Choices*. San Francisco: Jossey-Bass.

Ledoux, Joseph. 1991. *The Emotional Brain: The Mysterious Underpinnings of Emotional Life*. New York: Simon & Schuster.

Lima-de-Feria, Antonio. 1995. *Biological Periodicity: Its Molecular Mechanism and Evolutionary Implications*. Greenwich, Conn.: JAI Press.

Margulis, Lynn, and Dorion Sagan. 1986. *Microcosmos: Four Billion Years of Evolution from Our Microbial Ancestors*. New York: Summit Books/Simon & Schuster.

_____. 1995. *What Is Life?* New York: Simon & Schuster.

Mayr, Ernst. 2001. *What Evolution Is*. New York: Basic Books.

Monk, Richard. 2000. "Why Small Businesses Fail." *CMA Management* 74(6): 12–13.

Morgan, Gareth. 1997. *Images of Organization*. 2nd. ed. Thousand Oaks, Calif.: Sage.

Nicholson, Nigel. 1998. "How Hardwired is Human Behavior?" *Harvard Business Review* (July–August): 135–147.

Norris, Floyd, and David Barboza. 2002. "Lay Sold Millions in Stock Last Year." *Pittsburgh Post-Gazette*, February 16, A1 (reprinted from *New York Times*).

Panksepp, Jaak. 1998. *Affective Neuroscience: The Foundations of Human and Animal Emotions*. New York: Oxford University Press.

_____. 2000. Emotions as Natural Kinds within the Mammalian Brain. In Lewis, Michael, and Haviland-Jones, Jeannette M. (Eds.). *Handbook of Emotions*. 2nd ed. New York: Guilford Press.

Peers, Martin, and Matthew Karnitschnig. 2002. "John Malone Marches on Europe." *Wall Street Journal*, February 14, B1.

Petzinger, Thomas, Jr. 1999. *The New Pioneers: The Men and Women Who Are Transforming the Workplace and Marketplace*. New York: Simon & Schuster.

Pierce, Barbara Decker, and Roderick White. 1999. "The Evolution of Social Structure: Why Biology Matters." *Academy of Management Review* 24(4): 843–853.

Pinker, Steven. *The Language Instinct: The New Science of Language and Mind*. London: Penguin.

Plutchik, Robert. 1994. *The Psychology and Biology of Emotion*. New York: HarperCollins.

_____. 2001. The Nature of Emotions. *American Scientist* 89(4) (July–August): 344–350.

Polanyi, Karl, Conrad M. Arensberg, and Harry W. Pearson, eds. 1957. *Trade and Market in the Early Empires*. Glencoe, Ill.: Free Press.

Pugh, S. Douglas. 2001. Service with a smile: Emotional contagion in the service encounter. *Academy of Management Journal* 44(5): 1018–1027.

Reader, Simon M., and Kevin N. Laland. Forthcoming in *Proceedings of the National Academy of Sciences*, as reported in *Science Times*, 116 (11): 161 (March 16, 2002). A study of primates linking problem-solving ability—discovering new skills, learning skills from others, and tool use—to brain size, particularly the so-called executive brain responsible for complex thinking. The larger the executive brain, the more skilled the problem-solver.

Ridley, Matt. 1996. *The Origins of Virtue.* London: Penguin Books.

Rothschild, Michael. 1990. *Bionomics: Economy as Ecosystem.* New York: Henry Holt.

Ruth, Matthias. 1993. *Integrating Economics, Ecology, and Thermodynamics.* Dordrecht: Kluwer Academic Publishers.

Schneider, E. D. 1988. "Thermodynamics, Ecological Succession, and Natural Selection: A Common Thread." In *Entropy, Information, and Evolution*, ed. B. H. Weber, D. J. Depew, and J. D. Smith. Cambridge, Mass.: MIT Press.

Sloboda, John A. 1985. *The Musical Mind: The Cognitive Psychology of Music.* New York: Oxford University Press.

Stanworth, John, David Purdy, Stuart Price, and Nicos Zafiris. 1998. "Franchise Versus Conventional Small Business Failure Rates in the US and UK: More Similarities than Differences." *International Small Business Journal* 16(3): 56–69.

Stewart, Ian. 1995. *Nature's Numbers: The Unreal Reality of Mathematics.* New York: Basic Books.

Tattersall, Ian. 2002. *Monkey in the Mirror: Essays on the Science of What Makes Us Human.* New York: Harcourt Brace.

Tooby, John, and Leda Cosmides. 1992. "The Psychological Foundations of Culture." In *The Adapted Mind: Evolutionary Psychology and the Generation of Culture*, ed. Jerome H. Barkow, Leda Cosmides, and John Tooby. New York: Oxford University Press.

————. 1995. "Toward Mapping the Evolved Functional Organization of Mind and Brain." In *The Cognitive Neurosciences*, ed. Michael Gazzaniga. Cambridge, Mass.: MIT Press: 1185–1196.

de Waal, Frans. 1996. *Good Natured: The Origins of Right and Wrong in Humans and Other Animals.* Cambridge, Mass.: Harvard University Press.

————. 2001. *The Ape and the Sushi Master: Cultural Reflections by a Primatologist.* New York: Basic Books.

Waddock, Sandra. 2002. *Leading Corporate Citizens: Vision, Values, Value Added.* New York: McGraw-Hill Irwin.

Whiten, Andrew, and Christophe Boesch. 2001. "The Culture of Chimpanzees." *Scientific American* 284(1): 60–67.

Wilson, Edward O. 1992. *The Diversity of Life.* London: Penguin Press.

Wilson, James Q. 1993. *The Moral Sense.* New York: Free Press.

Wrangham, Richard, W. C. McGrew, F. B. M. de Waal, and P. Heltne. 1994. *Chimpanzee Cultures.* Cambridge, Mass.: Harvard University Press.

Wright, Robert. 1995. *The Moral Animal: Evolutionary Psychology and Everyday Life.* New York: Random House.

Appendix

Three Blind Mice: A Suggestive Analogy

Neuroscientists recently discovered the location of the retina's cells that set a person's biological clock (Blakeslee 2002). These cells let the body know when to wake up and when to go to sleep, and they operate on a twenty-four-hour schedule. This clock is reset every day as light levels change with the Earth's movement around the sun. The discovery overturns the prevailing belief that other retinal cells, called rods and cones, were resetting the circadian clock, which caused one scientist to describe the finding as "heretical."

Another said, "We thought we knew everything about the retina. Now we find we have two separate systems in the eye, one for vision and one for setting the clock. We have a new way of thinking about how light is interpreted by the nervous system."

Still another said that the traditional view of how light is handled in the eye has held for more than one hundred years. The rods and cones were supposed to perform both functions. Now a deeper understanding of the new photoreceptors might lead to novel treatments for disturbances of the body's internal clock. It may turn out that people who have defects in the newly described system could suffer from "time blindness" similar to color blindness.

I can't resist suggesting an analogy to this paper's account of the Evolutionary Firm. If it is true that business behavior is a function of ancestral neural algorithms embedded within the human brain, motivating business practitioners to economize and their companies to have a potential for symbiotic-moralizing outcomes, all within a highly charged emotive setting, then we have made a new discovery, thanks to neuroscientists and evolutionary psychologists.

Tracking the language of the scientists who discovered the eye's clock-setting cells, one might even be able to say, as they did, that we thought we knew everything about business. Now we find we have two separate but inter-related systems for understanding how business behaves. We have a new way of thinking about business motives and morals.

Moreover (continuing the analogy and paraphrasing the language used above), the traditional view of how business behaves has held for well over one hundred years. Character and culture, the managerial equivalents of those rods and cones, were supposed to contain all the answers. Now a deeper understanding of the way the human brain works might lead to novel solutions to some of the moral disturbances of the business system. It may turn out that business practitioners whose decisions are ruled by economizing and power-aggrandizing algorithms suffer a "moral blindness" similar to time blindness and color blindness. Some scholars may even believe the new way of thinking to be heretical.

It may or may not be analogically significant that the eye experiment was carried out on three blind mice, or that the findings of cognitive neuroscience and evolutionary psychology seem invisible to some people.

THE POSSIBILITY OF MORAL
RESPONSIBILITY WITHIN CORPORATIONS
AS COMPLEX SYSTEMS:
A RESPONSE TO WILLIAM C. FREDERICK

Mollie Painter-Morland

Abstract: This paper addresses the inherent danger of relativism in any naturalistic theory about moral decision-making and action. The implications of Frederick's naturalistic view of corporations can easily lead one to believe that it has become impossible for the evolutionary firm (EF) to act with moral responsibility. However, if Frederick's naturalistic account is located within the context of his and other writers' insights about complexity science, it may become possible to maintain a sense of creative, pragmatic moral decision-making in the face of supposedly deterministic forces. Business's most creative response to moral dilemmas takes place "at the edge of chaos," where a temporary order comes into being via self-organization. This process of self-organization is influenced by a great number of variables. Some of these variables are the x-factor configurations of individuals and groups, which cannot necessarily determine, but can influence the moral-decision-making process. Moral responsibility becomes part of a complex process through which creative, value-driven solutions emerge.

1. Introduction

Suggestions with regard to the possible relationship between the natural sciences and ethics are usually controversial. One of the central objections that is leveled against establishing links between the natural sciences and business ethics is derived from the age-old philosophical contention that one should not deduct an "ought" from an "is." According to this dictum we should not be looking to the natural sciences' views of what "is" when we want to determine how we ought to behave in business. It is a proposition that relies on a number of very specific suppositions with regard to both the natural sciences and ethics. But these suppositions are themselves contentious. It is based on the dualistic paradigm we inherited from modernism's urge towards specialization (I will argue this point in more detail later). Alternative positions in this regard of course have different implications. Personally, I have adopted a position that allows moral deliberation to be informed (though not determined) by a number of (sometimes divergent) forces, including the natural sciences. From this perspective, Frederick's articulation of the dynamics of the evolutionary form (EF) represents a valuable contribution to the debate around ethics in organizations. The natural sciences represent a wide and complex arena of enquiry with many competing models and theories. In his development of the notion of the evolutionary firm, Frederick seems to draw primarily on evolution theory. However, Frederick's enquiries into the field of the natural sciences are not limited to this model. Elsewhere in his oeuvre, he also explores the insights and implications of complexity theory.

Complexity theory represents an especially exciting new front in scientific enquiry. It has generated a number of new insights and concepts that may prove very meaningful within the context of business ethics. It is on these insights then that I will draw as I reflect on Frederick's conception of the evolutionary firm. In what follows I will first of all try to identify the main objections that are likely to be leveled against Frederick's position. I will attempt to formulate a response to these from the perspective of complexity theory. In addition, I will show how complexity theory sheds new light on some of the issues and concerns that Frederick raises. Finally I will outline in broad terms the possibilities and opportunities that complexity theory affords those who feel themselves firmly implicated in the logic of the evolutionary firm.

William Frederick's paper deals with a number of very basic issues. I believe that the position that he develops in this paper, is likely to incur resistance with regard to at least the following concerns:

1) The danger of determinism: Are all a firm's actions necessarily determined by its evolutionary struggle, it's economizing attempts to avoid entropy in the face of thermodynamic selection? Is there no room for principled ideals?

2) Closely related to the issue of determinism, is the age-old debate about nature versus nurture. To what extent are we able to intervene in and influence the actions of firms and how should this be done? If we agree that a firm naturally responds to an environment that poses competitive demands, are we also compelled to accept that a firm's leaders have limited power over their organization's actions, and by implication therefore, also limited responsibility?

3) Can a business organization be considered subject to the same evolutionary imprinted imperatives as natural organisms? Is Frederick right when he proposes that we see firms as a coalition of biological organisms, which therefore display the symptoms of the same evolutionary struggle?

4) Is the second law of thermodynamics, stating that *all* systems tend to-wards disorder, still the most dominant view in the natural sciences? Complexity theorists argue that the second law may not be an adequate description of all systems: some systems tend towards order, not disor-der. This discovery represents one of the major contributions of the science of complexity (Lewin 2001 p. 183). With this realization, other Darwinian elements that have long been taken for granted come under scrutiny. Is natural and thermodynamic selection still the prime ex-planatory concepts in terms of developments in the natural sciences? As has been mentioned, I believe that insights from the science of complexity sheds new light on all these issues and concerns. Frederick himself alludes to certain aspects of complexity science in his paper and has in fact written exten-sively on the subject elsewhere. I will start therefore, with a brief enumeration of some of the basic tenets of complexity science and indicate why and how I be-lieve it can be of practical use for dealing with ethics in a business environment.

2. Insights From Complexity Science (CS)

2.1. What is Complexity Science?

Why bring complexity science to bear on this discussion? Science has only recently come to grips with the kind of realities that we encounter in business, i.e., complex nonlinear systems that don't necessarily respond predictably. Lewin (2001 p. 11) indicates that for three centuries, science has successfully uncov-ered the workings of the universe by means of the mathematics of Newton and Leibniz. The linear world they described was characterized by repetition and predictability, and it remains a very important part of our existence. Most of nature, however, is nonlinear and unpredictable. The weather is an obvious example: it encompasses many components interacting in complex ways, which makes it extremely unpredictable. These nonlinear complex systems may seem complex, even chaotic on the surface, but its complexity may in fact be gener-ated by relatively simple sets of subprocesses. Interactions between related parts within a complex system also leads to the emergence of a global order, a whole set of fascinating properties that could not have been predicted from what we know of the component parts.

Complexity science also provides new perspectives on evolution and the processes of natural selection. Lewin indicates that, in Stuart Kaufmann's view, pure Darwinism leaves one without an explanation of the generation of biological forms. He (2001, p. 182) quotes Kaufman as saying: "In the pure Darwinian view, organisms are just cobbled-together products of random mutation and natural se-lection, mindlessly following adaptation first in one direction, then the other." Complexity science reformulates Darwinian theory to include self-organiza-tion, by which order emerges as a result of the complex interactions within the organism itself. New theories in CS about the dynamics of complex adaptive systems seem to indicate that there are also internal, rather than merely external engines for change of the species as a community. Order arises out of the local interactions of complex dynamic systems and the system settles at the highest level of energy. CS theorists refer to this condition as the position "at the edge of chaos." An important characteristic of systems at the edge of chaos is that small changes to the system may have huge effects. Stability in this context is an emergent property. Complex adaptive systems fluctuate among three states—stasis, chaos, and the condition described as one "at the edge of chaos." The system is most creative when in the third of these states, therefore—"at the edge of chaos."

2.2. Can Theories About Complexity Provide Us With Useful Insights for Business Ethics?

In a 1992 Harvard Business Review article entitled, "Is Management Still a Science?" David Freedman argues that: "management may indeed be a science, but not the science most managers think." He argues that managers may still follow an outdated scientific mind set, namely the mechanistic, reductionist perspective. Lewin (2001, p. 199) traces this mechanistic reductionist perspective on management back to its origins in Taylorism. Taylor was strongly influenced by the prevailing thought of the 1910s, i.e., Newton's laws of motion and the new science of thermodynamics. Together these theories allowed scientists to calculate how a machine would operate with maximum efficiency. Taylor, a reductionist, analyzed the system down to its component parts and then sought the best method to ensure the efficiency of the system. Taylorism's machine-like model led to huge increases in productivity in the workplace, and is still influential today.

Yet, the recognition that much of the world, also the business world, is nonlinear and organic, characterized by uncertainty and unpredictability, has brought into relief the limitations of reductionism and the mechanistic management model. Lewin and Regine (2001, p. 198). argue that when business is viewed through the lens of complexity science it becomes clear that businesses do not merely resemble natural ecosystems. Instead businesses and natural ecosystems share fundamental properties. Both businesses and natural ecosystems are complex adaptive systems, displaying nonlinear processes. According to Lewin and Regine (2001, p. 197) we should recognize that businesses are complex adaptive systems that evolve to a critical point poised between chaotic and static states. Here, at the edge of chaos, a business' response is most creative and it is here therefore, that it is likely to be at its most profitable.

Lewin and Regine do however draw an important distinction between businesses and natural ecosystems: in economies, conscious decisions are made by people, whereas in biology there is no conscious intent of that kind. This introduces the question as to what exactly the difference is between natural systems and cultural or social systems.

3. Are Corporations Subject to the Same Evolutionary Imprinted Imperatives as Natural Organisms?

The crucial question here is whether Frederick can prove that a corporation is subject to the same laws and dynamics that dominate the natural world. Frederick argues that the firm is a coalition of biological agents and displays the same behavior and reactions as natural organisms. In his view, therefore, there is no meaningful difference between a corporation and a natural organism. What he is in fact saying is that the corporation *is* a natural organism. It is for this reason that he feels justified in utilizing evolutionary models to describe the dynamics of corporations.

Complexity theory offers a further justification for utilizing insights from the natural sciences in understanding corporations. It argues that a corporation *is* a complex system just like any other natural organism. The qualifying characteristic that allows one to extrapolate from complexity science to corporations does not necessarily reside in the fact that it is composed by biological agents. Theorizing about complex systems encompasses a wide variety of phenomena, including social or cultural systems, e.g., Lewin's (2001, p. 6) analysis of Anasazi civilizations in the Chaco canyon, Mark Taylor's (1997, p. 326) virtual webs, the brain, and ecosystems. In my own research, I have tended to treat the notion of complex systems as a metaphor. In other words, I assumed that corporations function *like* complex systems. However, reading Mark Taylor's work on the dynamics of complex systems in biology, cultures and virtual reality (non-totalizing structures as he calls them), I have realized that a much stronger statement can be made. From Mark Taylor's perspective, the rejection of a correspondence theory of truth, i.e., that words and theoretical models provide a picture-depiction of objects and events in the real world, opens a new perspective on what scientific theory actually does and can claim to do. Our descriptions of reality, *is* in fact our reality. The virtual world becomes the real world and the real world becomes our descriptions of it. What we are dealing with in science, is an array of endless layers of meaning behind which nothing is hiding. We do not reveal the truth about something, we construct it. If one treats perspectives from the natural sciences in this way, science becomes less of an instrument of control and prediction, and more a process of tracing the complex relationships between events, entities and the meaning(s) we attach to them.

Complexity theory as a scientific view is extremely effective in helping us understand the complex layers of meaning. It demonstrates how the physical survival struggle of biological organisms are intricately linked to the cultural and social life in a system, as well as the external pressures and opportunities of the environment in which organisms operate and of which they are also an intricate part. Subject-object dualisms dissolve in an intricate web, and it becomes difficult to identify and sustain a distinction between nature and culture. I concur therefore with Frederick's insistence that the dichotomy between culture and nature has become meaningless. In a very real sense, culture is nature and nature is culture.

4. IS the Danger of Determinism Looming in Frederick's Thesis?

What are the implications of a position that sees values as cultural and social responses to nature, influenced by biological and physical realities? To what extent is our behaviour determined by natural forces? It is an important question for ethics, since ethical directives become impossible in a situation where all actions are explained and even justified from a determinist perspective.

Objections to what is seen as naturalistic determinism often represent nothing more than yet another mutation of the inherent dualistic tendencies of most philosophical ethics. It is characterized by an insistence that nature should not determine values, but that behavior should instead be directed by values. However, if the dualism between values and nature is dissolved, values and ethical reasoning become just another aspect of our natural existence. It becomes possible, as Petersen (1999) described it, to "judge from our guts," or to "think with our hands." This view is much more consistent with recent studies on the origin of emotions, or consciousness. Our brain is the prime example of a complex system where order emerges from complex interactions between emotions, abstract reasoning, language, and sensory experience.

We might no longer be the transcendental subject who with abstract reasoning rules over nature and directs our own behavior, but neither are we now passive objects determined by nature. Frederick has described the complex nature of economizing in another study: *"Today, economizing among humans is clearly a blend of genetic processes and sociocultural symboling, the latter much elaborated beyond a genetic level but still resting on and continuous with that underlying genetic process and capability"* (Frederick 1995, p. 42). As a commentator on Frederick's book, Timothy Fort (1996, p. 148). noted: *"To reduce nature to ruthless competition misses the complexity of the ecologizing and power-aggrandizing elements of life just as business without concern for ethical responsibilities misses what any human enterprise is about. Frederick's description of technologizing also emphasizes human ability to solve problems, utilize symbolic processes, reason abstractly, and display creative behavioral features."*

It is important to keep in mind, however, that though our behavior may not be completely determined by ruthless selection, we are not in the "driving-seat," exercising complete control, either. We are in fact part of complex systems that self-organize towards order. These systems respond to our creative energies, it interacts with us and impacts on us, it evolves in, with, through and even despite us.

5. Is Human Responsibility an Outdated Notion?

Dissolving the subject-object distinctions between ourselves and the natural world raises questions as to whether we can in fact still argue for human responsibility in a business context. Can we still significantly influence the system that we are part of? What is the measure of our influence and how does this change the nature of our ethical pursuits in business?

In Frederick's Ruffin paper, which is under discussion in this volume, he chooses to elaborate on businesses' economizing function. Seen in isolation from the rest of Frederick's work, this focus may be misconstrued to mean that no matter what we argue in business ethics, corporations are always going to be ruthless profit-maximizers. Clearly this is NOT what Frederick has in mind.

In his book, *Values, Nature, Culture and the American Corporation (VNC)*, Frederick (1995, p. 39) distinguishes between various developments in thermodynamic theory. In *Entropy I: The Austere view*, he describes the two laws of thermodynamics and the struggle against entropy much like he did in this paper. The second section, *Entropy II: Order from disorder*, describes another view of thermodynamic effects. It argues that thermodynamic processes provide way stations—life oasis—on a road that otherwise inevitably leads to ultimate doom. This is an acknowledgement of the fact that complex dynamic systems do not necessarily always tend towards disorder, some systems display the counter-tendency that embodies order, organization, patterns and regularity. Here Frederick (1995, p. 39) elaborates on his view of human responsibility: *"In the human arena, invention, creativity, self-awareness, social awareness, intellectual exploration, symbolic forms, and technological complexity appear."* Ultimately, it is this self-organizing activity that makes sustained existence possible.

I would like to add a few thoughts on what level of responsibility becomes possible, and should be expected of us within the business context. I would also like to venture a suggestion with regard to Frederick's analysis of the economizing, ecologizing, and power-aggrandizing value clusters in his book [VNC] (Frederick 1995, p. 20). More also needs to be said about the moralizer-evaluator function of the evolutionary firm. Economizing and power-aggrandizing values should in my view be balanced by a value strategy that can deal with the paradoxical struggles between different value clusters.

Frederick proposes in his paper that: *"the moral traits, features and habits of the EF are the product of contradictions embedded in diverse neural algorithms."* That these paradoxes exist, cannot be denied, and if they are not identified and effectively dealt with, Frederick may well be right in concluding that: *"EF is not only it's own worst enemy but cannot avoid moral condemnation by others both inside and outside the firm."* However, this need not necessarily be the case. If we acknowledge the fact that we are all part of ever-evolving, self-organizing complex systems, our symbolic capabilities allow us to make pragmatic sense of the paradoxical notions we encounter in the business world. I want therefore, to take up Frederick's challenge to bring pragmatism to bear on businesses as complex adaptive systems.

In describing the firm's moralizer-valuator function, Frederick balances the economizing tendencies of the firm with the important mutualizing tendencies that are part of human life. Cooperative, symbiotic behaviors emerge as a result of the fact that cooperation makes survival (economizing) sense. Economizing motives sometimes override mutualistic tendencies and Frederick describes this irony as *"the algorithmic crossroads where one finds the most intractable moral dilemmas of EF."* Clearly we need a way out of the paradox in which economizing causes mutualistic tendencies whilst at the same time in some cases undermining it. Frederick presents us with another challenge when he describes the way in which opposite and conflicting emotions and emotive reactions coexist in the same individual and firm. What are we to do with what Frederick calls *"a veritable tangle of overlapping, inconsistent and ultimately contradictory neural algorithms lying at the heart of today's business practitioners?"*

Frederick's analysis of how the evolutionary firm (EF) makes choices under these conditions embraces both natural selection and thermodynamic selection, but still comes to the conclusion that LEE (logic of evolutionary effect) will consistently select *economizing* algorithms and that this remains the dominant motivating force behind the evolutionary firm's actions. He qualifies this position by recognizing that the moralizer/ valuator function of the firm comes into play. He also acknowledges the fact that each of individual represents a unique and diverse moral configuration that can be a rich source of independence, creativity and moral imagination. In addition, some creativity and imaginative intelligence is allowed for as part of the firm's innovator/ generator and enabler/ stabilizer functions. He further acknowledges that mutualisms abound in all systems, and that a firm's values can act as strange attractors that orientate the EF in an ever-shifting fitness landscape. Having said this, we are still led to the somewhat fatalistic conclusion that economizing considerations ultimately trump all others. Our only alternative is to somehow augment Frederick's value clusters with something that can mediate the paradoxes inherent in them.

I think Frederick's (1995, p. 187) chapter on techno-logics in VNC provides us with some useful points of departure. It makes provision for a pragmatic logic that links organizational logic, cooperative-coordinative logic, unifying logic, and civilizational/ humanizing logic, with the notions of combinatory logic, cumulative logic, and progressive logic. I want to argue that we need to creatively find mediating concepts to act as strange attractors that mediate between paradoxical notions and apparently contradicting moral demands. These mediating concepts could be developed by combining pragmatist techno-logics with what Frederick (1995, p. 119) refers to as x-factors. These x-factors are value-configurations that arise within the individual and group as a result of the complex interactions of diverse tendencies, beliefs, motivations, capabilities etc. The x-factors cause unexpected contributions to come into play, which is then mediated by pragmatist techno-logics. In this way, creative, value-driven solutions emerge. These new solutions allow us to manage the inherently paradoxical tendencies in corporations meaningfully and effectively. What I would therefore like to do is to adjust Frederick's value-cluster diagram to reflect the emergence of mediating value concepts. (See diagram 1 below.) This corresponds with Dewey's instrumental pragmatism (Frederick 1995, p. 274), which argues that values emerge from human experience in socio-cultural-economic communities. In the new diagram, therefore, values are seen as those properties that emerge within complex systems if the pragmatist techno-logic of human participants in organizations, and their unique x-factor configurations, are brought into play in situations where the three value clusters make conflicting demands. These emerging mediating values (such as trust and respect in the diagram) should however always be seen as contingent, contextual responses to specific moral dilemmas.

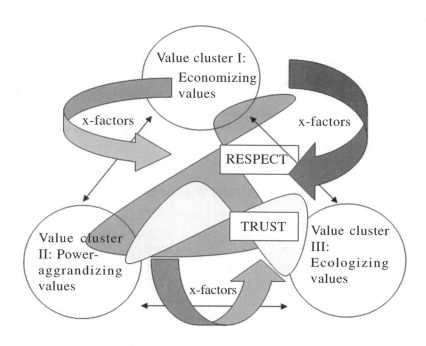

Diagram 1

6. Answering the "So What" Question: What Practical Insights Can Be Gained for Business Ethics?

6.1. Dealing with Diversity

Complexity models show that the emergent order in a complex adaptive system will be richer, more creative and adaptable if there is a diversity of agents in the system, agents with different characteristics and different behaviors. I believe this is caused by the interaction between the unique x-factor configurations of individuals, and the increased pragmatic capabilities of actors in complex systems, which creates the conditions necessary for the emergence of mediating concepts that can enhance the system's performance at the edge of chaos. This sends a strong message to business leaders to enhance diversity if they wish to enhance creativity. Agents who are part of the system must also attempt to enhance the conditions within which diversity and pragmatist, creative logics can flourish. Therefore "managing," or rather facilitating the organization as a complex adaptive system requires a specific form of leadership.

6.2. Leadership and Management

Complexity science argues against the managerial control advocated by traditional Taylorism. It argues that managers must give up the illusion of control, and instead create an environment in which creativity can flourish. Yet the message of complexity science does not merely amount to a new version of determinism that paralyzes managers by forcing them to accept the system's natural selection and self-organization. Too little direction and involvement is as misguided as too much. Management practice guided by complexity theory does not necessarily replace mechanistic management, but instead encompasses it in a larger context. Managers can no longer control their organizations from a mechanistic perspective, but they can influence where the company is going and how it evolves (Collier and Esteban 2000, p. 207).

6.3. Dealing With Internal Contradictions in Organizations

Paradox denotes contradictory yet interrelated elements—elements that seem logical in isolation but absurd and irrational when appearing simultaneously. These elements include perspectives, feelings, messages, demands, interests or practices. A further characteristic of paradoxes is that they are constructed. It is the way in which actors attempt to make sense of an increasingly ambiguous world by polarizing reality into either-or distinctions that conceal complex relationships. Paradoxes become apparent through self- or social reflection that reveals the seemingly absurd and irrational coexistence of opposites (Lewis 2000, p. 761). Paradoxes can therefore be reframed by the creative generation of mediating concepts. Complexity science makes it possible to break out of

self-organizing system that permits, for a time, the thwarting of entropic processes and increasing rather than decreasing levels of organization).

- This naturalistic perspective suggests that there are a limited number of forms—and functions or "objective functions" (cf. Jensen, 2000)— that an evolutionary firm can legitimately follow. Frederick rightly argues that the core function that dominates today's firm is economizing, supplemented by power aggrandizing driven by primary human emotions (fear, rage, panic, lust, care, play, and seeking).

- By the LEE (logic of evolutionary effect), nature creates a template or predisposition for humanity and its creations (e.g., firms) in the name of economizing at the firm level, which if left to its own devices, would ignore the need for greater ecologizing to sustain the societal (and ecological) level.

By integrating cognitive development and a combination of chaos, complexity, and ecological systems theory into Frederick's framework, perhaps we can, at least within specified time constraints, see how the forces of entropy can be managed within the evolutionary firm and its broader social context.

The Multiple Possibilities of Evolution

Biologically appropriate forms in nature and human civilization are not of a single type, but of many, despite a (mostly) common DNA structure for most living things. Biologically capable/appropriate entities range from viruses to bacteria, from plant to animal, from fish to mammal, from unconscious (at least to our knowledge) to conscious in a rational sense. Biologically appropriate forms can live in a wide range of conditions, from extreme cold to heat, wet to dry, high to low levels of oxygen, and so on. From the days when near-life forms first emerged out of the "soup" of possible materials (Kauffman, 1995) to the complex organisms we know today, however, we see emergence—and evolution—to increasingly complex systems at multiple levels (life forms, families, tribes, villages, and ultimately complex nation-states).

Complex systems tend become more, not less, complex over time (Capra, 1995; Kauffman, 1995) thereby seemingly thwarting the forces of entropy for at least a time (which, ultimately will catch up with them, presumably, if the universe or at least the earth devolves into chaos). If biological entities are multi-form, perhaps so too can be organizations, which, after all, are formed without DNA to constrict them. Such non-biological forms can conceivably be based, as Frederick himself acknowledged, on the more creative imaginings of human beings. Further, it is more than likely that neither biological processes nor societal ones have ceased their evolutionary—and adaptive—cycles; thus, over time firms too can be expected to "evolve." Indeed, this evolution happens within the lifetime of most firms, as they morph from simple sole proprietorships to partnerships or corporations, then from functional structures to divisional and ultimately multi-divisional forms. This evolutionary process was, of course the great insight of Alfred Chandler (1962). Evolutionary firms as we know them today are, in all likelihood, and as will be argued further below, a social construction rooted in the time period out of which the dominant form arose. Indeed, the past two decades have witnessed the emergence of the network structure with its boundary-less construction arising from the potentialities of instant and global communication capacity.

Since Frederick admits that evolutionary firms are not bound by their DNA structure, arguably, evolutionary firms can then (at least in theory) take multiple forms. These forms depend not only on the environmental and biological conditions out of which they arise but perhaps also on the social conditions (and attendant levels of social, cognitive, and moral development of founders and societies), as well as evolutionary selection processes (Miller, 2001) that shape them (cf. Wilber, 1995; Logsdon and Yuthas, 1997; Waddock, 2002). To say that companies are economizing entities is perhaps an accurate description of the way they have evolved to the present moment (maybe, even, the form they have today is the most "efficient" from a firm perspective, as Jensen [2000] would argue), and is at least partly a result of the system constraints they currently face. But other goals and agendas are conceptually at least possible and were even been part of firms' explicit "social contract" in the early days of their existence (Derber, 1998), when they were defined and designed to serve a broader objective than shareholder wealth, i.e., with societal good in mind. Other possibilities of corporate form and function may, thus, also (eventually) be in accord with nature's imperatives, particularly, as will be discussed below, if we take a more societal (systemic and ecological) perspective.

We can see a range of organizing possibilities in the intersection of different types of organizations operating in different spheres that are dominated perhaps by different imperatives and therefore somewhat different "bottom lines" for their entropic processes. For example, civil society organizations, such as religious organizations, educational organizations, hospitals, and activists organizations may be dominated by goals that "civilize" rather than by profits and growth (Waddock, 2002). Governmental organizations may be driven more by power aggrandizing motives (Etzioni, 1961; Waddell, 2001). Not even all business organizations find the entropic imperative towards growth that Frederick so strikingly lays out in his paper as a motivating force, albeit those businesses that don't grow tend to be sole proprietorships and small partnerships. This is not to say that thermodynamics don't enter into the equation but that stasis, at least for a time may "satisfice" some business practitioners.

There are two possible keys to a somewhat more optimistic view of the future of the firm than what I read in this paper that build on what Frederick has accomplished here. They are offered as (intellectual) food for future thought.

One possibility to re-conceive the firm as part of the *natural* tendency to *ecologize* as well as to economize (and power aggrandize) (Frederick, 1995), working from the ecological and social systems level. The second possibility is to re-conceive the firm as part of an *evolutionary* and *developmental* process that is also related to advances in human cognition, morality, and awareness that are potentially available to but typically not accessed by everyone (Wilber, 1995), not as set in stone today—and ever. In the next section, I will address the ecologizing systems perspective.

Ecologizing and Economizing: A Systems Perspective

In true naturalistic systems, i.e., those actually devised by nature, the predominant force—arguably from the same source of thermodynamic energy flows as drives formation of the corporation—may well be *ecologizing*, not economizing (see Frederick, 1995; Capra, 1995). Ecologizing relies as much on collaboration and symbiosis (Capra, 1995; Maturana and Varela, 1998) as it does on the competition of natural selection. And, importantly, despite that entropy is still at work, *there are few "externalities" in nature's ecologizing systems* (albeit there is dissipation of energy to the broader universe over time) at least at the planetary level because what is waste to one system generally becomes food for another system. Further, natural systems from the planet to the universe (including the evolution of human societies) appear to have become more, not less, complex over time, creating self-sustaining anti-entropic forces in a process of self-organization (for an undetermined period of time) (Kauffman, 1995; Lovelock, 2000). And at least one recent book has argued that the second law of thermodynamics may not, in fact, always apply in natural systems (Wolfram, 2002)

Thus, the first key to avoiding conceiving of the evolutionary firm's having been biologically determined and now immutable in its tendency to economize—and therefore externalize its wastes—may lie in conceiving the firm as an integral part of a broader ecological and social system that is both evolving and self-organizing. Some ecologists and strategists (e.g., Hawken, Lovins and Lovins, 1999; Hawken, 1993; Moore, 1997; Senge, 1990) already do conceive the evolutionary firm, as an *ecological* system and as truly *evolutionary*, i.e., not static. Here it needs to be acknowledged, as Frederick rightly argues, that all living creatures *are* subject to the forces of entropy. But arguably complexity theory provides insight into the emergent processes involved in the *evolution* of complex systems—into higher evolutionary forms, i.e., more complex systems (perhaps part of the growth process) that stabilize them at least for a period of time.

The Evolution of Consciousness—and Evolutionary Firms

Evolutionary (all) firms exist within a context that is biological in a naturalistic sense and, arising out of that, social or societal (as well as natural/ecological). My reading of the biology and psychological/cognitive development literature suggests that human *awareness* may, under certain circumstances, have the capacity to *transcend* biological imperatives of the economizing and power-aggrandizing sort. Rational thought does, I believe, sometimes exist and, occasionally, there are individuals in positions to shape social structures who have motives in mind other than immediate personal or company gain in the economizing sense. Granted, these folks are still relatively rare, however, cognitive development theory would suggest that humankind has made *significant* progress within the past 10,000 years (e.g., Jaynes, 2000; Wilber, 1996; Kegan, 1994, Torbert, 1991). Some, indeed, would argue that human consciousness is still evolving and may indeed be on the edge of another revolution similar to what humankind has undergone in its evolution from ape to man (Wilber, 1996; Ray and Anderson, 2000; Gebser, 1984). Such an on-going evolutionary process may have significant implications for the evolutionary firm.

Arguably, cognitive (and to some extent spiritual) developmental theorists might disagree with the evolutionary biology perspective that the "brain seems not to have changed one single bit since the first appearance of *homo sapiens*, some 150,000 years ago" (Mayer, 2001, 252, cited in Frederick, 2004). Cognitive (moral) development theorists might argue vociferously that the human capacity for self-awareness, rational thought, consciousness, and *conscience* have in fact evolved rather significantly, not just within the past 150,000 years since ape became man, but even more radically within the past 10,000 years (Jaynes, 1974; Gebser, 1984; Wilber, 1996; Wade, 1996). Such development may not be true for everyone but be true at least for some minority of people on the developmental *edge* of human consciousness, a group that some call "cultural creatives" (Ray and Anderson, 2001). Among this group, there are individuals who conceivably have higher levels of self-awareness, more cognitive capacity (Kegan, 1984), and more related capacity for moral thinking (Kohlberg, 1976), and thus more insight into the interconnectedness between man and nature, mind, spirit, and body (not to mention among all things at the quantum level) (Wilber, 1996; Capra, 1995, 1984). Some (relatively greater than in previous times) portion of individuals in the world today, that is, appear to have moved beyond the conventional and into the post-conventional and—for the shamanistic few—even post-post-conventional stages of cognitive, moral, and other forms (e.g., spiritual) development (Wilber, 1995, 1996). What, if true, are the implications of this development for the evolutionary firm?

Business (evolutionary) firms as we know them today are little more than 100 years old, albeit the structural elements of hierarchy, economizing, and power aggrandizing that, in Frederick's theory, characterize them can be found also in much older entities, such as the Catholic church and military organizations of all types. Corporations, while not giving up their profit seeking, have also "evolved" and changed significantly within the past twenty-five years (certainly the last 100), arguably moving away from their original social contract to serve society (Derber, 1998) into "serving" the great maw of investor capitalists with *only* wealth maximization for investors seemingly held in mind.

Further, it is important to recognize that the evolutionary firm we know today is a man-made construction, very likely developed from a specific level of cognitive and moral development (state of consciousness or awareness). Most probably that stage can best be classified as "conventional" from a developmental perspective (Kegan, 1982, 1994; Kohlberg, 1975; Wilber, 1995, 1996), where the majority of adult managers today can be found (Fisher, Rooke, and Torbert, 2001). Wilber (1995) suggests that these stages of cognitive development, which are the same as those of Kohberg (1975) and Gilligan's (1982) stages of moral development, are universal throughout the world, although they go by different names in different systems.

If it is true that human consciousness is still evolving, then biological forces of nature may also be pushing humankind and the societies generated by humans beyond current capacities into new evolutionary forms of organizing. Witness the emergence of strategic and social partnership alliances and other collaborative forms of organizing that integrate economic motives with others during the past several decades, not to mention the network structure within corporations. Witness the technological interconnections—and immediacy of interactions—made possible by the global web of electronic networking. If we conceive of Chandler's organizational forms, the multi-divisional form as the appropriate form for the time and technology of the early 1960s, then the network form, with its more systemic and relational orientation, may be the appropriate form for today. As time has gone by and technology has developed, networked organizations with more relational requirements have become not only more feasible but arguably the predominant form of organizing. This development speaks of evolution in its rawest form.

Linking Evolution, Ecological Thinking, and Consciousness

Higher stages of development—post (and post-post) (Wilber, 1996, 1995) conventional stages—are more systemic, more ecological in their orientation. A more systemic approach to organizing the evolutionary firm would recognize the embeddedness of the firm in its broader systems of human civilization and in nature—and its inherent and inextricable *relationship* in an ecological sense to that broader societal—and naturalistic—context. From this more systemic—ecological—perspective, a naturalistic approach would recognize the need for long-term sustainability (perhaps using the core function of innovator/generator that Frederick suggests does offer some degree of hope of positive improvement) (e.g., Hawken, 1993; Hawken, Lovens, and Lovens, 1999). Such systemic accountability, of course, requires also a shift in the types of externalities that are created so they feed into other systems systemically.

That said, the evolutionary firm, as we know it today, is a man-made conception and it is a conception that arguably arose out of a certain level of consciousness, i.e., the conventional level of consciousness development (Kohlberg, 1976; Kegan, 1982, 1994; Wade, 1996; Wilber, 1995). As a result of when the firm evolved and the general level of consciousness of its developers, today's evolutionary firm can itself probably be firmly placed at the conventional level of development (Logsdon and Yuthas, 1997; Waddock, 2002). The evolutionary firm as we know it, if this proposition is correct, arises from a consciousness imbued with the Cartesian split between mind and body and a relatively linear and hierarchical way of conceptualizing the world.

The conventional level is not ecological in its orientation, preferring one-way transactions rather than more systemic and integrated approaches. In its conventional level conception the firm produces goods/services and also wastes, which it tries to get rid of while growing as much as possible to thwart entropy. Because, however, the firm is conceived linearly rather than cyclically, little thought is given to ensuring that "waste" that is externalized is "digestible" by some other entity. That digestibility, which is exactly what happens in nature, is what is, in effect, demanded by deep ecologists and other advocates of sustainability (Freeman et al.; 2000; Hawken, 1993; Hart, 1008; Gladwin, Kennely, and Krause, 1995; Hawken, Lovins, and Lovins, 1999). Sustainability theorists suggest that planet earth cannot long sustain human civilization under the operational modalities of the current stage of development of the evolutionary firm, which spews out toxic wastes and uses up resources that cannot be replaced without regard for their ultimate re-use in other systems.

Continuing Evolution?

Can we possibly expect that evolutionary firms will *continue* to evolve, to be more systemic and holistic in integrating their own economizing activities with the ecologizing on which *natural* systems are based? There is some hope. E.g., an article in a recent *BusinessWeek* described Bill McDonough and Michael Braungart's theory (in a book entitled *Cradle to Cradle*) of ecologically-driven business enterprise:

> Fabrics you can eat. Buildings that generate more energy than they consume. Factory with wastewater clean enough to drink. Even toxic-free products that, instead of ending up as poison in a landfill, decompose as nutrients into the soil. No more waste. No more recycling. And no more regulation (Conlon and Raeburn, 2002, p. 70).

People who think in this way have clearly moved beyond conventional to more systemic ways of thinking, ways that can conceive the firm as part of its broader ecological environment. This conception could allow for a transformation of what are today externalities and waste into usable fodder for some other creature's or human's use. Thus, there is hope for the evolutionary firm and its place in a sustainable society, arguably, if we link sustainability approaches premised on ecologizing to developmental theories that suggest that in fact the evolutionary firm can evolve.

Is There a Next Stage?

Can mankind escape the predisposition of economizing that is integral to the evolutionary firm as we know it today and that Frederick believes is deterministic of evolutionary firms' fate and operating mentality? If you believe in the logic of the evolution of increasingly complex systems combined with higher levels or stages of awareness that I have ever so briefly delineated, perhaps so, especially if we focus at the systemic level using an ecological framing.

As part of nature, the firm—and our concept of what the firm is—does presumably change and evolve. If we remember that the firm today has been in existence for at most a couple of hundred years (and really as we know it, less than 150 years), then we can see that evolution is still possible, that perhaps it did not stop 150,000 years ago, either at the individual or the corporate form level. In the span of evolutionary time, this is a remarkably short period. And, as we begin to see when we look carefully, even today, the processes that are integral to evolution appear to still be at work.

No, I am not one hundred percent optimistic, because all of the terrible news that Frederick cites in the paper is certainly true, not to mention the lack of sustainability of our current ways. And those who are able to think beyond today's rewards to tomorrow's systemic implications are fewer than we might wish, but they exist. Isn't that the promise of evolution?

Bibliography

Capra, Fritjof. 1995. *The Web of Life*. New York: Anchor Doubleday.

———. 1983. *The Turning Point: Science, Society, and the Rising Culture*. New York: Bantam Books.

Chandler, A. 1962. Strategy and Structure. Cambridge, Mass.: MIT Press.

Conlin, Michelle, and Paul Raeburn. 2002. Industrial Evolution. *BusinessWeek* (April 8): 70–72.

Derber, Charles. 1998. *Corporation Nation: How Corporations Are Taking Over Our Lives and What We Can Do About It*. New York: St. Martin's Press.

Etzioni, Amitai. 1961. *A Comparative Analysis of Complex Organizations*. New York: Free Press.

Fisher, D., D. Rooke, and W. Torbert. 2001. *Personal and Organizational Transformations: Through Action Inquiry*. Boston: Edge\Work Press.

Frederick, William C. 1995. *Values, Nature, and Culture in the American Corporation.* New York: Oxford University Press.

Frederick, William C. 2004. "The Evolutionary Firm and its Moral (Dis)Contents," in *Business, Science, and Ethics,* ed. R. Edward Freeman and Patricia H. Werhane. Charlottesville, Va.: Philosophy Documentation Center, pp. 145–176.

Freeman, R. Edward, Richard H. Dodd, and Jessica Pierce. 2000. *Environmentalism and the New Logic of Business: How Firms Can Be Profitable and Leave Our Children a Clean Environment.* Oxford: Oxford University Press.

Gebser, Jean. 1984. *The Ever-Present Origin,* trans. by N. Barstad with A. Mickunas. Athens, Oh.: Ohio University Press.

Gilligan, Carol. 1982. *In a Different Voice: Psychological Theory and Women's Development.* Cambridge, Mass.: Harvard University Press.

Gladwin, Thomas N., James J. Kennelly, and Tara-Shelomith Krause. 1995. "Shifting Paradigms for Sustainable Development: Implications for Management Theory and Research." *Academy of Management Review* 20(4) (October): 874–907.

Hart, Stuart L. 1997. "Beyond Greening: Strategies for a Sustainable World." *Harvard Business Review* (January–February): 66–76.

Hawken, Paul. 1993. *The Ecology of Commerce.* New York: HarperBusiness.

Hawken, Paul, Amory Lovens, and L. Hunter Lovens. 1999. *Natural Capitalism: Creating the Next Industrial Revolution.* Boston: Little Brown.

Jaynes, Julian. 2000. *The Origin of Consciousness in the Breakdown of the Bicameral Mind,* 2nd edition. Boston: Houghton-Mifflin.

Jensen, M. C. 2000. "Value Maximization and the Corporate Objective Function." In *Breaking the Code of Change,* ed. M. Beer and N. Nohria. Boston, Mass.: Harvard Business School Press: 37–57.

Kauffman, Stuart. 1995. *At Home in the Universe: The Search for the Laws of Self-Organization and Complexity.* New York: Oxford University Press.

Kegan, Robert. 1982. *The Evolving Self: Problem and Process in Human Development.* Cambridge, Mass.: Harvard University Press.

———. 1994. *In Over Our Heads: The Mental Demands of Modern Life.* Cambridge, Mass : Harvard University Press.

Kohlberg, Lawrence. 1976. "Moral Stages and Moralization: The Cognitive-Developmental Approach." In *Moral Development and Behavior: Theory, Research, and Social Issues,* ed. Thomas Lickona; Gilbert Geis and Lawrence Kohlberg, consulting editors. New York: Holt, Rinehart and Winston.

Logsdon, Jeanne M., and Kristi Yuthas. 1997. "Corporate Social Performance, Stakeholder Orientation, and Organizational Moral Development." *Journal of Business Ethics* 16: 1213–1226.

Lovelock, James. 2000. *Gaia: A New Look at Life on Earth.* New York: Oxford University Press.

Maturana, Humberto R., and Francisco J. Varela. 1998. *The Tree of Knowledge: The Biological Roots of Human Understanding,* revised edition. Boston: Shambala Press.

Miller, Geoffrey F. 2001. *The Mating Mind: How Sexual Choice Shaped the Evolution of Human Nature.* New York: Anchor.

Moore, James F. 1997. *The Death of Competition Leadership and Strategy in the Age of Ecosystems.* New York: HarperBusiness.

Ray, Paul H., and Ruth Anderson. 2001. *The Cultural Creatives: How 50 Million People Are Changing the World.* New York: Crown.

Senge, Peter. 1990. *The Fifth Discipline.* New York: Free Press.

Torbert, William R. 1991. *The Power of Balance: Transforming Self, Society, and Scientific Inquiry.* Newbury Park, Calif.: Sage Publications.

Waddell, Steve. 2001. "Core Competencies: A Key Force in Business-Civil Society Collaborations." Working Paper.

_____. 2002. "Six Societal Learning Concepts in an Era of Engagement." *Reflections: The SoL Journal* 3(4) (Summer).

Waddock, Sandra. 2002. *Leading Corporate Citizens: Vision, Values, Value Added.* New York: McGraw-Hill.

Wade, Jenny. 1996. *Changes of Mind: A Holonomic Theory of Consciousness.* New York: State University of New York Press.

Wilber, Ken. 1995. *Sex, Ecology, Spirituality: The Spirit of Evolution.* Boston: Shambala Publications.

_____. 1996. *A Brief History of Everything.* Boston: Shambala Publications.

Wolfram, Stephen. 2002. *A New Kind of Science.* Champaign, Ill.: Wolfram Media, Inc.

DE RERUM NATURA

Edwin M. Hartman

Abstract: Aristotelian naturalism is a good vantage point from which to consider the moral implications of evolution. Sociobiologists err in arguing that evolution is the basis for morality: not all or only moral features and institutions are selected for. Nor does the longevity of an institution argue for its moral status. On the other hand, facts about human capacities can have implications concerning human obligations, as Aristotle suggests. Aristotle's eudaimonistic approach to ethics suggests that the notion of interests is far subtler than many have realized, and leaves open the possibility that cooperativeness may be adaptive, virtuous, and a good thing for the agent. Lawrence and Nohria argue along remarkably similar lines, and they provide evidence against those who would question the existence of character. But promising as the Aristotelian approach is, it seems to give an inadequate account of our moral responsibility to those who are not members of our community.

I would indeed that love were longer-lived
And vows were not so brittle as they are.
But so it is, and nature has contrived
To struggle on without a break thus far.
Whether or not we find what we are seeking
Is idle, biologically speaking.
—Edna St. Vincent Millay

Introduction: Naturalism

Like Lucretius, whose title I borrow, some of the scientists whom we have been considering in this conference offer a similar message: what science says we are greatly determines what we ought to do. That is a characteristically naturalist view. Contemporary naturalists hold that the venerable distinction between sentences that express what is the case and those that express or imply what ought to be the case cannot be maintained, and that the natural and social sciences are not cleanly distinguishable from moral philosophy. You can see what the consequences of this view are for the field of business ethics.

Contemporary moral realists hold that moral propositions may be true or false, defensible, vulnerable to defeat by evidence, and useful in causal explanations like this one: "Clinton was impeached in part because he behaved dishonestly, in part because many of his political opponents were partisan and vindictive." Evidence for the claim would include facts about his opponents' motivation and Clinton's false statements. In the jargon, the event of Clinton acting dishonestly *supervenes on* the event of Clinton telling self-serving untruths.[1]

Moral statements have a feature that some non-moral ones lack: they imply a positive or negative attitude towards the fact that they express. That is because most people believe that there is reason to act morally. But many factual statements, too, give us reason to act. Consider "Wet Paint," or "Our building is on fire." Naturalism does not deny that moral utterances imply reasons for action, or that morality by its nature is taken seriously and often engages the emotions. "You ought to do A" is a form of advice. "You are dishonest" is not merely a statement, accurate or not. But the same is true of "You are stupid." "That would be stupid" is a form of advice as well.

Realists typically believe that there are good moral theories, on the basis of which one can make moral judgments. A good moral theory is a coherent theory that explains the intuitions and confident moral judgments of sane and well-informed people in much the same way as a scientific theory explains their observations and observation statements. In contemplation and conversation we try to develop a coherent set of moral principles that fit with most of our mature intuitive judgments about particular situations and kinds of situation.[2] Our intuitions may appropriately involve emotional reactions, and may make reference to virtues. So our view that an act is dishonest or cowardly will count for something, as will our feeling of shame or disgust. Lawrence and Nohria (2002, esp. 95) and others claim that our moral intuitions and emotions are innate, the unreflective result of our evolution, acquired without much explicit instruction and fairly uniform from one culture to the next.

Neither principles nor judgments are foundational: to achieve coherence we may adjust our judgments, as for example by deciding that after all it is not morally wrong to take actions in war that result in civilian casualties. Or we may adjust our principles, as for example by deciding that act utilitarianism isn't right.[3]

Aristotle might say that a morally good person has defensible intuitions, but may act on them without working out the defense. So a person of courage is not deterred by fear from taking appropriate risks, and has a sense of what level of risk is appropriate. This involves the faculty that we now call moral imagination, the ability to see which principles are salient in a certain real or contemplated action.[4] Essential to this faculty is the appropriate emotion: we are supposed to be indignant at dishonesty, contemptuous of cowardice, and so on. In fact, Aristotle holds that lapses in rationality are sometimes the result of emotional failure, for the wrong emotion can cause one to misapprehend the situation. Compare Lawrence and Nohria's argument (45ff.) that emotion is somehow the trigger of reasonable action.

An Aristotelian realist, an ethicist who takes virtue seriously, can reasonably claim that Jones showed courage rather than foolhardiness in criticizing his boss, or that Smith's success was based on her intelligence rather than on mere luck. Virtues supervene on psychological states, and they justify behavior as they explain it.

You might think that Aristotle is the last moral philosopher that one would want to involve in a conversation about science and business ethics, since he not only has a discredited teleological scientific method but also believes that businesspeople cannot achieve genuine happiness or moral standing. But conversing about science or business and ethics requires understanding naturalism, whose father is Aristotle. His biology and "first philosophy" form the basis of his psychology, on which in turn his ethics is based. He holds that good character is in some way a natural state, and that it is morally good for people that they and their faculties operate naturally—that is, to achieve their appropriate ends.

Ends? Wasn't Darwin supposed to have expunged teleology? Can we get anything sensible out of this?

Let us try. I am going to consider sociobiology, a strong form of naturalism, as a possible source of insight on morality, and raise some doubts. But I accept that we must take certain ascertainable facts about ourselves into account as we try to design ethical practices and institutions. Next I am going to consider what history has to tell us about morality, and then what the social sciences, ably represented by Messick, might say about the limits on morality. Finally, I am going to review what Aristotle says about some of these issues. He sounds remarkably like Lawrence and Nohria. But there are questions about the welfare of people outside the community that Aristotle and the biologists of morality do not answer very well.

We start with some evolutionary scientists.

Darwin and Sociobiology

Darwin's theory seems to some readers to imply that predatory behavior is, in the jargon, *selected for.*[5] Social Darwinists like Spencer inferred that it was natural for predators to win out in human societies too—hence morally acceptable for the life of the weak to be nasty and brutish, and above all short. Spencer argued from facts about the success of predatory behavior to conclusions about its moral appropriateness.

Darwin himself offered a very different argument: the community as a whole will be better able to survive to the extent that its members are trustworthy, cooperative, public-spirited, even sometimes altruistic. So nature selects for communities whose members are moral in those respects. The specific lesson is that we should be kind to our family first of all, but to our fellow community members too. And indeed there is some reason to believe that what is moral is what supports the survival of a community, as opposed to that of certain individuals.

This view appears to be supported by much animal behavior. For example, when a predator approaches a flock of birds, the birds nearest to the predator sound the alarm. This is good for the flock, but the birds that sound the alarm are putting themselves at risk by becoming the likeliest to be caught by the predator. We are invited to infer that community-preserving behavior is selected for.

I do not think this will do. Today many evolutionary biologists believe that it is not the community or even the individual but the gene whose survival drives animals' behavior. But isn't the bird who raises the alarm being self-sacrificing and gene-sacrificing? Yes, in a way, but that is the wrong question. The right question is this: What sort of predisposition stands a bird and its gene in the best stead? And the answer is that all of the birds in the flock, and all of their genes, are better off if they all are predisposed to sound the alarm when the occasion arises. Those familiar with the commons and the Prisoner's Dilemma will recognize that the willingness of any individual to cooperate in situations of this sort is a good long-term strategy for all the individuals. Being that sort of bird helps preserve your genes. My colleague Trivers (1971; see Lawrence and Nohria, 2001, 84f.) and others have argued that what is somewhat oxymoronically called reciprocal altruism is selected for.

Birds do not deliberate. To believe that they bravely cast aside the opportunity for self-preservation and hold the line for the sake of their beloved flock is worthy of a romantic poet. (As one might say, "Ah, Nature! Where the courage of the bird/Leads to an act Ayn Rand would find absurd.") They're just wired to sound the warning cry when the big predator appears. It is just as well; for if a bird were smart enough to figure out that its act was preserving the flock, it could probably figure out that it would stand a better chance of surviving if it let some other birds call the warning while it survived as a free rider hiding somewhere in the middle of the flock. For familiar reasons, this attitude would be bad news for the flock and the genes that dwell therein.

In fact, we may think that rationality has bad consequences for cooperation and the commons that it preserves, since rational maximizers will ruin the commons because each will note that s/he is better off being greedy whether or not his/her neighbors are. In that case, a certain kind of sociobiologist will draw the inference that morality as we understand it has no basis at all where cheating is possible. But Trivers, de Waal (1996, esp. chap. 4), and others have provided evidence that even among primates capable of deception, reciprocal altruism is common.

Of course not every property of every extant species is selected for in the strict sense, and our social arrangements are not all the result of natural selection. Many properties are results of some other properties that are selected for; others are the result of physical conformation, or chance, or sexual selection or, as Lewontin et al. (1984) have argued, interaction with the environment. That we are rational beings is itself an accident, in the sense that it might have turned out otherwise. Nor is every property that is disadvantageous to its owner winnowed out. Modesty and forbearance are still with us, or at least with most of this audience. Some people are dumb or ugly, and they have children. So reciprocal altruism is present but may not have been selected for in the strictest sense.

If reciprocal altruism is selected for, is it therefore by definition morally good? Must an institution that survives be a good institution? Must a trait that survives be a virtue? Surely not. It is natural for us to care more about our families and our neighbors than about strangers, and that sort of division of labor is morally appropriate. But its appropriateness does not follow from its naturalness. It is natural in the same sense for us to eat more food than is good for us, because storing up fat has been selected for.

Here some sociobiologists might claim that our morality is a useful fiction.[6] Societies in which people falsely believe that there are some well-based moral principles that are binding on them, as religious people believe in a God who rewards and punishes justly, will fare better than they otherwise would. But those beliefs are false, according to this argument: what is true is only that reciprocal altruism under a range of circumstances has social advantages. But if people learn that their moral beliefs are false, then they will cease to hold to the socially useful fiction of morality, with nasty results.

Lawrence and Nohria (95) may have this argument in mind as they raise the question whether morality is "a convention of obligation and duty constructed from mode and custom" or "moral concepts are derived from innate emotions." I take it that they would hold that if morality is socially constructed rather than innate, then it is a socially useful fiction that we'd better not analyze very much lest it deconstruct in our hands. But surely some conventions are good conventions just because they are useful.[7]

They claim that if, as they believe, the innateness view is right, then the naturalistic fallacy is not a problem. " '[O]ught' becomes simply a logical means to a human purpose." Aristotle would find this claim attractive, but I do not. It seems to be based on one of two assumptions: (1) that every human purpose is good from a moral point of view, or (2) that we're only talking about good purposes here. The first assumption has no chance of being true; the second leaves us with the problem of separating the good purposes from the bad ones. How is that to be done? Surely not by saying that the innate ones are good. There appear to be two further assumptions, of which I grant neither: (3) that we have a way of distinguishing between "B is the purpose of A" and "A caused B" when A is not an action of an animate being, and (4) that all of our innate emotions are the result of evolution.

I do not believe that morality has or needs a basis in evolution. If a certain trait contributes to the continuation of a community, that is a reason for calling it a virtue, even if it is not selected for. If predatory deceitfulness keeps a gene going, that is not a reason for calling it a virtue. I am no expert in this field, as must be evident, but I have the impression that something like this is going on. Some sociobiologists believe that moral philosophers have been assuming that our moral principles are demonstrably sound because they are somehow firmly based on the truth, which is to say on science, and in particular on the facts about evolution. And when it turns out that morality is not selected for, so that

evolutionary biology does not uphold morality, moral philosophers are supposed to be reduced to babbling confusion.[8]

Hobbes characterized the state of nature as a war of all against all, and
held that civilization involves getting out of that state. He would have been
amazed at any suggestion that we are in the state of nature and that the state of
nature somehow indicates what morality is. Of course not all sociobiologists
agree that the state of nature is general war. Nor would Rousseau or Locke.

The Cultural Evolution of Morality

There is far more to be said on this issue than I can say in this essay, but some
summary remarks may be useful.

Biologists are not the only scholars who claim that what has survived is
somehow natural, hence good. The same idea has occurred to some historians,
and it provides a kind of *reductio* of facile naturalism.[9] Lawrence and Nohria
speak of cultural evolution (50, 89) without committing themselves to any
ambitious claims about the morality of traditional practices. But there have
been historians who have baptized what has survived—or, in the case of Marx-
ists, what eventually will. Some conservatives—Burke and Hayek, perhaps—
have wanted to justify certain traditional practices in a sort of sociobiological
way. Isn't it arrogant of us, they ask, to question the pillars of traditional morality, particularly as it relates to sex and private property, which has evolved
over a long time and survived much change? (We are presumably supposed to
forget about traditions like slavery and female genital mutilation.) Most attempts to improve matters generate bad unintended consequences.

Consider feminism. The traditional arrangements have served our purposes in more ways than we can comprehend. The liberal rationalist should
take how things are as strong evidence for how they ought to be, and avoid the
unintended consequences of social engineering. But surely we can also see
why the traditional arrangements, useful as they may have been, are no longer
appropriate. Social scientists may help us understand practices of which we do
not see the point so that we can assess them from a moral point of view and
more rationally decide whether to accept them.

One might find a parallel to evolution in the way in which our notions of
human rights and tolerance expanded as a result of economic development.
The consequent emergence of the nuclear family, dependent as it was primarily
on just two adults, gave people a greater range of choices and duties and hence
encouraged the notion that they should have corresponding rights and responsibilities.[10] What Lawrence and Nohria call the Great Leap gave humans the
ability to deliberate and choose. The opportunity to make a range of important
choices became available to ordinary people later; it is one of the marks of the
modern era and perhaps also of western society. But we had better be careful to
avoid the tempting but false conclusions that because people have few options
their rights are unimportant.[11]

We want to avoid an evolutionary theory of society that equates morality with viability and adaptability, because a society can be viable but bad. That is why we have politics. Aristotle claims that human beings are by nature civic creatures, but not that politics is an easy undertaking. If nature selects for political leaders like Hitler or Saddam, then so much the worse for nature.[12]

Our form of government is fragile; it is not foolproof or knaveproof. When civic society does not rise to the level of reciprocal altruism, each citizen may contribute to the destruction of the commons by demanding, for example, ever lower taxes to be achieved by reducing everyone else's benefits. Thus our citizenry becomes a sort of poster child for Darwinism: each of us protects our genes and those of our families, but the cost is bad schools, traffic jams, and dirty air—the destruction of the commons. This does happen.

One of the factors that can help ensure the kind of cooperation that a good community requires is trust: I need to believe that my cooperation will be reciprocated according to a social contract that probably cannot be closely enforced. We turn now to the examination of a natural process that helps create the conditions for trust.

Dealing with the Way Things Are

Some years ago, in a Ruffin lecture on which I had the pleasure of commenting, David Messick (1998) offered a nice example of how science can discover facts about human nature that moral philosophy ought to take into account. Messick presented evidence for the familiar thesis that the tit-for-tat strategy in games like Prisoner's Dilemma works better for the individual than does uncritical cooperation or relentless exploitation. He went on to show that the kind of self-fulfilling trust that can support cooperation is sometimes based on apparently arbitrary marks distinguishing those who deserve trust from those who do not. This is not altogether surprising: it would be hard to find a fully rational basis for confidence that one can gain from cooperating with another person whom one does not know. This pattern of behavior has benefits for a community. Widespread exploitative behavior leads to a worse outcome overall than does cooperation, as the Prisoner's Dilemma and commons arguments show. Messick does not claim that biological determinism is at work here: the selection mechanisms are likely cultural as well as genetic.

As I noted earlier, among birds and some other animals the winning behavior in the evolution game is the one that promotes the survival of the gene; the survival of the community is secondary. Human beings, who are smarter than birds, may have problems with free riders ruining the commons because each of us can assess the selfish advantages of being a free rider. There is good moral reason to create communities in which people do not ride free. Creating communities of this sort requires some combination of developing mechanisms for enforcing cooperative behavior and encouraging people to think differently about what might reasonably motivate them. That is, we have to think about both politics (including the politics of organizations) and morality, and we have to think about them together. To put it in Aristotelian terms, human beings are rational animals and political animals. That they are rational makes it both necessary and possible for them to be political in a way that birds are not.

A certain kind of naturalism is not supported by these considerations. That birds seem to be altruistic in certain circumstances does not imply that we have a moral obligation to be altruistic, or reciprocally altruistic. Another kind of naturalism, on the other hand, is. That being a cooperator-no-matter-what is a losing strategy is a strong fact-based consideration against the claim that one ought to be a cooperator-no-matter-what. The facts of the matter about human nature do limit and shape what people ought to do. There is reason to be what Messick calls a pragmatist: one should cooperate only with actual or potential cooperators.

Original Christian doctrine demands that one act generously even when one's generosity will be exploited. Kantian doctrine seems to demand much the same. Kant, the ultimate anti-naturalist, cites with approval the old line "Fiat iustitia, ruat coelum"—let there be justice even if heaven should fall—without any sense that the falling of heaven might indicate something wrong with one's notion of justice. He has been criticized for holding that, in effect, it is wrong to lie to the Nazis about whether your Jewish neighbors are hiding in your basement. The Kantian view seems to be that one ought to act as though one were in the Kingdom of Ends even though one manifestly is not. A moral realist would argue that it makes a moral difference that one is not. Similarly, if Messick is right, the moral realist will notice that certain human traits that seem morally problematical are functional. We are clannish because our clannishness gives us a fairly good answer to a difficult and important question: how do I decide whom to trust, so that I can reap the benefits of cooperation while minimizing the risks? That the traditional answer—trust one of us but not one of them—has endured this long is an indication that it is a useful rule even though it does not sound particularly acute. It is the sort of rule that we should keep in mind in creating organizations and other communities. But while we can make good use of it, we must also be careful with it. Racism and sexism are morally unacceptable.

Management and politics, sciences of the possible, are crucial to ethics because they create the conditions in which people know that they can behave ethically without being wiped out. Making the world safe for pragmatists while making money is not easy; nature does not do it for us. But Messick argues persuasively that nature helps show us how to do it.

There is a lesson about justice as well. When we are trying to decide whether discrimination based on a certain sort of distinction is just, we need to look at the role that that distinction plays in a community and consider whether it is a useful role. That is the kind of question that an anthropologist or a psychologist or an organization theorist is supposed to ask and answer. Its answer is the beginning of a judgment about justice.

Messick does not infer from the survival of a human practice that it is good from a moral point of view. On the contrary, he argues that understanding how a practice has survived may be a step in the direction of improving it. He suggests that questionable practices ought to be subjected to scrutiny to determine, if possible, what purpose they might ever have served and whether the conditions that gave rise to them still hold. Due consideration would have to be given to the emotions and expectations of those who had grown accustomed to taking the practices seriously. This is preferable to just accepting, say, genital mutilation because it is traditional. It may be no accident that it is traditional, that it serves some purpose of someone; so let us consider what purpose it serves and whose purpose that is. But there is no presumption that it serves a good purpose.

The disposition to create in-groups based on arbitrary distinctions leads to some moral problems, which may become more serious as globalization advances. The traditional criteria of inclusion will no longer do. We shall have a difficult time reaching a consensus on what the new ones should be, but we shall have to find some ways of deciding whom to cooperate with.

Cooperation and Morality

Somehow we do manage to cooperate, and that is a good thing, for otherwise there would be no communities, no organizations, and a terrible economy. Some scientists and their philosophical interpreters have considered cooperation and said that we have learned altruism, or something like it. But morality is not only about cooperating, and talking about altruism is not altogether helpful.

What is an altruist? A person who acts to satisfy the interests of others and takes a loss in doing so? Then what would a whole society of altruists be like? On whose interests would they act? Does it even make sense to speak of an altruist having interests? Perhaps an altruist is someone who always cooperates, whether or not others do. In that case, altruists will likely pay a heavy price.

Reciprocal altruism entails sacrificing self-interest—that is, the opportunity to be a free rider—by cooperating in support of the commons. This attitude is to be encouraged, but it is hardly selfless, since it is the winning strategy for all. In this case the reciprocal altruist has certain personal interests, separate from those of others in the community. Morality is essentially a matter of cooperating where there is reason to believe that cooperation will be forthcoming in response, or can be elicited. I believe that that is a fairly common view.

Let me suggest an Aristotelian alternative. Aristotle too holds that good citizenship in a good community is essential to being a good person: in fact, a good community is a necessary condition of being a good person. He also claims that a person of good character enjoys doing the right thing (*NE* II 3 1104b5ff.). In Aristotle's case that entails not only being a good citizen but also acting in ways that are consistent with one's own excellence—one's courage, wisdom, justice, and so on.

To make sense of this, we must understand that Aristotle is a *eudaimonist*: he holds that the moral person is the one whose soul is in a state of fulfillment (or flourishing or well-being or profound happiness or some other word that doesn't quite capture the idea). A teleologist as well, Aristotle holds that this state is the natural culmination of human life. It is a state of heightened rationality, to begin with, since humans are by nature rational creatures, but also of all other virtues. As human beings are civilized creatures too, the excellent state of one's soul is such that the person of good character is a good family member, friend, citizen. One is in a state that no one can have any good reason not to want to be in, a state that a wise person does want to be in.

Instead of addressing the question, "Why is it in my best interests to be moral?" Aristotle states why my acting in my best interests will be a good thing from others' point of view. Of course acting on the basis of short-term pleasures that coarsen the soul and alienate others is not in one's best interests. But suppose someone objects to Aristotle, "But I don't want to speak truth to power, and I don't want to help the poor. Acting bravely and generously aren't in my best interests; they're in someone else's best interests." Aristotle would reply, "Yes, I know. That's because you're a stingy coward. If you were courageous and generous, you'd enjoy speaking truth to power and helping the poor, and it would be in your best interests. And people who are brave and generous have better lives than those who are not." To which the stingy coward replies, "No they don't. They risk getting fired and they lose a lot of money, and that's bad." And Aristotle replies, "You remind me of the person who says, 'I'm glad I don't like spinach, because if I liked it I'd eat it, and that would be bad, because I hate it.'"

Aristotle holds that at least some people are naturally capable of achieving *eudaimonia*, but they must have the right kind of upbringing and education, in which one learns not only facts and correct principles but also the right desires and emotions. True happiness is not just a matter of getting what one wants but rather a matter of wanting the right sort of thing and getting that. So in the educational process *one learns to have certain interests*. If one is stingy or cowardly, one fails to achieve fulfillment and deep happiness not because one does not get what one desires but because one does. The gratification of the wrong desires may make one an outcast, may disappoint one, may ruin one's liver.

The greatest possible autonomy would be the ability to decide what shall be in one's interests. If that were possible, one could hardly make the decision on a selfish basis, since one is deciding what is to count as selfish. Yet it would be rational to choose interests that are consistent (so don't aspire to enjoy both smoking and good health) and achievable under likely circumstances (so don't aspire to be a billionaire). It would be rational to cultivate interests that do not seriously interfere with others' interests, as well as interests that can be served in the sort of society in which one will likely live. This is not so different from saying that there would be good reason to aspire to be a person of good moral character.

In carrying out this project one would have to recognize some limits. One cannot choose to live well without food, for example. And biologists have a lot of interesting news about what living well requires. If Aristotle is right, it cannot be in one's best interests to be alone, with no friends or fellow-citizens. It cannot be in one's best interests to be cowardly or greedy or stupid or irrational or unjust. Anyone of that sort will fare poorly in a good community, and cannot count on thriving in a bad one. Somewhat more controversially, Aristotle suggests that we ought to care more for our own children than for others' or for those outside the community. Messick gives reasons for believing that too.

Aristotle infers from our nature as communal and rational creatures that he can describe in some detail what will necessarily be in our best interests. Some of his proposed limits seem to us too strict, as they exclude women, farmers, the working class, and businesspeople. Those of us who are liberals in the applicable sense will allow that there is a broader range of ways in which people can be happy and fulfilled. We resist Aristotle's brand of naturalism when he holds that "Jones is a municipal bond salesman" entails "Jones is at best only superficially happy and is not truly virtuous." Yet we recognize limits on the possible forms of happiness, and we agree that one can mistakenly believe that one is happy, and can want some things that are not good for one. Perhaps any coherent and sustainable set of desires is a legitimate basis for happiness, so that one can be happy without being virtuous. But in a good community virtues are more sustainable than vices. That is in part an empirical matter, and therefore a reason for being a naturalist.[13]

What, then, does the Aristotelian approach have to do with evolution?

For one thing, evolutionary theorists imply that our nature puts some serious limits on what we want and what we need, and on what our communities can be like. Family bonds are not optional. Cooperation is possible and highly desirable. Aggression is not going to go away. As Lawrence and Nohria say, we are disposed to acquire, to bond, to know, and to defend. Any possible conception of happiness has to take those facts into account.

Second, we should not be sure that cooperation is always an expression of altruism. If Aristotle's view of self-interest is right, people may be self-interested and cooperate because they do not want the other villagers or the other prisoner to suffer unfairly. Even those not highly virtuous in Aristotle's sense have interests that are not separate from others', not narrowly selfish in the way that is presupposed by how we sometimes talk about game theory or economics.[14]

Eudaimonism is not standard egoism. It is compatible with other-directed morality. The person of good character, a civilized creature, is a good citizen and friend, and for that reason accepts principles that permit all people who are able to achieve *eudaimonia* to do so. In an Aristotelian utopia, every citizen capable of doing so achieves this state of fulfillment; none interferes with anyone else's fulfillment.[15]

The eudaimonistic approach does address some problems that sociobiologists and philosophers have raised. Those who believe that the evolution of our brains leads us to be rational maximizers ask why we should be moral in the standard sense. Why should I help someone in need? Why shouldn't I just be a free rider? Some who believe that helping behavior is selected for—Ruse, for example—raise the same problem. They talk as though evolution has fooled us into not being rational maximizers by implanting cooperative beliefs in us. But why should we continue to hold these beliefs if they are not true instead of just being a maximizing free rider?

The Aristotelian response is this: "You are asking the wrong question. The right question is this: 'Why should I be the sort of person who takes pleasure in helping those who are in need?' And the answer to that is that in so doing you will fulfill your nature and achieve well-being, and contribute to a community in which others will cooperate with you in achieving well-being." And how do we know that? "Just look at human nature," Aristotle replies. "We are social creatures whose need and pleasure is to live in a community and exercise our rationality. Morality is in our best interests when we get our best interests right."

Talk about altruism and self-interest obscures this insight. Talk about co-operating because it is the right thing to do as opposed to cooperating for prudential reasons obscures it in the same way. This is unfortunate, because Aristotle's position is one that evolutionary scientists and moral philosophers alike ought to welcome.

Despite his teleological tendencies, Aristotle does not claim that what is natural is morally good because it is natural. Good character is not automatic; in fact, it is rare. It requires serious education and the right kind of community environment. Aristotle takes human nature into account in describing good character. The well-being of human beings, for example, is not the same as the well-being of animals or of gods; and their sort of well-being would not suit us. But he does not believe that nature by itself is driving us towards the good life. In this he is right.

An Interesting Similarity

Lawrence and Nohria have views remarkably similar to Aristotle's. For example, Aristotle holds that the virtues that produce *eudaimonia* are means between extremes. Lawrence and Nohria locate themselves in the Aristotelian tradition in suggesting that happiness is a kind of harmony among the drives. We can think of the four drives that they identify as continua of dispositions, and of the Aristotelian virtues as lying on the mean of one of those continua, with vices at one of the extremes. So, for example, courage is at the mean on the continuum of the drive to defend, and greed is at an extreme of the drive to acquire. People who have achieved *eudaimonia* in Aristotle's sense appear similar to those that Lawrence and Nohria describe as having the right amounts of the four drives. They share weaknesses, too. Aristotle's notion of the mean is not of much help to anyone trying to work out whether, for example, a certain act is courageous, nor does he claim that it is. Lawrence and Nohria offer no independent test of whether one's drives are in balance.

Aristotle argues that one can be a person of good character and *eudaimonia* only if one lives in the right kind of *polis*. Lawrence and Nohria argue in chapter 11 that a good organization is one that accommodates its employees' drives. Human beings are social creatures, and good societies must meet their needs. But must a profitable organization meet its employees' needs? Can we show that a morally good organization is characteristically stable and profitable, or are we making the mistake of taking stability and profitability as criteria of moral goodness?

I think that the answer is something like this. Stable societies and successful organizations depend on cooperation, hence social contracts, hence trust. Like communities, organizations need social capital. If people act on the basis of rational self-interest in the standard sense, as the Prisoner's Dilemma and the commons argument illustrate, then managers will have a difficult task (228f.). But Lawrence and Nohria deny, as Aristotle does, that people are always motivated by self-interest narrowly understood. Whatever may be the merits of postulating drives, they understand clearly that bonding, for example, does not require a basis in the drive to acquire. Perhaps they would accept Aristotle's claim that a person of good character is happily motivated by socially useful and personally fulfilling considerations.

Here an extreme anti-naturalist might say that there can be no necessary identity between happiness (or whatever we call the object of morality) and any state as empirically described, for people want different kinds of life. An extreme naturalist, perhaps Aristotle himself, would say that the fairly narrowly describable state that is the culmination of human nature is by definition *eudaimonia*. As a compromise, we might say that the good life is a matter of getting what one wants, but also a matter of wanting things whose acquisition enables us to fulfill our short-term and long-term desires. We can find out what those things are by considering the ways in which our nature and our community affect our ability to develop wants and satisfy them. To the extent that our community interferes with our ability to develop and satisfy our desires, which will differ from one person to another within certain limits, it is *prima facie* immoral. That is why Aristotle says that ethics is ultimately about politics.

Earlier I noted that Lawrence and Nohria make much of the question whether morality is conventional or innate. No doubt it is innate—or, as Aristotle would say, natural.—to some degree. But Aristotle argues that good character is a product of instruction and the right environment as well. How much does the environment count? Does it count so much that there is no point in postulating character? We turn to some social psychologists who have argued just that.

A Possible Problem about Character

For a naturalist it is appropriate to assess a theory of virtues as one would any theory that undertakes to explain human behavior. Certain social psychologists and their philosophical allies have raised doubts: they do not believe that postulating virtues is a good way to explain behavior. For one thing, some names of virtues do not denote anything unitary: people are brave or talkative in one sort of situation but not in another. And just where we would think virtues would motivate actions, agents seem to be swayed more by situational factors and considerations of convenience. The Milgram experiment shows an appalling lack of moral courage in two-thirds of all subjects. The Good Samaritan experiment (Darley, 1973) shows that even many seminary students will not help a stranger in apparent need, particularly if they are late for a lecture. This topic is a Ruffin Lecture in itself, but let me make an observation or two, with thanks to Robert Solomon, who shared an unpublished paper on this subject. It has now been published (2003) along with a reply by Harman (2003).[16]

To begin with, when people act out of character under pressure or the influence of the environment, or alcohol, or too little sleep, we should infer that their character is of finite strength and durability, which is to say that they are not saints or villains. And when we do act under pressure, we sometimes exhibit one of the more expedient virtues, such as docility, perhaps because we do not possess all of the nobler ones to the extent that we think we do; or, if we do, they are only strong enough to make us regret what we have done.

There is no basis in the experiments for denying that some people are good at making moral judgments and acting on them while others are not. A number of people walked away from the Milgram experiment. Nor does a virtue ethicist need to deny that context counts. The officers of Enron no doubt acted under both pressure and temptation. On the other hand, there is no evidence that Jim Burke or Roy Vagelos would have done what they did. Part of the reason for that may be that Jim Burke and Roy Vagelos thought it important to create a corporate environment in which those pressures and temptations were unlikely to arise. What that shows, as Solomon argues (echoing Lewontin *et al.* in a different context), is that we should not facilely separate character from environment, since the two interact complexly. That is not news to Aristotle.

It is certainly necessary to pay attention when social psychologists provide evidence that virtues are more complicated than we believe, and in some respects contrary to nature. You may be courageous when confronting the dean but terrified of the dentist. It may be that our moral taxonomy does not map neatly onto our psychological taxonomy. In that respect some virtues are like rationality (not surprising, Aristotle would say): we can be rational about some things but not others. Does this mean that there is no such thing as rationality? No, but both courage and rationality are harder to achieve than we have thought.[17] Aristotle emphasizes that good character is a difficult accomplishment rather than an automatic gift of nature. It would be a good thing if all people had enough moral imagination, including the right emotional makeup, to act correctly when there is a conflict between courage and cooperativeness, as in the Milgram case, or between generosity and punctuality, as in the Good Samaritan case. In fact many do not.

Lawrence and Nohria provide support for Aristotle by adducing evidence about the brain to help explain what Aristotle calls character, but they surely do not believe that either rationality or the good *polis* is automatic. They know as well as anyone how hard management is, but they see in human nature the potential for good and productive citizenship in the workplace. They would agree that rationality makes it possible for persons to be political animals in the right way. No doubt they would agree with Aristotle that no one can achieve personal excellence who does not live in an excellent community.

The father of communitarianism as well as of virtue ethics, Aristotle argues for a eudaimonism that supports moral behavior and attitudes towards others in one's community. But what about strangers?

Strangers: The Need for Broad Principles

One of the great lessons of the parable of the Good Samaritan was that the man that he rescued was a stranger, from a different community. There seems to be no place in Aristotle's views or in those of evolutionary scientists, for kindness towards those in the out-group. If Aristotle cannot justify kindness to strangers, can we?

Up to a point, Aristotle's view is consistent with our intuitions. Fort (2000, 728) elaborates on Messick by citing the anthropologist Dunbar as claiming that, given our limited cognitive abilities, solidarity and consensus are hard to achieve in groups of more than 150. (Aristotle puts the population of the ideal community a bit higher than that.) After all, one develops one's moral identity face to face with others (729f.). We cannot monitor or much affect the lives of those far from us. It is not surprising that we lack the emotional support that moral action requires as we consider their fate. Is that a bad thing? Not altogether, since things work well in general if we assign primary responsibility to families and secondary ones to neighbors, and develop virtues and emotions accordingly. Our obligations must take account of what we are. But Aristotle shows signs of not understanding that what we are is contingent upon historical and cultural facts as well as scientific ones.[18] For things might change: for example, telecommunications technology might make more vivid to us the plight of the distant poor, and other improved systems might make it easier for us to assist them.

We should appreciate what Aristotle has done. He has started with the notion that ethics is about the good life, and has described the best sort of life for a human being. He makes a strong case that the agent who is deeply happy has a good character. That is comforting, even more comforting than the endurance of reciprocal altruism.

It is one thing, however, to believe that we cannot realistically cooperate with strangers or extend to them the same obligations or the same emotions that we do to family. It is another thing—a serious error—to say that we should have less respect for them or consider them inferior to us in any morally pertinent sense. Aristotle does not seem to comprehend this. He does not worry about any sort of obligation to barbarians, or even about slavery. Thereby he shows the limits of morality insofar as morality is based on the possibility of cooperation, which leads to the desirability of reciprocal altruism or, on Aristotle's theory, a more elaborate and sophisticated relationship.

It is a point supportive of morality that the recognition of ourselves as conscious and deliberative beings requires that we understand others as being the same. Aristotle does suggest that language binds a community; so did many of his fellow citizens, who called foreigners barbarians because they went "barbarbarbar" instead of speaking properly. But in his writings on what we now call the philosophy of mind and psychology (he does not distinguish them) he does not ponder consciousness deeply. He does not notice that, as Wittgenstein and others have argued, one can know about one's own mind only the sort of thing that one can know about the minds of others. Nor, therefore, does he infer that one can be self-conscious only if one is conscious of others, or that therefore it is natural for language-users to grasp intuitively that other language-users are feeling and aspiring creatures like themselves. To grasp that point and to see that it holds for strangers who speak a different language is not to grasp the whole of morality, but it is important. Regarding oneself as one person among many—a capacity crucial to justice and to moral principle—does not play a sufficiently large role in Aristotle's ethics, which is primarily about the good life for oneself, though the good life is a social one.

We can make the same criticism of ethics based on evolutionary theory. No doubt one's ability to know what someone else is thinking is the kind of advantage that any gene would want to have on its side, but it is not clear that evolution selects for the ability to draw any inference from morality about the usefulness of that ability, still less for the disposition to care very much about strangers upon whose kindness we shall never depend.

We learn a great deal about morality from understanding what permits individuals and communities to survive through time. We learn something further about morality from understanding the good life in depth. But there are some aspects of morality that even this valuable information about human nature does not teach us.

Morality is not only about cooperation or about reciprocal altruism, or about *eudaimonia*. It is about treating humanity in all its forms as an end in itself. It involves principles, which systematize our intuitions. It may well be, as Lawrence and Nohria (95) find many scientists and my colleague Colin McGinn claiming, that our innate or early learned intuitions cover a good deal of the ground in morality. At some point, however, we begin to think about them and to want them to make sense and be consistent. In the process of thinking and talking about them, we develop principles that we then test against the intuitions. Eventually we may find ourselves asking questions like this: Does someone else's membership in some group alien to mine justify treatment different from what I offer one of my own? Yes. Does it make that person less reliable? Maybe. Less honest? Probably not. A less worthy person? Not at all.

If Donaldson and Dunfee (1999) are right, this process, undertaken in a multitude of widely separated communities, leads to a set of fairly substantive principles that represent a remarkable consensus.[19] The wide acceptance of these hypernorms does not guarantee global solidarity, but it is useful for people in different communities to understand that there is this consensus on principles that apply across community lines. It may be that these principles are too broad to be very useful, but it is good news that they have widespread support, and good news that we share some intuitions about morality. The consensus gives hope that through reflective equilibrium, which bears a close resemblance to Aristotle's dialectic, or some similar process we may be able to create a coherent set of intuitions and principles that reaches beyond our narrow communities towards something global. It is a further reason for optimism that there appears to be a widespread human desire to be reasonable—that is, to act according to principles that any sane human being would recognize as giving an agent good reason to act. I do not know where that desire came from, but it is good that we have it.

We shall always choose up sides. We shall always ration our trust and limit many of our affirmative obligations. Built the way we are, we cannot do otherwise. But we ought always to think of all other people, built the way they and we are, as having dignity and deserving respect quite apart from whether we can ever cooperate with them, apart from whether thinking of them that way comes naturally to us or does us any good.

Notes

The author gratefully acknowledges the support of the Prudential Business Ethics Center at Rutgers.

1. The latter event, in turn, supervenes on some complex events involving Clinton's state of mind, which in turn supervene on events and states of atoms and the void. Moral events and states supervene on non-moral ones in the sense that there cannot be two events alike in all non-moral respects but different in some moral respects, nor can a person or a state alter in some moral respects without altering in some non-moral respects. Supervenience, which is also sometimes said to hold between mental and physical events, does not entail reducibility: there is no implication that we can find bridge laws between non-moral and moral states or events, still less that we ought to stop using moral language and stick to scientific language.

2. This form of argument is at least as old as Socrates. Rawls (1971) elaborates on it by offering what he calls reflective equilibrium.

3. One might object that the analogy between perceptions and intuitions is a bad one, since intuitions, unlike perceptions, are not based on anything solid and might be

false. Indeed, our intuitions might be false. If, for example, we have been raised to believe that women should be subordinate to men, we may have a strong intuition that feminism is bad. But our perceptual judgments may be false as well. If we have been raised to believe that women who behave in certain bizarre ways are witches (rather than, say, paranoid schizophrenic), then we might say, "I know from observation that there are witches. I just had a really bad conversation with one." We shall have better moral intuitions and better perceptual judgments if we have better theories about what is morally required and what causes bizarre behavior.

4. I do not mean to suggest that we can solve problems of any kind by inventing a name for a faculty that by definition solves them.

5. In the next several paragraphs I am indebted to O'Hear (1997).

6. Ruse (1993) admits to believing this sometimes but not always; see esp. 503f.

7. The point may be that there is no self-regarding reason to be moral. I shall argue that that is not true, and that Lawrence and Nohria themselves do not believe it. Nor are they as anti-convention as they seem to be in passages like this one.

8. That morality gives the agent a reason to act does not imply either that all moral acts are self-interested or that morality is selected for.

9. O'Hear (1997) discusses this issue.

10. See M. Hartman (2004).

11. A situation like this may lead us in an Aristotelian direction. We are inclined to think that human beings are innately capable of choice and of creating the future for themselves, and that a community that thwarts that natural capacity harms them in some essential way even if they don't mind. But Aristotle himself does not take rights seriously.

12. Lawrence and Nohria (206f.) quote Putnam's description of the divergent ways in which northern and southern Italy evolved—the latter disastrously.

13. Over the years Ronald Duska and to some extent Gerald Cavanaugh and others have sought to talk me out of the permissive view, and I have begun to think that I should move a bit in their direction, in part for reasons that follow.

14. The Aristotelian position needs to be distinguished from the genuinely trivial form of psychological hedonism that holds that all of our acts, charitable or not, are self-interested. Aristotle believes, correctly, that people do act contrary to their own interests, though he does not find it easy to explain.

15. Aristotle spoils this picture by suggesting that truly happy people will depend to some degree on the labor of Epsilons and others who cannot achieve the highest state.

16. Others who raise questions about character are Doris (2002), Ross (1977), and Ross and Nisbet (1991).

17. Rationality has come under skeptical criticism much as the virtues have, but I am a realist about rationality—about logic, sound reasoning, etc.—as I am about morality. Dennett (1995) postulates "memes," self-reproducing ideas and patterns of thought that colonize and dominate our minds though mechanisms not related to their rationality. Unless one is a very strong sort of pragmatist, one might find this difficult to believe. For one thing, giving a rational argument for it would involve the proponent in a self-contradiction. The more plausible view, held by both O'Hear and Lawrence and Nohria, is that rationality stands its owners in relatively good stead. It would follow that memes that undermine rather than support rationality will fail in their evolutionary obligation to the gene.

18. This is not surprising. Aristotle fathered not only naturalism but also the related doctrine of essentialism. In the past fifty years, as positivism has faded away, philosophers have tended to argue that some apparently necessary truths are in fact contingent, and essential items accidental.

19. Hypernorms may be procedural (having to do with voice within and exit from a community), structural (having to do with political and social organization generally), or substantive (having to do with the fundamentals of right and wrong). Donaldson and Dunfee claim that substantive hypernorms, as opposed to procedural and structural ones, are "discovered" as we contemplate the "convergence of human experience and intellectual thought" (53). I think that all of the hypernorms can come out of a process of reflective equilibrium extended across boundaries. Aristotle might well agree with Donaldson and Dunfee, provided they agree in turn that the hypernorms are subject to some exceptions.

Bibliography

Aristotle. 1894. *Ethica Nicomachea*, ed. I. Bywater. Oxford: Clarendon Press.
————. 1999. *Nicomachean Ethics*. Translated, with Introduction, Notes, and Glossary, by Terence Irwin. Second Edition. Indianapolis: Hackett Publishing Company.
Darley, J. M. 1973. "'From Jerusalem to Jericho': A Study of Situational and Dispositional Variables in Helping Behavior." *Journal of Personality and Social Psychology* 27: 100–108.
Dennett, Daniel C. 1995. *Darwin's Dangerous Idea: Evolution and the Meanings of Life*. New York: Simon and Schuster.
Donaldson, Thomas J., and Thomas W. Dunfee. 1999. *Ties that Bind: A Social Contract Approach to Business Ethics*. Boston: Harvard University Business School Press.
Doris, John. 2002. *Lack of Character: Personality and Moral Behavior.* New York: Cambridge University Press.
Fort, Timothy L. 2000. "On Social Psychology, Business Ethics, and Corporate Governance." *Business Ethics Quarterly* 10: 725–733.
Harman, Gilbert. 2003. "No Character or Personality." *Business Ethics Quarterly* 13: 87–94.
Hartman, Mary S. 2004. *The Household and the Making of History: A Subversive View of the Western Past.* New York: Cambridge University Press.
Lawrence, Paul R., and Nitin Nohria. 2001. *Driven: How Human Nature Shapes Our Choices.* New York: John Wiley and Sons.
Lewontin, Richard, Steven Rose, and Leon J. Kamin. 1984. *Not in our Genes: Biology, Ideology, and Human Nature.* New York: Random House.
Messick, David M. 1998. "Social Categories and Business Ethics." *Business Ethics Quarterly*, Special Issue No. 1: 149–172.
O'Hear, Anthony. 1997. *Beyond Evolution: Human Nature and the Limits of Evolutionary Explanation.* New York: Oxford University Press.

Prior, William. 2001. "Eudaimonism and Ethics." *Journal of Value Inquiry* 35, 325–342.

Rawls, John. 1971. *A Theory of Justice.* Cambridge: Harvard University Press.

Ross, L. 1977. "The Intuitive Psychologist and his Shortcomings." In *Advances in Experimental Social Psychology* 10, ed. L. Berkowitz. New York: Academic Press.

Ross, L., and R. Nisbet. 1991. *The Person and the Situation: Perspectives of Social Psychology.* New York: McGraw-Hill.

Ruse, Michael. 1991. "The Significance of Evolution." In *A Companion to Ethics,* ed. By Peter Singer. New York: Blackwell Publishers, Ltd.: 500–510.

Solomon, Robert C. 2003. "Victims of Circumstances? A Defense of Virtue Ethics in Business." *Business Ethics Quarterly* 13: 43–62.

Trivers, Robert L. 1992. "The Evolution of Reciprocal Altruism." *Quarterly Review of Biology* 46: 35–57.

Vidaver-Cohen, Deborah. 2001. "Motivational Appeal in Normative Theories of Enterprise." In *The Next Phase of Business Ethics: Integrating Psychology and Ethics,* ed. by John Dienhart, Dennis Moberg, and Ronald Duska: 3–26.

de Waal, F. B. M. 1996. *Good Natured: The Origins of Right and Wrong in Humans and Other Animals.* Cambridge, Mass.: Harvard University Press.

Werhane, Patricia H. 1999. *Moral Imagination and Management Decision Making.* New York: Oxford University Press.

CAN SCIENCE TELL US WHAT IS RIGHT? AN ARGUMENT FOR THE AFFIRMATIVE, WITH QUALIFICATIONS

Lisa H. Newton

Abstract: We argue that the goal of natural excellence, discoverable by scientific observation of the species, is appropriately called good, and the proper object of human development and education. That affirmation stands, but we are forced to acknowledge several conceptual difficulties (in the deliberate creation of "natural" excellences, for example, and in cases of plurality of excellences) and a final inability to reconcile human freedom—surely part of the natural excellence of human life—with the need to prevent humans from using that freedom to sacrifice it (through, for instance, drugs, self-indulgence, and emotional enthusiasms).

After a paper to the likes of which we have just been treated by Edwin Hartman, one rises to the podium with mixed feelings. On the one hand, there is the sheer pleasure of contemplating the argument, spreading it out on the table at different angles, holding it up to the light, enjoying it, playing with it, doodling comments and responses all over the margins. On the other hand, there is the necessity of *following* it on the program, with some presentation that will not badly disappoint the audience, which has been thoroughly spoiled by its experience so far in this session.

In the present case, the pleasure quickly overcomes the dread, for this argument in particular restores me to my Aristotelian roots, and licenses me— by its journey over the ground of moral realism and naturalism—to consider some slices of the problems of our business and political systems in light of Aristotle's approaches in the *Nicomachean Ethics* and the *Politics*, always the best starting points for such discussions. I will attempt to address examples presented in Hartman's paper, just to keep the discussion focused.

I take the "naturalist" position as the generally Aristotelian disposition to treat all natural growth to maturity (to excellence, defined by the ability to fulfill one's function) as good. We will follow the naturalist argument as far as it can take us, as it were growing the core of the argument, the central trunk from which all branches of qualification will spring. We will note these qualifications as we go along. Although they are powerful, and although they grow very close to the ground, we will conclude by arguing that a sense of "the natural" as the good for human life and associations is highly useful—if only for the purposes of telling us where to put our barriers against the normal play of human nature.

Let us see what the ancients can tell us about discovering the Right and the Good. The central claim is that what is natural is good, and the first objection is obvious: where does that "natural" falls in relation to the boundary that David Hume erected between fact and value; does it contain the notion of "good" within it? It does, sort of; for any species that can easily fall short of its highest and best maturity, what is "natural" is not the usual easy outcome of following the path of least resistance. It is the unusual and difficult achievement of full maturity, the highest normal endpoint of growth, the highest possible ability to fulfill one's normal function—and that is its good. We will call that assertion Proposition One (P1). For most of creation, the distinction does not apply. Rocks, bacteria, and most other plants and animals up to the simplest of mammals, simply are what they are. If they are not blighted by disease or run over by a truck, whatever they end up as is the highest they can be. Higher plants can be cultivated to become better than they would be in the wild; fish can be grown in farms to be larger and healthier than they would ordinarily be. But those variations in achievement are not of primary interest for purposes of this paper. (There are problems with farm-raised fish, but those also are not to our present purposes.)

The ancients, possibly Plato more than Aristotle, began to get interested in creatures only when they were advanced enough to be educated. Most domestic animals do not qualify. For the cows and the chickens, all we add to their lives is feed and water, and their DNA takes over from there; they will be what they will be. Horses and dogs are more interesting, which is why Plato keeps using them as examples. Take the Labrador Retriever, for instance. It is a hunting dog. Its function, in Aristotelian terms, is to retrieve ducks from the waters of the bays and rivers over which the ducks are shot. The function entails sitting in absolute silence in a blind for freezing hours, remaining unmoved when a huge shotgun goes off beside their ears, then leaping, on command, into freezing waters, swimming out to where the duck has fallen, picking it out of the water so gently that not a feather is misplaced, swimming back to the blind and dropping the duck at its master's feet. Then the sitting begins all over again, with icicles wreathing the chin. Anyone who thinks that behavior is "natural" in the sense of coming about without intervention, hasn't ever watched an untrained dog. For while that behavior is "natural" in the sense of "in the repertory" of the dog, it will not come about without strenuous efforts on our side. If we treat the dog like a chicken—just feed it twice a day, give it water, and keep it confined so it can't get onto the thruway—it will grow up to be an immensely happy unhousebroken canine, lying around all day and chewing unprotected bedslippers. That is its "normal" unguided path to maturity. But for Plato and Aristotle, it is sadly lacking; the training necessary to make the dog capable of performing the function for which it has been bred is a necessary part of the dog's reaching a genuine maturity, genuine happiness.

The key to the persuasiveness of that argument, to the extent that it has any, is the phrase, "for which it has been bred"; the function of the Labrador Retriever is not a matter of uninstructed nature, but carefully selected by us for purposes of our own. In accordance with that selection, we have bred the Labrador to have exactly those qualities which fit it for its assigned task—the layer of fat to keep it warm in the water, the strong swimming muscles, the apparent lack of irritability in its nervous makeup, and the wondrously soft mouth. The Labrador itself, forsooth, is not a natural object at all. It is a result of our purposes, as much an artifact as a knife. The natural virtue of a knife is sharpness, given the function for which it was manufactured. It can have no other end than that. The natural end of the Labrador is to retrieve ducks. Was that the Labrador's choice, or ours? Was it a good choice?

Qualification One, then (Q1), from the trunk of the natural development to natural excellence, is the possibility that natural excellences can be changed by human interventions. But, by naturalism, is this right? Do we have a right to screw around with the natural excellences? Do we have the *right* to create, by selective breeding, a dog whose natural excellence is different from the natural (God-created) dogs, or wolves, from which it was derived? It's hard to see, in general, why not. On the other hand, there are surely limits. In breeding dogs, we tend to accept the retrievers, spaniels, hounds, and shepherds as perfectly natural working dogs, and approve of them. But the Pomeranian and Yorkshire Terrier clearly have to be kidding.

Q1 is more serious than it might appear on the surface. Consider a problem recently brought up in the *Hastings Center Report*. The problem is one raised by the defenders of animal rights. We get our marvelously inexpensive eggs, as most of us probably know, from vast laying areas called batteries, where "battery hens"—hens kept all their lives in tiny cages, force-fed specially concocted foods—lay two or three eggs a day into a conveyor belt that carries them off. Never are the hens permitted to run, or scratch, or see the sun, or build a nest. They are unhappy. (You may not know how you would ever tell if a hen is unhappy, but those who raise the hens know: they start pecking each other through their cages, for one thing.) Because they are unhappy, the animal rights movement insists that they should be treated differently—allowed to run, allowed to eat outside, allowed to nest. They should be allowed to be happy.

Of course, their unhappiness comes from the fact that they are aware of their confinement. It does not seem to be possible to breed out the brains, such as they are, in hens. But it might be possible to get brainless, or better yet headless, chickens through genetic engineering, possibly with some interference with fetal development. Assuming it is possible, should we do that? Chickens without heads would be perfectly adapted to the task now set for battery hens. They would be aware of nothing, feel nothing, experience nothing, but would come into and go out of existence without any idea of what a normal chicken might be doing with its time. So the animal rights proponents are answered; the hens in this facility used to be in pain, but now they are not any more. So the problem is solved. Is it? Why do we have a sneaking suspicion that things are not better, but worse?[1]

We have here the first stand-off, or branch point One in our tree. Growth to excellence in fulfillment of one's natural potential is unquestionably good. But we can change natural excellence, if we so desire. We humans can bring about many (not all) changes through selective breeding, slowly; we can bring about the even more changes, probably much more quickly, through techniques of genetic engineering. Is it good to modify natural excellence in useful directions? If it's wrong, why is it wrong? If it's right, why do I feel so bad about it? What applications suggest themselves for human beings?[2]

What new issues arise when this screwing around with nature hits the business scene? Is it ethical to use and sell genetically modified organisms (GMOs) for food crops—strawberries with flounder genes to protect from frost, canola resistant to Roundup, corn engineered to poison corn borers? We tend to think so, but Europeans tend to disagree strongly.[3] Is it ethical to patent them, and to sue any and all farmers who turn out to have your patented plants in the field, no matter how they got there?[4]

Let us grow the tree a bit further. We deal with educable animals. The assumption we make with Labradors, children, and many species in between, is that they possess innately the potential for an excellence that is natural for them but will not develop "naturally," that is, without interference—they must be educated in certain ways in order to achieve their potential. As Aristotle put it, "the virtues are implanted in us neither by nature nor contrary to nature; we are by nature equipped with the ability to receive them, and habit brings this ability to completion and fulfillment."[5] This education is in accordance with the nature of the student, and is therefore, by naturalism, good, as is any aid, assistance, or enablement provided to permit a natural being to achieve its natural end. We'll call this Proposition Two (P2). Aristotle would have children first educated in much the same way we train Labrador Retrievers. First there is the rule, enforced in whatever way suggests as most effective: reward, punishment, repetition. Dogs and children need to be housebroken, taught to be attentive, obedient, and amenable to a daily routine. Through well-enforced obedience to rules, the dog or child acquires habits of good behavior. Training, or education, then continues to encompass the physical and other skills for excellence; the dog needs to learn to sit, fetch, and give, and the child needs to learn how to hit a baseball off a tee. At that point, save for continuing practice, the dog's education is complete. The child, as we know, continues on.

Aristotle would teach no ethics until good habits had been completely inculcated. Then the process is easy. You do not have to persuade students to adopt good behavior, even if that were possible, which it rarely is. All you have to do is teach the reasons for the original rules, and if possible suggest that a few key propositions ground all (or most) of them in one logical system. The student internalizes the reasons for the rules; after all, he has no reason not to, since he is already doing what they instruct, and the reasoning makes his life more coherent, which he likes. Thereafter, they are his own reasons, and he can order his future behavior around a more flexible understanding of the way the rules work. Through consistent and reflective practice of appropriate behavior in all parts of his life, the student becomes truly virtuous—not just a man, Aristotle would say, who acts justly, but who performs acts of justice as a just man would perform them.[6]

The tree has reached its next branch point. Supposing we have a normal dog, or child, one fully educable to his true potential, how do we figure out just what education is appropriate for that potential? In part, this is a question of means, not ends. For instance, we want all children to learn to read. That said, there are dozens of "schools" of literacy methods, claiming to have the best way of accomplishing that end. But in larger part, it is a question of the ordering of natural excellences, for they are many. The very qualities, for instance, that make a Labrador Retriever good at sitting in a blind for hours, tolerating cold, boredom, and guns going off in his ears, swimming in freezing water without detriment, carrying dead ducks without damaging the feathers, and placidly obeying every command of half-baked hunters, make him ideal for life around young children. There is little they can do to injure him, he will not bite them no matter what they do, and he can easily be trained to play harmlessly with them. For most of the same reasons, Labradors have been found to be excellent Seeing-Eye dogs and companions for otherwise disabled persons. Neither function—companion for thoughtless young children or trained helper for the infirm—played any part in the choices surrounding the breeding of Labradors. It just happens that the constellation of qualities that make a good duck hunter makes for competence in other functions as well. We'll call this Qualification Two (Q2): while training and education to natural function is good and (by definition) conducive to virtue, it may be that there are several other functions that such virtues serve equally well. So the good life for the Labrador Retriever may not be as determinate as its breeders would think. (It would follow, incidentally, that there are roles for which one might attempt to prepare a Labrador that would not accord with these qualities—as attack dogs, for instance. Initial question: would it be *wrong* to train the Labrador for that function, on the assumption that he might, in some inferior way, be able to fulfill it?)

What makes Aristotle so sure that there is one correct path of educational development for humans? For starters, he isn't so sure, pointing out in the *Nicomachean Ethics* that in this field, we are not looking for mathematical certainty (*pace* Plato of *The Republic*) but only for "what is true for the most part."[7] Next, he eliminates vast classes of humans. He seems to consign the tradesmen and that lot to the category of Labrador Retriever, to be subjected to ordinary obedience training with regard to their betters in the *polis*, then apprenticed for a terminal degree in handicrafts to some master or other, there to spend their lives. The active life of reason that he concludes is the best for human beings, the life of deliberation and choice, is reserved for a very small number—males, of good family, and of sufficient wealth (inherited) that they need not spend significant waking hours worrying about making a living. (For some, the life devoted to study—the life of contemplation—is possible,[8] but in this context we will not consider this possibility.)

Third, he thinks he knows how people ought to live—how they will be happiest. There was a consensus on the matter. Before we laugh too uproariously, we should point out that that consensus has a fair amount of staying power. All he wants us to accept is that the most fulfilling life for a human being is not (the most obvious alternative), the life of physical pleasure, Big Macs and Big Shakes by day and beer and brothels by night, but a balanced life of activity and leisure, curiosity and routine, and above all responsibility, public and private. I think we can find similar ideals in Mill, Santayana, even Aldo Leopold. Part of human capability involves not just living a good life (life according to a rational principle, the passive life of reason), but in taking an active part in forming those principles through deliberation. For the P2 phase of the investigation, those principles apply only to the individual life.

The moral education he suggests already blocks the expression of certain tendencies that we might be inclined, based on biology, to call "natural." For example, take the tendency, verified by the sociobiologists (or evolutionary psychologists) to kill your stepchildren. Robert Wright's *The Moral Animal*, tracking Darwinism (and Darwin), provides an excellent Darwinian explanation of the tendency to kill the stepchildren.[9] Many animals do. If the mate of a nursing female dies, a male interested in a larger harem will take her over. The first thing he does is kill her cubs. That brings her into heat, he mates, and the new litter bears his genes. Stands to reason. The point, after all, is to get your genes into the next generation. Although, of course, that's the wrong way to put it. The lion has no intention of "getting his genes into the next generation." But that lions who through some cruel trait of stepchildren-hatred always kill the cubs of the lioness they take over after the death of her mate, seem to have more cubs in the next generation with their genes. Since step-cub killing is probably a gene-mediated trait, step-cub killing will show up more in every generation, until its alternative, step-cub nurturing, fails completely from the species.

Evolutionary psychology tells us quite a bit about what we ought to do "by nature." First of all, men should look for women who are young and pretty. Why? Well, pretty means more likely to be healthy, and young means more likely to conceive and bear many children. Meanwhile, women should look for powerful older men for husbands. Every child they bear will have their genes, so there is no need to be picky about male physique or good teeth. Their major problem is getting food and protection for all their children until those children are themselves of reproductive age. For that they need a man powerful enough to compel the community to feed him and his family, and to scare away men who might want to poach. On the other hand, men should not be faithful to their wives. Why? Because the more women they have intercourse with, the more likely their genes are to show up in the next generation. Of course the same men should not tolerate infidelity on the part of their wives. If women have the least margin of permission to wander, the likelihood is that a man will end up (unintentionally) raising a child not his own—that is, preserving someone else's genes in the next generation. That is contrary to evolutionary imperatives, so a habit of slaughtering unfaithful wives (and their possibly bastard children) will result in the increase of their genes in the next generation, relative to others. Women should be faithful to their husbands, because their husbands will stop protecting them and their children if they suspect infidelity, and they need protection and nurturing (food, shelter and the like) if they want to raise their children to the age of sexual reproduction—which must happen, if their genes are to get into the succeeding generations.

Here is where rational upbringing enters the picture. There is more to life than ensuring ones' genes enter the next generation. Let us grant that stepfathers often would like to eliminate their stepchildren from the picture (the fathers of the fairy tales surely thought so). They won't do that, at least not openly. There are good societal reasons for having them care for stepchildren, so they will find a certain amount of social encouragement. But more importantly, they will have become the sort of person that does not slaughter blameless children. There are things that lions can do that humans cannot and remain human. It is a good thing for the society if we breed/train all humans to be peaceable, tolerant, and accepting of all sorts of people, for as a society we have less interest in how individual gene pools come out and more interest in keeping the peace. So in this particular instance we have erected a strong barrier against fulfilling nature. If a biological process results in a distribution of genes that leads to a distortion of human action (according to the usual standards by which we judge actions) then we will not do what the gene supposedly commands, but will raise up barriers against it—by legislating, perhaps, that family love trumps all, and that anyone who wishes to act less than loving for the child will lose control of it. And so forth. Barriers against nature raised in order to live more completely human lives will form part of any good life.

Again, let us take a fleeting sideways glance at the problems of business ethics that develop at this juncture. Business is all about sales. Pleasure Now is the easiest sell there is. Virtue Much Later is one of the hardest sells. Is there some obligation on a business to produce only those products, marketed through only those channels, in only that way, that will conduce the customer/consumer to adopt a more balanced, gentle, and responsible life—preferably the most reflective and responsible life of which he or she is capable? If so, we find very little evidence in the market that that duty is being fulfilled.

Can the capabilities that lead to the rational life of deliberation and choice lead also to other lives that are fully human and fully good? Let's start out by distinguishing three senses of that question. First, that question might mean, are there numerous, mutually incompatible, lives that are fully human and fully good? The answer to that is clearly yes; but if you leave it to you and me and Aristotle to say what they are, all the lives we might suggest will turn out to be lives of deliberation and choice. Second, it might mean, are there human lives that are *not* lives of deliberation and choice that can be called good? There certainly are—in fact, all human lives of those who are not capable of this level of thought, if they are to be good at all, must participate in some goodness other than the active life of reason. For Aristotle, the good life lived by the honest shoemaker, the hard-working farmer, and the brave foot-soldier were good lives, but not the highest life that humans could live. But the meaning we are after is a third one: do the capacities for deliberation and choice fit the human for a life that somehow uses them but somehow does not require them for their original function, yet is a fully good life utilizing all capabilities (as the life of a Seeing Eye dog is a fully good life for a Labrador Retriever)?

The only life that could fit the requirements would be one in which the life of deliberation and choice is fully achieved, and then freely renounced. We have a model for that renunciation, in our doctrine that "service to the Highest is perfect freedom." The life that competes with the active life of reason is the life of complete devotion, in which reason, as well as all other faculties, are freely put at the service of some Deity, nation, or cause. There is precedent for such decisions.

The life of renunciation of freedom is exemplified (ironically, in one of its least objectionable forms) in the life of Obedience as practiced by those in vowed religious orders. The claim that this is truly a case of freedom renounced rests on a double foundation. First, if the vow is to have any meaning, the person making the vow must be fully mature, fully rational, in complete possession—emotionally and every other way—of a life well understood. You have to have a self to give, or the giving of the self really makes no sense. So the person about to make a vow of obedience has to be fully autonomous, living a life of deliberation and choice. Second, if the vow is to have any meaning, it must mean what it says—obedience. You will obey your superior as if he or she were (in the Christian orders) Christ himself. Ideally, you are not even supposed to think about whether the orders you receive are good or bad; like the loyal foot-soldier you have just chosen to be, you just obey. Can this life qualify as fully human and fully good?

This is not an easy question to answer, largely because it's badly tangled. Let's start to untangle it. First tangle is that the vow rarely comes alone. Religious orders also demand vows of chastity (in effect, celibacy) and poverty, problematic enough in their own rights. We'll try to consider the question apart from those accompanying vows, simply because they confuse the issue. Celibacy, for instance, now broadly under attack, may or may not lead to the atrocious acts for which it has been blamed. In any case, parish priests take no vow of obedience and are therefore outside the scope of the question. The second is that the vow is rarely understood as absolute. There are orders that are not to be obeyed, just as in the armed forces. (That reservation may be taken as an acknowledgement that the religious superior is not, in fact, Christ, but makes mistakes, sometimes bad ones.) The third is that however the vow of obedience bears in theory, in fact once a member of religious order passes the novitiate, he or she is rarely supervised to the point where choices, even serious choices, are unnecessary. The life of a mature member of the religious order, in fact, has about as much independence in decision making as that of any professional. The life cannot be condemned as an abandonment of reason, for although it claims to place all reason at the service of the superior, in fact the obligation to think and choose kicks in whenever the superior or his orders become vague or questionable. The vowed life is at best not a clear example of an alternative to autonomy.

Better examples abound, clearer because they do not have the experience-tested safeguards of the vowed religious life, but much more problematic because it is so hard to call them "good." These are the lives of religious or national fanaticism, where the reason, fully trained and educated, passionately renounces its privileges and responsibilities to some Higher Authority, through which it expects to receive meaning for its life on this earth and salvation in some hereafter. It is foolishness to dismiss the suicide bombers and their supporters as uneducated peasants with no conception of what they are doing. Possibly the bombers themselves are immature victims with no adult conception of options and values in this life. But the people behind them, the "teachers" who fill them with hatred through speaking and writing, the trainers who promise the young-sters undying pleasures in heaven, the millionaires who provide the cash rewards for supportive families, the tenured professors who justify these crimes in learned articles about historic rights and ethnic despair, all these are people who have all the education they need to be rational and have chosen not to be in defense of values they conceive to be higher than the rational life. We can condemn them; but where among the armaments of reason is the principle by which we can say that it is plainly wrong so to use reason in the service of fanaticism, excuse me, higher values? When have we ever been able to say for sure that we ought not to sacrifice our reason to God—that if God wanted it, we shouldn't give it, or better yet, that we know for sure that God does not want it?

In part, we have here the paradox of voluntary slavery: there may be something wrong, undesirable, inadvisable, about selling yourself into slavery, but who can call it wrong—especially if you have good financial reason for doing so? If reason cannot choose totally to commit itself to an ideal worthy of its heroic efforts, in what sense can we call it free?

Yet the dangers of this development are all around us, tragically now in the random slaughter of civilians in the name of Allah, and throughout history in the name of the Emperor, the Motherland, the Czar, Jesus Christ, Whoever. With the advance to reason as a possible way of life, we open up also the pos-sibilities of a thousand unreasonable renunciations of reason. Q2, then, is far-reaching. Branches this luxuriant, spreading thickly from the point where reason becomes a possibility, threaten to turn our tree of nature into a bush once and for all. Where do we go from here?

For social animals, the individual is not the last stage of growth, accord-ing to Aristotle, nor is it the most important. The fundamental science of human life, he reminds us more than once, is not Ethics but Politics—the study of the *polis*. In the second chapter of the first book of the *Politics* he sketches the growth of the *polis* through comprehensible steps, all presupposing that for a social animal, the development of its natural collective home is a good and natural process, and that the achievement of that community is a natural goal properly commanding the energies of the animal in question. We will take that assertion as Proposition Three (P3), and it will constitute the next section of the trunk of the tree.

The point of developing the *polis* at this juncture, as far as we are concerned, is that we desperately need something to control individual fanaticism. Note that we do not need anything in particular to control individual aggressiveness, selfishness or greed (except by the rulers!). No society prior to the modern has ever had much difficulty doing that, and Aristotle would not have been able to conceive of a society that could not quickly and efficiently eliminate those whose selfish proclivities threatened the welfare of the whole. (The whole would have to be *really* threatened. Aristotle allowed, as Plato did not, for a robust competition of interests in the state, to be resolved in the ongoing negotiation of the political process.) But we really need a collective structure of reason, backed by collective force to use as necessary, to guide people away from the emotional excesses that seduce individual reason away from its proper role as governor of the individual life.

Aristotle grows the reasonable state as he does the reasonable person, by human guidance of natural (innate) proclivities.[10] Thus the Household is formed much as any animal mates, and nests, and secures the services of necessary others to carry on the work of survival. The Household grows into a Village as the extended family of the original Household forms little households of its own. At this point we have a (tribal) settlement, guided by custom and tradition from that founding Household (or so, at least, their legends would have it), operating mindlessly according to that tradition from generation to generation. Except for its ability to manipulate tools and fire (and make up stories), the tribe is only slightly different from the other troops of primates in its initial habitats. But then something intervenes—some new threat, an outside invader, or some new opportunity, the appearance of trading vessels off the shore—and the tribes find a reason to form a common fort or market or both. The motives that bring the tribes together into a distinctly non-tribal association may be entirely pragmatic, but the community that results has intriguing possibilities that were not there before. Because no single tribe dominates the arrangement (as Aristotle sees it), the living arrangements of the *polis* will have to be worked out by negotiation, that is, by collective deliberation and choice. The use of clear conceptual language becomes essential, as especially suited to the exchange of judgments of "the useful and the useless, the just and the unjust," in which the negotiation is carried on.

The *polis* completes the natural process sketched to this point. For the people who carry on those negotiations are, of course, the very citizens trained in virtue, supplied with reason, and prepared to take responsibility for their own lives, for the welfare of their families and villages, and now for the *polis* as a whole. The city becomes the source of the good and reasonable rules that govern the lives of families, hence of youngsters before they reach the age where they can understand the reasons behind what they are expected to do. In the *polis* we have the completion of human reason; in the establishment of collective deliberation and choice as the only possible way of governing a people that share no common tribal tradition, we have placed reasonableness as the ruling virtue in the state, and therefore established it as a permanent bulwark against the growth of fanaticism.

But of course it doesn't always work, and that sad fact is the base of Qualification Three (Q3), viz., that *if you can get away with it,* the path of least resistance—the path of most intense pleasure—will prevail in the human life no matter what rules and models are set down. All the reasonable state can do is minimize the amount and effect of the falling away from reason. And in a very reasonable state, that task is more difficult still. Consider some instances.

The three most salient examples of lives that fall away from reason, for us, are, first, the one just mentioned—the life of emotional overindulgence in cults, causes, nations and gods, sacrificing life, family, wealth, and future to some divine demand. Such lives are far more common than we generally admit in the U.S. alone. LIFE magazine at one point chronicled a historic meeting in Chicago of Father Divine of Philadelphia, Prophet Jones of Chicago, and Daddy Grace of Newark, New Jersey. They all wore their mink coats, and no doubt traded tips on how to keep their poverty congregations loyal to them. Since then, the cult communes of Jim Jones and David Koresh, not to mention the survivalist camps in Idaho, surely cast into doubt any beliefs we may have had about the inevitable triumph of reason in human life. Yet how can we crush the cults without abolishing freedom of religion?

The second example brings us back to the business system. In the absence of the kinds of formal and informal restraints that used to govern the business system, all limits on the pursuit of individual wealth among the group of higher executives of the business system (CEOs, corporate officers, corporate counsel and the like) seem to be off. Levels of annual compensation hovering around $8 to $10 million not that long ago rapidly escalated to $50 million, then to $150 million, then (last count) the five highest paid executives in the world made over $220 million each. That's compensation per year.[11] Hostile take-overs, unheard of in my father's generation, are now commonplace. Every gimmick to avoid taxes and increase wealth, through the use of offshore shell corporations and money laundries, has been exploited. Enron is not the only corporate sinner, nor Arthur Andersen the only corporate pander, in this wave of self-enrichment. Plato hypothesized that if the honest shepherd Gyges should ever find the magic ring of enrichment through concealment, he would throw morality to the winds and become the worst exploiter that ever was. Having found the magic Cayman Islands ring, our corporate shepherds seem determined to prove him right.

We suggested before that plain old greed, selfishness, was not that much a problem for most civilizations. It isn't really; corporate tax havens fly no planes into tall buildings, blow up no supermarkets. As soon as patient lawmakers find out the routes by which funds exit the US and return tax-free, that route will be stopped, and that abuse will be ended. It is a mark of the disorganization of a state that such practices can grow either undetected, or so well protected that nothing can be done about them until hundreds of millions of dollars have been lost to the public treasury. How much interference in the free market would be necessary to make sure that such abuses never happened again?

A third problem illustrative of the difficulty of holding the Aristotelian community on track is the tragic problem of street drug abuse. In a way, this is the simplest of problems. The drug promises (and delivers) pleasure. Every educational outlet we have, schools, YMCA, churches, billboards, whatever, proves that that pleasure is not worth it, that far better pleasure is to be found in continuing with the disagreeable effort of school and college and seeking a rewarding career. Yet the problem continues, and not only among the most disadvantaged of the society. How much do we have to tighten up on individual freedoms to root out illegal drug use in the society?

These three problems are emblematic—or symptomatic, or merely symbolic—of the problems a rational society deals with. The dilemma they illustrate is between freedom and order. The society envisioned by Aristotle and the naturalists is one of order freely chosen, internalized within each member of the society, so that the most perfect external order is preserved with a minimum of external controls. But such a society is very difficult to achieve. You can't achieve perfection without massive control, abolishing the freedom. When you attempt to control the abuses, you lose the room individual reason needs to operate even for normal life, and you certainly lose the room collective reason needs for innovation and experiment. There is no ideal solution.

We are left with three Aristotelian segments of the trunk of natural life seeking natural fulfillment—the natural animal seeking healthy maturity (P1), the rational human seeing the active life of reason (deliberation and choice) (P2), and the *polis*, or political association, seeking justice (P3). We have asserted the inherent rightness and goodness of all these. We are also left with three sets of very un-Aristotelian qualifications, not all of them known to Aristotle. Q1 points out that not all nature is natural; Q2 points out that not all choices of the reason are reasonable; Q3 points out that not all community arrangements can fulfill the goals of order and freedom at the same time—as a matter of fact, given the disastrous proclivities of human nature, maybe none of them can.

Notes

1. Bernice Bovenkerk, Frans W. A Brom, Babs J. Van den Bergh, "Brave New Birds: The Use of 'Animal Integrity' in Animal Ethics," *Hastings Center Report* 32(1) (January–February 2002):16–22.

2. There is a literature on "human cloning" that goes back for more years than I can count, reaching periodic peaks (most recently with the Raelians and their claim to human clones, who turned out not to be). While most Americans welcome genetic interventions to abolish genes for disease, a profound squeamishness (can one be squeamish profoundly?) attends suggestions for all other genetically designed humans. Why?

3. Lizette Alvarez, "Consumers in Europe Resist Genetically Altered Food," *The New York Times,* February 11, 2003, A5.

4. Poor Percy Schmeiser, who never bought or planted genetically modified canola (rape) seed—always used his own saved seed from the best plants of the year before—found himself sued by Monsanto when genetically modified canola volunteered in his fields, all Roundup Ready and quite unintended. Monsanto won the suit; it had patented Roundup Ready canola, and the way patent law reads, it doesn't matter how you got hold of the patented design, you have to pay royalties to the patent holder if you sell the product. No point complaining that the seed blew on to his land, as canola seed blows all over the lot; the law is the law. Marc Kaufman, "Farmer Liable for Growing Biotech Crops; Court Says Canadian Used Company's Plants," *The Washington Post,* March 30, 2001, A3. Schmeiser was still fighting in January 2003; Hanneke Brooymans, "Farmer Attacks Genetically Modified Food; Tells Audience Chemical Company Threatens Livelihood," *The Edmonton Journal,* January 10, 2003, A6.

5. Aristotle, *Nicomachean Ethics,* book II, line 1103a25.

6. Ibid., book II, lines 1105a30, 1105b.

7. Ibid., book I, line 1094b25.

8. Ibid., book X, line 1178b30.

9. Robert Wright, *The Moral Animal: Why We Are The Way We Are—The New Science of Evolutionary Psychology,* New York: Pantheon Books, 1994.

10. Aristotle, *Politics,* book I, chap. 2.

11. In the spring of 2001, we wrote: "As this computer rolls in early April of 2001, stocks have undergone a sudden 'correction,' read, gone very far South, and shareholder wealth has decreased substantially. Do we find CEO compensation humbly bowing to the facts of the ROI? Not in the least. 'While typical investors lost 12 percent of their portfolios last year [2000], based on the Wilshire 5000 total market index, and profits for the Standard & Poor's 500 companies rose at less than half their pace in the 1990s, chief executives received an average 22 percent raise in salary and bonus.' So we find out from a Special Report on Executive Pay from the *New York Times* on April 1, 2001 (First Business Page), and that was no April Fool. Among the best-paid executives were Steven Jobs at $775.0 million for the year, Sanford Weill of Citigroup at $315.1 million, Lawrence Ellison of Oracle at $216.4 million, Dennis Kozlowski of Tyco at $205.2 million, and trailing the Top Five, John Welch of General Electric at $144.5 million." *Taking Sides: Clashing Views on Controversial Issues in Business Ethics and Society,* ed. Lisa Newton and Maureen Ford, Guilford, Conn.: Dushkin McGraw-Hill, 2002. Since then, the figures have only increased.

BRIEF REMARKS ON
THE EVOLUTIONARY METHOD

Robert A. Phillips

Abstract: There are explicit claims to Darwinian thinking in numerous fields of study. A common temptation associated with this method across disciplines is to call some attributes "natural" and others "cultural" in origin. But this distinction can be dangerous—particularly when applied to ethics. When employing the Darwinian method, ideas should be evaluated in the same way whether the characteristics are described as natural or as cultural. We should ascertain the moral usefulness of a trait irrespective of its genetic basis or lack thereof. The nature/culture distinction is irrelevant to ethics. If Darwinian thinking connotes or implies an important difference, it is a dangerous idea to moral theory. I don't believe the method denotes such a distinction, and in fact helps ethicists ask and answer many interesting questions that would not have arisen without it. But great care should be taken.

In the closing section of *Darwin's Dangerous Idea,* Daniel Dennet writes, "There is no denying, at this point, that Darwin's idea is a universal solvent, capable of cutting right to the heart of everything in sight."[1] Indeed, Dennett's claims are persuasively argued and there are explicit claims to Darwinian thinking in psychology, sociology, anthropology, political science and, more recently, literary criticism and "biohistory."[2] Dennett goes on to caution, however,

> I have learned from my own embarrassing experience how easy it is to concoct remarkably persuasive Darwinian explanations that evaporate on closer inspection. The truly dangerous aspect of Darwin's idea is its seductiveness.[3]

In the course of commenting on Edwin Hartman's fine Ruffin Lecture, I would like to briefly echo this caveat—particularly as Darwin's method is applied to ethics. The danger is particularly acute given the method's roots in biological science and the connotations involved in calling a trait "natural" or "cultural" in origin.

I am in the somewhat difficult position as a respondent of agreeing, I think, with most of what Professor Hartman says in his lecture. To test the extent of this agreement, therefore, I would like to propose extensions of his paper that I believe are consistent with what he writes, but may go a bit farther than he is willing to go.

Hartman insightfully observes that, "Biologists are not the only scholars who claim that what has survived is somehow natural, hence good. The same idea has occurred to some historians" (p. 206). To this, and the list above, I would add that the method has also occurred to those who study organizational economics. Rather than adaptability or fitness, however, organizational survival is taken as a sign of efficiency. To my knowledge, however, these scholars do not suggest that the organization features leading to such efficiency are either natural or cultural—the question is typically not addressed. And yet, the method is remarkably Darwinian and the conclusions often impressive and convincing.

This leads me to wonder what value is added, particularly to considerations of ethics and politics, by asking whether a given characteristic (or trait) is natural or cultural. I propose that it is something like relative prominence of a human trait across cultures that is relevant to ethics and not the source of the trait in nature or culture. If all, or nearly all, humans exhibit a norm or characteristic (reciprocity, for example), then we may, indeed should, use this fact in designing political and organizational institutions.[4] Hartman rightly sees Messick's work as an exemplar of the sort of science we may reference in rendering moral judgments. But, to quote Hartman, "Messick does not claim that biological determinism is at work here: the selection mechanisms are likely cultural as well as genetic" (p. 207). The same holds for de Waal's and Cosmides' work. We must evaluate the results of all such work in the same way whether the characteristics described are natural or cultural. From the perspective of Hartmanism we must ascertain the usefulness of a trait for the preservation of the community and contribution to human excellence irrespective of its genetic basis or lack thereof. The findings of evolutionary psychology would be equally interesting with or without the modifier "evolutionary" and the occasional implications of natural being superior or immutable. Darwin's method is extraordinarily useful in generating good questions, but can be more pernicious when the time comes for interpreting results.

If nature/culture is a distinction that makes no difference, time spent placing various norms or traits into the taxonomy is time better spent on other endeavors. For example, thinkers since at least Mandeville have asked whether moral precepts are real or merely a "useful fiction."[5] Hartman and Lawrence and Nohria[6] consider this question as also am I right now. My purpose, however, is to state explicitly what I believe is implied by Hartman's discussion—the question makes little or no difference to ethics.

At his most direct, Hartman writes, "I do not believe that morality has or needs a basis in evolution" (p. 205). We should not, however, throw out the methodological baby with the "greedy reductionist" bath water. Dennett, among others, describes the Darwinist method as similar to that of reverse engineering. Hartman employs such reverse engineering to the task of social criticism when he writes (p. 209),

Messick does not infer from the survival of a human practice that it is good from a moral point of view. On the contrary, he argues that understanding how a practice has survived may be a step in the direction of improving it. He suggests that questionable practices ought to be subjected to scrutiny to determine, if possible, what purpose they might ever have served and whether the conditions that gave rise to them still hold. Due consideration would have to be given to the emotions and expectations of those who had grown accustomed to taking the practices seriously. This is preferable to just accepting, say, genital mutilation because it is traditional. It may be no accident that it is traditional, that it serves some purpose of someone; so let us consider what purpose it serves and whose purpose that is. But there is no presumption that it serves a *good* purpose.

Similarly, Cosmides[7] rightly points out that the Darwinian method allows us to ask questions that are unlikely to even be considered in its absence. The fecundity of the method does not depend in the least on the nature/culture distinction—though the distinction still lurks in the background. Here's one question that occurred to me while reading Hartman's rhetorical questions about altruists and their interests: What if free-riders, non-cooperators, and otherwise ignominious characters MUST exist because an entire world of altruists is a non-evolutionarily stable strategy? If a certain amount of defection is required for equilibrium, what does this imply for as we design institutions and organizations? I will confess that I'm not sure, but it strikes me as in interesting point of consideration that was facilitated, if not made possible entirely, by Darwin's method.

But the question of natural vs. cultural is not only distracting. It also risks falling into the various traps involved in attributions of Truth—with a capital "T." Hartman ably debunks the idea that "what is selected for is by definition morally good" while allowing for the possibility that there may be good reasons for continuing to respect "intuitions that have their roots in the dead past"—though I believe he may underestimate the usefulness of such intuitions. Despite Hartman's arguments to the contrary, however, continued emphasis on the nature/culture distinction and the status of evolutionary theory as science will lead many to perceive a hierarchy. We should certainly continue to employ the methods of science to root out which human tendencies are more general—or even universal. But inasmuch as our uses for this information do not change based on the source of the trait or characteristic studied, dispensing with the question of natural or cultural may help avoid the severe problems associated with Herbert Spencer's social Darwinism—problems that placed the *method* into disrepute for a time and continues to haunt Darwinian thinking.

In his review of Daniel Dennett's book *Darwin's Dangerous Idea*, Richard Rorty invokes another of Dennett's famous works, *The Philosopher's Lexicon*. Rorty writes:

This book [*The Philosopher's Lexicon*] is made up of plays on the names of great thinkers (e.g., "It's buried so deep we'll have to use a heidegger"). The most famous definition in the book, perhaps, is that of "chomsky." This adjective "characterizes the attempt to derive very broad philosophical conclusions from very specialized scientific results, as in 'The conclusions drawn from Godel's Theorem are even chomskier than those drawn from Heisenberg's Principle'"[8]

There is a strong possibility that evolutionary theory will prompt the chomskiest work to date. The nature/culture distinction is irrelevant to ethics. If Darwinian thinking connotes or implies an important difference, it is a dangerous idea to moral theory. I don't believe the method denotes such a distinction, and in fact helps ethicists ask and answer many interesting questions that would not have arisen without it. As with all universal acid, though, we would do well to take great care in its use.

Notes

1. Daniel Dennett, *Darwin's Dangerous Idea* (New York: Simon & Schuster, 1995), p. 521.

2. David P. Barash and Nanelle Barash, "Biology as a Lens: Evolution and Literary Criticism," *The Chronicle Review* (October 18, 2002): B7–B9. Robert S. McElvaine, "The Relevance of Biohistory," *The Chronicle Review* (October 18, 2002): B10–B11.

3. Dennett, p. 521.

4. Robert A. Phillips and Joshua M. Margolis, "Toward an Ethics of Organizations," *Business Ethics Quarterly* 9(4) (1999): 637–656.

5. Bernard Mandeville, *Fable of the Bees*, ed. F. B. Kaye (Oxford: Oxford University Press, 1725/1924).

6. Paul R. Lawrence and Nitin Nohria, *Driven* (New York: Jossey-Bass, 2002).

7. Leda Cosmides and John Tooby, "Knowing Thyself: The Evolutionary Psychology of Moral Reasoning and Moral Sentiments," in *Business, Science, and Ethics*, ed. R. Edward Freeman and Patricia H. Werhane (Charlottesville, Va.: Philosophy Documentation Center, 2004), pp. 93–128.

8. Richard Rorty, "Cranes and Skyhooks," *Lingua Franca* 5(5) (1995).

EXPLANATION AND JUSTIFICATION: THE RELEVANCE OF THE BIOLOGICAL AND SOCIAL SCIENCES TO BUSINESS ETHICS

Joseph DesJardins

Abstract: This paper attempts to sort through some of the challenges facing those of us who look to empirical science for help in doing normative business ethics. I suggest that the distinction between explanation and justification, a distinction at the heart of the difference between descriptive social science and normative ethics, is often overlooked when social scientists attempt to draw ethical conclusions from their research.

Philosophical ethics in the West has had a long and ambiguous relationship with science. While both Plato and Aristotle thought we could draw normative conclusions from a proper understanding of human nature, only Aristotle thought that the empirical sciences (although a very different conception of science than our own) provided relevant information concerning human nature. Much later, in the earliest years of modern science, Hobbes sought to create an explicitly scientific basis for politics and social ethics. Indeed, it is fair to identify Hobbes as the prototypical philosopher who thought that a scientific account of human nature should be the basis from which to draw normative conclusions.

Within a century things had become much more uncertain. David Hume, explicitly modeling his own method on the work of Newton, thought that only careful empirical observation could distinguish between reasonable beliefs and "sophistry and illusion." His conclusions were that while science could tell us all that we can know about human nature, it cannot provide the basis for drawing normative conclusions from that nature. Empirical science could provide a rational basis for judgments about the world, and it could explain the origins of moral sentiments, but empirical science could provide no rational justification for normative judgments. The only empirically discoverable basis for morality was found in human feelings and sentiments, notoriously subjective bases for judgment. After all, one can find a vindictive or spiteful sentiment for every sympathetic and benevolent one. Thus, here in Hume we find the initial formulation of what has become canonized as the "is/ought" or "fact/value" gap.[1] Empirical science can discover facts about what is or is not the case, but questions of value and oughts are to be found only by looking within one's "own breast" for a "feeling or sentiment" of approbation or disapprobation. Needless to say, it was exactly this sort of conclusion that awoke Kant from his dogmatic slumbers to attempt the rescue of ethics from the attack by empiricism. The autonomy of practical reason, or the rational will, allowed Kant to maintain a rational, although not empirical, basis for morality.

For the past two hundred years, moral philosophers in the West have seldom strayed far from the boundaries established by Hume and Kant. Those in the Humean tradition tend to understand morality as a matter of sentiments or feelings. These are typically interpreted as subjective and therefore nonrational. Thus, while we can offer an empirical account of the *origin* of moral sentiments, we cannot obtain an empirical *justification* of those sentiments. Facts and values are distinct logical categories. Kantians focus on moral judgments rather than sentiments, and seek a rational basis for them. Kant essentially accepts Hume's account of moral sentiments and their independence of rational assessment; but he denied that sentiment exhausted the moral domain. For Kant, morality essentially involves practical judgments about what ought or ought not be the case rather than empirical judgments about what is or is not the case. Practical judgments can be subject to non-empirical rational assessment. Both sides, however, continued to discount the relevance of empirical science in determining what was, or was not, ethically justified.[2] For most of those two hundred years, the challenges of the fact/value, is/ought gap (or the "naturalistic fallacy" in the twentieth-century language of G. E. Moore and later dubbed the "open-question" argument by William Frankena) remained in force. Facts alone do not establish the validity of a moral judgment. No matter what the facts, the normative conclusion one should draw from those facts always remains an "open question."

By the 1970s this sharp divide was changing. Rawls's interest in moral psychology, the blossoming of applied and professional ethics, and the growing interest in Aristotelian virtue ethics began to open the door for an increased interest in the empirical sciences. While the reasons for these changes are many and varied, the fact is that at present many philosophers seem open to investigating the relevancy of the empirical sciences to ethics.

Two other trends suggest the time is ripe for a closer integration of ethics and empirical sciences especially for those of us interested in business ethics. First, empirical scientists themselves are looking more carefully and systematically at issues of moral judgment, moral sentiments, and moral behavior in both humans and non-human animals. Kohlberg's pioneering yet flawed psychological research has given way to more sophisticated empirical studies of, for example, Leda Cosmides. The early speculation of primatologists such as Jane Goodall and Dian Fossey has evolved into the very interesting work of Frans de Waal. Second, colleagues in the business-related disciplines, many of whom are themselves experienced social scientists, have turned their attention to ethics. Thus, groups such as the Society for Business Ethics and the European

Business Ethics Network count many social scientists among their membership. The work of Bill Frederick and Paul Lawrence reflects this trend. My own inclination is that the empirical study of morality can make important contributions to normative ethics in general and to business ethics in particular. Nevertheless, there are many pitfalls along the way and I find myself uneasy about many of the particular attempts to carry out such an integration. While the gap between facts and values may not be unbridgeable, we are nonetheless well-advised to mind the gap. In what follows, I attempt to sort through some of the challenges facing those of us who look to empirical science for help in our important work of doing normative business ethics.

Explanation and Morality

Let us begin with a simple question. What is it that we are after when we turn to the empirical sciences for help in our work in ethics? To answer, simply, that we seek to "understand" morality is not enough. Nor is it enough to cite the "ought implies can" principle and look to empirical science to discover what humans "can" do. We already know quite well that ordinary humans are capable of a wide variety of behaviors ranging from the extraordinarily heroic to the despicably evil. There is enough for ethics to work with within that broad range of capacities without needing verification from sophisticated empirical science.

When we look to the scientists' own statements we find a mixed bag of answers. Frans de Waal asks "to what degree has biology *influenced and shaped the development of moral systems?*" [emphasis added here and in what follows] and answers by suggesting that "human moral systems might be the *product of* natural selection."[3] In the very title of one of his books, de Waal alludes to "*the origin*" of right and wrong. Paul Lawrence talks of "the biological *base* of morality" and proposes "a unified *explanation* of human morality as an innate feature of human minds" involving innate "drives" and "skill sets." Lawrence goes on to say that "Morality . . . *arises from* the existence in humans of the drive to bond."[4] Focusing on firms rather than individuals, William Frederick tells us that "the business firm's motives, productivity, organization, strategy, markets, and its moral significance *are a function of—a direct outgrowth of*—evolutionary natural forces." The locus of such forces, and the beginning of moral analysis, are to be found in an evolutionary understanding of the human brain that "nature has bequeathed to business and to humanity." In summing up his paper, Frederick tells us simply that his goal is the "*explanation* of business behavior."[5]

It strikes me that there are some deep ambiguities involved with such claims. Reference to biological, evolutionary, adaptive, and psychological "forces," "drives" and "influences" which "produce" and provide the "basis" "origin" and "prerequisites for" "morality" which "arises from" them is, at best, imprecise. It seems fair to say that there are very different conceptual models at work here. Sorting through some of these ambiguities and models can help us attain a better understanding of the relevance of science to ethics.

I think, in general, each of these authors would agree that their immediate goal is to, in some sense and to some degree, explain morality. But this seemingly innocent goal is fraught with dangers for what constitutes both an *explanation* and *morality*. Within the sciences, and particularly within the social sciences, there are some very different models for what constitutes an adequate scientific explanation. Within philosophy, there are competing models for understanding the nature of morality.

On one hand, these authors sometimes seem to be making a reasonably uncontroversial claim. Morality is a fact of human (and perhaps other non-human animal) life. As such, there must be some antecedent biological and psychological occurrences that accompany moral activity. Moral judgments, like all judgments, involve brain activity. Moral behavior, like all human behavior, involves psychological and physiological activity. Moral sentiments, like all human sentiments, can be traced to biophysical activity within the body. Few today would deny this. If all that is involved here is the claim that cognitive, psychological, physiological, neurological, and biological factors are necessary conditions for human judgment, behavior, and feelings, I doubt anyone would disagree. Even such a dualist as Descartes would admit that there are biological, physiological, and neurological events accompanying such mental activity as judging, feeling, acting. All this seems true, and perhaps trivially so.

Obviously there must be more involved than this. In turning to the empirical sciences to "explain" morality (as both Lawrence and Frederick explicitly suggest), these authors are hinting at something more than just a mere correlation between morality and scientifically discoverable facts about the world. They seem to be after a *causal* explanation of morality. Perhaps this should be no surprise given the close connection between this social science research and business management. Understanding the causes of moral behavior will provide the tools for managers to control, shape, and influence moral (and immoral) behavior. From this perspective, we would have explained morality when we can identify the antecedent causes responsible for bringing it about. Lawrence tells us that a broader theory developed by evolutionary biologists and various behavioral and social scientists will explain the role of human nature in "shaping" human choices.[6] De Waal, at times, seems more explicit, looking to biology for what has "influenced and shaped" and what provides the "origin" of moral systems. Frederick speaks of a "function of—a direct outgrowth of— evolutionary natural forces" and explicitly acknowledges the "deterministic" implications of this.[7] Cosmides is even more explicit when she asks "Is there evolved neurocognitive circuitry that *causes people* to punish free riders in collective action contexts?" While she thinks that the evidence is not yet sufficient to answer affirmatively, the question itself accurately identifies a central aspect of her research program.[8]

No doubt many philosophers (and others) will get nervous at such claims. Suggesting that morality is "caused by" biological and physiological factors raises deep questions not only in ethics but in epistemology, philosophy of mind, philosophy of science, and metaphysics as well. Before considering this issue in more depth, let us first turn to some ambiguities in the talk about "morality."

Philosophers have often called attention to descriptive and normative uses of words such as "morality," "ethics," and "ethical." When used descriptively such terms designate a domain of human experience that can be contrasted with such things as etiquette, politics, prudence, law, religion, and the like. The converse of this descriptive sense is the non-ethical. Thus, to use Hobbes' famous example, while it might be a matter of "small morals" or etiquette that one not pick one's teeth at the table, it is not particularly an ethical or moral question. When the social sciences study morality in this descriptive sense, they would examine charity as often as miserliness, cooperation as often as competition, love as often as hatred.

The normative use of these terms carries with it an evaluative component and is to be contrasted with unethical or immoral. To identify some judgment, act, or sentiment as "moral" in this sense is to identify it as deserving praise and commendation, as being in some sense justified, right, correct, decent, respectable, or good. While this seemingly simple distinction between descriptive and normative uses of morality can be controversial in ways that we need not explore here, it is crucial that we recognize its relevance for scientists studying moral phenomena.

First, scientists need to articulate a descriptive account of morality if it is to be studied empirically at all. Simply put, scientists need to identify the domain that they propose to study. Methodologically, we need an independent account of what morality is before we can, for example, determine if apes and bonobos have one.[9] I suspect that much of the controversy over de Waal's work, for example, stems from this issue. Critics might be relying on a definition of morality which makes it impossible, by definition, for animals other than humans to be moral beings. For example, if morality is defined in cognitively sophisticated terms of making universalized prescriptive judgments, then it seems highly unlikely that animals can be moral beings. A definition for the descriptive use of morality will determine whether de Waal's question is an empirical or a conceptual one.[10]

Second, some of the anxiety surrounding the empirical study of morality surely comes from the fear that the descriptive and normative uses are being conflated. When applied to the *normative* use of morality, talk about a biological "base," "origin" or "cause," or viewing it as a "function of" or a "direct outgrowth of" evolutionary forces confronts the is/ought issue straight on. To claim that there is a biological base of morality—in the normative sense—seems to say that what we ought to do is determined by biological factors. On the other hand, to claim simply that there is a biological basis for moral—as opposed to non-moral—behavior is to flirt with triviality.

It is worth noting in this regard that the focus for many of these recent empirical investigations has been on morally praiseworthy behavior. Many of the present authors seem particularly concerned to show that altruistic behavior, sentiments, and drives are as natural as egoistic ones. Such usage clearly involves the normative sense of morality. As evidence that apes have a "morality," de Waal looks to such morally praiseworthy factors as empathy, reconciliation, consolation, and altruism. Apparently it is a less interesting, and far less controversial, question to study if apes act deceptively or vindictively. Likewise, Cosmides looks to evolutionary biology for evidence to support cooperation and cheater detection. Free riding and cheating apparently don't need a scientific explanation, but punishing free riders and detecting cheaters do. But why wouldn't it be just as interesting to discover an evolutionary or biological basis or origin for conflict or cheating itself? When Lorenz argued for a biological basis for aggression in the 1963, the controversy was not, as it is now for de Waal, over whether this provided evidence that animals were moral beings (in the descriptive sense).[11] People seem readily willing to attribute such value-laden characteristics as aggression, selfishness, and rivalry to animals. Why is it that there is not the kind of doubt concerning a biological basis for these characteristics as there is concerning a biological basis for cooperation, empathy, and truth-telling?

A second ambiguity concerning the language of morality involves its object. The adjective "moral" is used normatively to characterize acts, sentiments (which I will take to include feelings, motivations, dispositions), and judgments. Viewed in isolation, it seems possible to identify each of these aspects independently. Hugging an individual injured in a fight can be identified as the moral act of consolation. Such a person can be said to be motivated by moral sentiments of empathy and sympathy. We can judge that one morally ought to offer support and comfort to those injured. Nevertheless, deep issues are hidden just beneath the surface here.

Some consequentialist moral theories are comfortable distinguishing moral actions from moral motivations and acknowledging that morally good (or evil) people can perform morally evil (or good) acts. By focusing on consequences, this approach can blur an important distinction between acts and behavior (a distinction that will be developed later in this paper) and thus can allow us to speak meaningfully about moral behavior independently of the motives or intentions that give rise to the behavior.

Likewise, philosophers in the Humean tradition speak meaningfully about moral sentiments that are independent of judgments about the moral legitimacy of those sentiments. Thus, one might speak about the sentiment of empathy or sympathy while maintaining neutrality concerning the judgment about whether one ought to be empathetic. In this way sentiments could be taken to be descriptive categories that can be identified and studied independently of any normative judgment about their appropriateness. This would be an attractive strategy for a social scientist wishing to study morality in a morally neutral way, for example.

However, unlike behavior and sentiments, moral judgments are essentially normative. A moral judgment is the act of assessing right or wrong, good or bad, decent or despicable. Judgments are inescapably intellectual and cognitive; they involve giving reasons and forming beliefs. Judgments are the home of justification and therefore are an essential and necessary component of the normative use of "morality." One simply cannot identify acts, consequences, drives, or sentiments as moral in the normative sense without having already made a judgment about the justification of that act or sentiment. I hope to make the significance of these distinctions clear in what follows.

Thus the seemingly simple goal of seeking to explain morality turns out to be full of difficulties. The dangers involved in navigating one's way through these difficulties range from triviality to logical incoherence. The following sections will try to sort through some of these challenges.

Causality and Intelligibility

So what are we after when we turn to the empirical sciences for help in explaining morality? Imagine someone who thought that they could explain why Minnesota voters elected Jesse Ventura governor by making reference to brain chemistry, adaptive mechanisms, and evolutionary forces. Or, imagine someone who thought they could explain why a meteorite fell to earth by appealing to that object's desire to seek its natural place. I suspect that most of us would think that both answers have gone seriously awry. The first question calls for an answer in terms of the thoughts, beliefs, values, desires, and goals of the Minnesota electorate. Instead, the answer is given in terms of antecedent physical causes. The second question is appropriately answered in terms of antecedent physical causes and forces, but instead is answered in terms of desires and purposes.

This distinction, of course, is at the heart of the fundamental philosophical problem of the social sciences. Social sciences are split on the relevance of causal and intelligible strategies of explanation. Naturalistic (or empirical, behavioral, positivist) social science maintains that human action can be explained causally and that, eventually, we will be able to discover causal laws that will help to predict and control human action. Interpretive (or hermeneutic) social sciences deny this and instead maintain that the goal of social science is to make human action intelligible.

Perhaps the best example of the interpretive explanatory strategy can be found in anthropology. When an anthropologist seeks to explain the practices of a foreign culture she is not looking to identify antecedent causes of those practices as much as she is seeking to make them *intelligible*. Intelligibility rather than causation is the mark of a successful explanation in anthropology, as it is in many other social sciences as well.[12] Interestingly, de Waal's own approach in primate studies seems much more akin to anthropology than neurology.[13] He has done a marvelous job in making primate behavior intelligible to us without being much concerned with brain chemistry and proteins. This distinction between causal and intelligible explanations of human action is fundamental and is, in my opinion, at the heart of many of the confusions concerning the relevance of science to ethics.

In the philosopher's taxonomy there is a conceptual distinction between causal and interpretive approaches, and therefore between physical and social sciences.[14] Interpretive explanations are purposive, intentional, forward-looking, and teleological; causal explanations are deterministic, mechanistic, and backward-looking. Admittedly, the real world of science is more complicated and the "behavioral sciences" of zoology, primatology, evolutionary psychology, and sociobiology have a foot in each camp. (I find it fascinating that de Waal, who is self-described as an ethologist, has more in common with the interpretive social sciences in his study of apes, than does the psychologist Cosmides, who is much more comfortable with the causal language of "computational machines," "encoding," "neural architecture" and "mechanisms" in her study of human psychology.) Despite the fact that the line between causal and interpretive explanations is not clearly drawn in practice, it is essential that it be drawn conceptually.

Let us consider causal explanations, and more specifically, one major criterion for the empirical and scientific legitimacy of causal explanations. Legitimate causal explanations, at least in so far as they claim to be empirical, require that causes be logically independent of effects. This requirement can be traced at least as far back as Hume's distinction between relations of ideas and matters of fact. Hume tells us that no matter how carefully we look at one billiard ball rolling down the table, we can never discover, from that ball alone, what effects it will have when it strikes the other ball. In Humean language, we can never learn the effects of a cause (or cause of some effect) *a priori*; only experience can teach us the effects of any particular cause. Conversely, if we can know the effect solely from reasoning about the cause *a priori*, then the connection is not a matter of fact but a relation of ideas, i.e., a tautology. If the relationship between cause and effect is logical rather than empirical and contingent, then the judgment that "*C* caused *E*" is a tautology. As a tautology, the explanatory power of an alleged causal relationship is circular and therefore empirically vacuous. Hume tells us that only empirical, i.e., contingent, relationships between causes and effects provide us with any information about the world.

Consider the following example.[15] Suppose your child is having difficulty in school and you seek advice from a school psychologist. The psychologist conducts several tests and announces a diagnosis of Attention Deficit Disorder (ADD). You ask for an explanation and you are told that ADD causes children to have short attention spans, distractability, impulsivity, and hyperactivity. Now imagine you ask for an explanation of ADD from the psychologist. What would *not* count as explanation would be a claim that ADD is a disorder in which children have short attention spans, are easily distracted, impulsive and hyperactive. You would rightfully point out that you know this already and are seeking an explanation—the cause—of this behavior. You want to know *why* your child behaves this way and, so far, you have only had his behavior re-described as ADD. This second explanation amounts to a re-description of the cluster of behaviors and would rightfully be thought empirically vacuous. Only a causal explanation provides the resources for addressing the ultimate goal of changing the behaviors.

Re-describing a set of behaviors as ADD leaves open the question of what is causing these behaviors. In order for some factor to be empirically established as the *cause* of these various behaviors, it is necessary that scientists be able to identify independent criteria for the existence of these factors. So, for example, they might claim that ADD is caused by a lower activity rate in certain areas of the frontal lobe and not with such environmental factors as eating too much sugar, watching too much TV, poor parenting, or incompetent teachers. Once a cause has been hypothesized, experiments can be set up to confirm or disconfirm the alleged connection. One implication of the logical separateness of cause and effect, of course, is the claim that causal and empirical hypotheses must be falsifiable. One would test the claim that ADD is caused by certain brain activity by, among other things, looking for children with ADD who do not have the relevant brain activity. Likewise, the alleged causal claim that ADD is caused by too much sugar is disconfirmed by the many cases of children with high sugar intake and no ADD. The mere re-description of ADD as a set of behaviors is unfalsifiable because, as a logical connection, it is impossible to have one without the other.

(This is not to claim that a diagnosis of ADD based solely on a collection of behavioral symptoms would be unhelpful. A re-description of symptoms *as* a known and not uncommon disorder can help parents understand their child, can make the child's behaviors intelligible in a way they previously were not, might relieve both the child and parent of guilt feelings, and so forth. Presumably this re-description of a set of behavioral symptoms as ADD also played an important role in the early stages of the discovery. Naming a phenomena is an important first step in understanding it.)

What's the significance of this? Ordinarily our explanation of human action makes reference to such factors as the beliefs and desires of the agent. This view is so normal that it is commonly taken to be a fundamental element of "folk psychology" and might be expressed by the following rule:

> For any agent a, if a desires d and a believes that some act x is a means for getting d, then a does x.[16]

If social scientists seek causal explanations of human action and if, as folk psychology suggests, reference to beliefs and desires are an essential part of explaining human action, then social science should seek causal laws connecting the beliefs and desires of an agent to that agent's action. So, for example, we might say that the voters in Minnesota elected Jesse Ventura *because* they wanted to express their frustration with the status quo of the major political parties and they believed that a vote for Ventura would, in the circumstances, be a way to express that frustration clearly.

In ordinary language explanations, we certainly talk in terms of actions being caused by beliefs and desires. Unfortunately, there are convincing reasons for thinking that such mentalistic concepts as beliefs and desires cannot function as empirically verifiable causes precisely because they are logically, and not contingently, related to the actions they are alleged to have caused. It is for this very reason that the interpretive method in the social sciences rejects the naturalistic and causal approach for explaining human action in favor of intelligibility. To make some action intelligible just is to make sense of it—to re-describe it—in terms of the beliefs and desires of the agent. If beliefs and desires cannot function as causes, then the behavioral sciences face two options: abandon (or re-interpret) the reference to beliefs and desires in the explanation of behavior and look for causes elsewhere; or, retain the legitimacy of beliefs and desires in the explanation of behavior, and abandon the search for causal explanations. Classical behaviorism, rational choice theory, and sociobiology take the first option; interpretive approaches in anthropology, sociology, psychology, and I daresay, primatology take the second.

I would like to suggest that something very much like this choice faces us when we look to the empirical sciences for help in ethics. Either we abandon the relevance of beliefs and desires in ethics, or we discount the relevance of causal explanations. The first option is unacceptable, I will argue, because it would force us to abandon the question of justification in ethics and thereby seriously distort the nature of morality. As the previous section suggested, judgments are the essential and primary aspect of the domain of morality. I will suggest that the second option does not require that we ignore causal explanations, only that their relevance is not what some apparently think.

Reasons and Causes

Can beliefs and desires be re-interpreted as, reduced to, or identified with, causes? Throughout this paper so far I have been using the terms "behavior" and "action" indiscriminately. It is important that we now distinguish them. Standard examples distinguish between a blink and a wink, or an arm raising and signaling a question. Behavior, often qualified with the adjective "mere," signifies bodily movement; actions are what we do, they are done for some purpose or with some intention. Bodily movements can occur without any actions, as when my heart beats throughout the night. Actions can occur without any body movements, as when I allow my journal subscription to expire by not sending in my dues. The same bodily movement, in different contexts or with different purposes, can constitute different actions. I raise my hand to ask a question or to signal my friend across the street. The same action can be performed by different bodily movements, as when I pay for groceries by signing a check or scanning a credit card.

The subject of social science, and certainly the subject of morality, is human action, not human behavior. It can be readily admitted that human behaviors can be causally explained, at least in principle if not in fact, by reference to antecedent events. The question, of course, is whether or not human *actions* can be explained in terms of antecedent causes. In ordinary language, beliefs and desires are not causes but function as *reasons* for an action. Explaining an action by reference to the agent's beliefs and desires make that act meaningful, intelligible, understandable, appropriate, indeed they make it reasonable and justifiable. These are all normative and evaluative concepts that would have no place in descriptive and causal explanations. If human acts cannot be explicated except in terms of such mentalistic concepts as beliefs and desires, and if such factors are logically connected to acts, then the answer to the causal question would seem to be "no." Put another way, unless reasons can be causes, naturalistic explanations of morality's "origins," "basis," or "function" will turn out to be mostly irrelevant for doing normative ethics. Conversely, alleging that moral action or sentiments are caused by the relevant beliefs and desires is akin to alleging that ADD is caused by distractability and short attention spans.

While the possibility of giving a reductionistic account of beliefs and desires remains somewhat of an open question in contemporary philosophy of mind, I think a very strong case can be made against the possibility. I turn to two (admittedly brief) arguments which suggest the logical independence of reasons from causes.

First, if beliefs and desires are to function as causes for action, then it must be the case (as described above) that beliefs and desires can be identified independently of their resulting action and the action described independently of the beliefs and desires. The standard method for doing this would be to formulate the alleged causal connection between beliefs/desires and acts as a prediction, set up an experiment and try to confirm or falsify it.

Consider a human case that parallels de Waal's example of consolation among bonobos. We witness an argument between two people, one of whom appears to suffer great humiliation. Soon thereafter, a bystander approaches that person, places her arm upon his shoulder, hugs him, pats him on the back, and smiles at him. An initial and plausible hypothesis would be that the bystander was trying to console and comfort the humiliated person. How would we verify empirically that this was an *act* of consolation brought about by (or has its "basis in" is "produced by" is a "function of" or a "direct outgrowth of" or is "influenced and shaped by") the *desire* to comfort that person and the *belief* that a hug and a pat on the back would provide consolation? The only way to do this empirically, of course, would be to hold two of the three variables (the act, the belief, and the desire) constant while testing for the third. (The other plausible way to verify this, of course, would be to ask the person!) But there is good reason to think this is not possible.

To see this, recognize that the presence of the relevant belief and desire is not by itself sufficient to bring about the action. One may desire to comfort the person and believe that a hug will do so, but any number of intervening variables might interfere (one may be unable to approach him, have other competing desires, believe that he would be offended by such an act, and so forth). So, the belief-plus-desire-causes-action hypothesis requires a fairly strong *ceteris paribus* clause, (e.g., there were no more pressing desires, contrary beliefs, preferable alternative actions, and so forth). In fact, unless we specify the *ceteris paribus* clause in great detail, it is unlikely that we could predict a person's behavior from an initial knowledge of just their beliefs and desires. But the more we specify the *ceteris paribus* conditions, the more likely it becomes that the beliefs and desires (the "causes") are not identifiable independently of the act (the "effect"). To say that someone consoled another is just to say that, under the circumstances and in this very specific set of conditions, they had a particular set of beliefs and desires. Put another way, the bodily behavior becomes an action by ascribing a particular set of beliefs and desires to the agent.

For example, how would we know that the bystander did not go over to pat the person on the back as a means of further humiliating that person? If she had another set of beliefs and desires (e.g., the desire to further humiliate a person and the belief that a pat on the back by a bystanding female would do that), then perhaps the action was one of insult rather than consolation. But how would we ever tell the difference without reference to the beliefs and desires of the bystander? Unless we can independently differentiate the belief, desire, and action—unless, for example, we can identify the act as one of consolation rather than humiliation without making reference to the agents beliefs and desires—then the connection between the act and the beliefs and desires begins to look much like the ADD case. We have re-described the act in terms of beliefs and desires, but we have not identified its cause.

A second way of explaining why reasons cannot be identified with causes involves the intentionality of beliefs and desires. To say that a belief or desire is intentional is to say that it has propositional content. We do not have beliefs *simpliciter,* we have the belief *that* such-and-such is the case. We do not simply have desires, we desire *that* such-and-such be the case. Beliefs and desires cannot be identified or differentiated without reference to their propositional content, i.e., what the belief or desire is *about.* You and I can and do have the same belief just in case that which we believe, the propositional content of the belief, is identical. My own beliefs are distinguished from one another just in so far as their propositional content is different. Beliefs are not differentiated by their spatial or temporal location (as they would be if they were identical with brain states, for example), but by their propositional content.

Compare this to any possible antecedent physical cause alleged to be identical with belief or desire, e.g., some brain state or neurological structure. There just does not seem any way to make sense of the claim that physical states have propositional content. And it seems a stretch, at best, to say that you and I have the "same" brain state. No physical activity can have propositional content unless it is interpreted *as* meaningful and, unless one postulates a ghost within the brain machine, there is no agent to do the interpreting of brain states.[17] If beliefs and desires are intentional (they cannot be individuated without reference to some propositional content), and if brain states (or any other physical structure) cannot have propositional content and can be individuated only spatially and temporally (*this* brain state right *here now*), then beliefs and desires cannot be identical to brain states and thus such mentalistic concepts cannot be reduced to or identified with physical causes.

Biological Drives as Causes

What does this rather esoteric discussion have to do with science and ethics? First, these distinctions will help us assess the nature of many allegedly empirical claims. I suspect some claims that appear to be empirical will, on analysis, turn out not to be. Second, the distinction between reasons and causes will also help bring clarity to the distinction between descriptive and normative claims within ethics. The question of ethical justification and judgment, so very central to philosophical work in normative ethics, depends crucially upon that distinction.

Consider the notion of "drives" that plays so central a role in Paul Lawrence's work.[18] Lawrence proposes, based on recent scientific work on the human brain, a "unified explanation of human morality as an innate feature of human minds." The two major discoveries he relies on are the "discovery of the locus and function of human [unconscious] drives" "genetically pre-wired" and "located in the limbic section of the brain," and the discovery of "innate skill sets" or "starter-kits" for "learning sophisticated skills." Based on such discoveries, Lawrence proposes that "morality arises from the existence in humans of the drive to bond" and that this drive "has led . . . to the evolution of a skill set for morality" and that this drive to bond "is the 'end,' the ultimate motive supplied by our biology, and the morality skill set is the 'means' to this end, also supplied by our biology."[19]

What are we to make of biological "drives"? The word drive itself is ambiguous, having use as both a verb and a noun. As a verb, the word suggests a mechanistic and causal model, as when the engine drives the power train to move my car. Talk of drives as "pushing humans toward," being "genetically hard-wired," and located in the brain further reinforce the interpretation of drives as physical causes that push or force behavior. In this sense, hunger, thirst, and sex might be considered as drives that impel people towards certain ends. In this way, the drive-as-brain-state can be logically distinguished from the behavior that is its end (e.g., eating or drinking). Thus, one could set up an experiment to confirm or falsify the alleged causal connection between the brain state and the behavior.

But as a noun, a drive is also used to mean a desire, disposition, inclination, or an impulse. "These drives provide the sense of purpose, meaning, and intentionality to all human behaviors."[20] People do not have drives *simpliciter*; they have drives to succeed, to compete, and indeed, to acquire, to bond, to learn, and to defend. Having a drive in this sense calls out for some action (captured by the infinitive verb form that follows) to fulfill it. But in this use, the drive cannot be logically distinguished from the end in which it is fulfilled.

The analysis offered so far suggests that Lawrence cannot have it both ways. "Drives" are either causal mechanisms that push us to behave in certain ways, or they are make behavior meaningful as actions by ascribing to that behavior certain purposes, meanings, or intentions.

The outcome of these drives, in all of Lawrence's examples, are human actions not behaviors. As a noun, a drive is an intentional concept in the sense described above. Drives, like beliefs and desires, cannot be distinguished from one another except in terms of what they are about, i.e., their propositional content. Humans, we are told, have the drive to acquire *valued* objects and *pleasurable* experiences, to bond with others in long-term *mutually caring* relationships, to learn and develop *beliefs that make sense of the world*, and to defend one's self, one's possessions, one's loved ones, and one's *beliefs*. But *prima facie* there is no way to individuate and distinguish the alleged cause (e.g., the drive to bond) from the effect (e.g., forming a long-term, mutually caring relationship"). That is, the "drive to bond with others" (as I suspect is true for all of these drives) is logically, not contingently or empirically, connected to its fulfillment (e.g., the tendency to form long-term mutually caring relationships).

Consider how this alleged connection might be verified or falsified. Since these drives are "located in the limbic section of the brain, lying just below and behind the pre-frontal cortex," one would, presumably, identify some brain state as the drive to bond and predict that when the brain state is present the person would *act* (not *behave*) in a manner that fosters long-term mutually caring relationships. Let us take the consolation example described above. Let us also assume that one could identify the brain state associated with (identified as?) the drive to bond. Would knowledge of that brain state help us predict whether or not that individual approaches the victim, and whether or not the act was done to console or humiliate him? It seems not.

First, the outcomes of the drive are radically underdetermined by the drives themselves. The drive to bond can result in a mutually caring relationship with one other individual or with all other human beings. Thus, the same drive could be the cause of both the consoling act (bonding with the victim) and the humiliating act (bonding with the perpetrator). Thus, it seems that no matter which act the agent performs, the same innate drive can be identified as the cause. Further, this drive can conflict with at least three other drives that can all vary in strength. So, if the predicted act is not performed one is always free to attribute this fact to the presence of some conflicting drive. This more than suggests that the only way of deciding which drive was causally effective is to first identify the effect and then attribute it to the relevant cause. But, as with the ADD example, this would trivialize any causal claim since the "strongest" drive is, by definition, whichever one results in the effect. Yet, we cannot know the effect (consolation or humiliation?) without knowing something of the agent's beliefs and desires. Further, we are precluded from the most obvious way to independently identify the beliefs and desires (i.e., by asking the agent) when we are told that the drives are unconscious. Because the drives are said to be unconscious we cannot even hope for guidance from the person herself since she herself would not be aware of what was driving her to act in the way she did. Moreover, "when the drives are in conflict, . . . *pushing for* incompatible lines of action, more deliberation ensues in search of a more creatively integrated solution. . . . [A] *deliberate choice* is made by an act of will that satisfices, not optimizes, in relation to the four drives."[21]

Consider where this leaves us. If drives are intentional concepts, then it seems unlikely that they can be identified with brain states. Even if we could identify some brain state with a drive to bond, that drive would not be enough to make a prior identification of the act that it will bring about. Thus, based on the presence of the brain state alone we have no way to predict its effects and therefore no way to confirm the causal hypothesis. If we witness an act we will not be able to distinguish it as an act of consolation or humiliation by studying the associated antecedent brain states since the same drive may bring about either of these conflicting acts. Further, if neither act occurs, this would not be counterevidence to the causal hypothesis since there can be intervening stronger competing drives. Thus, even if we can identify the act and not discover the accompanying cause, we would still be unable to falsify the alleged causal chain. The connection is made even more unfalsifiable by the claim that drives are unconscious, suggesting that they are there as the underlying cause even if we have no evidence that they are. Finally, we can only know which drive was active if we know the outcome of the deliberative choice of the agent, an act of the will which chooses between competing unconscious desires. Thus, the effective drive seems to be determined, after all, by the relevant beliefs and desires of the agent.

It is important to note that I have used Paul Lawrence's work only as an example of a much more general approach to the scientific study of human action. By no means do I think Lawrence is the only researcher to face such challenges. A strong case can be made for the claim that classical behaviorism succumbed to these very problems.[22] I also suspect that the concept of sentiments and feelings that plays major roles in some of this work might be subject to similar challenges. It is easy to interpret sentiments/feelings as some physiological state yet it is difficult to specify sentiments (or feelings) without a purposive, teleological, intentional, or propositional content. The general point is that there may be insurmountable difficulties in trying to apply the methods of natural science, with its goal of developing causal laws to explain and predict, to the study of human action in general and morality specifically.

Meaning and Intelligibility Among Animals

In the prologue to *The Ape and the Sushi Master* de Waal encourages the social sciences and humanities "to carefully reconsider their own chosen domain—often defined in opposition to biology—and see how broadly it applies. They can export their ideas to students of animal behavior."[23] It is clear from de

Waal's work that what he has in mind is extending the concepts and categories of morality and culture to the study of animal behavior. Extending the framework of interpretive social science seems most inline with what de Waal does himself. De Waal's insight is that conduct otherwise viewed as "mere behavior" becomes intelligible when we interpret them as purposive and intentional acts of consolation, mediation, sympathy, empathy, and sharing.

A similar approach characterized much work in classical anthropology. At first glance, some activities of indigenous cultures appeared irrational and bizarre to Western anthropologists. But over time, as the scientists came to understand the beliefs and desires of the native culture, they were able to understand cultural practices as meaningful and intelligible. Of course, de Waal's work is fascinating exactly because he adopts this same approach for the study of non-human animals. Just as the behavior of an alien culture can be understood as meaningful and purposive, so can the culture of bonobos and chimps. In my own opinion, he has done this in a thoroughly convincing manner.

Perhaps the greatest challenge to the interpretive approach among social scientists is that it is ultimately vacuous. Since one understands some practice when one can explicate it in terms of the beliefs and desires of the participants, social science appears to do little more than document the obvious. Imagine a researcher who models de Waal's work in the study of humans announcing as a significant discovery the fact that humans have been observed sharing food, reconciling disputes, consoling injured parties. For this reason, there seems no way to improve on the explanatory and predictive success of an interpretation beyond what the native participants could already have done. A scientific explanation, within interpretive social science, is nothing more than what any self-reflective participant could have provided. Thus, as *science*, this interpretive approach seems unable to progress much beyond common sense and "folk psychology."

Perhaps because of this, some interpretive social scientists tend to ignore the explanation of individual actions and concentrate on underlying, unconscious, deeper meanings, functions, and structures. Explicating such "deeper" meanings would not be merely to document the obvious since individuals are seldom conscious of such explanations. Freud, Marx, critical theory, and functionalism are obvious examples of this approach. Interestingly enough, at this deeper level causal explanations can re-emerge as both Freud and Marx would have claimed. In this respect, both evolutionary theory and sociobiology can be understood as offering deeper-level functional and causal explanations of social phenomena.

But, of course, de Wall is not documenting the obvious. His thesis is that some animals act in ways that can only be understood as moral and that these actions are communicated culturally rather than being merely the products of evolutionary and biological forces. Chimpanzees and bonobos act so as to reconcile damaged relationships, empathize with and console hurt individuals, share food with others, cooperate for mutual benefit, and mediate disputes. In other words, chimps and bonobos act in ways that can be understood as meaningful when we interpret those acts in terms of moral purposes and intentions.

In terms of our earlier topics, de Waal clearly is concerned with the normative sense of morality. The existence of morally praiseworthy acts among primates is reason to think that morality (as opposed to immorality) "in all likelihood arose during the course of evolution and was only refined in its expression and content by various cultures."[24] Thus, we can talk about the "biological origin" of morality. The behavior of individual primates can be interpreted as moral acts, but the presence in various species of the capacity to so act can be explained in evolutionary and causal terms. At the level of individuals, de Waal explains morality in the mentalistic and intentional language of desires, expectations, beliefs; at the level of evolutionary biology, morality is explained in terms of adaptive functions. But what exactly is the sense of "morality" of which de Waal speaks?

Chimpanzees and bonobos presumably are not moral beings in the Kantian sense of autonomous agents forming and acting from universalized reasons. As far as I have seen, no one has yet suggested that non-human animals are capable of such abstract reasoning. Rather, chimps and bonobos are said to be moral in several other ways. First, they behave in ways that can appropriately be described in morally praiseworthy terms. They share food, they mediate disputes, they console injured individuals. Second, these acts seem motivated by such morally praiseworthy sentiments as empathy, sympathy, and care. Thus, if we can make a distinction between moral judgments, moral acts, and moral motivations or sentiments, de Waal's work suggests that the last two components at least can be ascribed to various primates.

Justification and Explanation

Let me begin to draw these various themes together and work towards some conclusions. To say that morally praiseworthy acts and sentiments are an "outgrowth of" or "arose during the course of" evolution and that they therefore are "innate" and have their "origin" or "basis" in biology is at first glance trivial. In so far as the capacity for all human (and non-human) acts and sentiments arose during the course of evolution, such a thesis is obvious.

To claim that any particular morally praiseworthy act or sentiment (as opposed to the mere species-wide capacity for such things) is brought about by biological forces would be more controversial. This would imply a biological determinism that few people seem willing to defend. Even the staunchest defenders of genetic influences on human behavior acknowledge that not every genetic disposition gets manifested in actual behavior.

Turning from acts and sentiments to moral judgments, the issues get murkier. Alleging a biological origin for our capacity to make moral judgments, as with any judgment, once again can be trivially true. Humans make all sorts of judgments, including judgments of fact and a wide variety of evaluative judgments. Presumably no one would deny that the capacity to make factual judgments arose in the course of evolution. But such a biological origin has no more to do with making a judgment morally sound than it would have to do with making it factually or scientifically sound. And herein lies the rub. In so far as drives, sentiments, feelings, actions, and motives are identified as moral in the normative sense, they presuppose a prior judgment that such things are morally justified or sound. Finally and crucially, the justifications embedded in moral judgments necessarily must be expressed as reasons and beliefs, intentional concepts that can only be logically but not causally related to action.

Consider the case of punishment as described by Cosmides. She hypothesizes that neurocognitive circuitry has evolved to "cause people to punish free riders." I believe that a persuasive case can be made for the claim that the very concept of "punishment" is conceptually connected to such other value-laden concepts as retribution and desert. Someone who harms another who does not deserve the harm, who inflicts a harm on another without the purpose or intent of paying back a wrongdoing, cannot be said to have punished the other. Such acts might attack, harm, hurt, inflict pain, negatively reinforce another, but they do not punish. Such behavior may even be caused by neurological processes that have evolved as a result of (not designed by) natural selection. But such causes cannot explain "retribution" "wrongdoing," or "desert" and therefore cannot, logically cannot, explain punishment. Punishment can only be explained in the sense of being made intelligible by reference to reasons, beliefs, and justifications.

A further crucial feature of moral justification, as so clearly presented by Hume, is that they are always underdetermined by the facts. That is, no type or amount of empirical data is sufficient to entail the judgment of practical reason that one ought, or ought not, perform any act or cultivate any sentiment. No amount of evolutionary facts alone can ever establish that one *ought or deserves* to be punished. Empirical data are surely relevant in practical reasoning and justification, but they are not conclusive.

All this would perhaps be obvious to the point of triviality were it not for the underlying connection that much of this research makes to evolutionary theory. Throughout the work of de Waal, Lawrence, Cosmides, and Frederick one finds both implicit and explicit claims that moral (in the normative sense of praiseworthy) action, sentiments, and judgments serve evolutionary and adaptive ends. Unfortunately (in my opinion), all too often these evolutionary claims are couched in teleological and purposive terms that imply normative conclusions that, in fact, are unjustified.

Consider just two examples from Cosmides' writings. The results of her research "suggests that the human computational architecture contains an expert system *designed for* (emphasis added) reasoning about cooperation for mutual benefit."[25] In discussing punitive sentiments and behavior, Cosmides asks if there is "evidence of special *design* . . . [that] is a solution to the problem . . . rather than a byproduct" of other biological mechanisms and she refers to evidence which shows such sentiments and behavior to "appear *well-designed to solve adaptive problems*" (emphasis added).[26]

I am not suggesting that Cosmides herself claims that evolutionary forces of natural selection are purposive and teleological. Presumably she would explicitly deny that they are. Nonetheless, the language is purposive and teleological and such language does have normative implications. To conclude that something fulfills its design or accomplished its purpose is, at least in some *prima facie* sense, to say that it is good. When such teleological language underlies the biological explanation of morally praiseworthy behavior, the normative conclusions from a factual description appears even more obvious. Even when the purposive terms are used metaphorically or casually, it is a very short step from the claim that cheater detection and punishment (or empathy, cooperation, bonding, or consolation) accomplishes its evolutionary design or purpose to the conclusion that it is, therefore, good because it do that. But evolution has neither a purpose nor design (whose would it be?) and, even if it did, accomplishing that purpose would not entail the normative conclusion.[27] Again, I am not attributing such a conclusion to any of these authors, but the pervasive ambiguities described at the start of this paper leave the door open to this unsound reasoning.

In summary, I have claimed that an essential part of normative ethics involves the question of justification. Justification of one's beliefs, whether they are empirical or ethical, must be done with the intentional language of reasons, not the causal language of empirical science. Consider this issue in terms of a self-referential challenge aimed at evolutionary psychology. Imagine someone who claimed to explain the origin of evolutionary biology in terms of "neurocognitive circuitry" that has evolved to cause people to conduct research in evolutionary psychology. Suppose such a person went on to conclude that this discovery "suggests that the human computational architecture contains an expert system *designed for* (emphasis added) reasoning about" evolutionary psychology. Since our brains seem designed for such thinking, we might be tempted to conclude that evolutionary psychology is true, justified, or legitimate. But this conclusion is as out of place in scientific debates as it would in ethical debates.

Implications for Business Ethics

It remains to say something about what conclusions should be drawn for our work in normative business ethics. One immediate implication is that these findings can be used to counter simplistic egoistic views in normative ethics. Business ethicists are familiar with support for ethical egoism and market-based policy recommendations on the basis of alleged facts about the egoistic nature of human beings. Indeed, significant support for the market comes from the alleged fact that humans are naturally selfish. Influenced no doubt by economic assumptions about self-interest, many argue that only self-interested reasons can be offered for normative prescriptions in ethics.

If it turns out that chimpanzees, bonobos, and other animals regularly act in unselfish and caring ways, and if clear evolutionary and biological explanations can be offered for this fact, then those who deny such abilities in humans face major obstacles in the defense of their claims. These facts would not decide the debate, of course, in the same way that the alleged facts of psychological egoism would not end the debate. The is-ought gap challenges altruistic facts as well as egoistic ones. But evidence of widespread empathetic, conciliatory, altruistic, and cooperative behavior among both humans and primates, and plausible evolutionary explanations for such behavior, may well shift the burden of proof onto those who—in economics, ethics, and management—offer only self-interested rationales for policies and recommendations.

This point can be made in terms of the oft-used expression "ought implies can." Some have claimed that ethical prescriptions requiring people to act altruistically are unreasonable in that they demand people act in way that they cannot. The scientific assertions we are discussing would count against this conclusion by claiming that, in fact, both human and other animals are quite capable of acting altruistically. But it would be an equal logical mistake to conclude that because we have the biological capacity to act from empathy or sympathy, we ought. Justification questions require something other than mere facts. If ought implies can, can does not imply ought.

I am less confident that there are many more direct implications for management theory. I suspect that there will be tendency to think that these behavioral sciences are developing or discovering causal laws about human behavior, laws that management theorists and practicing managers might then be able to use to influence employee and consumer behavior. In a passage referenced earlier, Linda Klebe Treviño explains that

> The social scientists who study business ethics . . . focus on the world as it exists and attempt to understand and predict how it works. . . . The dominant social science paradigm assumes human behavior is influenced by a combination of individual and contextual factors. . . . These contextual factors are particularly interesting to management scholars because managers have some control over the context within which people work. Thus the assumption is that managers can influence their subordinates' ethical conduct.[28]

From a perspective such as this, the goal of behavioral sciences is to discover causal regularities that explain and predict individual behavior. Unless such regularities are causal rather than mere correlations, the explanatory and predictive power of the discoveries is lost. Such regularities, eventually identified as "laws of human behavior," can then guide those who seek to manage others.

Reminiscent of Frederick Taylor's call for scientific management, and later generations' flirtations with such social theorists as Abraham Maslow and Lawrence Kohlberg, the goal would be to use discoveries in neuroscience or evolutionary psychology to better manage and influence behavior. One can imagine managers seeking to design a workplace that would facilitate the natural drive to bond, or that would enable the brain's neurological subroutine specialized for cheater detection to flourish. Human resource managers might test for highly developed neurological cheater-detection subroutines when seeking to hire an auditor. One can imagine marketing managers designing an advertising campaign based upon the "four innate drives . . . hard-wired in the brain." The innate drive to acquire seems a marketer dream, and the drive to bond could certainly be useful for branding and product loyalty issues.

What I have said throughout this paper suggests that such hopes are conceptually and ethically misguided. Managers who seek to influence their subordinate's ethical conduct would be much better advised (both practically and ethically) to speak with their subordinates, listen to them, engage them in conversation. Knowledge of their individual beliefs, desires, values, interests, and motivations will be much more effective in influencing their behavior than will knowledge of arcane laws of neurophysiology, brain chemistry, innate skill sets, computational architecture. Managers who appeal to employees' or consumers' beliefs and desires in the attempt to influence behavior will also be engaged in the morally justified act of persuasion. Managers who seek causal laws that can be used to influence behavior are engaged in the morally suspect act of manipulation. Knowledge of brain chemistry and evolutionary psychology will prove as relevant for understanding the fraudulent behavior of Enron and WorldCom executives as it is for understanding the behavior of Minnesota voters who elected Jesse Ventura. For those of us interested in preventing repeats of both, our time will be better spent engaged with those individual human beings whose actions we hope to influence.

Notes

1. While some ambiguity exists concerning Hume's exact meaning—he never did explicitly deny that one can derive an *ought* from an *is*—the textual evidence seems unambiguous that he did believe that reason cannot infer evaluative judgments from facts. See especially Hume's *Treatise*, Book III, Part I, section 1.

2. Of course, in the utilitarian tradition following Hume, empirical science proved very helpful in determining appropriate means for attaining valued-laden goals, but remained at least neutral concerning the value of the goals themselves. Thus, in the clearest example of market economics as it developed following Hume's friend Adam Smith, individuals are left free to choose for themselves what they value, and the role of economics is to determine how to optimize the satisfaction of individual preferences. A similar judgment can be made about how utilitarians viewed the relevance of political science.

3. These quotes are taken from the opening abstract of "Any Animal Whatever: Darwinian Building Blocks of Morality in Monkey and Apes," *Journal of Consciousness Studies*, 7, No. 1–2, 2000, pp. 1–29, by Jessica Flack and Frans de Waal. Emphasis added. See p. 7 of this volume.

4. Paul Lawrence, "The Biological Base of Morality?" in *Business, Science, and Ethics*, ed. R. Edward Freeman and Patricia H. Werhane (Charlottesville, Va.: Philosophy Documentation Center, 2004), pp. 59, 61. Emphasis added.

5. William C. Frederick, "The Evolutionary Firm and its Moral (Dis)Contents," in *Business, Science, and Ethics*, ed. R. Edward Freeman and Patricia H. Werhane (Charlottesville, Va.: Philosophy Documentation Center, 2004), p. 166. Emphasis added.

6. Lawrence, "The Biological Base of Morality?" p. 59.

7. This perspective has been described quite clearly by Linda Klebe Treviño in "Business Ethics and the Social Sciences," published as chapter 18 in *A Companion to Business Ethics*, edited by Robert Frederick (Malden, Mass.: Blackwell Publishing, 1999).

> The social scientists who study business ethics . . . focus on the world as it exists and attempt to understand and predict how it works. . . . The dominant social science paradigm assumes human behavior is influenced by a combination of individual and contextual factors. . . . These contextual factors are particularly interesting to management scholars because managers have some control over the context within which people work. Thus the assumption is that managers can influence their subordinates' ethical conduct. (pp. 218–219)

8. Michael Price, Leda Cosmides, and John Tooby, "Punitive Punishment as an anti-free rider psychological device," *Evolution and Human Behavior* 23(3) (2002): 203–231.

9. Of course, our conception of morality might itself develop in light of what one learns about bonobos. Our concepts and experiences can shape each other. Nevertheless, without at least an initial conception of morality to start with, science would risk begging the question with an alleged discovery that bonobos have one.

10. De Waal reviews similar challenges to his work on the question of "culture" in *The Ape and the Sushi Master* (New York: Basic Books, 2001); see especially chapter 6.

11. Konrad Lorenz, *On Aggression* (London: Methuen, 1963). In *The Ape and the Sushi Master*, de Waal concludes that, with proper qualifications, Lorenz "remains fundamentally right on the point that aggression is an innate human potential" (p. 95). It is interesting to note that despite Lorenz's massive evidence from animal studies concerning aggression, de Waal believes that forty years later it still remains to be shown that animals possess "moral" sentiments.

12. This approach can be traced to Max Weber's concept of *Verstehen*. See his *The Methodology of the Social Sciences*. A helpful collection of essays on this topic can be found in William Outhwaite, *Understanding Social Life: The Method called Verstehen* (London: George Allen & Unwin. 1975).

13. Indeed, much of de Waal's book, *The Ape and the Sushi Master*, is an explicit defense of ethologists against behavioristic approaches.

14. The incompatibility of these approaches is, of course, philosophically controversial. Among those who would argue that explanations in terms of intelligibility are incompatible with causal explanations are Charles Taylor, *The Explanation of Behavior* (London: Routledge & Kegan Paul, 1964); G. E. M. Anscombe, *Intention* (Ithaca, N.Y.: Cornell University Press, 1958); A. I. Melden, *Free Action* (London: Routledge & Kegan Paul, 1961); and Richard Taylor, *Action and Purpose* (Englewood Cliffs, N.J.: Prentice Hall, 1966). Among those who defend the compatibility of causal and intelligible explanations are Donald Davidson, "Actions, Reasons, Causes," *The Journal of Philosophy* 60 (1963): 697; and Alvin Goldman, *A Theory of Human Action* (Englewood Cliffs, N.J.: Prentice Hall, 1970). The compatibility thesis generally rests with the claim that not all causal explanations are mechanistic or deterministic. My own point in what follows could be expressed as well by substituting "empirical" for "causal" explanations and thus avoid much of this particular controversy.

15. The literature is full of similar examples. My two favorite are the all human acts are motivated by self-interest and that satisfying one's desires will cause one to be happy. When challenged by disconfirming evidence, both tend to dissolve into vacuous tautologies.

16. For this characterization of folk psychology and much of what follows in the next sections, I rely on Alexander Rosenberg, *Philosophy of Social Science* (Boulder, Colo.: Westview Press, 2nd edition, 1995).

17. One could, of course, hypothesize another brain state which "interprets" the initial ones. Yet this would simply push the same question back one step further: how does *this* brain state "contain" the propositional content necessary for interpreting some physical state *as* meaningful? Perhaps there is a third such state which interprets it, and so on into an infinite regress. This point is developed in Rosenberg, pp. 48–49.

18. Lawrence, "The Biological Base of Morality?" developed in more detail in *Driven: How Human Nature Shapes our Choices*, by Paul Lawrence and N. Nohria (San Francisco: Jossey-Bass, 2002).

19. Lawrence, "The Biological Base of Morality?" pp. 59–61.

20. Ibid., p. 60.

21. Ibid., p. 61, emphasis added.

22. See Rosenberg, *Philosophy of Social Science*, chapter 3, for a convincing version of this argument.

23. *The Ape and the Sushi Master*, p. 29.

24. Jessica C. Flack and Frans de Waal, "Any Animal Whatever: Darwinian Building Blocks of Morality in Monkeys and Apes," *Journal of Consciousness Studies* 7(1–2) (2000), p. 2. See Flack and de Waal, "Monkey Business and Business Ethics: Evolutionary Origins of Human Morality," in *Business, Science, and Ethics*, ed. R. Edward Freeman and Patricia H. Werhane (Charlottesville, Va.: Philosophy Documentation Center, 2004), p. 8.

25. Leda Cosmides and John Tooby, "The Cognitive Neuroscience of Social Reasoning," in *The New Cognitive Neurosciences*, ed. Michael Gazzaniga (Boston: MIT Press, 2000).

26. Michael Price, Leda Cosmides, and John Tooby, "Punitive Punishment as an Anti-Free Rider Psychological Device," forthcoming in *Evolution and Human Behavior*, pp. 2 and 17.

27. Of course, the natural law tradition has ready answers to these challenges. Nature reflects the design and purpose of the Creator and therefore attaining God's purpose is to attain the good. Presumably, contemporary evolutionary psychology does not make such assumptions.

28. "Business Ethics and the Social Sciences," *op. cit.*, pp. 218–219.

EVOLUTIONARY BIOLOGY RESEARCH, ENTREPRENEURSHIP, AND THE MORALITY OF SECURITY-SEEKING BEHAVIOR IN AN IMPERFECT ECONOMY

Ronald K. Mitchell

Abstract: This article investigates whether there is an underlying morality in the ways that human beings seek to obtain economic security within our imperfect economy, which can be illuminated through evolutionary biology research. Two research questions are the focus of the analysis: (1) What is the transaction cognitive machinery that is specialized for the entrepreneurial task of exchange-based security-seeking? and, (2) What are the moral implications of the acquisition and use of such transaction cognitions?

Evolutionary biology research suggests within concepts that are more Darwin- v. Huxley-based, an underlying morality supportive of algorithm-governed economizing arising from the behaviors that are most worthy of long-term reproduction. Evolutionarily stable algorithm-enhanced security-seeking is argued to be a new view of entrepreneurship, but one that, somewhat ironically, is grounded in a primordially-based entrepreneurial morality that is at the core of economic security.

Introduction

Is there a primordially-based global entrepreneurial drive toward ever-escalating levels of economic exchange—the continual creation of new value-adding transactions that are at the core of economic security (Mitchell, 2001; Venkataraman, 1997)? And if so, is there an underlying morality in the ways that human beings seek to obtain economic security within our imperfect economy that can be illuminated through evolutionary biology research?

Ideas that contribute possible answers to these questions were presented at the Ruffin Lectures on Business, Science, and Ethics, held at the University of Virginia in April 2002. These lectures, and subsequent research and development, make possible a further assessment of relationships among evolutionary biology research, entrepreneurship, and the morality of security-seeking behavior within the imperfect economy that characterizes our present business and ethical environment.

© 2004 *Society for Business Ethics and the Darden School Foundation*   pp. 263–287

From Ruffin Lecturers we learned that:

- Social exchange is an ancient, pervasive, and central part of human social life (Cosmides and Tooby, 2004);
- Evolutionary biology research leads us to look for things that we otherwise would not search for (Cosmides and Tooby, 2004);
- The existential challenge for an organism is to live and adapt while staying ahead of the entropy it creates (Frederick, 2004);
- The modern corporation (understood by me to represent more basically: the transacting system) is the main life support system for homo sapiens (Frederick, 2004);
- There are both economizing and algorithmic moral dilemmas posed in the security-seeking process: economizing (transacting) moral dilemmas—because survival requires economizing/ transacting (i.e., it is not an option), and economizing/ transacting produces entropy (the extent of which is variable) that is exported to the community and is *dis*order creating; and algorithmic (cognitive) moral dilemmas—because coalition members within a security-seeking society carry with them ancestral algorithms, which cue prior-age responses (algorithmic impulses) that can be, and often are morally contradictory (Frederick, 2004).

The foregoing ideas guide the formulation of two more precise research questions that are the focus of this paper: (1) What is the transaction cognitive machinery that is specialized for the entrepreneurial task of exchange-based security-seeking? And, (2) What are the moral implications of the acquisition and use of such transaction cognitions?[1]

In this paper I shall explore the four conceptual connections implied by the foregoing questions, those being the relationship between:

- Evolutionary biology research and exchange-based morality,
- Evolutionary biology research and transaction cognitions (economizing/ transacting and algorithmic reasoning/ cognitions),
- Transaction cognitions, entrepreneurship, and security-seeking behavior, and
- Entrepreneurial security-seeking behavior and morality.

Evolutionary Biology Research and Exchange-Based Morality

The presenters during the Ruffin Lectures argued persuasively that there is a relationship between evolutionary biology research and exchange-based morality. Some of the concepts and logic contained in their arguments are as follows:

- Socioeconomic exchange involves an approximate logical form: *If person A provides the requested benefit to or meets the requirement of person or group B, then B will provide the rationed benefit to A*: and we refer to the resulting behaviors as a social contract. (Cosmides and Tooby, 2004);

- This social contract arises in response to the long-enduring problems that humanity faces (Cosmides and Tooby, 2004), (e.g., as I interpret these remarks: obtaining food, shelter, and in sum, attaining economic security: "provisions in store for an uncertain future" [Durant, 1935: 2]);

- This social contract also results in cooperative socioeconomic behavior generated by cognitive machinery specialized for that task (Cosmides and Tooby, 2004): e.g., a support system;

- The support system that leads to economic security is not the same as the moral system that is created to guide the process (Flack and de Waal, 2004);

- There exists a hierarchy of moral prerequisites that flows from the necessities of operating the support system, which includes (in order) sympathy, norms, reciprocity, getting along, and trust (Flack and de Waal, 2004);

- The support system—which in its essence must accommodate and utilize competition, differs from the moral system—which in its essence must engender reconciliations among competing (group) aims and those of individuals (Margolis, 2004);

- Evolutionary biology research suggests that exchange-based morality was not devised to subjugate the independent economic interests of individuals, but rather emerged out of the interaction of both individual and group interests (Flack and de Waal, 2004).

Evolutionary Biology Research and Transaction Cognitions

As earlier noted, Frederick has suggested that both economizing and algorithmic-based behaviors have moral implications (Frederick, April 20, 2002). A clear understanding of the nature of economizing (transacting in an imperfect economy), and of algorithmic responses (security-seeking based upon transaction cognitions) is therefore a prerequisite for the analysis of the moral implications of entrepreneurially-driven socioeconomic behavior, one of the key objectives of this inquiry. In the following paragraphs I conduct this analysis by rigorously defining what is meant by the terms: transactions, economic imperfections, and transaction cognitions.

Transactions

Aristotle noted the centrality of transactions when he stated: "There would be no society if there were no exchange" (DelMar, 1968 [1896]: 1). Exchange forms the basis for transacting. A rigorous definition of a transaction ought therefore to specify the irreducible components of exchange. This assertion poses a challenging question: Does the transaction have a basic form, analogous, for example, to the planetary model developed by Niels Bohr for field of nuclear physics, or the double helix developed by Crick and Watson for the field of genetics?

In his extensive analysis of human creativity, Gardner (1993: 9) relies on a model proposed by Csikszentmihalyi (1988) to explain the essence of a transaction. Each of three components specified—the individual (creator), the work (the creation) and other persons (the other party to the transaction)—adds a necessary element. All must be present at the same time for a transaction to occur. Any two alone are insufficient to accomplish a transaction. Thus, there can be no transaction when an individual offers to transact without creating anything to sell (the work). Nor can a transaction occur where an individual creates a work but has no buyers (other persons) to which to sell. And, the idea of a product (the work) being for sale to buyers (other persons) without a creator (the individual) is undefined. Arguably, then, although a transaction may occur using more elements than the three specified, it may not exist with fewer. A preliminary representation of a basic transaction is shown in Figure 1.

Figure 1
The Elements of a Basic Transaction

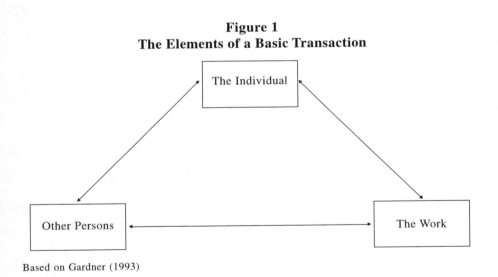

Based on Gardner (1993)

However, each component of the transaction introduces imperfections into the exchange. The individual introduces limitations to thinking processes: bounds to rationality; the work by its nature is specific: candles not crops, buns not beer, guns not butter; and other persons introduce opportunism: self-interest seeking with guile. In the following paragraphs, these attributes of an imperfect economy are discussed, and are specified in terms of their effects on transaction basics.

An Imperfect Economy

The two decades encompassing the mid-1960s through the mid-1980s saw the development of economic theories that attempted to relax the neoclassical economic assumption of perfect rationality to take into account behavioral assumptions (Cyert and March, 1963; Nelson and Winter, 1973; Simon, 1979; Williamson, 1975; Williamson, 1985) that more accurately identify the sources of imperfections within an economy. Helpfully, these assumptions also relate economic outcomes to cognitions of individuals about themselves, about others, and about the work that they produce, i.e., cognitions about the elements of the basic transaction (Figure 1).

One of the more comprehensive of these theories is transaction cost economics, which is especially suited to the articulation of the *economizing* roots of moral dilemmas in transacting (Frederick, April 20, 2002), and which specifies three attributes of frequent transacting under uncertainty: bounded rationality, opportunism, and asset specificity (Williamson, 1985: 31). Bounded rationality refers to the cognitions that convert intendedly rational behavior into limitedly rational behavior (Williamson, 1985: 30). Opportunism—a behavioral condition of self-interest seeking with guile (1985: 30)—creates the cognitions of social friction due to moral hazard and distrust. Asset specificity refers to cognitions surrounding the non-trivial investment in transaction-specific (non-redeployable) assets (Williamson, 1985; Williamson, 1991: 79). These attributes create transaction costs, and the attributes themselves arise due to particular cognitions. A brief explanation of these assertions about transaction costs and cognitions follows.

Transaction costs

Transaction costs are defined as the costs of running an economic system (Arrow, 1969: 48), and are one way of describing the entropy that Frederick (April 20, 2002) suggests is disorder-creating as it is exported into the community. The notion of transaction costs is quite useful in the development of a model of transacting in an imperfect economy, because it calls for us to specify the behavioral features of the economic environment that are not perfect—the factors which cause costs, and are therefore at the core of economizing moral dilemmas. Transaction costs in socioeconomic systems are thus thought to be the equivalent of friction in physical systems (Williamson, 1985: 19).

At the organizational level of analysis, the concept of transaction costs has been utilized extensively to argue that hierarchies (firms) and markets are alternative systems for governing transactions based on transaction cost-driven "substitutions at the margin" (Coase, 1937: 387; Williamson, 1975). But there appears to be no reason to suppose that the application of transaction cost-driven substitution at the margin is limited solely to questions of how firms form when markets fail (Coase, 1937). Theoretically, transaction costs could explain a variety of alternative system choices at various levels of analysis, including the individual level.

Thus, for example, there are well-documented instances reported as "prospect theory" (Kahneman and Tversky, 1979) where (in psychological prospect) losses loom larger than gains (1979: 288), and individuals' actual utility has been found to be less than expected utility—a difference likely due to transaction costs.[2] Or a person's choice between a job and self-employment might also be explained by a transaction cost-induced substitution at the margin (a decision to transact with a "boss" v. with multiple customers in a marketplace), as perhaps could success or failure in a job or a venture ("in" or "out" of a particular economic governance system: e.g. "boss" system or industry system).

Cognitions

Cognitions are the algorithmic root of moral dilemmas in the security-seeking process. Thus, there is strong support for an explanation of market imperfections which, though economic, appeals to psychology. In his Nobel Prize acceptance speech, Simon (1979) reaffirmed Marshall's proclamation that economics is a psychological science (Marshall, 1920; Simon, 1979: 493). Also, Maurice Allais, 1988 winner of the Nobel Prize for economics for his theories on economic markets and the efficient use of resources, advanced (although not included in the Nobel citation) the Allais paradoxes (1953, published by himself over the objections of his reviewers), which—while virtually ignored for several decades—provided a psychological explanation (Lopes, 1994: 203) for irrationality in the economic behavior of individuals (Allais, 1953). Furthermore Arrow (1982), when he observed that failures of the rationality hypothesis in economics are compatible with the observations of cognitive psychologists (Arrow, 1982: 5), pointed to a branch of psychology within which one could look to find relevant models. Thus, generally, there is reason to suggest the use of psychological constructs as the basis for theory that describes security-seeking transacting in an imperfect economy; and specifically, to suggest further examination of the social cognitive model as a theoretical engine that can drive an explanation of important relationships.

Transaction Cognitions

The making of transacting choices among alternatives in economic systems may thus be thought of as relating to the cognitions—specialized mental models (Arthur, 1994)—that surround individuals' responses to the three previously noted sources of market imperfections: bounded rationality, opportunism, and specificity. This model of entrepreneurially-driven socioeconomic behavior may therefore be characterized as a transaction-cognitive model. Williamson (1985) argues that the world of contract (which may be broadly interpreted to include economic relationships in general, i.e., *social* contract) is variously described as one of: (1) planning, (2) promise, (3) competition, and (4) governance/ hierarchy, depending (respectively in each instance) upon the presence/ absence combination of the sources of market imperfections as illustrated in Table 1 (as adapted from Williamson, 1985: 31).

Table 1
Some Attributes of the Contracting Process

Behavioral Assumption			Implied Contracting Process
Bounded Rationality	Opportunism	Asset Specificity	
0	+	+	Planning
+	0	+	Promise
+	+	0	Competition
+	+	+	Governance

0 = absence
+ = presence

Adapted from Williamson (1985: 31)

Interestingly, although his argument appears to be bi-directional, Williamson utilizes only one of the directions in his analysis of hierarchies v. markets. That is, he suggests (for example) that the absence of bounded rationality in the presence of asset specificity and opportunism implies planning (i.e., bounded rationality is inversely related to planning); but leaves under-utilized the logical extension that planning should therefore be useful in managing situations characterized by those same two conditions (because planning reduces transaction costs that arise from bounded rationality). The same logic follows for transaction costs created by opportunism and asset specificity. Each (respectively) should be affected by promise (trust) and by competition (value-based bargaining).

Thus, the specialized mental models that individuals possess about planning (e.g. mental models that assist in developing analytical structure to solve previously unstructured problems), promise (mental models that help in identifying and prioritizing stakeholders thereby building trust in economic relationships), and competition (specifically mental models that can create bargaining positions—small or large[3]), are expected to impact the success of transacting as a security-seeking behavior. The utilization of transaction costs through the employment of specialized cognitions has significant implications for transacting in an imperfect economy.

As noted previously, transaction cognitions about the self, the work, and others are impacted by bounded rationality, opportunism, and what might in its general form be termed "work"-specificity. That is, cognitions about the self in relationship to the work and others are shaped primarily by bounded rationality. Correspondingly, cognitions about other persons, in relationship to the individual and the work, are shaped primarily by opportunism. And finally, cognitions about the work in relationship to the individual and others are shaped primarily by work-specificity. It stands to reason, then, that cognitions about any of the dyad-based relationships (e.g. individual/ work) will be primarily shaped by only two of the three behavioral conditions if influenced by the specialized mental models identified in the preceding paragraphs. Williamson's analysis suggests in the general transacting case, that planning therefore ought to influence the effects of transaction costs related to bounded rationality when constrained by work-specificity and opportunism, etc. as illustrated in Figure 2.

Figure 2
The Source of Transaction Cognitions

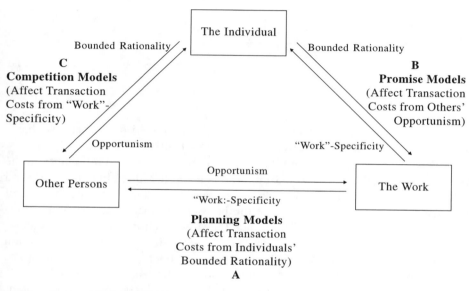

Based on Gardner (1993); Williamson (1985)

Figure 2 illustrates the likely effects of specialized cognitions about planning, promise, and competition, and in doing so provides the basis for a rigorous derivation of transaction cognitions. That is, to the extent that individuals possess or can gain the specialized algorithmic knowledge for planning, promise, and competition, their ability economize on the transaction costs that impact the dyadic relationships illustrated should be enhanced. If the objective of entrepreneurially driven socioeconomic behavior is to increase economic security through the success of transactions, then entrepreneurial security-seeking behavior can be characterized as the utilization of transaction cognitions to economize on transaction costs.

Evolutionary biology research suggests the existence and profound influence of primordially-sourced cognitive machinery that has been specialized for social exchange-based tasks (Cosmides, April 20, 2002). And in his Ruffin lecture, Frederick (2002, Figure 2) suggests in his analysis of the natural substrate that gives rise to phenomena such as transaction cognitions, the equivalent of planning, promise, and competition cognitions.[4] I now turn to a discussion of the relationships among transaction cognitions, entrepreneurship, and security-seeking.

Transaction Cognitions, Entrepreneurship, and Security-Seeking

For most people, the accepted way to accomplish economic security is getting and keeping a stable job. However, this course of action is becoming less and less reliable as Western economies yield to the pressures of globalization (Friedman, 2000). Some commentators have begun to claim that for many Americans, economic security no longer exists (Mandel, 1996). One response to this growing economic insecurity is the increasing emphasis on entrepreneurship in both the private and public sectors of the economy. In response to such interest, the research community has expended extensive effort to better understand entrepreneurship (please see for example reviews by Duchesneau and Gartner [1990] and Wortman [1987]), under the implicit assumption that should entrepreneurship be better understood, more jobs might be created (Birch, 1981; Birley, 1986; Kirchhoff and Greene, 1995; Kirchhoff and Phillips, 1988), with a resultant increase in economic security.

Figure 3 illustrates the three decision zones in this security-seeking process. Interestingly, the three previously identified sets of transaction-cognitions appear to apply sequentially to this decision process as also shown in the decision tree diagram. In a 1986 study, Leddo and Abelson (1986: 121) noted that cognitive scripts occur in a decision order that begins with "entry" and then proceeds to "doing." Read (1987) also documents that scripts proceed according to a known or relatively standard sequence.

The transacting sequence illustrated is no exception (Mitchell, 2001; Vesper, 1996). The decision sequence in the accomplishment of economic results proceeds with the successive answering of the following age-old economic questions:

1. Will I seek economic security? (Will I prepare something of economic value to offer?)

2. How shall I seek this economic security? (Can I agree upon a socioeconomic exchange with another person or group?) and,

3. Can I successfully complete this economic exchange? (What will I do to deliver on this promise?)

Put in terms of transaction cognition theory, the cognitive scripts required to support/ or not support the accomplishment of economic results can be represented by the decisions that must be made to answer the foregoing questions. These choices are also represented in the decision tree shown in Figure 3 (p. 272).

As a general model, this depiction permits us to represent people's use of transaction cognitions as three steps in a standard sequence. Through the successive use of Competition, Promise, and Planning cognitions as steps in a standard decision sequence, individuals attain greater economic security through successfully completing transactions.[5] Thus, using transaction cognition theory we can derive a simple representation of the cognitive machinery that is specialized for the tasks of the security seeker. This observation suggests that an investigation of the workings of the cognitive transaction process

Figure 3
Security-Seeking Decision Tree

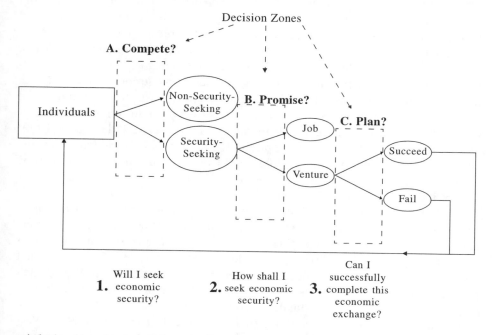

might lead to a better understanding of entrepreneurially driven security-seeking in imperfect markets.

Why does the process of security-seeking by individuals work the way that it does? To account for the empirical evidence available with respect to individuals' security-seeking decisions (as revealed by demographic research), it is necessary to identify the reasons for the security-seeking *status quo* behaviors of individuals in an imperfect economy. In the process, I seek in answer to the questions highlighted by the decisions illustrated in Figure 3 (Why do some people seek economic security while others do not? Why do some seekers of economic security choose job employment while others choose self-employment? and, Why do some entrepreneurially driven security seekers succeed, while others fail?), to examine the morality of security-seeking behavior in an imperfect economy through the lens of evolutionary biology research.

Entrepreneurial Security-Seeking Behavior and Morality

The diagram in Figure 3 graphically illustrates the alternatives available to economic security-seeking individuals.[6] As shown, some people don't seek economic security; some don't venture (utilize entrepreneurially based behaviors to seek economic security); and some don't succeed whether they venture or not. Echoing Coase (1937) cited earlier in the article, each of these choices involves making substitutions at the margin, based upon the influence of entropy as represented by transaction costs. If theoretically robust, the model that has been developed should provide an explanation for the choices made by individuals in each of these three decision zones, and should also provide the basis for the assessment of the moral dilemmas posed by entrepreneurially-based choices.

The moral implications of the choice-making process in economic security-seeking can be assessed from a variety of vantage points (and has been in various forms and in a variety of non-evolutionary biology research settings e.g., (Kant, 1909; Rawls, 1971; Weber, 1985 [1930]), and others). However, of particular applicability to this analysis is an assessment of the moral implications of entrepreneurially-driven security-seeking behaviors using the lens offered by evolutionary biology research. In the following paragraphs I first summarize some of the pertinent concepts offered by Ruffin Lecturers, and then second, demonstrate how these ideas can be used to assess moral implications of the security-seeking sequence (Figure 3).

Concepts from Evolutionary Biology Research

Each of the Ruffin Lecturers presented concepts from, or in relationship to, evolutionary biology research that have implications for assessing the moral implications of economic behaviors. It is my intention in this section to present concepts that appear to be applicable, to thereby assemble a rough evolutionary biology-based framework for use in the assessment of the moral implications of the entrepreneurially-driven security-seeking behavior that occurs within our imperfect economy. These concepts, summarized in order of each distinguished lecture, are as follows:

1. Frans B. M. de Waal—April 19, 2002. In his Ruffin Lecture entitled "Monkey Business and Business Ethics: Evolutionary Origins of Human Morality," Professor de Waal suggested following:

- The degree to which the tendency to develop and enforce moral systems is universal across cultures, suggests that moral systems do have biological origins and are an integral part of human nature;

- Common benevolence nourishes and guides all morality, but its morality is based upon reciprocity;[7]

- Unlike simultaneous co-operation or mutualism, reciprocal altruism involves exchanged acts that, while beneficial to the recipient, are costly to the performer (and, by extension, occur in sequence).

2. Paul R. Lawrence—April 20, 2002. The following concepts from the Ruffin Lecture by Professor Lawrence entitled "The Biological Base of Morality" further contribute to the assessment of the morality of entrepreneurially-driven security-seeking behavior:

- Morality arises primarily from the existence in humans of the drive to bond with others, which, as suggested by Darwin (1894) occurs "due to the small strength and speed of man, and the want of natural weapons."

- Morality also arises because "good" can be defined in terms of the support of human drives as follows:

Drive	Rationale for What is Good
Acquisition	Preserving property; facilitation of pleasurable experiences
Bonding	Keeping promises; fair dealing
Learning	Telling the truth; sharing information; respecting another's beliefs
Defense	Helping v. harming; Protecting; Not abandoning

3. Leda Cosmides—April 20, 2002. Professor Cosmides, in her Ruffin Lecture entitled "Breaking Faith: The Evolutionary Psychology of Moral Reasoning and Moral Sentiments," suggested additional concepts from evolutionary biology research:

- Willingness to participate in a collective action is a public good (i.e., is moral);

- Incentives in many collective action problems (citing game theoretical analyses) are insufficient to promote voluntary contributions by individual, and instead favor free riding as the equilibrium outcome;

- Willingness to participate in collective action (contribute to the public good) can be evolutionarily stable as long as free riders are punished, along with those who refuse to punish free riders.

4. William C. Frederick—April 20, 2002. Entitled "The Evolutionary Firm and Its Moral (Dis)Contents," the Ruffin Lecture by Professor Frederick contributes the following as concepts that are relevant to the assessment of the morality of entrepreneurially-driven security-seeking behavior:

- The evolutionary firm is an internal and external contradiction due to diverse neural algorithms;

- Nature has bequeathed the motivator-driver function to humanity; and it is not likely to go away (and, quoted with permission):

  Business firms are first and foremost economizing organizations, made that way by nature. The firm's moral problems arise from contradictions rooted in behavioral impulses of the human psyche in interaction with an entropic universe. Culture and reason can channel, moderate, and reconfigure—but cannot eliminate—these behavioral predispositions. Virtuous character can confront but not seriously deflect the natural course of embedded neural algorithms. Social contracts can design but cannot enforce or guarantee fair exchanges. Stakeholder claims on the corporation cannot exceed or violate the firm's entropic limits. Philosophic principles and ideals not consistent with the firm's natural architecture cannot be expected to stand.

- Moral action is a reconciliation, using adaptation, survival, creativity, experimentation, exploration, imagination, and expansion of the quantity and quality of life.

5. Edwin M. Hartman, April 21, 2002. In this final Ruffin Lecture, entitled "De Rerum Natura," Professor Hartman suggested the following:

- If a certain trait or attribute contributes to the continuation of a community, that is reason for calling it a virtue;

- We want to avoid an evolutionary view of society that however, simply equates morality with viability and adaptability, because a society can be viable but bad; and (quoted with permission):

> Human beings . . . may have problems with free riders ruining the commons because each of us can assess the selfish advantages of being a free rider. There is good moral reason to create communities in which people do not ride free. It requires some combination of developing mechanisms for enforcing cooperative behavior and encouraging people to think differently about what might motivate them. That is, we have to think about both politics (including the politics of organizations) and morality, and we have to think about them together. To put it in Aristotelian terms, human beings are (both) rational animals and political animals.

- Reciprocal altruism entails sacrificing self-interest—that is, the opportunity to be a free rider—by cooperating in support of the commons;

- Aristotle too holds that good citizenship in a good community is essential to being a good person: in fact, a good community is a necessary condition of being a good person. He also claims that a person of good character enjoys doing the right thing;

- (Morality) is about treating humanity in all its forms as an end in itself. It involves principles, which systematize our intuitions.

A Preliminary Assessment Framework

From the principles offered by Ruffin Lecturers, we can construct a preliminary assessment framework. Morality criteria[8] summarizing these comments are presented in Table 2.

Table 2
Selected Morality Criteria from Ruffin Lectures

Ruffin Lecturer	Selected Morality Criteria—Behavior is moral when based upon:
Frans B. M. de Waal	Common benevolence rooted in reciprocity
Paul R. Lawrence	The support of human drives: acquisition, learning, bonding, defense
Leda Cosmides	Punishment of free riders along with those who refuse to punish free riders
William C. Frederick	Reconciliation of economic imperatives using a values hierarchy
Edwin M. Hartman	Good citizenship while treating members of humanity as ends in themselves

What is to be assessed using these criteria? The security-seeking decision tree (Figure 3) suggests that the object of assessment should be the decisions that lead to security-seeking behaviors because the transaction cognition model of security-seeking that has been developed herein is intended to: (1) provide the cognitive context for the economizing choices made by individuals in each of these three decision zones, and (2) provide the basis for the assessment of the moral dilemmas posed by such choices.

Each decision illustrated in Figure 3 has moral implications. Decision 1 (Compete?) while doubtless involving the individual choice between security-seeking and non-security-seeking, also requires a decision of whether or not to contribute to the commons. In this regard, some of the dilemmas/ questions that occur at this decision point call for moral assessments regarding free riders, disabled persons, and a determination of the nature of acceptable modes of competition.

Decision 2 (Promise?) requires the specification of what ends (in the form of social contracts) will be agreed to in the security-seeking process. This second decision zone entails the evaluation of the job v. venture choice (and with it the level of risk and uncertainty that it is moral to ask/ permit to be assumed), as well as the evaluation of the validity of underlying motives of a security-seeking system that enables venturing to become a viable security-seeking choice.

Decision 3 (Plan?) requires the specification of what means will be chosen to accomplish the agreed upon ends. Some of the dilemmas/ questions that occur at this stage of the analysis include: the examination of our definitions of success, and what behaviors are defined to be permissible for its attainment; reflection upon the extent to which we are to condone the success-driven treatment of human beings who participate in the production of products or services as means v. ends.

Thus, based upon criteria selected from the remarks of Ruffin Lecturers (Table 2), the contents of each set of essential transaction cognitions (competition, promise, planning) suggest morality criteria as shown in Table 3 (p. 277).

Using these criteria, then, it is possible to examine morality aspects of decision making at each stage in the transaction sequence: security-seeking, venturing, and success or failure.

Security-Seeking

Because it is at this beginning point in the security-seeking process (Figure 3, point A) that the decision is made whether to bargain/ exchange/ transact, or not, the choice between security-seeking and non-security-seeking invokes the specialized mental models that individuals possess about competing economically (specifically mental models that can create bargaining positions—small or large[9]). The reasons that some people do not engage in economic security-seeking flow from the definition of the construct—the need for economic security—itself. Where the need for economic security is defined to be the desire to have "provisions in store for an uncertain future" (Durant, 1935: 2), then

Table 3
Implications of Morality Criteria for Security-Seeking Decisions

Ruffin Lecturer	Morality Criteria	Implications for security-seeking decisions based on:		
		[1] *Competition Cognitions:* Mental models that can create bargaining positions—small or large	**[2]** *Promise Cognitions:* Mental models that help in identifying and prioritizing stakeholders thereby building trust in economic relationships	**[3]** *Planning Cognitions:* Mental models that assist in developing analytical structure to solve previously unstructured problems
		Decision to compete or not:	**Decision on choice of ends:**	**Decision on choice of means:**
de Waal	Common benevolence rooted in reciprocity	For the able, exchange-based security seeking is good; non-exchange based security seeking (e.g., robbery) is bad	Moral promises should provide for two-way and mutually beneficial exchanges	Moral plans are reciprocal over the long term, which suggests long- AND short-term planning
Lawrence	The support of human drives: acquisition, learning, bonding, defense	Security seeking decisions that add to/preserve property (provisions), or that help, protect, or prevent abandonment, are moral	Decisions that lead to keeping promises and fair dealing in forming economic relationships are moral	Plans for goal attainment consistent with acquisition, learning, or not harming are moral
Cosmides	Punishment of free riders along with those who refuse to punish free riders	Non-security-seeking behaviors should be closely scrutinized for free riding (e.g., welfare fraud audits)	Choice to accomplish (promise) job or entrepreneurship is moral where optimal contribution is enabled (e.g., intellectual property protections, protections of bankruptcy laws, fair labor standards, etc.)	Plans and systems should provide for detection and punishment of free riders
Frederick	Reconciliation of economic imperatives using a values hierarchy	Prima facie morality of both security and non-security-seeking behavior should be assessed	Values-consistent jobs and ventures should be encouraged	Means must be reconciled with, v. justified by, ends
Hartman	Good citizenship while treating members of humanity as ends in themselves	Competing or not competing within market systems is moral depending upon both the quality of society and quality of life for its members	Promises that are more stakeholder-impact-based are better than those that are narrow-beneficiary-based	Humanity and citizenship-supportive plans are those most sought

logically, the reason why an individual may not be seeking economic security should relate to the absence of this need. According to the definition, absence of the need for economic security, and therefore the choice of non-security-seeking behavior, could arise due to lack of desire, lack of uncertainty, or both, each with moral consequences.

For example, in every society there are individuals who lack the desire or ability to accumulate provisions in store. The lens of evolutionary biology research can help us to assess the morality of such choices. The economizing stance characterized by this lack of desire/ ability to accumulate might (non-exhaustively) be due to a specific value choice (e.g. self-denial for a spiritual purpose), due to age (e.g. individuals too young or old to care for themselves), due to a disability (e.g. lack of awareness of need due to developmental difficulties), or merely due to an individual judgment that provisions in store are sufficient given the perceived level of uncertainty (e.g. an individual or a societal group is rich, or rich enough), which of course also varies by case. In other instances, the accumulations (such as savings and pension) might be perceived by an individual to be adequate given the present level of uncertainty, but inadequate in times of high inflation, war, or natural disaster. Thus—depending upon the case—society, parents, or individuals themselves provide for the economic security of non-security-seeking individuals.

Further, due to perceptions of an individual's circumstances when compared to perceptions of opportunity or threat in the environment, variations occur in levels of uncertainty. Thus, the level of security-seeking, and thereby the propensity to "compete" might be higher or lower given specific circumstances. As previously argued, economizing on transaction costs is expected to account for the alternatives: non-seeking v. seeking. For those who do not seek economic security, the transaction costs of competing for it are just too high. For those seeking economic security, the transaction costs of *not* seeking it are unacceptable. Thus there is reason to expect that,

> Proposition 1: The choice between security-seeking and non-security-seeking behavior is associated with transaction cost minimizing substitutions at the margin of one state of seeking for its alternative.

This proposition, while appearing to be morality-neutral because ostensibly it is driven by the notion of cost minimization, nevertheless has implications that can be evaluated according to morality criteria suggested by evolutionary biology research. For example, we can intuitively assess the non-security-seeking decisions of the young, old and/ or disabled as being moral using the criteria summarized in Table 3, Column [1]. It is also intuitive to expect that punishing the non-security-seeking decisions of economic free riders will be deemed to be moral under Cosmides' criteria; or that regulations to limit restraint of trade or unfair competition practices are moral under criteria offered by de Waal. Perhaps less intuitive might be the use of evolutionary-biology-research-based criteria to assess the morality of those individuals and groups whose decisions and behaviors have the potential to damage the security-seeking system itself.

For example, questions relating to the morality of anti-globalization or anti-WTO protest—as phenomena that can impact the viability of the prevailing security-seeking system (a global economy)—may also be assessed using the criteria summarized in Table 3, Column [1].

Venturing

Once the group of individuals who are not security-seeking are accounted for in the model (Figure 3), the status of the remaining individuals[10] may be described using either the level of venturing, or the level of job-holding—since these alternative states of economic security-seeking appear to be reciprocal. Making the choice between venturing or job-holding requires the use of the algorithms that individuals possess about promise (mental models that help in identifying and prioritizing stakeholders thereby building trust in economic relationships) to predict which course or action is likely to be more reliable. Promise-based cognitions assist individuals in assessing the likelihood that those with a "stake" (Clarkson, 1995; Mitchell, Agle, and Wood, 1997) in the economic well being of that individual will, in fact, contribute to economic security.

The transaction-cognitive model developed in this article appears to shed light on this decision point also. As noted earlier in the article, transaction costs represent the consequences of socioeconomic friction on economic security-seeking, and thereby enable the model to account for a variety of "alternative-system" substitutions at the margin. Under these assumptions, the social commitments made by individuals—such as choosing a job v. self-employment—ought to be related to costs that attend the transactions associated with that social choice. Thus, where the mental models of an individual might result in work-specificity (whether the preferred work is job- or self-employment) the costs of transacting in the alternative system become prohibitive. For example, if my mental models for security-seeking center on "work that I like and can do," and if work that I like and can do involves using highly sophisticated equipment that is only available to people who take jobs in particular organizations, I may have high transaction costs relative to self-employment and see more "promise" in employment with such an organization. Alternatively, if I have been raised in a setting where the self-employment algorithms have been readily available and have been internalized by me with positive self-efficacy (Gist and Mitchell, 1992), then I may have high transaction costs relative to seeking job employment, and see more promise in a venture. The transaction-cognitive model is therefore likely to account—through a logical extension of transaction cost economic theory—for the broad range of social commitment/ promise decisions made in pursuit of economic security. Accordingly it is expected that:

> Proposition 2: The choice between job v. venture employment is associated with the transaction cost minimizing substitution at the margin of one state of individual transacting for its alternative.

Proposition 2 appears to suggest that this second decision in the security-seeking sequence (Figure 3, point B) might also be a morality-neutral cost-based calculation of sorts. But while the extent of calculation v. visceral reaction to the choice of ends (what shall I do to obtain/ enhance my economic security?) may vary somewhat by individual or by societal group, it appears to be likely that this decision has moral implications to which evolutionary-biology-research-based criteria apply using, for example, the criteria summarized in Table 3, Column [2]. Recall that according to transaction cognition theory, promise cognitions are the algorithmic basis for making this decision, and that promise cognitions are defined to be: mental models that help in identifying and prioritizing stakeholders thereby building trust in economic relationships. Based on promise cognitions, individuals are therefore expected to assess the likelihood that stakeholders (those with a "stake" (Clarkson, 1995; Mitchell, Agle, and Wood, 1997) in the economic well being of that individual) will, in fact, contribute to their economic security.

In the venturing case, the assessment of such a promise is an assessment of ends in two respects: (1) because the focus of this choice is the selection from among a variety of economic relationships with potential stakeholders, those economic relationships that have the most promise to produce economic security, and (2) because the venture that results from this nexus of relationships (Hill and Jones, 1992) does itself make both express and implied promises to stakeholders, and these promises have consequences beyond those that strictly apply to the entrepreneur. As such, the decision to venture to gain economic security can also be assessed using the principles offered by evolutionary biology research.

Accordingly, in the first case, that of attempting to assess the morality of the individual choice between job- or venture-based security-seeking, one might apply the concepts articulated by Lawrence and Cosmides (Table 3, Column [2]). Lawrence suggests concepts that lead us to regard either choice that is made and enacted according to fair dealing, to be moral. Cosmides suggests that the moral choice for individuals is the one that leads to the making of an optimal contribution. Furthermore, where institutional barriers, or barriers due to cultural norms exist, then the incidence of decisions to venture v. to hold a job might be expected to vary (Mitchell et al., 2000; Mitchell et al., 2002b), and the reasons for such variations (institutions, culture, etc.) might have moral significance that merits analysis.

In the second case, that of attempting to assess the morality of underlying motives of the security-seeking (economic) system that enables venturing to become a viable choice, one might utilize criteria offered by Frederick and by Hartman (Table 3, Column [2]). Frederick encourages values consistency in promise-based choices, and Hartman's lecture may be interpreted to suggest the superiority of promises that are more stakeholder-impact-based, than those that are narrow-beneficiary-based. Thus, where the motive purpose of ventures (Mitchell, 2002) is recast from the maximization of profits for stockholders to serving the interests of stakeholders (Venkataraman, 2002: 54) one can assess as more consistent with the moral principles suggested by evolutionary biology research, a conception of the venture that is broader v. narrower in its citizenship (Mitchell, 2002: 224). This is because in the case of the former, an entrepreneur creates a venture within an environment of genuine uncertainty, by assembling resources to pursue an opportunity through ensuring fixed payments to other parties such as employees and suppliers, and by retaining residual rights (Dew, Velamuri, and Venkataraman, 2003: 2; Knight, 1921). The right to the residual is often construed to limit the moral scope of the venture to production-essential stakeholders at its widest, and to only stockholders at its most narrow. In the case of the earlier-noted broader conception of the venture, such a firm is created through a social contract of mutual promise to share in benefits and costs (v. only in revenue and expenses), which thereby widens the scope of accountability within which the morality of the decision to venture and consequent venturing behaviors can be assessed (Mitchell, 2002).

Success or Failure
The third decision that every security-seeking and, venturing individual must make from time to time, is whether or not it is possible to remain so engaged—a decision we can term the success or failure decision (Figure 3, point C). Transaction cost theory suggests that an alternative governance system will be invoked when the costs of organizing an extra transaction within the existing governance system become equal to the costs of carrying out the same transaction through an exchange on the open market (Coase, 1937: 396). Thus, when exchange behavior is no longer effective, transaction costs will drive the transactions into the open market (i.e. a venture will fail). Thus, transaction failure and venture failure are closely related (Venkataraman, Van de Ven, Buckeye, and Hudson, 1990). According to the transaction-cognition model, ventures fail when plans fail, because the mental algorithms that individuals possess about planning (e.g. mental models that assist in overcoming the limitations of bounded rationality) are expected to impact the economizing on transaction costs to effect success in transacting.

This simple but powerful idea appeals to the very essence of transaction cost economics: in short, confirming the notion that economizing (on transaction costs) is the best strategy/ plan (Williamson, 1991: 76, 90). Williamson suggests that transaction cost economizing (e.g. waste elimination) can have as much as a 10:1 influence on results as compared to the effect of the ordinary cost and pricing decisions made in exchanges (1991: 79). It stands to reason then—once again using the other half of this bi-directional argument—that lack of a plan for transaction cost economizing will have a great deal to do with the failure of security-seeking behaviors. For example, the plan to manage opportunism in a competitive marketplace can save a job or save a customer, which is a far more important result than the successful negotiation of wage rates, or sale prices. It is likely that the success or failure of ventures will be highly correlated with the effective planning for (first order economizing on (Williamson, 1991: 78)) transaction costs—a huge public policy opportunity (e.g., cut waste, not wages; increase productivity, not prices). Thus it can be expected that,

Proposition 3: The choice between venture success and failure is associated with the transaction cost economizing substitution of hierarchy for its alternative, the market, at the margin.

Proposition 3 suggests that success or failure involves an element of cognitive choice, contrary to the research-literature-rejected, but still popular-press-accepted conventional wisdom (Mitchell et al., 2002a). And where there is conscious choice, success or failure decisions cannot be stripped of their moral consequences. Thus, according, for example, to de Waal, plans that lead to short-term "success" (say, quarterly profits) that do not include long-term reciprocity (say, environmental sustainability) cannot be considered to be moral plans (Table 3, Column [3]). Or, according to Cosmides notion of Darwinian selection (which is not *survival of the fittest* but is rather *survival of the fittest to reproduce necessary behaviors*), plans that lead to evolutionary instability (e.g., plans that fail to detect and punish free riders, or further, plans that restructure ventures—such as laying people off—without regard to their skill at reasoning procedures involving social conditionals of exchange, interpreting their meaning, and successfully solving the inference problems they pose) would be a morally questionable planning decision on the choice of means.

Planning decisions, as decisions involving the choice of means, also have more far-reaching moral consequences, especially as they relate to the propensity of decision makers who view the business firm in technical-rational terms (Scott, 1987), and consequently view human beings to be means of production v. as ends in themselves. Both Hartman and Frederick (Table 3, Column [3]) are adamant on the moral necessity for recognizing *homo sapiens* as ends.

Conclusion

The notion of an imperfect economy—one where perfect, logical, deductive rationality rarely, if ever, prevails—has been used to denote a marketplace where individuals' rationality is bounded due to complexity, and the inability to perfectly predict the actions of others (Simon, 1979). Such a setting demands that individuals utilize inductive and/ or algorithmic reasoning to be able to identify patterns within the complexity, to simplify decisions by using previously identified patterns to construct adaptable mental models/ hypotheses/ schemata, and to continually test these mental models for usefulness, replacing those with bad track records and retaining those with good ones (Arthur, 1994: 406). In an imperfect economy, therefore, the mental models that individuals possess about the best ways to satisfy security needs, compete for preeminence within the minds of individuals, and also between individuals (1994: 409).

As argued by Ruffin Lecturers and in other research articles (e.g., Holland, Holyoak, Nisbett, and Thagard, 1986), this competition forms an ecology of cognitions that evolves over time. In this article I have argued that security-seeking individuals utilize such cognitions subject to the friction of transaction costs that arise from bounded rationality, opportunism, and asset specificity

(Arrow, 1969: 48; Williamson, 1985: 19, 31), and that as a result a reliable security-seeking sequence exists that can be assessed for moral implications, using principles from evolutionary biology research.

Is there therefore an underlying morality in the ways that human beings seek to obtain economic security within our imperfect economy? Conclusions drawn from the analysis in this article suggest both the feasibility of a systematic explanation for security-seeking decisions in an imperfect economy, and a means for assessment of the moral implications of such decisions using concepts from evolutionary biology research. What emerges is an underlying morality that originates in the evolutionarily long-lived notions of (for example): reciprocity (de Waal), consonance with the basic human drives (Lawrence), discouragement of free riding (Cosmides), values-based dilemma reconciliations (Frederick), and good citizenship—where human beings are ends, not means (Hartman). The emergence within evolutionary biology research, of concepts that are more Darwin- v. Huxley-based, suggests an underlying morality supportive of algorithm-governed economizing arising from the behaviors that are most worthy of reproduction. The morality of security-seeking behaviors in an imperfect economy may thus be assessed based upon the likelihood that such behaviors will be evolutionarily stable.

Thus, if the continual creation of ever-increasing levels of new value-adding transactions in a modern economy by ever-increasing numbers of entrepreneurs is a global innovation, then it seems prudent to observe that the conditions are now ripe for society to move from producing entrepreneurial security seekers who are idiosyncratic early adopters (old-style entrepreneurs), to producing entrepreneurial security seekers who are systematically trained in the necessary cognitions/algorithms (sustainable entrepreneurs). It is appealing, therefore, to consider the logical outgrowth of this reasoning: the prospect that economic security is, in fact, compatible with entrepreneurship (a notion that—without the lens offered by evolutionary biology research—would not be intuitive); and is also consistent with a conception of morality that is supported by research in evolutionary biology. This, because new cognitions (algorithmic responses) can produce entrepreneurial behavior that is more secure: sustainable entrepreneurship that creates social and environmental sustainability, in addition to economic sustainabililty.

Although the articulation of many of the fine points, the exploration of new research questions, and the empirical testing of the propositions suggested remains to be accomplished, new maps (as Cosmides persuasively argues) appear to suggest new methods. Evolutionarily stable algorithm-enhanced security-seeking represents a new view of entrepreneurship, but one that is grounded in a primordially-based entrepreneurial drive that is at the core of economic security. And, according to the foregoing analysis, this new "sustainable" entrepreneurship appears to be possible across all imperfect market economies. The critical question which then remains for twenty-first century society to answer is this: People wanted security—did entrepreneurship deliver?

Notes

1. Henceforth within this article, the term "cognitions" may be taken to mean algorithms (e.g., Frederick, April 20, 2002) and, alternatively, cognitive machinery (e.g., Cosmides, April 20, 2002) or mental models (Arthur, 1994).

2. Prospect Theory (Kahneman and Tversky, 1979) provides one of the clearest illustrations of the transaction costs that arise from bounded rationality. Essentially Kahneman and Tversky found that the actual value of economic choices made by individuals (actual utility) was less than the possible value (expected utility) because individuals ignored or overweighted highly unlikely events, or neglected or exaggerated highly likely events due to: *reflection effects* (emphasis in original)—risk aversion in the positive domain and risk seeking in the negative (1979: 268), and *isolation effects*— disregarding the commonly shared attributes of decisions to focus on the distinguishing ones (1979: 271). According to Prospect Theory, these effects arise due to cognitive errors that occur in individuals' *coding, combination, and/or cancellation* (1979: 274) of relevant information, which taken together limit/bound rationality.

3. A small numbers bargaining position occurs when, if you are a seller for example, and the number of sellers is small, negotiations in the transacting process lead to a division of the surplus that would not be the case in a competitive market. (That is not to say that the negotiation is not competitive, only that the seller for example, is able to raise the price above his lowest acceptable sale price in the course of the negotiation.) A large numbers bargaining position occurs when, if once again you are a seller and the number of sellers is large, negotiations in the transacting process are more perfectly competitive, and lead to prices that are at or near the point of lowest acceptability.

4. Although in a different order, the parallels suggested (with the three center constructs in the model in Frederick's Figure 2) are planning: organizer/ coordinator, promise: innovator/ generator, and competition: enabler/strategizer.

5. The reader is invited to note that Figure 3, as bounded by the limits of the analysis attempted in this paper, illustrates only the entrepreneurially driven security-seeking pathway to increased economic security.

6. Note: However, if all pathways were illustrated, the diagram would represent an extensive form game (Watson, 2002: 9) and would thereby be further linked to the concepts suggested by evolutionary biology research, as noted by Cosmides (April 20, 2002).

7. The Ruffin Lecturers appear to use the terms reciprocity, reciprocal altruism, and social exchange interchangeably.

8. Please note that these criteria do not purport to represent the fully developed argument of a given Ruffin Lecturer. Rather, they are selected and presented to support an illustration of the manner in which concepts developed within evolutionary biology research can be applied to assess some of the moral implications of the security-seeking sequence represented in Figure 3.

9. See note 3, above.

10. Admittedly there are those who at this point in the sequence choose to engage in ventures or jobs who have low levels of security-seeking (e.g. they engage for the fun, the challenge, or a passion, more than for the security). Although there may be reason to examine the theory developed herein for application to non-security-seeking venture v. job, and non-security-seeking success v. failure decisions at the margin, such an analysis is beyond the scope of this article and is therefore left for subsequent consideration.

Bibliography

Allais, M. 1953. Le comportement de l'homme rationnel devant le risque: critique des postulats et axiomes de l'Ecole Americaine. *Econometrica* 21: 503–546.

Arrow, K. J. 1982. Risk perception in psychology and economics. *Economic Inquiry* 20: 1–9.

———, ed. 1969. *The organization of economic activity: Issues pertinent to the choice of market versus nonmarket allocation.* Washington, D.C.: U.S. Government Printing Office.

Arthur, W. B. 1994. Complexity in economic theory: Inductive reasoning and bounded rationality. *AEA Papers and Proceedings* 84(2): 406–411.

Birch, D. A. 1981. Who creates jobs? *The Public Interest* 65: 3–14.

Birley, S. 1986. The role of new firms: Births, deaths, and job generation. *Strategic Management Journal* 7(4): 361–376.

Clarkson, M. B. E. 1995. A stakeholder framework for analyzing and evaluating corporate social performance. *Academy of Management Review* 20(1): 92–117.

Coase, R. H. 1937. The nature of the firm, Economica New Series 4. In *Readings in Price Theory*, ed. G. J. Stigler and K. E. Boulding. Homewood, Ill.: Irwin: 386–405.

Cosmides, L., and J. Tooby. 2004. Knowing thyself: The evolutionary psychology of moral reasoning and moral sentiments, in *Business, Science, and Ethics*, ed. R. E. Freeman and P. H. Werhane. Charlottesville, Va.: Philosophy Documentation Center: 93–128.

Cyert, R. M., and J. G. March. 1963. *The behavioral theory of the firm.* Englewood Cliffs, N.J.: Prentice-Hall.

DelMar, A. 1968 (1896). *The science of money* (2nd ed.). New York: Franklin.

Dew, N., R. Velamuri, and S. Venkataraman. 2003. Dispersed knowledge and an entrepreneurial theory of the firm. *Journal of Business Venturing* (forthcoming).

Duchesneau, D. A., and W. B. Gartner. 1990. A profile of new venture success and failure in an emerging industry. *Journal of Business Venturing* 5(5): 297–312.

Durant, W. 1935. *The Story of Civilization.* New York: Simon and Schuster.

Flack, J. C., and F. B. M. de Waal. 2004. Monkey business and business ethics: Evolutionary origins of human morality, in *Business, Science, and Ethics*, ed. R. E. Freeman and P. H. Werhane. Charlottesville, Va.: Philosophy Documentation Center: 7–41.

Frederick, W. C. 2004. The evolutionary firm and its moral (dis)contents, in *Business, Science, and Ethics*, ed. R. E. Freeman and P. H. Werhane. Charlottesville, Va.: Philosophy Documentation Center: 145–176.

Friedman, T. L. 2000. *The Lexus and the olive tree.* New York: Anchor Books-Random House, Inc.

Gist, M. E., and T. R. Mitchell. 1992. Self-efficacy: A theoretical analysis of its determinants and malleability. *Academy of Management Review* 17(2): 183–211.

Hill, C. W. L., and T. M. Jones. 1992. Stakeholder-agency theory. *Journal of Management Studies* 29(2): 131–154.

Holland, J. H., K. J. Holyoak, R. E. Nisbett, and P. R. Thagard. 1986. *Induction.* Cambridge, Mass.: MIT Press.

Kahneman, D., and A. Tversky. 1979. Prospect theory: An analysis of decisions under risk. *Econometrica* 47: 263–291.

Kant, I. 1909. *Foundations of the metaphiysics of morals.* London: Longman's Green.

Kirchhoff, B. A., and P. G. Greene. 1995. Response to renewed attacks on the small business job creation hypothesis. In *Frontiers of Entrepreneurship Research*, ed. W. D. Bygrave, B. J. Bird, S. Birley, N. C. Churchill, M. Hay, R. H. Keeley, and W. E. Wetzel, Jr. Babson Park, Mass.: Babson College.

Kirchhoff, B. A., and B. D. Phillips. 1988. The effect of firm formation and growth on job creation in the United States. *Journal of Business Venturing* 3(4): 261–272.

Kirzner, I. 1980. The primacy of entrepreneurial discovery. In *The prime mover of progress*, ed. A. Seldon. Lancing, Sussex: The Institute of Economic Affairs: 3–26.

Knight, F. H. 1921. *Risk, Uncertainty and Profit.* New York: Kelley and Millman, Inc.

Leddo, J., and R. P. Abelson. 1986. The nature of explanations. In *Knowledge Structures*, ed. J. A. Galambos, R. P. Abelson, and J. B. Black. Hillsdale, N.J.: Lawrence Erlbaum Associates, Inc.: 103–122.

Mandel, M. J. 1996. *The High Risk Society: Peril and Promise.* New York: Times Business Books.

Margolis, J. D. 2004. Responsibility, inconsistency, and the paradoxes of morality in human nature: De Waal's window into business ethics, in *Business, Science, and Ethics*, ed. R. E. Freeman and P. H. Werhane. Charlottesville, Va.: Philosophy Documentation Center: 43–52.

Marshall, A. 1920. *Principles of economics* (8th ed.). New York: Macmillan.

Mitchell, R. K. 2001. *Transaction cognition theory and high performance economic results* (First ed.). Victoria, B.C.: International Centre for Venture Expertise: www.ronaldmitchell.org/publications.

————. 2002. Stakeholders of the world unite: Assessing progress on the path toward a stakeholder theory of the firm. In *Proceedings of the Thirteenth Annual Conference, June 27–30, 2002*, ed. D. Windsor and S. A. Welcomer. Victoria, B.C.: International Association for Business and Society: 223–225.

Mitchell, R. K., B. R. Agle, and D. J. Wood. 1997. Toward a theory of stakeholder identification and salience: Defining the principle of who and what really counts. *Academy of Management Review* 22(4): 853–886.

Mitchell, R. K., B. Smith, K. W. Seawright, and E. A. Morse. 2000. Cross-cultural cognitions and the venture creation decision. *Academy of Management Journal* 43(5): 974–993.

Mitchell, R. K., J. B. Smith, E. A. Morse, K. W. Seawright, A.-M. Peredo, and B. McKenzie. 2002a. Toward a theory of entrepreneurial cognition: Rethinking the people side of entrepreneurship research. *Entrepreneurship Theory & Practice* 27(2 [Winter]).

Mitchell, R. K., L. Busenitz, T. Lant, P. P. McDougall, E. A. Morse, and J. B. Smith. 2002b. Are entrepreneurial cognitions universal? Assessing entrepreneurial cognitions across cultures. *Entrepreneurship Theory & Practice* 26(4 [Summer]): 9–32.

Nelson, R. R., and S. Winter. 1973. Toward an evolutionary theory of economic capabilities. *American Economic Review Proceedings* 63: 440–449.

Rawls, J. 1971. *A theory of justice.* Cambridge, Mass.: Harvard University Press.

Scott, W. R. 1987. *Organizations: Rational, Natural, and Open Systems.* Englewood Cliffs, N.J.: Prentice-Hall, Inc.

Simon, H. A. 1979. Rational decision making in business organizations. *The American Economic Review* 69 (September): 493–513.

Venkataraman, S. 1997. The distinctive domain of entrepreneurship research. In *Advances in entrepreneurship, firm emergence and growth*, ed. J. Katz. Greenwich, Conn.: JAI Press: 119–138.

————. 2002. Stakeholder value equilibration and the entrepreneurial process. *Business Ethics Quarterly: The Ruffin Series* 3: 45–58.

Venkataraman, S., A. H. Van de Ven, J. Buckeye, and R. Hudson. 1990. Starting up in a turbulent environment: A process model of failure among firms with high customer dependence. *Journal of Business Venturing* 5(5): 277–295.

Vesper, K. H. 1996. *New Venture Experience.* Seattle: Vector Books.

Watson, J. 2002. *Strategy: An introduction to game theory.* New York: W. W. Norton & Company.

Weber, M. 1985 (1930). *The Protestant Ethic and the Spirit of Capitalism.* Boston: Irwin.

Williamson, O. E. 1975. *Markets and Hierarchies.* New York: The Free Press.

————. 1985. *The Economic Institutions of Capitalism.* New York: The Free Press.

————. 1991. Strategizing, economizing, and economic organization. *Strategic Management Journal* 12(S): 75–94.

Wortman, M. S. J. 1987. Entrepreneurship: An integrating typology and evaluation of the empirical research in the field. *Journal of Management* 13(2): 259–279.

TO PROPAGATE AND TO PROSPER: A NATURALISTIC FOUNDATION FOR STAKEHOLDER THEORY

Tara J. Radin

Abstract: This article examines the contribution of nature and the sciences toward a deeper understanding of business. Integrating these disciplines with stakeholder theory opens up new avenues for thinking about business that will potentially offer greater success in addressing the disconnect between moral discretion and the behavior of businesspeople. The specific focus is on integration of modern Darwinism (evolutionary psychology) and business theory. According to modern Darwinism, there are insufficient resources for all genes to reproduce. Natural selection occurs as genes compete to reproduce and those best suited for survival are able to reproduce. During the struggle, human beings are motivated by impulses intended to further reproduction, which lead them into many fruitful endeavors—such as participation in corporations. As genes strive to be passed on to the next generation, a consequence is their contribution to productivity and prosperity. By developing insight into the evolutionary process, we can create mechanisms that help us to manage human behavior in order to promote moral behavior. Connecting people with their natural selves provides for a more robust understanding of business.

Nearly ten years ago, William C. Frederick asserted that "business values contain the key to much that is troubling the business world today" (Frederick, 1995: 5). His words frame an ongoing search within the field of business ethics for a deeper understanding of the connection between morality and business. This search has encompassed the pursuit of an appropriate paradigm for business—one which reconciles the conflicting demands of morality and profitability. Our quest continues with the new millennium being ushered in by a host of corporate scandals involving business leaders and public figures such as Martha Stewart. In the wake of the egregious situations that have surfaced during the past couple of years—Enron, WorldCom, Adelphia, Tyco, Merck, and so on—where managerial irresponsibility has resulted in significant harm to a multitude of corporate stakeholders, we continue to explore alternative models in order to find new was to motivate good behavior in business—in terms of both moral and financial performance.

© 2004 *Society for Business Ethics and the Darden School Foundation*   pp. 289–310

More recently, Frederick has spearheaded an engaging inquiry into nature and the sciences for a new approach to thinking and theorizing about business (Frederick, 1995; Frederick, 1998; Frederick, 2004; Fort, 1999; Fort, 2000; Nicholson, 1997; Nicholson, 1998). As champion of this endeavor to incorporate learnings from nature and the sciences in our examination of business, Frederick has liberated the management discussion and opened it up to a whole new array of considerations. In addition, he invites us to reconsider former topics of conversation within the new context of a naturalistic approach.

The purpose of this paper is to join the host of scholars who are participating in the process of exploring nature and the sciences in order to develop of a more viable business model. Although nature and the sciences are not traditionally incorporated in business theory, integrating these disciplines with stakeholder theory opens up new avenues for thinking about business that will potentially offer greater success in addressing the disconnect between moral discretion and the behavior of businesspeople.

Overcoming the Separation Thesis

According to R. Edward Freeman, the source of the disconnect between ethics and business lies in what he has called the Separation Thesis (Freeman, 1994). We have become accustomed to allowing the separation of discourses—such as among academic disciplines and functional areas of business, including business and ethics (Freeman, 1994). This actually serves to impoverish the practice of ethical behavior in business:

> As long as the discourse distinguishes "business" and "ethics" we will need business ethicists to make it up as we go along—holding business, piece by piece, to the light of reason. And, as long as business ethics is separate, business theorists are free to make up supposedly morally neutral theories such as agency theory which can be used to justify a great deal of harm. (Freeman, 1994: 412)

In other words, by separating ethics from business, we send the message that ethical behavior is optional. If our goal is to promote ethical behavior, it would seem that our business models should incorporate moral decision-making as inherent.

The result of our continuing implicitly or explicitly to subscribe to the Separation Thesis is "to close off discussion and to silence conversation" of the sort that would prompt us to challenge the disconnect between business and ethics in order to repair the moral compass (Freeman, 1994: 419). Freeman has concluded that overcoming the Separation Thesis is integral to business development: "Unless we get on with this work of redescription that crosses the bright lines between discourses that have been established by theory and practice, talk of human progress, as difficult as it is, is likely to come to a rather immodest and abrupt halt" (Freeman, 1994: 419).

This is exactly what Frederick has done, that is, to cross the "bright lines between discourses." Frederick has reexamined existing theories of the firm and found them all incomplete (Frederick, 1995; Frederick, 2004). A theory of the firm must answer five questions:

(1) What motivates firm behavior?
(2) What generates business productivity/profitability?
(3) What shapes the business organization?
(4) What drives business strategy?
(5) What determines the firm's moral posture?

Existing theories of the firm tend to fall into three general categories: economics, moral philosophy (business ethics), and social sciences (corporate social performance). Economic theories of the firm neglect moral analysis or sublimate it to positivist thinking. Moral theories overemphasize motivation and moral posture to the exclusion of consideration of the other questions, such as regarding productivity and profitability. Social sciences theories focus on the structure and strategy of the organization with attention to the moral posture without adequately addressing motivation or productivity and profitability. All of these theories thus leave gaps. Understanding nature and the sciences, according to Frederick, enables us to fill in the gaps. Nature is what is all around us and part of us—it is what shapes our behavior and determines our potential. In addition, it is what creates the forces that act upon us. Frederick contends that integrating principles of science and how they influence organizations helps to establish the foundation for a more viable model for business.

Frederick has reframed the challenge issued by Freeman:

> Our inquiring enterprise must seek and find new ground, must break out of well-worn ways of thinking about business's ethical and social dilemmas, must build on what is presently known about human nature and human values, must infuse ethics and values inquiry with a larger range of scientific insight than is customarily used, must be willing to relinquish the tight grip on cherished concepts, must help forge a new normative synthesis out of the best that philosophy, social science, and the natural sciences can offer. If we, as scholars, do not encourage the building of new perspectives from constantly evolving, multiple sources of knowledge, how can we expect business practitioners to grasp the realities and complexities on which ethical discourse must go forward? (Frederick, 1995: 300)

For business ethics to progress, the Separation Thesis must be abandoned in favor of shared learnings that span the disciplines. Nature and the sciences hold promise for becoming one avenue through which useful and effective linkages can be created.

Organizations and Personhood

In order to address questions surrounding the possible shortage of values guiding business decisions, it is important first to identify the moral decision-makers. The personhood of corporations has been widely discussed by both legal and business scholars (Hovencamp, 1988; Nesteruk, 1988; Blumberg, 1990; Laufer, 1994). Dialogue has addressed both the legal and moral dimensions (Phillips, 1992). It tends to be accepted that corporations are, at the very least, legal persons—particularly in the United States, where firms incorporate in specific states (Dodd, 1932; Mayer, 1990; Dan-Cohen, 1991). Treating corporations as legal persons enables the legal system to enforce rights and responsibilities for and against corporations.

Legal personhood does not translate into moral personhood, however. In fact, the moral status of corporations has been the subject of considerable debate. It has been argued that corporations are moral persons because of the collective nature of their operations and actions (French, 1979; French, 1984; French, Nesteruk, et al., 1992). The view is that, since the combined behavior of individuals acting on behalf of corporations have moral consequences apart from those of the individual actors, the corporation must itself be a moral person. The difficulty lies in the absence of dignity—an attribute unique to human beings (Velasquez, 1983). Corporations lack the autonomy necessary to perform the primary actions of moral persons (Werhane, 1985). Although they function similarly to "real, autonomous, individual entities," the reality is that corporations merely reflect the behavior of the individuals who operate on their behalf. Corporations are thus secondary moral agents, in that, even though they are not capable of moral reasoning, they are morally accountable for the consequences of the collective actions of their members (Werhane, 1985).

This is significant in that it poses a challenge for scientists—evolutionary scientists, in particular: How can firms, with neither the dignity nor the autonomy of human beings, engage in inherently human undertakings?

One approach is to consider the organization with regard to its collective influence. Frederick (2004) introduced us to what he has called the Evolutionary Firm (EF). According to Frederick, the EF is the characterization of the business firm as linked to evolutionary natural forces—it is a non-organic entity that evolves in reaction to natural forces:

> [T]he firm has organic (and nonorganic) parts but is not itself organic or genic. The firm's organic core is a coalition—an alliance, a collective, a team—of biological agents (i.e., people) who act collectively and symbolically as an adaptive unit, displaying a suite of organic behaviors and interacting with environment as do all organisms. (Frederick, 2004: 147–149)

Frederick identified five core functions of the EF—motivator/driver, innovator/generator, organizer/coordinator, enabler/strategizer, and moralizer/valuator—and suggested that careful examination and delineation of these functions offers a framework for moral inquiry into behavior within firms (Frederick, 2004).

Another approach is to focus on the behavior of individuals—the evolutionary organisms that comprise organizations (see, for example, Nicholson, 1998). As organic entities, human beings naturally evolve. People are both moral persons as well as evolutionary beings. Determining how science influences their moral decision-making as participants in and contributors to business organizations provides insight into the values that exist in business.

Role of Nature

Nature is what exists all around us. It encompasses the birds that sing, the rain that falls, and the atoms that collide. It is what gives us life and then takes it away. In spite of the all-encompassing influence of nature, it paradoxically remains what we often take most for granted. Except for those long walks in the woods that we take when we need a break and have the time, nature is what we virtually ignore in our professional lives.

This is unfortunate, in that scientific inquiry has provided us with many valuable and transferable learnings about animals, people, nature, and human nature. Things in nature tend to operate in predictable ways, and it is that predictability that we have endeavored to capture. Scientists have labored to identify, analyze, and categorize the patterns that exist in nature in order to derive principles, rules, and theories to explain the natural or naturalistic behavior of animate and inanimate objects. The principle of inertia, for example, informs us that objects at rest remain at rest until acted upon by contrary forces. Science explains that, to move an object, we must apply force to the stationary object.

Understanding the rules of nature empowers us by enabling us to predict the consequences of our actions and thereby control the sorts of actions in which we engage in order to achieve desirable results. Integrating scientific principles in theories about business allows us to escape a sort of intellectual inertia.

Business and the Environment

The relationship between nature and business initially appeared somewhat antagonistic. For many years, business seemed to view the environment as an obstacle to overcome. It has only been during recent years that the natural environment has acquired increasing relevance and respect. Businesses in general previously operated as if their actions were without moral consequences. It was not until the past thirty years or so that we have begun to confront firsthand the significant harm that businesses and industrial development can cause to the environment and our natural resources. It has been during this time that we have begun to recognize and accept accountability for the impact of business on nature and the environment. In some instances, the environment has even been labeled a stakeholder in order to make certain that businesses are encouraged to mitigate the harmful byproducts of their activities—i.e., the exploitation and pollution of natural resources (Phillips and Reichart, 2000).

If business people do not act responsibly, their behavior can cause devastating human and environmental consequences. Tragedies such as the fire at Cuyahoga River, the groundwater contamination at Love Canal, and the horrific chemical release in Bhopal, India, have prompted the adoption of a host of environmental laws and regulations (Marks, 2002). In addition, society has begun to demand more from businesses, and business people, in turn, are accepting increasing responsibility for the consequences of their actions—at least regarding the environment.

The Environment and Business

The relationship between business and nature is not one-sided—it is not just about conserving resources and treating the environment with respect. While we have traditionally treated the environmental as an external concern vis-à-vis how business affects it, what is becoming increasingly apparent is that the environment, nature, and the sciences together influence the behavior of business people in their firms as well. Indeed, there is a degree of reciprocity in that nature and the sciences also help to describe business behavior and can potentially serve a normative role as well.

The argument underlying the approach of scholars is that learnings from the sciences contribute to the development of business theory—both as a useful metaphor as well as an essential ingredient. Traditional metaphors of business tend to involve games, sports, or even violence. Such images portray business as a solitary endeavor. A more useful metaphor of business—one derived from nature—might be that of a bee hive. Such an analogy captures the interconnectedness of the members of an organization. Further, one of Frederick's primary criticisms of existing theories of the firm is that they neglect nature. The Separation Thesis tends to lead us to isolate our professional selves from the surrounding environment and its potential influence. We operate as if we in business are separate from who we are in nature. But how can this be? The answer is that we cannot truly isolate ourselves depending upon the sphere of life in which we are operating. We are susceptible to the principles of science and nature that frame our physical evolution and shape the development of our natural environment, regardless of whether we are at work, home, or anywhere else. It is not just that principles of science contribute to business thinking, but also that any theory that ignores the very principles that explain and determine the development of organisms such as ourselves is incomplete.

It is for such reasons that Frederick has criticized the separation and isolation of the disciplines and the stifling of shared learnings:

> The role assigned to economic behavior is peculiar inasmuch as it is generally ignored, denigrated, or dismissed as harboring unworthy and unsavory motivations. And there is no role spelled out for nature—no room at the inn, so to speak. Nor is technology given any better treatment, being ignored by most ethicists or, when noticed, it

is said to be anti-normative, morally neutered, or amoral in ethical significance. (Frederick, 1995, 242)

Frederick has instigated conversation about the connection between business values and nature and the sciences in an attempt to integrate insight from the sciences in our thinking about business.[1] As Frederick has asserted, "[B]usiness values lie at the very core of human existence and survival. Those values are an expression of the most fundamental natural and cosmic forces known to science" (Frederick, 1999). Active incorporation of nature and the sciences into thinking about business contributes to a more comprehensive and integrated view of business, the individuals in business, and the natural environment in which business is embedded.

A Naturalistic Approach

Possible contributions from nature and the sciences to business theorizing are abundant—virtually innumerable. We could derive potential insight from almost any area of the sciences. Quantum physics, for example, has generated heated discussion regarding implications for business through innovative applications of chaos theory to organizational behavior (Wheatley, 1992). Incorporating learnings from nature and the sciences creates the basis for a naturalistic approach to business. A body of scholarship has developed that endeavors to examine this interconnectedness between nature and science and the business spheres of our life. Foremost among the contributors in this arena is Frederick, who has been instrumental in developing an exciting and challenging new lens through which business can be examined—the naturalistic lens (Frederick, 1995). This is part of an ongoing dialogue surrounding the relationship between business and the sciences, advanced through the contributions of leading scholars from a range of disciplines (Cosmides and Tooby, 2000; Flack and de Waal, 2000; de Waal, 1996; Lawrence and Nohria, 2002). Indeed, it seems almost counterintuitive not to incorporate science in business thinking. According to noted evolutionary biologist Richard Dawkins,

> [W]hether you're a CEO or a chimney sweep, you're brain-dead if you don't want to know where you came from and why you exist. My main message to laypeople, therefore, is: Think for yourselves. Don't rely on the scientists to interpret everything for you. Try to understand the issues for yourselves. Scientific literacy is its own reward. (Coutu, 2001, 163)

Each of the physical and social sciences—anthropology, biology, chemistry, psychology, physics, and so on—holds its own particular promise of learnings. In addition, a new field has developed, evolutionary psychology, which reflects the convergence of anthropology, behavioral genetics, comparative ethology, neuropsychology, paleontology, and social psychology (Nicholson, 1998; Cosmides and Tooby, 1987, 302; Caporael and Brewer, 1991; Caporael, 2001). Evolutionary psychology captures the view that "human culture can be explained by cognitive patterns laid down in the hunter-gatherer societies of pre-history, patterns (or modules) that are written in our genes" (Egerton, 2001; Flint, 1995). While the goal of this paper is not to diminish the value of input from other scientific disciplines, the focus here is limited to exploring the potential of involvement of evolutionary psychology in new thinking and theorizing about business.

More than a century ago, Charles Darwin proposed a theory of evolution (Dennett, 1995). The fact that organisms change over time—that they evolve—was not news. Darwin's major contribution was the notion of natural selection, that is, the view that reproduction is the process through which the beings with the most viable genes mate and reproduce such that less viable genes disappear over time through this natural process (Rose, 1999; Thomson, 1997). According to natural selection, three things are true: (1) like organisms mate and reproduce with slight to moderate variations between parents and offspring; (2) reproduction results in overpopulation—more offspring than can breed and survive; therefore, (3) the organisms with the genes best suited for survival in the natural environment are those that breed successfully and those are the genes that are perpetuated. In other words, those organisms with less suitable genes are less likely to breed and so, in time, as a result of lack of breeding, those genes disappear from the gene pool (Rose, 1999).

Although Darwin's theory of evolution and natural selection has been studied throughout the past century, interest has been revived with renewed vigor with the emergence of evolutionary psychology, also known as modern Darwinism. Scholars in evolutionary psychology suggest that modern Darwinism informs our understandings of business. Watching how animals evolve and develop emotions such as empathy and sympathy can arguably guide us in our development of business insight regarding cooperative and competitive behavior in business (Flack and de Waal, 2004). Some evolutionary psychologists go a step further in arguing that an understanding of science is necessary in order not only to develop, but to follow through successfully with, social contracts (Cosmides and Tooby, 2004; Frederick and Wasieleski, 2002). Since social contracts are increasingly viewed as integral to business, it is essential that we figure out how to incorporate scientific principles in our understanding of business ethics (Donaldson and Dunfee, 1999).

Modern Darwinism is clearly linked to Darwin's original thinking. It builds upon traditional Darwinism, creating a more robust view of human evolution and the community. According to evolutionary psychology, the human community is comprised of organisms with genes that create impulses to which they react. Human beings evolve and, as they do so, the gene pool narrows such that the genes that continue to be passed along are those that are best suited to facilitate the process of reproduction. The human mind evolves just as do human organs and bodies (Cosmides, 1989; Cosmides and Tooby, 2000). Human minds and bodies are predisposed toward the sort of society from which they came, that is, "the highly social clan life of mobile hunter-gatherer existence" (Nicholson, 1997).

Natural selection is the result of the reproduction process. According to Nigel Nicholson, "All living creatures are 'designed' by specific combination of genes. Genes that produce faulty design features, such as soft bones or weak hearts, are largely eliminated from the population" (Nicholson, 1998: 136). This takes place in two ways: environmental selection and sexual selection. Environmental selection occurs as the genes that do not support survival against environmental conditions gradually disappear as the holders of those genes die off without reproducing. Similarly, sexual selection is what happens when inferior genetic traits cause people not to mate and reproduce. The combined iterative effect of the two types of natural selection is to create a species that naturally and continually rejects the genes for weaker traits. Over time, the process of natural selection thus strengthens the species. The broad mission of evolutionary psychologists is primarily to identify how genes influence behavior in this way.

There is a theme echoed throughout modern Darwinism that the guiding motivator of genes is the goal of reproduction. According to Steven Pinker,

> The ultimate goal of a body is not to benefit itself or its species or its ecosystem but to maximize the number of copies of the genes that made it in the first place. Natural selection is about replicators, entities that keep a stable identity across many generations of copying. Replicators that enhance the probability of their own replication come to predominate, regardless of whose body the replicated copies sit in. (Pinker, 1997)

In other words, the view is that genes exist to be reproduced; therefore, where there are more genes than can be reproduced, the genes best suited for reproduction tend to be those passed on from one generation to the next (Dawkins, 1976; Wilson, 1993).

Although a popular criticism of this sort of thinking is that it is overly deterministic, in that it suggests that genes control behavior, modern Darwinism does not inherently translate into determinism (Konkola, 1999). In fact, the prevalent belief is that genes control influences on behavior, not the behavior itself. Genes affect behavior, but they do not literally manipulate behavior. As Pinker has explained, "Sexual desire is not people's strategy to propagate their genes. It's people's strategy to attain the pleasures of sex, and the pleasures of sex are the genes' strategy to propagate themselves" (Pinker, 1997: 44). The presence of a strategy that works sometimes does not create determinism.

The larger question that provokes controversy is that of whether organisms are born as they are or whether they develop into what they become. This is often framed as the question of nature vs. nurture.[2] One view is that a person is born as a "blank slate," and it is his or her life experiences that write upon that slate to create the person that he or she becomes. Darwinism is often perceived in opposition to this because of the role played by genes. In reality, though, it is possible to interpret the two views as compatible. There is room, within evolutionary psychology, for the perspective that, even though a person is born with certain genes, his or her particularized behavioral responses have a nurturing effect in contributing to the specific development of the individual. In other words, instead of wondering whether organisms are influenced by nature *or* nurturing, the more fruitful inquiry might lie in exploring the complementary roles of nature *and* nurturing (Pinker, 2003; Harris, 1998; Herrnstein and Murray, 1994; Thornhill and Palmer, 2001; Goode, 2000).

Evolutionary psychology expands the horizons of Darwinism and sheds additional insight about human behavior by exploring new dimensions of evolution and natural selection, such as the development of the human mind and the connection between the evolution of humans and animals.[3] By venturing into these new intellectual territories, learnings have emerged regarding interpersonal behavior.[4] Research by Frans B. M. de Waal, for example, indicates that both animals and humans share an innate desire to dominate (de Waal, 1989: 187–191). According to de Waal, people engage in altruism (i.e., charity) and, it follows, cooperation, because of an underlying belief that there will be a reciprocal positive impact on their status (de Waal, 1996: 136–154. Similarly, in studying the human mind, Leda Cosmides and John Tooby have conducted research that suggests that mental algorithms that assist people in identifying and punishing cheaters might actually indicate that human beings are naturally inclined toward social exchange (Cosmides and Tooby, 1987; Cosmides and Tooby, 1989; Price, Cosmides et al., forthcoming). They have provided support for the natural development of social contracts by demonstrating that significant improvement occurs for performance on certain tasks where such preexisting agreements establish that the receipt of a benefit is contingent upon the payment of a cost (Cosmides, 1989; Frederick and Wasieleski, 2002).

Evolutionary psychology remains still in the early stages of development. Scholars from multiple disciplines are stretching the limits of their understanding of evolution in order to develop further insight into behavior. While this body of knowledge is itself still evolving, significant milestones have been achieved and exploring how they relate to business clearly represents a worthwhile and rewarding endeavor.

Darwin and Business

Although it can be argued that it is important for people to anticipate the future, that is not what evolutionary psychology aims to accomplish. The particular contribution of modern Darwinism lies on increasing intellectual linkages between the present of the human species and its iterative past as it has evolved in order to develop greater understanding of the reasons for the changes that have taken place. The evolutionary psychologists create these linkages to enable us then to predict the nature of future changes and perhaps to play a role in shaping how those changes manifest themselves. Existing scholarship offers a sort of "map" of the current status of the intellectual territory, one subject to ongoing development—just as is the landscape around us (Cosmides, Tooby et al., 1992).

The purpose here is not to debate the specific beliefs of individual evolutionary psychologists, but to explore the consequences of their collective thinking, particularly with regard to business, assuming that their assumptions are valid. In other words, quite simply, how does modern Darwinism affect our thinking about business—its foundation and its operation? Scholars are beginning to explore the ways in which the sciences assist in thinking about businesses and other organizations (Ben-Ner and Putterman, 2000; Clark, 1996; Duening, 1997; Grossnickle, 1997; Saad and Gill, 2000). Frederick (2004), for example, has drawn from the sciences in order to explain the behavior of firms. Nicholson (1998), on the other hand, has incorporated learnings from modern Darwinism to predict the behavior of businesspeople and to address common concerns. Further examination of the relationship between evolution and business, within the context of the major tenets of evolutionary psychology, results in a series of paradoxes, the resolution of which suggests additional ways in which modern Darwinism can contribute to a more robust theory of business.

Paradox of Propagation

A common theme in modern Darwinism is that the goal of genes is to survive in order to propagate (Wilson, 1993). A corporation does not reproduce; how is it or its survival linked to human beings?

Since corporations are not moral persons, it is the genes within human beings and their alleged urge to be reproduced that is relevant. The role played by corporations within the context of evolution is to create common goods and services that enhance the ability of human beings to prosper and thereby reproduce. Corporations provide for the pooling of efforts and the division of labor such that the results are greater than any one individual could accomplish alone. Further, the sheer size and expanse of some corporations enable them to perform tasks that individuals acting alone could not, and it can be argued that these tasks are integral to the survival of the genes.

In addition, it is possible to argue that corporations offer a venue that facilitates the satisfaction of natural impulses. The corporation, for example, offers a peaceful forum through which people are able to exercise their innate desire to dominate. The extensive hierarchy that exists within many corporations provides numerous opportunities for people to dominate one another, and climbing up the corporate ladder affords them the occasion to participate in the struggle toward achieving domination. In addition, corporations also facilitate social contracting. The corporation itself can be viewed as a partner to social contracts; further, it serves as a locus through which other human beings are able to engage in these sorts of arrangements (Frederick and Wasieleski, 2002).

This suggests that a broad purpose for corporations can be interpreted from modern Darwinism: to facilitate the fulfillment of natural urges, whether the urges are linked to basic needs (i.e., sustenance, shelter, and so on) or interpersonal behavior (i.e., dominance, social contracts, and so on). Corporations serve as vehicles through which people are able to satisfy primary urges.

Paradox of Relationships

Evolutionary psychology tends to limit caring to the familial relationship. In other words, modern Darwinism neither views caring as a rational basis for connecting with other human beings nor provides the basis for a common set of shared morals. How does consideration of stakeholder relationships make sense within the context of evolution?

According to current laws in the United States, stakeholders as a group are not recognized by the corporation vis-à-vis their holding of general stakes. The legal landscape recognizes specific stakeholders (i.e., stockholders, employees, and so on), but their potential recognizable claims tend to be limited to named situations. An increasing number of corporations are nevertheless integrating attention to stakeholder concerns in their decision-making process.

The mission of genes as explained by evolutionary psychology is to provide for survival of the organism so that they can be passed on to the next generation. This isolates genes in that the perception is that, for some genes to survive, others will not. At the same time, organisms must engage in relationships in order to mate. Further, inherent in genes is interconnectedness, for each organism is influenced by multiple genes, which, together, must enable the survival of the organism in order to be replicated in the next generation.

In addition, even though modern Darwinism does not necessarily provide an obvious foundation for caring relationships, there is evidence that human beings are inherently social.[5] Social cooperation for mutual benefit is not a new phenomenon (Frederick and Wasieleski, 2002). As Cosmides and Tooby have pointed out, "Social exchange is not a recent cultural invention. . . . [It is] universal and highly elaborated across human cultures, presenting itself in many forms" (Cosmides and Tooby, 1995: 1202). There is support for relationships based on need and the satisfaction of mutual goals (Cosmides, 1989). It can be said that stakeholders exist in these sorts of relationships with one another that are based on need and the satisfaction of mutual goals. Interestingly, the metaphor in nature for groups of organisms recognizes this inherent interconnectedness. The ant hill and the bee hive, for example, are common examples of how animals work together in nature. Perhaps these are better metaphors for business enterprises as well. The reality is that stakeholders are engaged in mutual relationships in which each individual relies upon others in order to attain personal goals.

This sort of a metaphor coincides with changing perspectives in the business ethics scholarship. Thinking about stakeholders is moving away from the original bilateral hub-and-spoke model offered by Freeman, which depicts all relationships as emanating from the firm, toward a model that takes a more network-based approach and stresses a multilateral, interconnected web of relationships. Integrating insight from modern Darwinism reinforces the direction in which stakeholder thinking has already been moving (Radin, 1999; Radin, 2003).

Consideration of stakeholder relationships is playing a growing role both in business practice and in scholarship (Waddock and Smith, 2000b; Ehin, 1998).

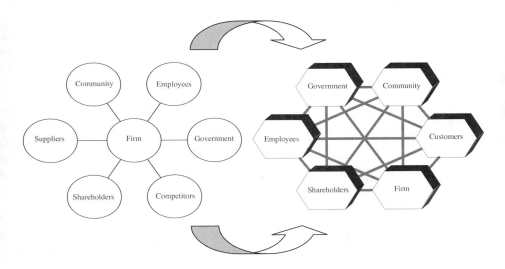

In fact, this sort of thinking causes us to reframe how we interpret specific stakeholders. Consideration of nature supports our reframing of how we view competitors. Although we have traditionally portrayed business as an aggressive, sometimes violent, sport, this is changing. As Jeanne Liedtka has pointed out, our perspective on business competition has changed and is moving away from the treatment of business as "dog-eat-dog":

> Rather than competing head-to-head against each other, firms have increasingly come to believe that they compete by learning, partnering, thinking, redesigning, and innovating faster than those they compete against. This new view of the nature of competition creates new possibilities for having a conversation that links business ethics and practice in powerful new ways. . . . This approach has been argued by Solomon (1993) to offer the best prospects for achieving impact on the world of business practice. (Liedtka, 1998, 258)

This coincides with views of competition derived from how animals behave in nature. Animals do not kill for pleasure—they kill for need (i.e., food or protection).

There appears an inherent connection between stakeholder thinking and modern Darwinism, in that both recognize the value of relationships built on trust and mutual respect, not on self-interest and exploitation at the expense of others. Although evolutionary psychology alone does not necessarily explain the depth of these relationships, it does offer possible insight into their foundation and formation.

Paradox of Fallible Managers

One of the most popular criticisms levied against stakeholder theory has been that it does not provide concrete guidance—a formula—for managerial decision-making.

Similarly, modern Darwinism does not account for the role of fallible human beings. How does the process of natural selection operate naturally if managerial decision-making accounts for which stakeholder concerns are addressed?

The problem here lies in the underlying assumption that taking care of some stakeholders inherently translates into harm to other stakeholders. People often belong to multiple stakeholder groupings. In other words, employees, for example, are also often members of the community and stockholders. Each narrow stakeholder grouping might have a discrete set of interests, but the stakeholders themselves—the people—manifest complicated webs of interests. A person who is a stockholder benefits when a company in which he or she owns stock cuts costs and is able to distribute greater returns; that same person also suffers if he or she is a victim of the round of layoffs to which the cut costs are attributable.

Stakeholders with conflicting interests can benefit from the same course of action—the difference is often a matter of magnitude in how much one group benefits versus another. Take, for example, a company that is reducing costs by polluting a neighboring stream. If the company adopts a new strategy that includes respect for the environment and decides to absorb the cost of alternative waste disposal methods, the company, the environment, and members of the community (particularly those who use the stream) benefit. While the environment and the community benefit from the cleaner water, the company also benefits from increased goodwill and positive public relations. Other stakeholders will also benefit, though perhaps not in the same way as if the stream were polluted. Stockholders, for example, might not receive the same short-term profits, but their long-term interests might be enhanced through the more favorable company image that develops as a result of its demonstrated respect for the environment.

The greater problem lies in our lack of faith in managers. We hire employees and managers because of who they are—the performance record they have exhibited, the skills they claim, and the appearance they make. Why, then, in the workplace, do we look for formulas to replace the particularized managerial decision-making judgment they have supposedly developed in order to reach the positions they occupy? It would seem that, if we are asking how to bypass the possibility of managerial fallibility, then we are asking the wrong question. We should instead perhaps be asking how we can train managers more effectively and make better hiring decisions.

It would seem that the paradox of the fallible manager is not really a paradox after all. Human error is only one of a host of environmental conditions that genes must overcome in pursuit of their survival and ultimate replication. Human error, like human beings, is part of nature.

Paradox of Evolution

Evolutionary psychology draws upon the sciences in order to explain behavior based on the history of the organisms involved—according to how they have moved through the process of evolution. Since evolution is an ongoing process, it would seem that explaining evolution involves the constant pursuit of a moving target. How is it possible to systemize learnings that are still developing? Key here is the underlying assumption that theories are stagnant, when modern Darwinism reveals is that they are in fact dynamic. A quest for such a theory of business is misguided. Nature is in flux—as is business. This does not mean that everything is changing, but that it is subject to change. Incorporating evolutionary thinking in a theory of business reinforces linkages to the past and assists in anticipating the future based on known behavioral patterns. Change should be embraced, not feared.

Nature and Stakeholder Theory

Exploring the apparent paradoxes reveals the contribution of evolutionary psychology to the foundation for stakeholder theory. The message is that corporations exist to enable people to accomplish more than they could alone. Because people work together as part of these enterprises, the underlying networks of stakeholder relationships become essential. Paying attention to stakeholder interests does not translate into satisfying every concern, because that is a virtual impossibility and not necessarily even desirable. Not all stakeholder claims are legitimate. Overall, successful management of stakeholder concerns does tend to benefit the array of stakeholders. It is essential to keep in mind that, while not every grouping of concerns can be addressed, most specific stakeholders belong to multiply groupings and their interests often overlap. Stakeholder theory and modern Darwinism both send the message that stakeholders matter.

The paradoxes and contributions offered here are far from comprehensive. They represent a start, a beginning, an open door. This is a project that scholars will hopefully continue, that is, the process of integrating the newest discoveries by modern Darwinism with traditional and ongoing thinking about business. As we learn more about the motivation and behavior of stakeholders, it enhances our ability to anticipate and address their needs in order to contribute to stronger firm performance.

A growing body of literature supports both the moral and financial interests in attending to stakeholder concerns (Anderson, 1999; Elliot, 2000; Nassutti, 1998; Waddock and Smith, 2000a; West, 2000). It is possible to "do well by doing good." The gene's quest to propagate—to be reproduced—can therefore enhance the ability of firms to prosper. As individuals are motivated to prosper, so will the organizations to which they contribute. A next step lies in figuring out what sort of moral signals and cues can embed in organizational training and decision-making processes in order to counterbalance negative genetic impulses and to build upon those that are supportive.

Moral Consequences

So, what does this all mean? Recent years have witnessed an ongoing search for a normative foundation for stakeholder theory (Evan and Freeman, 1988; Rowley, 1998; Bishop, 2000; Donaldson and Preston, 1995). Answering that question does not inherently assist us in resolving individual moral dilemmas or meeting the challenge of increasing the presence of moral values in business. A naturalistic understanding of and approach to business does, though, suggest new avenues through which we tackle morality in business.

First, if our lives are defined by the underlying mission of our genes to reproduce, then it is important that we recognize that. Further, on behalf of the organization, it behooves us to recognize these influences that will affect the performance of stakeholders of the organization. It might be necessary for us to change our expectations and to create internal mechanisms that reinforce the priority of organizational goals. The message must be sent that there are personal consequences that can outweigh the short-term benefits of pursuing satisfaction of the genetically-created urges. If we recognize that these urges exist, then we can fight them.[6]

Second, evolutionary social contracting provides a vehicle for increasing social interconnectedness and productive collaborative behavior (Frederick and Wasieleski, 2002). Mutually beneficial relationships should be developed and encouraged. It is important to emphasize the stakeholder metaphor of the corporation as a web of interconnected relationships in order to prevent the absence of moral values that accompanies feelings of disassociation and lack of connectedness.

Third, organizations need to embed moral values in their cultures such that, as individuals pursue their innate desires to dominate, the message is reinforced that domination occurs through increased moral decision-making. Our businesses are learning that that is how they succeed in business, that is, "doing well by doing good." It is time for individuals in business to receive the same message about their personal success.

Fourth, it is essential that individuals be reminded that they are the organization. In other words, they will bear the consequences of poor performance—in moral or financial terms. If a corporation endorses irresponsible behavior, they as stakeholders will feel those consequences personally. This information must be factored into the responses by individuals to the impulses that their genes create.

Fifth, overcoming the Separation Thesis, particularly as it relates to humans and nature, is crucial. As we search for role models, we have overlooked many of the most obvious candidates—those that exist in nature around us. As the scholarly discussion has focused on the unnatural limitations that are created by our dividing the disciplines, we, too, have missed the underlying consequences on a personal level. People will develop deeper understanding of themselves—why they behave in certain ways—if they are able to recognize their connection to nature and natural processes. Addicts—alcoholics—feel inner impulses to engage in destructive behavior. Once the alcoholic recognizes that urge and the potential consequences, he or she then knows what to fight and how.

With regard to organizations, we speak often of empowerment. True empowerment on an individual level is derived by enabling people to battle their urges by enabling people to recognize them and understand their origin. This we can accomplish by reintroducing people to nature—by emphasizing the interconnectedness.

Conclusion

According to Freeman, "[O]ur task is to take metaphors like the stakeholder concept and embed it in a story about how human beings create and exchange value" (Freeman, 1994). The project begun by scholars such as Frederick, of which this article is part, is not a new story, but a very old one, about where we came from, how we became who we are, and where we are going. Interestingly, it is not a story about us as individuals but about us as a species. At first blush, this might seem a bit absurd; upon reflection, however, it becomes apparent that the absurdity lies not in the pursuit of connections between nature and business, but rather in thinking that we are disconnected from nature—even as businesspeople.

To Frederick we are grateful for opening the door to a paradigm of business that portrays organizations as life-sustaining enterprises. If the sciences offer insight that can inform our assumptions about human interaction, then it only makes sense to reconnect ourselves with our past. The naturalistic approach to business is not the only approach; it is, however, one rich with potential and one we should not ignore.

Notes

A summer research grant from the Zarb School of Business at Hofstra University made this research possible.

1. Not everyone agrees that the Separation Thesis has played a major role in chilling interdisciplinary thinking and theorizing. Richard Dawkins, for example, cites the "cross-fertilization between fields" as a longstanding and beneficial tradition (Coutu, 2001). See also Foss (1994), who has pointed out that there is a longstanding history of drawing analogies between evolutionary biology and economics. The difference between Dawkins' view and Freeman's and Frederick's perspective is that the isolated and occasional borrowing facilitates the perpetuation of the barriers between disciplines. Frederick would likely argue at the very least for more systemic cross-fertilization; Freeman has maintained that the separation itself should not exist—that ethics should naturally be subsumed into what is meant by business.

2. Pinker has asserted, "Many intellectuals and social critics have still not moved beyond the simplistic dichotomy between heredity and environment to acknowledge that all behavior comes out of an interaction between the two" (Pinker, 2003).

3. See, for example, Flack and de Waal (2000), in which animal behavior in activities such as food-sharing and conflict resolution is explored. In addition, there is discussion of emotions, such as empathy, sympathy, and consolation. A better understanding of how such emotions develop and exist in animals could contribute to an understanding of how they could be better developed and managed in human beings.

4. It has even been contended that language patterns have evolutionary roots (Dunbar, 1997). Since language structures communication, understanding the development of language can contribute to deeper understanding of human interaction (Kaschak, 1992).

5. Emerging research regarding emotions and animals suggests that scientific research—particularly regarding animals—might lend support for the development of caring relationships (Lawrence, 2004; Wright, 1994).

6. Nicholson (1998) suggests specific ways of managing human behavior (i.e., propensity toward "gossip").

Bibliography

Anderson, J. A. 1999. "Doing Well by Doing Good." *Black Enterprise* 29(12): 105–107.

Ben-Ner, A., and L. Putterman. 2000. "On Some Implications of Evolutionary Psychology for the Study of Preferences and Institutions." *Journal of Economic Behavior and Organization* 43(1): 91–99.

Bishop, J. D. 2000. "A Framework for Discussing Normative Theories of Business Ethics." *Business Ethics Quarterly* 10(3): 563–591.

Blumberg, P. I. 1990. "The Corporate Entity in an Era of Multinational Corporations." *Delaware Journal of Corporate Law* 15: 283–375.

Caporael, L. R. 2001. "Evolutionary Psychology: Toward a Unifying Theory and a Hybrid Science." *Annual Review of Psychology* 52: 607–628.

Caporael, L. R., and M. B. Brewer. 1991. "Reviving Evolutionary Psychology: Biology Meets Society." *Journal of Social Issues* 47(3): 187.

Clark, C. 1996. *Choice, Chance and Organizational Change: Practical Insights from Evolution for Business Leaders and Thinkers*. New York: Amacom.

Cosmides, L. 1989. "The Logic of Social Exchanges: Has Natural Selection Shaped How Humans Reason? Studies with the Wason Selection Task." *Cognition* 31(3): 187–276.

Cosmides, L., and J. Tooby. 1987. "From Evolution to Behavior: Evolutionary Psychology as the Missing Link." *The Latest on the Best: Essays on Evolution and Optimality*. J. Dupre. Cambridge, Mass.: MIT Press: 277–306.

———. 1989. "Evolutionary Psychology and the Generation of Culture, Part II: Case Study: A Computational Theory of Social Exchange." *Ethology and Sociobiology* 10(1–3): 51–97.

———. 1995. "From Function to Structure: The Role of Evolutionary Biology and Computational Theories in Cognitive Neuroscience." *The Cognitive Neurosciences*. M. S. Gazzaniga. Cambridge, Mass.: MIT Press.

_____. 2000. "The Cognitive Neuroscience of Social Reasoning." *The New Cognitive Neurosciences*. M. S. Gazzaniga. Cambridge, Mass.: MIT Press.

_____. 2004. "Knowing Thyself: The Evolutionary Psychology of Moral Reasoning and Moral Sentiments," in *Business, Science, and Ethics*, ed. R. E. Freeman and P. H. Werhane. Charlottesville, Va.: Philosophy Documentation Center: 91–126.

Cosmides, L., J. Tooby, and J. H. Barkow. 1992. "Introduction: Evolutionary Psychology and Conceptual Integration." *The Adapted Mind: Evolutionary Psychology and the Generation of Culture*, ed. L. Cosmides, J. Tooby, and J. H. Barkow. New York: Oxford University Press: 3–15.

Coutu, D. 2001. "What is Science Good For? A Conversation with Richard Dawkins." *Harvard Business Review* 79(1): 159–163.

Dan-Cohen, M. 1991. "Freedoms of Collective Speech: A Theory of Protected Communications by Organizations, Communities, and the State." *California Law Review* 79: 1229–1267.

Dawkins, R. 1976. *The Selfish Gene*. New York: Oxford University Press.

Dennett, D. C. 1995. *Darwin's Dangerous Idea: Evolution and the Meanings of Life*. New York: Simon & Schuster.

Dodd, E. M., Jr. 1932. "For Whom Are Corporate Managers Trustees." *Harvard Law Review* 45: 1145–1163.

Donaldson, T., and T. W. Dunfee. 1999. *Ties that Bind: A Social Contracts Approach to Business Ethics*. Boston: Harvard Business School Press.

Donaldson, T., and L. Preston. 1995. *The Stakeholder Theory of the Corporation: Concepts, Evidence, and Implications* 21(1): 65–91.

Duening, T. 1997. "Our Turbulent Times? The Case for Evolutionary Organizational Change." *Business Horizons* 40(1): 2–8.

Dunbar, R. 1997. *Grooming, Gossip, and the Evolution of Language*. Cambridge, Mass.: Harvard University Press.

Egerton, M. 2001. "Evolutionary Psychology Undermined?" *Lancet* 357(9252): 318–319.

Ehin, C. 1998. "Fostering Both Sides of Human Nature—The Foundation for Collaborative Relationships." *Business Horizons* 41(3): 15–25.

Elliot, M. 2000. "Doing Good While Doing Well." *Newsweek* (Dec./Feb.): 68–71.

Evan, W. M., and R. E. Freeman. 1988. "A Stakeholder Theory of the Modern Corporation: Kantian Capitalism." *Ethical Theory and Business*, ed. T. Beauchamp and N. Bowie. Englewood Cliffs, N.J.: Prentice Hall, Inc.

Flack, J. C., and F. B. M. de Waal. 2000. "'Any Animal Whatever': Darwinian Building Blocks of Morality in Monkeys and Apes." *Journal of Consciousness Studies* 7(1/2): 1–29.

_____. 2004. "Monkey Business and Business Ethics: Evolutionary Origins of Human Morality," in *Business, Science, and Ethics*, ed. R. E. Freeman and P. H. Werhane. Charlottesville, Va.: Philosophy Documentation Center: 7–41.

Flint, A. 1995. "Do We Still Think Like Stone-Agers." *Boston Globe* (Aug. 21): 25.

Fort, T. L. 1999. "Business and Naturalism: A Peek at Transcendence?" *Business and Society* 38(2): 226–236.

————. 2000. "On Social Psychology, Business Ethics, and Corporate Governance." *Business Ethics Quarterly* 10(3): 725–733.

Foss, N. J. 1994. "The Biological Analogy and the Theory of the Firm: Marshall and Monopolistic Competition." *Journal of Economic Issues* 28(4): 1115–1136.

Frederick, W. C. 1995. *Values, Nature, and Culture in the American Corporation.* New York: Oxford University Press.

————. 1998. "Creatures, Corporations, Communities, Chaos, Complexity." *Business and Society* 37(4): 358–389.

————. 1999. "Relativism, Feminism, and Theology: A Naturalist Response." *Business and Society* 38(2): 237–245.

————. 2004. "The Evolutionary Firm and Its Moral (Dis)Contents," in *Business, Science, and Ethics*, ed. R. E. Freeman and P. H. Werhane. Charlottesville, Va.: Philosophy Documentation Center: 143–174.

Frederick, W. C., and D. M. Wasieleski. 2002. "Evolutionary Social Contracts." *Business and Society Review* 107(3): 283–308.

Freeman, R. E. 1994. "The Politics of Stakeholder Theory: Some Future Directions." *Business Ethics Quarterly* 4(4): 409–421.

French, P. 1984. *Collective and Corporate Responsibility.* New York: Columbia University Press.

————. 1979. "The Corporation as a Moral Person." *American Philosophical Quarterly* 16(3): 207–215.

French, P. A., J. Nesteruk, et al. 1992. *Corporations in the Moral Community.* New York: Harcourt Brace Jovanovich College Publishers.

Goode, E. 2000. Human Nature: Born or Made? *New York Times* (Mar. 4): F1.

Grossnickle, W. F. 1997. "Choice, Chance and Organizational Change: Practical Insights From Evolution for Business Leaders and Thinkers." *Personnel Psychology* 50(3): 807–809.

Harris, J. R. 1998. *The Nurture Assumption: Why Children Turn Out the Way They Do.* New York: Free Press.

Herrnstein, R., and C. Murray. 1994. *The Bell Curve: Intelligence and Class Structure in American Life.* New York: Free Press.

Hovencamp, H. 1988. "The Classical Corporation in American Legal Thought." *Georgetown Law Journal* 76: 1593–1689.

Kaschak, E. 1992. *Engendered Lives.* New York: Basic Books.

Konkola, K. 1999. "Theology and Evolutionary Psychology." *Skeptic* 7(2): 74.

Laufer, W. S. 1994. "Corporate Bodies and Guilty Minds." *Emory Law Journal* 43: 648.

Lawrence, P. R. 2004. "The Biological Base of Morality?" in *Business, Science, and Ethics*, ed. R. E. Freeman and P. H. Werhane. Charlottesville, Va.: Philosophy Documentation Center: 59–79.

Lawrence, P. R., and N. Nohria. 2002. *Driven: How Human Nature Shapes Our Choices.* San Francisco: Jossey-Bass.

Liedtka, J. 1998. "Constructing an Ethic for Business Practice: Competing Effectively and Doing Good." *Business and Society* 37(3): 254–80.

Marks, P. D. 2002. "Workbench: Tools to Improve Environmental Compliance." *Maryland Bar Journal* 35(4): 10–15.

Mayer, C. J. 1990. "Personalizing the Impersonal: Corporations and the Bill of Rights." *Hastings Law Journal* 41: 577–667.

Nassutti, C. 1998. "Doing Well by Doing Good." *Journal of Accountancy* 186(3): 51–54.

Nesteruk, J. 1988. "*Bellotti* and the Question of Corporate Moral Agency." *Columbia Business Law Review* 1988: 683–703.

Nicholson, N. 1997. "Evolutionary Psychology: Toward a New View of Human Nature and Organizational Society." *Human Relations* 50(9): 1053–1078.

———. 1998. "How Hardwired is Human Behavior?" *Harvard Business Review* 76(4): 134–147.

Perry, J. 2000. "Doing Well by Doing Good—for Credit Community Service may be an Assignment." *U.S. News & World Report* (Sept. 11): 1.

Phillips, M. J. 1992. "Corporate Moral Personhood and Three Conceptions of the Corporation." *Business Ethics Quarterly* 2(1): 435–460.

Phillips, R. A., and J. Reichart. 2000. "The Environment as a Stakeholder? A Fairness-Based Approach." *Journal of Business Ethics* 23(2): 185–197.

Pinker, S. 1997. "Against Nature." *Discover* 18(10): 92–95.

———. 1997. *How the Mind Works.* New York: Norton.

———. 2003. "The Blank Slate: The Modern Denial of Human Nature." *Skeptical Inquirer* 27(2): 37.

Price, M. E., L. Cosmides, et al. Forthcoming. "Punitive Sentiment as an Anti-Free Rider Psychological Device." *Evolution and Human Behavior.*

Radin, T. J. 1999. "Stakeholder Theory and the Law." Charlottesville, Va.: Darden Graduate School of Business Administration, University of Virginia.

———. 2003. "700 Families to Feed: The Challenge of Corporate Citizenship." *Vanderbilt Journal of Transnational Law.*

Rose, S. 1999. "Evolutionary Psychology—Biology Impoverished." *Interdisciplinary Science Reviews* 24(3): 175.

Rowley, T. 1998. "A Normative Justification for Stakeholder Theory." *Business and Society* 37(1): 105–107.

Saad, G., and T. Gill. 2000. "Applications of Evolutionary Psychology in Marketing." *Psychology and Marketing* 17(12): 1005–1034.

Thomson, K. S. 1997. "Natural Selection and Evolution's Smoking Gun." *American Scientist* 85(6): 516–518.

Thornhill, R., and C. Palmer. 2001. *A Natural History of Rape: Biological Bases of Sexual Coercion.* Cambridge, Mass.: MIT Press.

Velasquez, M. G. 1983. "Why Corporations Are Not Morally Responsible for Anything They Do." *Business and Professional Ethics Journal* 2(3): 111.

de Waal, F. B. M. 1989. *Chimpanzee Politics: Power and Sex among the Apes.* Baltimore, Md.: Johns Hopkins University Press.

———. 1996. *Good Natured: The Origin of Right and Wrong in Humans and Other Animals.* Cambridge, Mass.: Harvard University Press.

Waddock, S., and N. Smith. 2000a. "Corporate Responsibility Audits: Doing Well by Doing Good." *Sloan Management Review* 41(2): 75–83.

———. 2000b. "Relationships: The Real Challenge of Corporate Global Citizenship." *Business and Society Review* 105: 47–62.

Werhane, P. H. 1985. *Persons, Rights, and Corporations*. Englewood Cliffs, N.J.: Prentice-Hall, Inc.

West, D. 2000. "Doing Well by Doing Good." *Pharmaceutical Executive* 20(10): 98.

Wheatley, M. J. 1992. *Leadership and the New Science*. San Francisco: Berrett-Koehler Publishers.

Wilson, J. Q. 1993. *The Moral Sense*. New York: Free Press.

Wright, R. 1994. *The Moral Animal*. New York: Pantheon Books.

NOTES ON CONTRIBUTORS

Leda Cosmides is Professor of Psychology at the University of California, Santa Barbara, and co-director of the UCSB Center for Evolutionary Psychology. She was educated at Harvard University (A.B. 1979 in biology; ph.D. 1985 in cognitive psychology), did postdoctoral work in psychology at Stanford University, and was a fellow at the Center for Advanced Study in the Behavioral Sciences before accepting a faculty position in 1991. She is best known for her work in pioneering the new field of evolutionary psychology. Her awards include the 1988 American Association for the Advancement of Science Prize for Behavioral Science Research, the 1993 American Psychological Association Distinguished Scientific Award for an Early Career Contribution to Psychology, and a J. S. Guggenheim Memorial Fellowship (1999–2000). In 1992, Cosmides and her colleagues published *The Adapted Mind: Evolutionary Psychology and the Generation of Culture*, the volume that introduced the field of evolutionary psychology to a wide scholarly community.

Joseph DesJardins is Professor in the philosophy department formed jointly by the College of St. Benedict and St. John's University. He is the author of *An Introduction to Business Ethics* (McGraw Hill) and co-editor, with John McCall, of *Contemporary Issues in Business Ethics*.

Jessica C. Flack is a post-doctoral researcher at the Santa Fe Institute and an Affiliate Researcher at the Living Links Center at Yerkes National Primate Research Center in Atlanta, Georgia. Her interests include the evolution of organization, robustness and stability mechanisms in biological and social systems, the distribution of power and conflict management in animal societies, representation of meaning and encoding and decoding processes in signaling systems, and information transfer across different levels of biological organization. She is also interested in the origins of a concept of rights.

Tim Fort is an Associate Professor of Business Law and Business Ethics. In 1998, he was named the Outstanding Junior Faculty Member of the Academy of Legal Studies in Business. Oxford University Press published his book, *Ethics and Governance: Business as Mediating Institution*, in 2001.

With Professor Cindy Schipani, he has launched a Corporate Governance and Peace Initiative through the William Davidson Institute. He and Professor Schipani are also co-Directors of the Corporate Governance and Corporate Social Responsibility Area of the Davidson Institute.

William C. Frederick is Professor Emeritus, Katz Graduate School of Business, University of Pittsburgh. He is author and coauthor of books on social auditing, business and society relationships, business ethics, and managers' values. His 1995 book *Values, Nature, and Culture in the American Corporation* (Oxford University Press) is part of the Ruffin Series on Business Ethics. He is past president of The Society for Business Ethics, past president of The Society for the Advancement of Socio-Economics, past chair of the Social Issues in Management division of The Academy of Management, and a present member of the editorial board of Business Ethics Quarterly. His PhD in economics and anthropology is from the University of Texas.

R. Edward Freeman is the Elis and Signe Olsson Professor of Business Administration and Co-director of the Olsson Center for Applied Ethics at the Darden Graduate School of Business. He is an internationally recognized authority on stakeholder management—how to understand and manage the multiple changes and challenges in today's business environment, and on the connection between business ethics and corporate strategy. Freeman has received numerous awards in recognition of outstanding teaching at Wharton, Minnesota, and Darden. In 2001 he was recognized by the World Resources Institute and the Aspen Institute Project on Corporate Responsibility with a Pioneer Lifetime Achievement Award.

Edwin M. Hartman is a professor in the philosophy department and the business school at Rutgers University. He is the author of *Substance, Body, and Soul: Aristotelian Investigations* (Princeton University Press, 1977), *Conceptual Foundations of Organization Theory* (Pitman [HarperCollins], 1989), and *Organizational Ethics and the Good Life* (Oxford University Press, 1996). He has also written a number of articles on ancient philosophy and business ethics. At Rutgers Professor Hartman has taught courses in organization theory and strategy, and in ethics, epistemology, and business ethics. He is the founding director of the Prudential Business Ethics Center at Rutgers.

Paul R. Lawrence is the Wallace Brett Donham Professor of Organizational Behavior Emeritus at Harvard Business School. During his forty-four years on the Harvard faculty, he taught in all the School's programs and served as chairman of the Organizational Behavior area and also of both the MBA and AMP programs. He did undergraduate work in sociology and economics at Albion College and did MBA and doctoral training at Harvard. He has been honored by the School's Distinguished Service Award and by the naming of the Paul R. Lawrence MBA Class of 1943 Professorship. His research, published in 24 books and numerous articles, has dealt with the human aspects of management. In particular he has studied organizational change and organization design. His 1967 book, *Organization and Environment* (written with Jay Lorsch) added "contingency theory" to the vocabulary of students of organizational behavior. In 2002 he co-authored *Driven: How Human Nature Shapes Our Choices* with Nitin Nohria, which offered a new theory on the evolution of four universal human drives and their role in organizational life.

Joshua Margolis is an Assistant Professor of Business Administration at Harvard Business School. His current research focuses on how professionals in a variety of settings perform "necessary evils," tasks that require harming other human beings in order to advance a worthy purpose.

David Messick was named the Morris and Alice Kaplan Professor of Ethics and Decision in Management at the Kellogg School of Management of Northwestern University in 1991. Previously he was a professor of psychology at the University of California, Santa Barbara, where he had been a faculty member since 1964. Professor Messick's teaching and research interests are in the ethical and social aspects of decision making and information processing, and the psychology of leadership. He is the author of more than 150 articles, chapters, and edited books and his scholarly work has been published in prominent academic journals. Recently he was named the Director of the newly endowed Ford Motor Center for Global Citizenship at Kellogg.

Ronald K. Mitchell holds the Francis G. Winspear Chair in Public Policy and Business at the University of Victoria, and is a jointly appointed Professor of Strategic Management at the Guanghua School of Management at Peking University, Beijing, PRC. His research interests focus on increasing economic well being in society—both domestically and internationally—through the study of entrepreneurs and stakeholders, and the development of transaction cognition theory.

Lisa H. Newton, Ph.D., is Professor of Philosophy, Director of the Program in Applied Ethics, and currently Director of the Program in Environmental Studies at Fairfield University in Fairfield, Connecticut. She has authored or co-authored several textbooks in the fields of Ethics and Environmental Studies, including *Wake Up Calls: Classic Cases in Business Ethics* (2nd ed. 2003), *Watersheds: Cases in Environmental Ethics* (3rd ed. 2001), *Taking Sides: Controversial Issues in Business Ethics and Society* (7th ed. 2002), and *Ethics and Sustainability: Sustainable Development and the Moral Life* (2003). She has authored over 70 articles on ethics in politics, law, medicine and business, and is presently updating Media and Society's 1990 series, *Ethics in America,* for which she was the writer and ethics consultant. She has been President of the Society for Business Ethics and the American Society for Value Inquiry, serves on the executive boards of the Association for Practical and Professional Ethics, the Society for Ethics Across the Curriculum, and the International Society for Environmental Ethics, and has made numerous presentations, here and abroad, on current issues in business and ethics. She is ethics consultant to several regional health providers, corporations, and professional associations.

Dr. *Mollie Painter-Morland* is the Director of the Centre for Business and Professional Ethics at the University of Pretoria, South Africa. She is also a senior lecturer in the Department of Philosophy and is responsible for the integration of ethics into the curricula of various professional scrhools. She consults in the field of ethics management and corporate governance and specializes in the skills and knowledge needed to facilitate and manage ethical values in the workplace.

Robert Phillips holds a joint appointment between the social/legal and management areas at the University of San Diego's School of Business Administration. He received his Ph.D. at the University of Virginia's Darden School and also holds MBA and BSBA degrees. His work on organizational ethics has previously appeared in *Business Ethics Quarterly* and *Journal of Business Ethics*, among others. He is also the author of *Stakeholder Theory and Organizational Ethics* (2003).

Tara J. Radin is Assistant Professor of Management and General Business at the Zarb School of Business, Hofstra University, where she teaches business ethics, business and society, and strategy. She is an active member of the Society for Business Ethics, the Academy of Management/Social Issues in Management Division, and the International Association of Business and Society. Her research encompasses topics such as

314 / Business, Ethics, and Science

employment, international labor practices, technology, privacy, corporate governance, and stakeholder theory, and includes publications in journals such as *Business Ethics Quarterly*, *Journal of Business Ethics*, and *American Business Law Journal*.

Saras Sarasvathy is Assistant Professor of Entrepreneurship at the University of Maryland. Trained in cognitive science and behavioral economics under Herbert Simon, Sarasvathy has developed a new baseline of entrepreneurial expertise called effectuation. Her current research involves the theoretical and empirical connections between effectuation, the economics of social choice and the philosophy of pragmatism. Sarasvathy received her Ph.D. in Information Systems and Entrepreneurship, and an MBA, from Carnegie Mellon University.

Robert C. Solomon is Quincy Lee Centennial Professor of Business and Philosophy and Distinguished Teaching Professor at the University Texas at Austin. He is the author of six books in business ethics, Above the Bottom Line , *It's Good Business*, *Ethics and Excellence*, *New World of Business*, *A Better Way to Think About Business* and *Building Trust* (with Fernando Flores) and many books on European philosophy and on the emotions.

John Tooby is Professor of Anthropology at the University of California Santa Barbara, and, along with Leda Cosmides, is co-director of UCSB's Center for Evolutionary Psychology. Tooby received his A.B., M.A., and Ph.D. at Harvard, and since graduate school has been known for his role in co-founding the field of evolutionary psychology. He has published widely in evolutionary biology, evolutionary psychology, cognitive science, neuroscience, and anthropology. Tooby has been President of the Human Behavior and Evolution Society, a Fellow at the Center for Advanced Study in the Behavioral Sciences, recipient of the National Science Foundation's Presidential Young Investigator Award and a J. S. Guggenheim Memorial Fellow.

Frans B. M. de Waal is a Dutch-born ethologist/zoologist world-renowned for his work on the social intelligence of primates, such as chimpanzees, bonobos, capuchins, and macaques. His first book, *Chimpanzee Politics* (1982) compared the schmoozing and scheming of chimpanzees involved in power struggles at the Arnhem Zoo with that of human politicians. Ever since then, de Waal has drawn parallels between primate and human behavior, from peacemaking and morality to culture. His scientific work, conducted first in the Netherlands and later at NIH-sponsored regional primate centers in the USA, has been published in hundreds of technical articles in journals such as Science, Nature, Scientific American, and outlets specialized in animal behavior and primatology. His award-winning popular books have been translated into more than a dozen different languages. These books and his regular appearances in the media have made Dr. de Waal one of the world's most visible primatologists. His latest work, *The Ape and the Sushi Master* (Basic Books, 2001), tries to bridge the nature/culture divide.

Dr. de Waal is C. H. Candler Professor in the Psychology Department of Emory University and Director of the Living Links Center at the Yerkes Primate Center, Atlanta, Georgia. He is Correspondent Member of the Royal Dutch Academy of Sciences.

Sandra Waddock is Professor of Management at Boston College's Carroll School of Management and Senior Research Fellow at BC's Center for Corporate Citizenship. She is editor of the *Journal of Corporate Citizenship* from 2003–2005. She received her MBA (1979) and DBA from Boston University (1985) and has published extensively on corporate responsibility, corporate citizenship, and inter-sector collaboration in journals such as *The Academy of Management Journal, Strategic Management Journal, The Journal of Corporate Citizenship, Human Relations,* and *Business & Society,* among many others. Her 1997 paper with Sam Graves entitled "Quality of Management and Quality of Stakeholder Relations: Are They Synonymous?" in *Business and Society* won the 1997 Moskowitz Prize. She is the author of *Leading Corporate Citizens: Vision, Values, Value Added* (McGraw-Hill, 2002). She was a Fellow of the Ethics Resource Center in Washington from 2000–20002 and is a founding faculty member of the Leadership for Change Program at Boston College. She is the co-editor of the two-volume series *Unfolding Stakeholder Thinking* (Greenleaf), published in 2002 and 2003.

Patricia H. Werhane holds a joint appointment as Ruffin Professor of Business Ethics at the Darden Graduate School of Business and Wicklander Chair in Business Ethics and Director of the Institute for Business and Professional Ethics at DePaul University. Werhane is a prolific author, an acclaimed authority on employee rights in the workplace, one of the leading scholars on Adam Smith, and founder and former Editor-in-Chief of *Business Ethics Quarterly*, the leading journal of business ethics. She was a founding member and past president of the Society for Business Ethics and, in 2001, was elected to the Executive Committee of the Association for Practical and Professional Ethics.